POSTHUMOUS AMERICA

POSTHUMOUS AMERICA

LITERARY REINVENTIONS OF AMERICA
AT THE END OF THE EIGHTEENTH CENTURY

· · · · · · · ·

BENJAMIN HOFFMANN
Translated by Alan J. Singerman

THE PENNSYLVANIA STATE UNIVERSITY PRESS
UNIVERSITY PARK, PENNSYLVANIA

Library of Congress Cataloging-in-Publication Data

Names: Hoffmann, Benjamin, 1985– , author. | Singerman, Alan J., translator.
Title: Posthumous America : literary reinventions of America at the end of the eighteenth century / Benjamin Hoffmann ; translated by Alan J. Singerman.
Other titles: Amérique posthume. English.
Description: University Park, Pennsylvania : The Pennsylvania State University Press, [2018] | Includes bibliographical references and index.
Summary: "An English translation of Benjamin Hoffmann's French monograph L'Amérique Posthume. Examines the literary idealization of a lost American past in eighteenth-century French literature"—Provided by publisher.
Identifiers: LCCN 2017060786 | ISBN 9780271080079 (cloth : alk. paper)
Subjects: LCSH: United States—Description and travel—Early works to 1800. | Travelers' writings, French—History and criticism. | St. John de Crèvecoeur, J. Hector, 1735–1813—Criticism and interpretation. | Lezay-Marnézia, Claude-François-Adrien, marquis de, 1735–1800—Criticism and interpretation. | Chateaubriand, François-René, vicomte de, 1768–1848—Criticism and interpretation.
Classification: LCC E164.H71513 2018 | DDC 917.304/33—dc23
LC record available at https://lccn.loc.gov/2017060786

Copyright © 2018 Benjamin Hoffmann
All rights reserved
Printed in the United States of America
Published by The Pennsylvania State University Press,
University Park, PA 16802-1003

The Pennsylvania State University Press
is a member of the Association of
University Presses.

It is the policy of The Pennsylvania State University Press to use acid-free paper. Publications on uncoated stock satisfy the minimum requirements of American National Standard for Information Sciences—Permanence of Paper for Printed Library Material, ANSI Z39.48–1992.

CONTENTS
....

Acknowledgments • vii

Introduction:
New World Paradoxes • 1

1

Saint-John de Crèvecœur and
Nostalgia for Colonial America • 16

2

Lezay-Marnésia and Nostalgia
for the American Golden Age • 77

3

Chateaubriand and Nostalgia
for French America • 124

Conclusion:
America, a Mobile Sign • 181

Appendix • 187
Notes • 189
Bibliography • 212
Index • 226

ACKNOWLEDGMENTS

This book is dedicated to my professional role models, Thomas M. Kavanagh and Christopher L. Miller, with my most heartfelt gratitude. I would like to thank the Beinecke Library at Yale University and the Whiting Foundation for the research grants they awarded me. I also wish to express my gratitude to Guillaume Ansart, Howard Bloch, Michel Delon, Pierre Frantz, Laurence Mall, and Maurice Samuels for the depth of their comments on my work. I likewise owe warm thanks to my editor, Kendra Boileau, for her generous and constant support, as well as to Alex Vose, who deftly guided the preparation of the manuscript. I extend most sincere thanks to the author of the present translation, Alan J. Singerman. Once again, it was a pleasure and a privilege to work with you. The idea of this book was born on a train between New Haven and New York City, during a conversation with my wife, Audrey. Thank you for your ideas, your support, and your love, from the outset of this project and at each and every step toward its completion.

INTRODUCTION

New World Paradoxes

... the United States is growing more quickly than this manuscript.
—Chateaubriand, *Mémoires d'outre-tombe*, 1:470

Ephemeral America

At the turn of the eighteenth century, America resembled Heraclitus's river where no one ever swims twice.[1] Numerous travelers, novelists, and memoir writers attempted, more or less successfully, to meet a monumental challenge: to portray America in writing.[2] Such a project bears in itself the seeds of its own failure, for at the end of the Enlightenment, America is constantly changing, and its reality never coincides with its written image at a given moment. In the interval between its discovery by a traveler and the publication of a text on its subject, this perpetually evolving country has already assumed a form that no longer resembles what had been observed by the writer. "It is difficult to present a durable picture of such a mobile entity as the United States. It is changing at the very moment at which I am writing . . . ," remarks the French Consul François Barbé-Marbois in 1782, summarizing in two sentences the difficulty America presents to a man of letters: the writing necessarily lags behind this metamorphosing entity.[3] What are the causes of this constant mutation?

The boundaries of the body of literature examined in this work are set by the publication of *Lettres d'un cultivateur américain* (1784) by Saint-John de Crèvecœur and *Mémoires d'outre-tombe* by Chateaubriand (1848). Between these two periods, the territory of the United States increased considerably. Beginning with the creation of four new states between 1791 and 1803,[4] the colonization of the American continent was completed during the course of the nineteenth century through acquisitions and military conquests.[5] While the shaky beginnings of the young Republic bred fear of the imminent failure of the union of the states that composed it—owing to the danger posed by the opponents of the federalists, the concurrent ambitions of the European nations, and the resistance of the Amerindians to the expansion of the new country into the territory beyond the Appalachians—the country founded by Washington, contrary to all expectations, managed to remain united and absorb the immense space between the Atlantic and the Pacific. This expansion was greatly facilitated in 1803 by the unexpected and providential acquisition from Napoleon's France of Louisiana, which represents 22.3 percent of the current geographical area of the United States.

This considerable territorial increase was accompanied by a remarkable rise in population. The thirty-six censuses completed by England between 1761 and 1775 allow us to trace the demographic evolution of the American colonies: on the eve of independence, they comprised 2,300,000 inhabitants.[6] The wave of immigration slowed between 1775 and the 1830s before surging even more: between 1851 and 1854, around 400,000 people arrived each year in the United States. Suffering from famine and sick of living in misery, the Germans and Irish constituted the most important contingent of new arrivals in the first half of the nineteenth century, joining their countrymen as well as the English, Dutch, Swedes, French, and Swiss who had preceded them. In 1830, the United States counted 12,900,000 inhabitants; in thirty years, its population nearly tripled, reaching 31,400,000 in 1860.[7] At the same time, the cities grew so rapidly that in the space of one lifetime an individual could witness the birth of a city and its transformation into a metropolis connected to the outside world by regular maritime routes.[8]

The uninterrupted demographic and territorial growth of the United States was accompanied by protean changes: the forests were decimated and cities arose from the ground; despite violent resistance and brilliant victories, the Amerindians were ultimately driven from lands they had occupied forever; and innumerable Europeans followed in the footsteps of their predecessors who had fled religious persecution or misery in the course of the preceding two centuries. They came from France and Santo Domingo during the Revolutions, gathering north of Philadelphia when, like Volney, Noailles, and La Rochefoucauld-Liancourt, they were not frequenting the high society of the New World after having set the tone for that of the Old World.[9] This rapid evolution of the American society and the territory it occupied made a man of letters's head spin when, like La Rochefoucauld-Liancourt, he set out to describe the country of Washington: "The United States is perhaps the one place in the whole world that is the most difficult to describe to those who have not traveled there themselves. It is a country that is growing everywhere; what is true today of its population, its establishments, its prices, its business was not true six months ago and will no longer be true six months from now. . . . The information that at the present time, and for many years to come, a traveler can and will be able to record the most carefully will only be memories, a means of comparison with future years."[10] Describing America thus presents an initial paradox: it slips away when you try to write about it. Devoting a book to it is like attempting to seize an object that perpetually eludes you.

An Elusive New World

At the turn of the eighteenth century, there is indeed an inevitable gap between a discourse on America and the current state of this land, such that no manuscript, to paraphrase Chateaubriand, could ever keep pace with the territorial and social mutations of the United States. They are like the train that recedes into the distance and can only be pictured at the place that it no longer inhabits—or like the star that may well already be dead when its light reaches us. In this respect, any literary representation of America at a particular time may be considered *obsolete* by definition, since it arises after the disappearance of its model: a text can at best only give a prematurely anachronistic image of a country that has already metamorphosed at the moment of its publication.[11]

This gap between reality and representation, however, is not caused by the speed of demographic and territorial change alone, for in the case of traveling French writers, the spacio-temporal distance between the two countries greatly contributes to its increase. René Rémond thus emphasizes the importance of the time factor in accounting for the divide between the reality of America and the image it has for the French public: "Information naturally lags behind the evolution of reality, and this gap is aggravated by the persistence of the images of a faraway country that are already fixed in the public imagination."[12] Although it may vary according to the season, the force of the winds, and the skill of the captain, the average length of a transatlantic crossing is always significant in the period that concerns us here: the normal length of a simple round-trip voyage is about seventy-five days.[13] To this period, a minimum to cross the Atlantic, one must add the time that passes before setting sail; it is normal to wait eight or ten days for the cargo to be loaded or for the winds to be favorable.[14] In the final analysis, it takes eighty days, on average, to receive in France the response to a letter sent to the United States; longer, in fact, for this period does not include the letter's travel by land. This considerable length of time is at the origin of two phenomena that take protean forms and have multiple consequences: the sedimentation of the image of America in French public opinion and its accompanying idealization.

Given that it takes a very long time to receive news from America in France, the conceptions that people may have formed of that country have ample opportunity to spread and provoke new commentaries that fix them in the minds of the contemporaries before potentially contradictory information might lead them to contest these impressions or at least to question what they thought they knew. Upon returning to France after twenty-seven years in North America, Saint-John de Crèvecœur discovered there a widely accepted idyllic representation of the United States that he did not hesitate to further with his personal testimony in order to profit from the popularity of America in public opinion to promote his *Lettres d'un cultivateur américain*, which were surprisingly successful throughout Europe. Likewise, after receiving numerous letters from people seeking to emigrate during his stays in Paris, Benjamin Franklin had attempted to propagate the extremely favorable opinion the French had formed of his country, widely associated with the popular but very vague concepts of liberty, tolerance, equality, and happiness. In his *Avis à ceux qui voudraient s'en aller en Amérique* (*A Word to Those Who Would Like to Go to America*; 1784), Franklin nonetheless tried to discourage the hope of making a quick fortune that the French nourished by insisting on the happy mediocrity of the lot of his fellow countrymen: if extreme poverty did not exist in his country, neither did extravagant wealth.[15]

Indeed, the distance between America and Europe allowed people to imagine El Dorado–like opportunities awaiting emigrants from across the Atlantic. As Rémond writes, "If America remains for the French imagination, in the first half of the 19th century, the height of the exotic, the reign of the fabulous, it doubtlessly owes it largely to its distance from the continent. It is thus predestined to be the locus of all utopias, whether political, social, or philanthropic; over there everything is possible, even the impossible."[16] A true land of milk and honey in the European imagination at the end of the eighteenth century, America undergoes an idealization that combines a variety of literary influences, among which the reminiscence of the golden age of antiquity and of Jean-Jacques Rousseau's novel *Julie ou la Nouvelle Héloïse* (1761) are the most frequently evoked. They are particularly prominent in the utopian project of the marquis de Lezay-Marnésia, a project whose exceptional importance is demonstrated by the number of people it involved and by the magnitude of its economic stakes, as well as by its repercussions in the history of France, the United States, and their interwoven images.[17]

In the end, the rhythm of the modifications that occur in Washington's land, the distance that separates the two shores of the Atlantic, and the length of time necessary to bridge it explain why the French representations of America at the turn of the eighteenth century regularly combine anachronism with inaccuracy. Nonetheless, the works that are the subject of this study stand out in the French literary production devoted to America in this period in that they do not produce an obsolete but rather a posthumous representation.

What Is Posthumous America?

A child is referred to as "posthumous" when it is born after the death of its father; likewise, a literary work is posthumous when it is published after the decease of its author.[18] According to this definition, posthumous America is a literary representation that focuses on a past—defunct—period of American history that the writer knew firsthand and that fills him with such nostalgia that he attempts to assuage it with a retrospective recreation whose goal is to give a literary revival to the period that preceded a break in historical continuity.[19] While an obsolete representation of America no longer gives an accurate image of the country, since it has transmogrified in the lapse of time between the experience of the itinerant writer and the publication of his work, a posthumous representation revives a historical epoch that has already vanished when the author who knew it takes up his pen.

It is still incumbent upon us to distinguish between a posthumous representation and a historical approach that would attempt to describe America's past as rigorously as possible, since unlike the historian, who has not necessarily witnessed the period he is examining and whose legitimacy rests in part on the dispassionate relationship he cultivates with the object of his study, the author of a posthumous representation of America has traveled to the other side of the Atlantic during the period that he is recreating after the fact. Moreover, while the traveling writer does not commit to tell the truth about his experience, the deontology of the historian demands veracity.

The author's breaches of historical truth are an integral aspect of the notion of posthumous America. They are explained both by the temporal distance and the nostalgia that the writer feels at the loss of *his* America. On the one hand, the author of a posthumous representation begins to write after several years of separation from the period he is describing. His retrospective evocation is thus open to factual errors that he does not bother to rectify, because he is only interested in describing things as he remembers them, associated with sensual impressions and permeated with the psychological color it had at the time of the experience—and absent the objective framework in which the memories were born. He makes no attempt to reconstitute the truth of the period by verifying the accuracy of his own memories or by purging them of his past and present subjective views but strives instead to reproduce the image he has of his past experience at the time of writing. On the other hand, the author of a posthumous representation's drive to write is in direct proportion to the force of his nostalgia, exacerbated by the feeling of loss he experiences in recalling a bygone period. His recollection takes the form of a retrospective idealization born of convenient additions and subtractions that allow him to illustrate the supposedly perfect felicity of a country now only inhabitable through the efforts of memory, and that pass over the inevitable imperfections of a period that is being presented as idyllic.

The posthumous representation of America cannot, however, be reduced to an elegiac literary construction, offering an outlet to the nostalgia felt by the author. It has, of course, the *commemorative* function of preserving the memory of a period whose disappearance is mourned by the author, but it also possesses secondary functions. One of these functions is *advertising*, in which the author tries to match his posthumous representation of America not to what he discovered in the course of his travels but to what he expects to find: in the rest of our study, this will be referred to as a "doxological America." Then there is the *analeptic* function in which the writer reinvents America not as he remembers it but as he would have liked to discover it during a period preceding his own travels. The *specular* function, finally, allows the author to evoke the situation in France through his reflections on America and to comment implicitly on the former's political functioning. The goal of this study is to show how these different functions are combined in the texts we examine and to what extent their identification sheds light on the aesthetic and political positions taken by the authors in the course of their retrospective evocation of their travels in North America.

When all is said and done, the posthumous representation of America implies a dialectic of loss and resurrection. Of course, as Chateaubriand writes, it is "with old bones and ruins" that an author constructs his work;[20] that is, with all the distant memories, the buried impressions, and the images he keeps of men and women who have disappeared. However, the writer's recognition of the disappearance of a historical epoch does not prevent him from bringing it back to life by creating a work that commemorates it. As Michael Riffaterre comments, "The *fact* of writing, in the very moment that it articulates a destruction, represents the victory of the monument over the ruins."[21] The America that the author knows no longer exists is reborn beneath his pen at the moment of writing. By the same token, the reader is carried back to a historical period that he knows to be long gone, but that he too brings back to life each time he reads a work by such authors.

The expression "doxological America," used earlier, needs to be explained. It means the imaginary construction produced by the sum of the discourses—the direct and indirect testimonies—of the literary, political, historical, and philosophical works that ultimately embeds itself in the minds of the members of a community as an adequate description of America despite the numerous gaps between this construction and its referent. As Jean-Philippe Mathy observes in his study of the discourse on America produced by French intellectuals in the twentieth century, if we look closely, we can see that the human mind possesses in fact a capacity for symbolization and rationalization whose inherent limitations and repetitious character are revealed over time: "[T]here are just so many ways of celebrating or denouncing such cultural realities as Incan sacrificial rituals, Chinese mandarinism, or American Modernity." "Despite the innumerable individual variations in the expression of beliefs and values," Mathy continues, "representations nevertheless form interpretive clusters around which people rally and sometimes mobilize."[22] What we call "doxological America" is simply one of these "interpretative groupings" constituted over time by the accumulation and progressive stratification of individually expressed opinions on the subject of America that are centered around recurrent argumentative positions. The definition of doxological America at the end of the eighteenth century is in fact organized around a limited number of themes, values, and historical and literary connections such that it can easily be summed up in a notion omnipresent in the literature of the period, "the Golden Age," establishing a direct aesthetic and philosophical link with the pastoral novel and the bucolic poetry whose influence can be detected notably in the style of authors depicting the New World. Despite the force of this imaginary construction in the minds of individuals, it is nonetheless subjected to slow and progressive reconfigurations when new positions thrust themselves into the debate over the meaning of "America." In this respect, the French Revolution had a considerable effect on the redefinition of doxological America. As eloquently witnessed by the evolution of Chateaubriand's discourse on the United States between the first writing of the *Voyage en Amérique* and the last version of the *Mémoires d'outre-tombe*, it began a process of reinterpretation whose fruits can still be found at the center of contemporary French discourse on America.

A Prematurely Old New World

The three authors at the heart of this study all devote themselves to the search for lost time with America as the setting. Their ambition reveals a second paradox of the New World: it is always too old when the traveler comes ashore there. At first glance, however, their works consistently set the youthfulness of the American continent in opposition to the decrepitude of the rest of the world and, in particular, of Europe. Saint-John de Crèvecœur makes multiple references, for example, to the radical newness of America, which he compares to a "hemisphere emerging from the depths of the water."[23] In his *Letters from an American Farmer* (1782) as in the 1784 translation, *Lettres d'un cultivateur américain*, the youthfulness of America is compared to the antiquity of Greece and Italy in order to dissuade the curious from visiting the ruins of the Old World and to encourage them to look instead toward what is, in his opinion, a more instructive model: that of new America. Fifty years after Crèvecœur,

Tocqueville sees in the United States an early image of what Europe is going to become when it too generalizes equality of social condition and concludes that it is greatly in the interest of the French to study the American example.[24] To look toward America is thus tantamount to getting a glimpse of what Europe is going to become, as if turning one's eyes to the west was the same thing as looking toward the future. Although it is six hours earlier in New York than in Paris, owing to the difference in time zones, a voyage across the Atlantic must have been, for a Frenchman, an exploration of the future itself.

Nonetheless, despite this regular celebration of the youth of America and of its people, the experience of a voyage on the other side of the Atlantic gave numerous travelers the opposite impression of arriving late, when the New World had already begun to lose what had aroused their dreams and hopes. Having come "too late to a world too old,"[25] these authors seek futilely in contemporary America, something that has apparently disappeared long ago. In many respects, these are the theses of Rousseau in the *Discours sur l'origine et les fondements de l'inégalité parmi les hommes* (*Discourse on the Origin and Foundations of Inequality Among Men*, 1755), which produced in his readers' minds a series of preconceptions about "primitive life" whose confrontation with the reality of the American experience proved to be a source of disenchantment, as was the case for Chateaubriand, who only presents himself as a "disciple of Rousseau" in the *Mémoires d'outre-tombe* in order to express his deception at the decrepitude of the American "natural state."[26] Disenchanted, these authors cultivate the nostalgia of an epoch in which the New World really deserved its euphoric image, an epoch that, it would appear, simultaneously began and ended with the discovery of America by Christopher Columbus. As Dominique Jullien observes regarding the famous explorer: "Creator of a world, but also destroyer of a world, Columbus embodies the traveler who came before; he infuses the American experience with nostalgia forever."[27]

The Unity of the Corpus

The concept of posthumous America facilitates a dialog between the works of Saint-John de Crèvecœur, Claude-François-Adrien de Lezay-Marnésia, and François-René de Chateaubriand by emphasizing the similarities of their literary goals and their themes, not to speak of the obsessions that haunt them. It behooves us to determine for what personal and ideological reasons and prompted by which historical events and currents of thought these authors came to produce a posthumous representation of *their* America: the one that they had discovered in the course of their stay on the other side of the Atlantic. Of course, it would have been possible to include in this study other writers besides the three around which it is organized. Nostalgia is in fact an experience that is inseparable from the individual discovery of America by a European, and it is the primary factor that motivates the retrospective writing of the tale of a voyage in which the author simultaneously rediscovers the memories of a historical era and of a defunct period in his existence. By paying attention to writings that are posterior to those that we have included here, it would be possible in particular to follow the evolution of the posthumous representation of America and to identify its invariant characteristics. "Evolution," for if the historical changes at the turn of the eighteenth century are exceptionally rapid and protean, they continue, of course, throughout the following decades and mark a break between the time of the writing of a work and any preceding period that is perceived as a new Golden Age for the person describing it. A continuation of this study could, for instance, bear on the Louisiana literature in the French language of the nineteenth century and on the retrospective idealization of the decades preceding the American Civil War. This literature manifests a clear break between a before and an after, given that it begins an attempt at political, cultural, and linguistic unification of the United States that is achieved at the expense of the Francophone and creole culture that the authors, in particular Alfred Mercier (1816–1894), try to preserve by means of their writings and their individual commitment.[28]

As for the invariant characteristics that such a continuation of this study could produce, one of them would certainly be an experience of deception as a precondition for the idealization of the past. This phenomenon may be observed in particular in a text written by Tocqueville during his stay in America between 1831 and 1832 and published after his death by Alexis de Beaumont, the *Voyage au lac Oneida*. In this short travel narrative, Tocqueville alludes to the authors of the preceding generation: "I do not believe that I've ever experienced such complete disappointment as I felt when I saw these Indians. My head was filled with the memories of M. de Chateaubriand and Cooper, and I expected to see in the countenance of the American savages some natural trace of those elevated virtues born of the spirit of liberty."[29] Although he compares his meeting with these "vile and mean-looking Indians"[30] to his memories of the reading of *Atala* and *Les Natchez*, Tocqueville experiences the same disappointment as Chateaubriand; just as the latter had been disappointed in seeing Amerindians dance to violin music,[31] Tocqueville is generally disillusioned by what he discovers in the American wilderness. The same scene plays out in an opposition between the present state of things and the preconceptions based on his reading of his predecessors that evokes an indefinite past in which the traveler would not have been confronted with a divorce between his dreams and the American reality they conceal.

Despite the obvious interest of pursuing this investigation beyond the admittedly vague limits of "the end of the eighteenth century," this study is devoted, for several reasons, to the American writings of Crèvecœur, Lezay-Marnésia, and Chateaubriand alone. On the one hand, the period of their travels coincides approximately with the French and American Revolutions: Crèvecœur lived across the Atlantic during the colonial period before witnessing both the War of Independence in the United States and the French Revolution, whereas Lezay-Marnésia and Chateaubriand observed the beginnings of the momentous events in France before leaving for the New World the same year. The fact that they were contemporaries of both of these major historical upheavals makes their discourse on America all the more interesting, since they visited it at a time of profound renewal while being positioned to make extremely pertinent comparisons between what they were observing across the Atlantic and what was happening in France in the same period. The French discourse on the United States always contains an implicit meditation on the homeland of its authors, and it proves to be particularly fruitful to examine it at a crucial moment in the history of the two countries.

In addition, the narratives on travel to America written at the end of the eighteenth century bear an affinity to the nascent form of the travel guide in that they attempt to prepare the itinerary of a reader who will become a traveler and to provide him with information that will be useful for his trip but is obviously doomed to rapid obsolescence. This practical dimension—which is accompanied by a quasi-journalistic ambition since the traveler, in revealing spaces largely unknown to his readership, is attempting to record and share his newly acquired knowledge of the New World—generally accords less importance to the aesthetic qualities of the text, the effort to improve its style and turn it into a literary work. Written on the spot, in the majority of cases these texts were quickly published after their authors' return to France. Therefore, among a copious production of narratives on travel to America—the bibliographies drawn up by Echeverria and Everett and those of Bernard Faÿ, Frank Monaghan, and Joseph Sabin are ample evidence of its extreme abundance—it is quite unusual to discover texts whose intrinsic literary qualities make them far more than the joy of a blissful historian, delighted to browse through a document that provides him with information on a faraway period, but works whose intellectual density and elegant style could in fact pique the interest of a reader not primarily interested in their relationship with America. No one doubts that these qualities are evident and possess a particular enchantment in the *Voyage en Amérique* and the *Mémoires d'outre-tombe*, but it remains to be demonstrated that they are also to be found in Crèvecœur's work, that is rarely read in French, and in Lezay-Marnésia's, whose *Letters Written from the Banks of the Ohio* has just been republished and is still in search of a readership. In short, it is the exceptional aesthetic value of these texts belonging to a genre whose principal interest is ordinarily related to history and not literature that justified their inclusion in this study.

Finally, and above all, these three works are brought together because of the intertextual character that links them; from a methodological viewpoint, it is easy to prove the relevance of a comparison when the authors concerned are familiar with each other's works and have left proof of this familiarity in their writings. There is an explicit relationship between the works of Crèvecœur and those of Lezay-Marnésia, since the latter, who has read *Lettres d'un cultivateur américain*, only pretends to differ from his predecessor in his own description of the United States, accusing him, not without justification, of multiple fabrications. Chateaubriand is likewise a reader of Crèvecœur, as is evidenced both by a letter sent to Fontanes and the publication in the *Mercure de France* of an article on the *Voyage dans la Haute Pensylvanie et dans l'État de New York depuis l'année 1785 jusqu'en 1798* (*Journey in Upper Pennsylvania and the State of New York from 1785 to 1798*).[32] By their complementarity, the numerous thematic convergences between these texts guarantee the unity of the corpus. Lezay-Marnésia and Chateaubriand both traveled to the United States in 1791, and the respective paths of these aristocrats—both hostile to the French Revolution—constructing projects that were equally chimerical although of a different nature (one dreamed of utopian colonies, the other of impossible conquests in isolated polar regions), crossed more than one time, leading them to reflect on identical questions after visiting the same places. Moreover, the fascination with the Native Indian culture is shared by these three authors, who describe it with the ambition of preserving through their writing a civilization that they all clearly perceived to be destined to disappear in the near future. They also have in common an attempt to stage a meeting between an imaginary America that preceded their voyage and their personal discovery of that country. This recurrent theme tends to prove that writing about travels in America is necessarily an intertextual undertaking during which the traveler compares his experience to the expectations that the reading of the works signed by his predecessors had previously aroused in him. There results a phenomenon of "circularity of representations" that consists in the repetition by different authors of a similar discourse on America whose power of persuasion increases along with its successive reconfirmations.

Limits of Posthumous Representation

The idea of posthumous representation is perpetuated after the end of the eighteenth century. Just as it would have been possible to increase its temporal extension, it would have been possible to increase the number of its objects, since America is obviously not the only country that might be represented posthumously. Of course, the inclusion of any other space than America would have eliminated the coherence of the present study, but it is possible to dream of other studies that would be organized around the paradigm of posthumous representation and would adopt the various functions that it is capable of exercising. One might speak, for example, of the commercial representation of France in *Bleu-Blanc-Rouge* (*Blue-White-Red*) by Alain Mabanckou, a novel in which the hero imagines a Parisian El Dorado similar to the one that exists in Africa in a postcolonial context.³³ The *Aventures de Télémaque* by Fénelon create on their part a critical picture of France through the evocation of a voyage carried out in a mythical Greece, illustrating by this fact the specular function by which the evocation of a society distant in time and space can be a way of describing indirectly the country of the readers in the period of its publication. As for analeptic representation, this is well illustrated in the narrative of Sylvain Tesson, *L'Axe du loup* (*The Route of the Wolf*), since, while walking from Siberia to India on the same path taken by escapees from the Gulag, the author accomplishes not only a voyage in space but also a journey in time in which he attempts to reproduce as closely as possible the prior experience of another in order to revive it. The concept of posthumous representation is therefore in no way linked exclusively to the American arena at the end of the eighteenth century, and just as one could use it to study a later text such as *L'Etudiant étranger* (*The Foreign Student*, 1986) by Philippe Labro, whose narrator recreates the memory of a stay in Virginia in the 1950s, it would be entirely conceivable to undertake the study of "posthumous France" as Ernest Hemingway reinvents it in *A Moveable Feast*. Although it is used here to characterize the work of three traveling writers bearing on the same space and the same period, the concept of posthumous representation may be applied to other territories in order to analyze works treating different periods and places. The psychological mechanisms of recollection, projection, and retrospective idealization are fully at play in the recreation of the past, whatever the place and period may be, as they are in the impression that individuals may have of foreign peoples and distant lands.

Texts from Beyond the Grave

Among the criteria previously specified to justify the linking of the works of Crèvecœur, Lezay-Marnésia, and Chateaubriand, their exceptional aesthetic quality has been stressed. Still, the works examined in this study have more often attracted the attention of historians than literature specialists. It is true that the American writings of Chateaubriand have been studied in works that are exclusively interested in their literary dimension. This notwithstanding, the major part of the bibliography devoted to the America of Chateaubriand consists of texts produced by a history of literature whose methods and means of interrogating a text are clearly obsolete today. Did Chateaubriand go to the United

States with the intention, as he claimed, of discovering the Northwest Passage, or did he just seize this pretext to flee the revolutionary turbulence that would cost the life of several members of his family? Had he really set out, as he claims in the preface of *Atala*, to write the "epic of the man of nature" several years before his 1791 trip?[34] Did he really explore the south of the United States as he suggests, or did he only take a much more traditional course through the northeast of the country? What literary sources did he consult to fill in the gaps in his memory of his experience? These questions—and others even more specific: did he really meet Washington?—are repeated in a number of articles devoted to the *Voyage en Amérique* and to the American books of the *Mémoires d'outre-tombe*, with the result that the question of the degree of credibility that the reader can grant to Chateaubriand's works has proved to be crucial to specialists who, from the 1830s to the present day, have responded to each other to complete or refute their respective writings.[35] This historical approach, which ultimately concerns far more what the work tells us about the author's life than about the work itself, is foreign, indeed contrary, to the one that is adopted in this study, which analyzes the methods and functions of the fictionalization of America: its imaginary and retrospective recreation at the end of a process in which, to adopt Chateaubriand's own term, fabulation eventually "metamorphoses" into truth.[36]

Similarly, one meets the names of Crèvecœur and Lezay-Marnésia much less frequently in a literary study than as a passing remark in a historical work. Unlike his *Letters from an American Farmer*—widely quoted by specialists of early American studies and placed on the same level as those early masterpieces of American literature, *Notes on the State of Virginia* (1785) by Thomas Jefferson and the *Autobiography of Benjamin Franklin* (1791)—the French-language writings of Crèvecœur are too often reduced to sources of information on the United States at the end of the eighteenth century. Indeed, the texts published in his mother tongue have scarcely been studied for their characteristic heterogeneity—not to reduce them to catalogs of various and sundry facts about the history of the United States but to reveal their underlying structure or highlight the formal innovations that they put into practice.[37] This interpretation of Crèvecœur's writings in French in which they are considered generally to be documents rather than complete works is evidenced most clearly in Françoise Plet's edition of the *Voyage dans la Haute Pensylvanie et dans l'État de New York*.[38] Although this edition is to be lauded for improving the availability of a work whose diffusion suffered from its comparison with *Atala* at the time of its publication, it nonetheless neglects its literary qualities by presenting it as the history of a "geography under construction"[39] and by excising large sections that are among the most stimulating in the book.[40]

Likewise, the *Lettres d'un cultivateur américain* is a work whose heterogeneity may discourage the reader and give him or her the impression that an organized and systematic work is still in the nascent stage. However, far from being a weakness for which we must absolve Crèvecœur, the very multifariousness of his letters, the diversity of the subjects they treat as much as the variety of the texts (excerpts from speeches, dialogs, tales with multiple narrators, etc.) are the tools of an ambitious undertaking that consists of nothing less than an attempt to transform America into language. To "express America"—in the vast variety of its spaces and its modes of settlement, in the diversity of its inhabitants, their origins and their manner of dress—is the goal that Crèvecœur has set for himself, and that he does not attempt to reach by means of a systematic work but through the kaleidoscopic representation of a constantly shifting reality. In his trilogy *U.S.A.*, John Dos Passos employs four distinct narrative modes in order to adopt a variety of viewpoints on multiple characters: free indirect discourse, stream of consciousness, newspaper articles, and biographies of historical figures. One hundred and fifty years before him, Crèvecœur foreshadows his techniques by integrating into his epistolary volumes a collection of anecdotes, the French translation of authentic newspaper articles, and the imaginary biography of exemplary characters (rich and poor colonists, immigrants from various nations with their typical virtues and vices, etc.). Just like the author of *Manhattan Transfer* (1925), Crèvecœur attempts as early as the 1780s to depict the United States by adopting a composite form.

In the end, Crèvecœur's reputation suffered greatly from the characteristic atomization of his works, which lend themselves to the deletion of fragments at the cost of a simplification, if not a caricature, of the whole in which they are inscribed. When he happens to be mentioned, he is regularly confused with the figure of the "American farmer" that he brought to life, while his discourse on America is often described as "idyllic" or "pastoral." But if we look closely, his bucolic tableaus are not spared the onslaught of violence and evil, and his political thought, sometimes reduced to a partisan championing of the young Republic, includes muted concerns about the future.[41] Following the pioneering writings of Bernard Chevignard, the time has come to do him justice by adopting a global reading of his work, bringing together the English and French texts instead of treating them as two separate bodies and pursuing a reading that resists the temptation to lift anthology pieces from his works without bothering to analyze those works in their entirety. There is no doubt that Crèvecœur will emerge more eminent from this reevaluation, achieving a stature that even he did not expect (the doubts about his literary talent are a recurrent theme), that of one of the last great French writers of the eighteenth century, offering in a rich body of work an example of the hypersensitivity, utopian visions, and incitement to tolerance of the waning years of the Enlightenment.

As for the *Letters Written from the Banks of the Ohio* by the marquis de Lezay-Marnésia, they have been victim of the same jaundiced reception accorded the *Lettres d'un cultivateur américain*. Published in 1792, immediately censured by the Girondins, they have just been republished for the first time since 1800.[42] And if the works of Roland-Guy Bonnel have greatly deepened our knowledge of the œuvre of Lezay-Marnésia and the context of their production, many riches in the *Letters Written from the Banks of the Ohio* remain to be explored, in particular their prefiguration of the "salad-bowl theory," their surprising anticipation of what might be called the "uchronotopian" genre (the fusion between the utopian and the uchronian genres), as well as their inherent ambivalence in the depiction of both a colonial project and a political utopia.

In many ways, the respective works of this reader and these writers resonate together. For these authors, the goal is to give the floor to voices from beyond the grave that commemorate a world that no longer exists. The same goes for the critic whose intention is to shine the spotlight on these works that have fallen into obscurity, to give them a place that literary history, necessarily selective, has refused them either by condescension or by negligence. Like these texts, that claim to bear witness to a bygone age whose last, fragile traces subsist in the memory of their author, this study proposes to exhume these buried works by correlating them with better-known opuses that are their explicit or implicit intertexts. In this manner, they will be integrated into the corpus of texts explored by the specialists of Enlightenment literature, utopia, and travel narratives, and will contribute to the field of both transatlantic and revolutionary studies, as well as to the history of the representations of America in French thought. A historical prologue is placed at the beginning of each of the following literary analyses, an indispensable prerequisite for a study bearing on works that are in constant dialog with the reality of their period. Intended to measure the influence of the social and historical context on the work of the authors and on the reception of their works, they will facilitate the appreciation of the gap between the reported facts and the posthumous representations that record them at the same time as they reinvent them.

SAINT-JOHN DE CRÈVECŒUR AND NOSTALGIA FOR COLONIAL AMERICA

> People complained in colonial times also; for it is man's fate: this time was nonetheless the true golden age of this new part of the world.
> —Crèvecœur, *Voyage dans la Haute Pensylvanie et dans l'État de New York*

Prologue: Saint-John de Crèvecœur's Fracture

A SPLIT SUBJECT

"Of course all life is a process of breaking down, but the blows that do the dramatic side of the work—the big sudden blows that come, or seem to come, from outside—the ones you remember and blame things on and, in moments of weakness, tell your friends about, don't show their effect all at once."[1] Just like the experience described by Fitzgerald, Saint-John de Crèvecœur's existence is proof that a deep-seated fracture is at the origin of literary creation, writing being an attempt to compensate for the pain that defines a before and an after in the flesh of a life. "I am no longer the person you formerly knew when I was happy and free,"[2] Crèvecœur declared following his imprisonment in 1779, but "a very different man from what I was before."[3] Why was he locked up in New York jails during the American revolution? In what circumstances did his second "self," of which he speaks previously, come into existence, and to what extent does this event coincide with Crèvecœur's entry into the realm of literature?

Everyone is an autobiographer who chooses, from among the nearly infinite range of experiences, a narrative that is able to describe for himself and for others the person he has become. In the case of Crèvecœur, this narrative constantly returns to the fault line that cuts his life in two, the break that defines not only two periods in his life but, in fact, two identities. The subjective representation of his past is crucial if one is to understand his work, which may be seen as the space in which his *second self*, haunted by a poignant nostalgia, strives to recreate the existence formally led by the *first*. Insatiable, this nostalgia nourishes and constantly refuels a literary undertaking that attempts to enter into communion with a past period that it eventually reinvents in an elegiac mode. As Bernard Chevignard writes, "*Letters* is thus the projection of a retrospective gaze that reinvents the past through contrast and lives it again like an inverse image of a present that has become unbearable."[4] One can only reach a similar conclusion in reading the *Lettres d'un cultivateur américain* (Paris, 1784 and 1787)[5] and the *Voyage dans la Haute Pensylvanie et dans l'État de New York* (Paris, 1801), texts to which the present chapter is devoted. But before proceeding to the analysis of the posthumous representation of America in his works, a prologue devoted to Crèvecœur's personal journey is essential: it will permit the reader to determine to what extent he has deformed or reinvented the original biographical material he shares, just as it is necessary to study the norm to be able to judge the extent of a variation from that norm.

THE YOUTH OF A PROTEUS

Crèvecœur's life has been studied in several very fine works that strive to retrace the various stages of the adventurous existence of the "American farmer." This is nonetheless a considerable challenge, because there is no lack of shadowy areas in the story of this elusive and wandering "Proteus."[6] As suggested previously, this story includes two distinct periods, a before and an after. Before the war, the destruction, before the abuses and the inner wavering caused by the metaphysical experience of evil, there was the first life of a man that in no way foreshadowed his future as the overzealous and suspicious advocate of the United States of America. Crèvecœur's father, heir of a family of provincial magistrates, was the first to raise his lineage to the level of the provincial elites. Guillaume-Augustin de Crèvecœur married into a distinguished family in the Norman aristocracy, the Blouet de Cahagnolles, and cultivated the friendship of the Turgots and the Houdetots, the latter of whom would one day become his son's protectors. On January 31, 1735, his son Michel-Guillaume-Jean de Crèvecœur was born in Caen. He studied at the Jesuit Collège du Mont, where he was particularly interested in mathematics, especially geometry. In 1751, he went to live with two aunts residing in England. The reasons for this "exile" are not known: Thomas Philbrick suspects that a quarrel between Michel and his father might have been at the bottom of it, but whatever the causes of this early emigration, it helped Crèvecœur learn English at a young age.[7] During his stay in England, he became engaged to a young lady whose name has been lost. Of her nothing is known, other than she was the only daughter of a merchant, and that she died before the marriage could be celebrated. The disappearance of his fiancée seems to have precipitated Crèvecœur's departure for Canada. In 1755, perhaps as early as 1754, he joined the free companies of the Navy and served in the artillery and the corps of engineers.

What kind of man was Crèvecœur when he embarked for the New World? Contrary to Chateaubriand, he was not a writer seeking a personal experience with the exotic;[8] unlike Lezay-Marnésia, he was not a mature man with extremely set ideas when he emigrated.[9] Crèvecœur was still a young man who, perhaps attracted by the appeal of adventure, his heart prematurely heavy with the loss of a loved one, set out to invent himself in America.

FROM CANADA TO THE ENGLISH COLONIES

Crèvecœur remained in Canada from 1755 to 1759. He devoted his first years to his profession as a cartographer and took long journeys that served as an opportunity to observe several American Indian tribes.[10] In 1757, he joined the Montcalm army and took part in the attack of Fort George before drawing a map of it that the famous explorer Bougainville (serving as captain in the dragoons in Canada since 1756) presented to King Louis XV. Begun with brilliant prospects, his military career nonetheless came to a brutal end.[11]

Following the fall of Quebec to the English (September 13, 1759), Crèvecœur left the army under ambiguous circumstances: cowardice in combat, independence of mind, and disgust with the war are all explanations advanced by biographers to explain his departure.[12] At the age of twenty, he broke his ties to the French army and traveled to the English colonies of America under the name of Mr. John Hector Saint-John. Why adopt this new identity at this pivotal moment of his life? "Saint-John" is the English translation of his given name, as Crèvecœur himself explained to Benjamin Franklin.[13] The choice of English suggests a desire to invent a new persona for himself in a new culture, to create a double that demonstrates by its "anglicized" identity his voluntary integration into the community of settlers in the New World. Conversely, the choice of the name Hector is more surprising: why adopt the name of a Trojan warrior? Did Crèvecœur give himself a heroic name to compensate for the cowardice in combat that he may have shown in Canada? Language would then be functioning as a revenge on reality, a corrective function more generally assumed by Crèvecœur's literary writings. Unless, after witnessing the fall of Quebec, he ultimately identified with the figure of Hector, another warrior vanquished after a murderous siege? Whatever may be the symbolic dimension of this new baptism, it is no less true that he was responding to a necessity: in entering the territory of the English colonies, it was clearly in Crèvecœur's interest to disavow his identity as a former officer in the army of the enemy.

Once he had passed into the colonies, he undertook a variety of activities. Surveyor, cartographer, peddler of books, medicine, and lace, he roamed from Newfoundland to the banks of the Mississippi. The richness of his knowledge of America and the length of his sojourn distinguish him from the majority of French travelers on the other side of the Atlantic, and from Lezay-Marnésia and Chateaubriand in particular, who explored a much smaller territory and stayed a little less than two years in the United States in the case of the first, and scarcely five months in the case of the second.[14] Naturalized on December 23, 1765,[15] in the colony of New York, Crèvecœur married four years later (on September 20, 1769) an Anglo-American, Mehetable Tippet, from a family residing in Westchester County. Three children were born of this union: America-Frances, or "Fanny" (December 14, 1770); Guillaume-Alexandre, or "Ally" (August 5, 1772); and Philippe-Louis (October 22, 1774). By the choice of these surnames, Crèvecœur was demonstrating his attachment to both his motherland and his adopted country and transmitted to his children the double heritage of their parents. On September 12, 1769, he acquired the fifty hectares of the Greycourt estate at Goshen in Orange County. In English first, then in French, his works will reinvent the decade that now opened for him.

LOST IN TRANSLATION

What is the relationship of Crèvecœur to these two languages, and how did they evolve over time? He wrote the Letters from an American Farmer (1782) in English. He translated the letters himself into French in 1784 and 1787: these are the Lettres d'un cultivateur américain. The first of the "Lettres servant d'introduction" to those of the "cultivateur américain," written by Lacretelle and sent to the editor of the Mercure de France on January 4, 1783, traces the linguistic evolution of Crèvecœur: "Having adopted, in his youth, an English motherland, he threw himself whole-heartedly into the language of the country; it is in that language that he read and wrote, to such an extent that his native tongue became for him a foreign language."[16] To say of Crèvecœur that he had almost forgotten his French upon his return in 1781 is hardly an exaggeration. Invited several times by Madame d'Houdetot, the former expatriate initially preferred to avoid her despite the honor that this great lady was doing him: "Seized with panic at the thought of exposing his shaky French and 'foreign manners' to a lady whose refinement was so well known, Crèvecœur pleaded illness."[17] Crèvecœur was in fact painfully aware of the weakness of his French: "I do not know what she saw in the style of my letter (that I wrote first in English and then translated as well as I could into French), but the odd turns of phrase, the use of words that I thought were French, *instead of making her feel scorn for a man who didn't even know his own language, increased her desire to see him.*"[18] He eventually yielded to the urging of the countess, however, and the deep gratitude that he later expressed to her may be explained in particular by the progress in the mastery of French that her company helped him to achieve.[19]

As his French slipped away in America, English was slowly replacing his mother tongue. He acquired it by following a method that he described in a letter to his son Ally: "Write one page every day in English and French; that will teach you spelling and style. . . . Make an outline first, as I always do myself when I write something important. Put that into writing that evening, then the next morning reread and correct it, and after that make a clean copy."[20] This immersion in the English language, accompanied by daily writing exercises, helped Crèvecœur wield it with a clarity that would be admired by D. H. Lawrence and lead his readers to think that it was his mother tongue.[21] In fact, in the *Letters from an American Farmer*, Crèvecœur wrote under the guise of an Anglo-American colonist having no other ties with Europe than the friendship of a noble Englishman to whom he was sending his missives. The specialists of the *Letters* have regularly denounced the naive reading of said letters, identifying the persona created by the author with the author himself. This confusion indicates, in any case, that the mastery of the English language by Crèvecœur was so remarkable that it could pass for his mother tongue.[22] From the beginning of the 1900s, excerpts of the *Letters from an American Farmer* were widely reproduced in anthologies of American literature. This is the case, notably, of the famous Letter III, titled "What is an American?," the "shining star of the Crèvecœurian constellation," to quote Edward White.[23] That a Frenchman was able to write what is often described as the first masterpiece of American literature is a veritable tour de force of linguistic adaptation of which there are very few examples in the history of world literature.

However, following the publication of the *Letters from an American Farmer*, Crèvecœur reserved the use of English for his personal correspondence. After writing a *Traité de la culture des pommes de terre* (Treatise on Potato Farming, 1782) for his Norman countrymen and finishing the French translation of the *Letters* in 1787, it is in French that he chose to continue his œuvre. In 1801, he published the *Voyage dans la Haute Pensylvanie et dans l'État de New York* (1801) before tackling the *Voyage aux grandes salines tyroliennes de Reichenhall* between 1808 and 1809. After having begun to learn to write in French, Crèvecœur decided to remain in this mode of expression. In addition, the political context at the end of the eighteenth century certainly influenced his choice of language: a publication in English in London like he had done with the *Letters* was no longer an option after 1792, at the time of the European coalitions against France, especially since the *Voyage dans la Haute Pensylvanie* begins with vibrant praise for the Premier Consul (Napoleon), described as the "Washington of France."[24] While he never returned to English or to the United States after 1790, Crèvecœur never stopped thinking about the New World, as is witnessed by the American memories that arise in his final work.[25]

FATE AND PLEASURES OF AN AMERICAN FARMER

In English, then in French, Crèvecœur spoke of the Pine Hill Estate that he bought in 1769. Despite the numerous pages in which he describes the "fate and pleasures" of an American farmer,[26] what he chose to publish under his name should not be confused with a documentary account of the life he led in the New York colony. Without expecting to find therein the truth of an experience that the *Letters*, and then the *Lettres*, would simply embellish, it is nonetheless stimulating to read the texts gathered in two volumes published after the death of the author, *Sketches of Eighteenth-Century America* and *More Letters from the American Farmer*, in order to note how they differ from *Letters from an American Farmer*. These works present fragments that the author refused to include in his 1782 collection and that remained unpublished until the twentieth century. They give an image of life in America in which the difficulties met by the farmers are not passed over as systematically as they were in *Letters* and a fortiori in *Lettres* and *Voyage*. In "Thoughts, Feelings and Pleasures of an American Farmer," the farmer of the *Letters* rejoices over the economic and political independence that forms the basis of his happiness: "I owe nothing to my country other than a pittance, a meager tribute to my king to which I add my loyalty and the respect that is due him. I know no other sovereign than He who reigns over the universe, to whom I owe the most sincere gratitude."[27] On the contrary, the narrator of the "Thoughts of an American Farmer on Various Rural Subjects" in *More Letters from the American Farmer* deplores the endemic indebtedness of farmers: *"flourishing as we may appear to a superficial observer*, yet there are many dark spots which, on due consideration, greatly lessen that show of happiness which the Europeans think we possess. The number of debts which one part of the country owes to the other would greatly astonish you. The younger a country is, the more it is oppressed, for new settlements are always made by people who do not possess much. They are obliged to borrow; and, if any accidents intervene, they are not enabled to repay that money in many years. The interest is a canker-worm which consumes their yearly industry."[28] Crèvecœur sets the euphoric discourse of Europeans on America against the more somber reality that is revealed to those who look more closely. In *Letters*, and even more so in *Lettres*, he demonstrates the same glowing ardor for America for which he reproached "superficial observers" when he lived in the English colonies.

GENERAL SHIPWRECK

Whatever may have been the degree of Crèvecœur's happiness during his time at Pine Hill, it is certain that worry and fear replaced it during the American Revolution. Crèvecœur depicts it as a historical and personal disaster that left him with a fragmented self, like those shipwrecked vessels that haunt his literary work. The War of Independence marks the fracture evoked in this chapter's prologue that splits Crèvecœur's existence into two distinct periods. While the expression "War of Independence" may call to mind the effort of a people to liberate itself from an oppressive foreign power, Crèvecœur depicts the conflict as a civil war during which friends, neighbors, and members of the same family joined opposing sides and slaughtered each other on the ruins of their former relationships.

The question of Crèvecœur's allegiance was in serious doubt in his time and still is in ours.[29] Was he a loyalist, a faithful subject of the King of England and determined to live under his aegis? Or a patriot, resolved to shed the yoke of the English occupier? The last of the *Letters from an American Farmer* depicts the dilemma of the narrator whose anguish very likely reflects Crèvecœur's own during the war: "If I attach myself to the mother country, which is 3,000 miles from me, I become what is called an enemy to my own region; if I follow the rest of my countrymen I become opposed to our ancient masters: both extremes appear equally dangerous to a person of so little weight and consequence as I am, whose energy and example are of no avail."[30]

At first glance, it would appear that Crèvecœur was leaning toward the side of the loyalists, since he couldn't bear to see the end of the existence he had been leading during the English reign; the crown afforded its distant subjects a liberty of action and enterprise that was consistent with his principles. Myra Jehlen has in fact described Crèvecœur's political ideal as the paradoxical a priori conjoining of monarchism and anarchism. The radical self-determination for individuals of which Crèvecœur dreamed is more easily reconciled, in his mind, with a monarchical government having minimal impact on local communities than with a democracy whose nature is to subject individual interest to the general will.[31] Nonetheless, despite his reticence regarding the cause of the patriots, Crèvecœur is in no sense a confirmed loyalist. It appears that he had wanted to stay above the fray, an attitude that, far from winning him the esteem of both sides, earned him hostility from everyone.[32]

At the beginning of 1778, he requested permission to travel to New York, at that time in the hands of the English. But after the month of July 1778 and the arrival of the French fleet, it was now the supporters of the British crown who held him in suspicion. Crèvecœur made contact with his countrymen, and rumors flew that he was frequenting La Fayette. In February 1779, he finally decided to leave for New York. During this journey, he was only accompanied by his son Ally; his wife and two other children remained at Pine Hill. Why didn't he leave with his whole family? In all likelihood, he preferred to have his wife take care of their property in his absence.

While awaiting the opportunity to embark for Europe, Crèvecœur survived in New York by plying his trade as a surveyor. But on July 8, 1779, suspected of spying by the English, he was imprisoned. With an energy that is characteristic of his writing when he expresses torments of conscience, Crèvecœur describes the experience of prison as a metaphysical crisis, marked by the sudden consciousness of the omnipresence of evil: "I suddenly became a Manichean; I thought I saw in man a degree of corruption which I had never suspected. Ah! What an image of human nature I entertained! What unholy questions I dared to ask the great Creator when I saw society as a group of lions tearing to shreds the weakest but most numerous of its members."[33] Crèvecœur was beginning to muse about suicide when his friend William Seton obtained his release.[34] The man who emerged from prison on September 17, 1779, was a deeply changed person. At the end of these two months of detention, his health had severely deteriorated, in regard to both his physical condition and his morale, but he had also developed new faculties, as is demonstrated in a most striking manner by a text edited by Chevignard in 1983:[35] "I became a new man: ashamed not to be able to laugh with others or share their gaiety, I avoided the company of my closest friends. In my solitude, I had discovered pleasures that I had never experienced before. I could meditate at length on the same subject without being disturbed. I could converse with myself and give rise through this conversation to ideas that simple meditation didn't produce. I could, finally, in the moments of calm remember those ideas and write them down."[36]

This passage reveals the mechanisms of a personal and artistic evolution. Solitude is the means of a new kind of meditation. Before the experience of imprisonment, this deep reflection was not only less extensive and less intense but was also monological: his thought applied itself to a problem more or less consistently from a single perspective. The moral consequences of the ordeals he had undergone during the Revolutionary War led him to embrace a dialogical approach: his thought became "an internal discourse that the soul pursued silently with itself," to use Plato's expression;[37] that is to say, the examination of a problem or of a situation is no longer carried out from a single viewpoint, that which an individual is spontaneously led to adopt on a question, but is henceforth opened up to a series of opposing hypotheses and contradictions that he spontaneously contemplates as if he embodied the two adverse parties at the same time. Undoubtedly, the metaphysical experience of the omnipresence of evil in the world, which had suddenly made him "a Manichean," had revealed to him the greater complexity of human nature and of historical events that only a dialogical style of reflection was capable of portraying for himself and his future readers. By opposing "conversation" to "meditation," Crèvecœur emphasized moreover the productive character of the former, given that it permits the rise of ideas that the latter would not have inspired. This is, however, only a first stage in the writing process, since these moments of solitude, in which the author confronts conflicting perspectives before giving birth to new ideas through an internal dialog, precede the moment of writing itself that records the results of this process of investigation and creation. In this essential text, Crèvecœur describes the effects of this crisis of the winter of 1779, following which he became a writer endowed with a superior power of concentration and analysis, the one who was going to publish just a few years later the *Letters from an American Farmer*.[38]

However, Crèvecœur's difficulties did not cease on the day of his liberation: he continued to live in misery until September 1780, at which time he finally managed to embark for Europe with his son. After a month's crossing, they reached Ireland, then England. On May 20, 1781, while passing through London, Crèvecœur sold the manuscript of the *Letters from an American Farmer* to the publishing house of Thomas Davies and Lockyer Davis. That a virtual unknown succeeded in having his first book published by such an important house is the sign of the burning interest this text held for the English people. Finally, on August 2, 1781, Crèvecœur set foot on his native soil.

RETURN TO THE MOTHERLAND

What man had Crèvecœur become after twenty-seven years in exile? The *Mémoires* of Brissot de Warville help us to understand.[39] The two men met in 1786 and were soon drawn together by "the most affectionate friendship."[40] With Étienne Clavière and Nicolas Bergasse, they founded, on January 2, 1787, an association intended to promote the intellectual and commercial relations between France and the United States: the Société Gallo-Américaine.[41] In the portrait that he draws of his friend, Brissot emphasizes the anguish that characterized him during this period: "Crèvecœur always had a somber look about him, a worried air; he seemed to fear being found out. He never shared his emotional turmoil; sometimes he even seemed frightened by the success of his work and appeared to have a secret that weighed heavily on his soul and that he feared might be revealed."[42] If we are to believe Brissot, Crèvecœur's melancholy on the eve of the French Revolution was the result of his political vacillation during the War of Independence: "This indecisiveness had bred in the Republicans a deep scorn for him; if they did not consider him a dangerous person, they saw him as a man with neither energy nor character, and closer to slavery than liberty."[43] Crèvecœur had good reason to conceal this ambiguous past when he translated the *Letters*.[44] On the one hand, he now belonged to a circle that was entirely behind the cause of the American rebels,[45] and this exerted a profound influence on his rewriting; on the other hand, the French public was then possessed of a "craze for America" that strongly predisposed it to praise for the patriots and would have led it to rebel against any discourse that was in any way favorable to perfidious Albion. A third reason was added to these first two in 1783 when the maréchal de Castries appointed Crèvecœur to the position of French Consul in New York: "[The Republicans] were understandably astonished that the French minister would give the first consulate in America to an enemy of the Revolution and of American independence. Himself overcome by his prodigious success in France, Crèvecœur feared being exposed and losing a position that he held very dear."[46]

It was thus with the anguish of being seen as a partisan of the British crown that the author of the *Letters from an American Farmer* translated them into French. As I attempt to demonstrate in the following part of this chapter, this context played a dominant role in the redefinition of both the aesthetics and the political discourse of his work in the French language. Ultimately, the war and its consequences created in Crèvecœur's existence a fracture that preceded the publication of his works and created two distinct periods with effects that were as lasting as those provoked by the powerful moral shocks experienced by more famous authors.[47] This notion of a split that his ensuing misfortunes only increased,[48] separating not only two periods but also two identities, helps us understand Crèvecœur's work as an attempt to recreate a past that, since it was lost forever, appeared infinitely desirable to him. The posthumous representation of America was thus not only an undertaking designed to protect a historical period in order to pass on its memory to future generations: for Crèvecœur, it simultaneously constituted an attempt to relive, through his writing, a vanished and otherwise unreachable happiness.

In Search of Lost America: The *Lettres d'un cultivateur américain* (1784–87)

THE *LETTRES* OF 1784: AMERICA RECOMPOSED

Frenchification and Idealization
When Saint-John de Crèvecœur moved into Madame d'Houdetot's home in the spring of 1782, his hostess's encouragements, the praise of their mutual friends, and the growing success of the *Letters from an American Farmer* soon convinced him to undertake a French translation of his work. Published in 1784,

the first two volumes of the *Lettres d'un cultivateur américain* were followed in 1787 by a new edition with a third volume. The numerous divergences between the English and French versions have been analyzed by Howard C. Rice[49] and Bernard Chevignard.[50] This question will be taken up again by highlighting two processes that organized the work of translation and rewriting undertaken by Crèvecœur, "Frenchification" (*francisation*) and idealization, in order to establish their internal logic, their diverse manifestations, and their role in the production of a posthumous representation of America.

Frenchification is making a literary text correspond to the expectations, aesthetic preferences, and values of French society in a given period, eliminating what the author assumes would go against its tastes or its prejudices and adding what, instead, appears to be likely to garner its approval. It concerns consequently a form of translation in a system of values that is socially constructed and subject to change, given that the definitions of the beautiful, of the good, but also of the proper are, of course, apt to evolve within a community. The "idealization" is a similar operation to the extent that it too comprises a double movement of addition and rejection. It consists of the production of a representation that is commensurate with the aspirations of its readers, eliminating what might render it less desirable and including, on the contrary, what may correspond to their highest expectations. Idealization presupposes the existence of a representation upon which there is already a consensus in the community of the audience of the work, just as a translation transfers a given text into a system of signs whose meaning is agreed upon by its users. By means of more or less numerous and subtle erasures and supplements that, rather than being detrimental to "truth," redefine it as they invent it, the author engaged in an idealizing process thus seeks the most precise correspondence between the representation that he is producing and the ideal image embedded in the collective consciousness, and for which he also serves as the guardian. The identification of these two processes helps us account for Crèvecœur's choices in the course of the translation of the *Letters from an American Farmer* and, ultimately, explain the difference between the posthumous America he constructs and its supposed referent.

Transposition and Adaptation

The Frenchification and idealization of the *Letters* are made possible by a theory of translation in the eighteenth century that is the antithesis of contemporary thought on this subject. In the history of translation, two methods came to be opposed: transposition (or faithful translation) and adaptation (or integral translation).[51] Although differing opinions were held in the eighteenth century, the adaptation approach generally won out.[52] A good translator transposed the ideas and the style of the source text into the target language with a view toward correlating them with the tastes of his new readership and correcting what he perceived as awkward turns of phrase or just plain bad writing.[53] His role consisted of lending to the author the language that he would have adopted if he had been not only his contemporary but his countryman. The liberty of the translator in relationship to the original work is still greater when, as in the case of Crèvecœur, he is also its author. The French translation of the *Letters from an American Farmer* belongs to the category of adaptation: it modifies the first text and adds numerous passages, so that the length of the French version far exceeds that of the original.[54] In the course of his work, Crèvecœur sought the counsel of six people whose advice turned out to have considerable influence on the final version of the *Lettres d'un cultivateur américain*: the comtesse d'Houdetot; Jean-François de Saint-Lambert, contributor to the *Encyclopédie* and author of *Les Saisons* (1769); the prince and princesse de Beauvau; Louis de Lacretelle, publisher of the *Mercure de France*; and Gui-Jean-Baptiste Target, a lawyer.

Several reasons explain Crèvecœur's receptiveness to the influence of his friends and protectors. When he decided to translate the *Letters*, his native tongue became a foreign language to him.[55] Painfully conscious of the weakness of his French, he asked the enlightened readers surrounding him to verify the correctness of his writing. In addition, Crèvecœur was never confident in his talent as a writer and felt that he had only come to literature by accident.[56] He thus took the advice of his protectors all the more willingly since he considered them to be arbiters of good taste and even models in the art of writing, since one of them, Saint-Lambert, was a member of the French Academy. Finally, Crèvecœur was caught in a knot of material and moral obligations that prevented him from ignoring the literary advice that his friends offered him so generously: he was in fact greatly in debt to the latter, who, not content to introduce him into the best society, used their influence with the highest authorities of the monarchy to obtain for him the highly coveted position of French Consul in New York. His protectors were thus implicated in each stage of the writing of the *Lettres d'un cultivateur américain*: they convinced Crèvecœur to undertake the translation of the *Letters*;[57] they recommended amendments and proposed their own works as models for him to learn from; they participated in the commercial launching of his work; and Crèvecœur went so far as to entrust to them the final revision of his text, which he was prevented from carrying out himself.[58] It was thus under their auspices that the *francisation* of the text accompanied its translation: following their advice, Crèvecœur adapted the *Letters* to the sensitivity and convictions, if not the prejudices, of his new public.

A Superficial Rousseauism
The Frenchification of America manifests itself particularly by the introduction of a superficial Rousseauism, that is, references that demonstrate the familiarity of an author with the literary and philosophical works of Jean-Jacques Rousseau.

Occasionally explicit, these references are more often simply implied, since the extremely widespread diffusion of Rousseau's writings, and the commentaries provoked by them, created in the minds of his contemporaries such a familiarity with his works that any allusion to the idea that his community of readers had of his intellectual production was immediately recognized by them. This idea, however, was little more than a simplified version, diluted and partially false, of works whose complexity proved to be irreducible to the process of simplification performed by the collective consciousness when it tried to come to grips with the aesthetics and the philosophical thought of Jean-Jacques Rousseau. This simplification, or popularization if you will, is the ransom of the success of operative philosophical concepts that, owing to their ability to grasp reality in order to make useful and fertile distinctions, lend themselves to endless reformulations during which their initial significance—enriched by its internal tensions, the examples and details provided by its creator—is progressively impoverished to the point of no longer being anything but a sign partially emptied of its substance. Such, for example, is the case of the concept of "state of nature," which, while recalling Rousseau's *Discourse on the Origin of Inequality* (1755), is most often, under the pen of Rousseau's imitators, only a pale version of this same concept, whose philosophical foundation is more apt to be the reductive idea that the contemporaries conceived than the meaning that was in fact given to it by the citizen of Geneva.[59] Similarly, the use of a pastoral tone in the description of a rural landscape, a certain effusion in the expression of sensibility, a variation on the theme of sovereign virtue accompanied by an irrevocable condemnation of the seductions of vice have as their referent the aesthetics of the *Nouvelle Héloïse* and are perceived as signs that the author who employs them adheres to the moral values that underlie the actions of Julie and Saint-Preux. This superficial Rousseauism, in which the adoption of a concept takes as its referent a philosophical system constructed elsewhere, while partially betraying it, in which the use of a literary tone expresses an aesthetic that it gradually caricatures as it systemizes its use, is also found in the *Lettres d'un cultivateur américain* and notably in the texts that concern the Amerindian world. It is true that the image of the Native American is sometimes threatening in the *Lettres d'un cultivateur américain*[60] and may be distinguished from the topos of the "noble savage" that is one of the principal clichés of superficial Rousseauism; several passages nonetheless dwell at length on a potential harmony between their society and that of the colonists, as in the case of a text particularly admired in Crèvecœur's time, the "Anecdote of the Wild Dog."[61]

Recounted for the first time in a passage that is not in the *Letters from an American Farmer* but was published by the editors of the *Sketches of Eighteenth-Century America*,[62] this anecdote reappears in a watered-down form in the *Lettres* of 1784 (1:199–211). Crèvecœur tells the story of a child believed to be dead after disappearing for a whole day in the forest before an Amerindian found him with the help of his dog. The scene in which the young boy is returned to his parents gives rise to an outpouring of tears and gratitude (204), and even the Native American warrior is moved and cannot hold back his tears in observing the extreme happiness he has caused. The next day, Le Fèvre (the father of the child) holds a meeting of eighty-three people—friends, neighbors, and servants—before whom he swears to the "savage" an eternal friendship: "Téwénissa, with this branch of wampum, I touch your ears; Téwénissa, I am speaking to you: my heart was broken, you cured the wound. I cried bitter tears for fear of having lost my child; you dried my tears by finding him with the help of your faithful dog. . . . My wife and I were like two grass snakes, stiff and lifeless; you revived us by bringing us close to the fire" (207–8).

This scene is a celebration of the marriage of the Western and the Amerindian worlds. Le Fèvre's borrowing of one of his benefactor's customs and of rhetorical practices that are characteristic of Amerindian eloquence accompanies a series of performative declarations. After giving him a very valuable carbine, Le Fèvre makes a first promise to Téwénissa: he will shelter him under his roof and take care of him if he were ever to fall ill or sought refuge in old age. Then he publicly announces a solemn adoption, recognizing his benefactor as a member of his family (208). Sanctified by the approval of the gathering, the fraternal bonds between the two men are made yet stronger by the second baptism of the rescued child; the name by which he had been known before his disappearance will be forgotten, and he will answer henceforth to that of "his liberator and uncle Téwénissa" (209). The latter then adopts Le Fèvre and swears a friendship that lasts after their disappearance, since their children likewise recognize each other as brothers.

By means of this anecdote, Crèvecœur presents an ecumenical image of the relations between the white settlers and the Native Americans. An image from the present, the harmony between the two peoples had always existed, if we are to believe Le Fèvre, who describes the appropriation of the ancestral lands of the latter by the former—a land grab that was accomplished by force, ruse, and broken promises—as the result of a willing gift that the Europeans received with gratitude: "I offer you no land, for you do not want any; it is from you and your ancestors that we received the land we cultivate" (208). The expression "received" implies the idea of a transfer that was effected with neither conflict nor abuse and casts a veil over the reality of the historical process, so much more somber and unjust, in the course of which the American national territory was constituted. At this time, the worlds to which the colonists and the Amerindians belong are not only able to coexist peacefully but are in fact intertwined: the cultural differences are overridden by the sharing of symbols and linguistic practices mastered by the members of the two groups owing to their long familiarity with each other. It is possible to travel between their respective territories, as is demonstrated by the presence of Téwénissa on Le Fèvre's lands and the trip of the latter's son to his adoptive uncle's village; a complex network of relations maintained over the years, as well as mutual obligations, gradually created a social fabric joining the two communities. While it is true that cultural difference is never completely surmounted, as evidenced by the fact that it must be occasionally transcended by means, for example, of the goodwill showed by Le Fèvre in adopting the customs of his benefactor on a solemn occasion, it nonetheless permits the creation of a shared universe whose harmony reaches its zenith in the course of ceremonies in which individuals are united in a common emotional experience. From beginning to end, a superficial Rousseauism infuses this anecdote in which the Amerindian protagonist demonstrates the generosity and selflessness that a reader of Rousseau expects from a "noble savage," while the philosophical message slipped in at the beginning of the text—"only wholesome morality and virtue are shared by all countries" (200)—prepares the intensely emotional spectacle of a reciprocal adoption between representatives of distinct cultures and serves discreetly as an echo of the outpourings of the "Profession du vicaire savoyard" ("Profession of Faith of the Savoyard Vicar") concerning the innate origin of our moral conscience.[63] The readers of Crèvecœur did not miss the reference and gave a particularly favorable reception to this anecdote that confirmed their preconceptions about an American state of nature inhabited by "savages" who demonstrate all the virtues originally rooted in the human heart.[64] This representation of a "primitive" world in which the natural goodness of human beings is given free rein is indissolubly linked to the philosophy of Rousseau or, more precisely, to what has been called here the superficial understanding of it. In any case, Rousseau's work is only the place where a discourse about the morally exemplary nature of the savage crystallizes, a discourse that originates in the first contacts between the New World and the Old.

In the sixteenth century, travelers such as Jean de Léry brought back to Europe a description of the mores, customs, and social organization of the inhabitants of the New World that contributed to the nascent image of America among his fellow countrymen. A reader of Léry, Michel de Montaigne describes the Amerindian society, in a famous essay titled "Des cannibales," as the most faithful to what he calls the "natural laws," questioning the so-called barbarity of the peoples of America and offering the European readers a comparison with their own vices.[65] Following Montaigne, the *Dialogues de Monsieur le Baron de Lahontan et d'un sauvage* (1704) contribute to the diffusion in European thought of the dream of a state of nature that is combined, in Lahontan's work, with a nostalgia for "the mythical situation of the feudal nobility when it was escaping the domination of the monarchy."[66] Rousseau, who was a reader of Lahontan, takes up again the question of the state of nature in the *Discourse on the Origin of Inequality* by describing, in solitary primitive man, characteristics bordering on animality.[67] While the state of nature, under Rousseau's pen, is a largely theoretical conceptual artifact, a tool allowing him to imagine the situation of the human race before the rise of property and society—and not the description of a particular historical moment in the evolution of mankind—the popularity of this theme contributed to its perception in the course of its multiple reworkings as an accurate description of the reality of primitive life.[68] For the imitators of Rousseau, the state of nature is not a fiction cast on the origins of human history: it becomes a proper description of man at the margins of European civilization, both a contemporary of the Europeans and a reincarnation of his ancestors by dint of belonging to a civilization considered primitive. When Crèvecœur tried his hand at representing the "primitive" world, the Rousseauist tropism was so strong that he could not resist it: the Amerindians were also noble savages, capable of sublime devotion and elevated sentiments. In this manner, he offered the guarantee of his vast experience to what had only been philosophical speculation and tireless repetition of the same themes.[69] Since it is confirmed by Crèvecœur, himself an "American savage" and soon to be consul of his very Christian majesty in New York, America must be, indeed, this Arcadia where European settlers and Amerindian hunters make merry together as he claims.[70]

The circularity of the representations achieves yet another rotation that reinforces its power in the collective imagination when travelers such as Brissot and Lezay-Marnésia go to the United States with expectations based on the reading of Crèvecœur's works. When Brissot visited America, he saw it through the lens of the *Lettres d'un cultivateur américain*; he did not describe the country he was discovering using his own sensitivity and judgment but rather by constantly calibrating his observations on those of Crèvecœur. It is those observations that he corroborated in publishing his own account in which the reader is constantly referred to the works of his predecessor, such that Brissot's journey, far from correcting the image he had of America before going there, has no other effect than to confirm the accuracy of this prior representation.[71] The French send back to each other a mimetic representation of the United States, their imagination influencing the observations they make in America before providing preconceived models upon which they narrate their memories.

In this respect, the composition of the French discourse on America is a particular case of a phenomenon that can be observed on the scale of Europe as a whole: "The New World was invented before it was discovered. Mythology preceded exploration; and discovery happily fitted previous invention," observes Marcus Cunliffe.[72] This discourse, organized around recurrent images and themes to which reality was summoned to conform by the very certainty that it had acquired during its innumerable repetitions, what Cunliffe calls a "mythology," referred to previously as a "doxological America," is subject to national variations and historical evolution. A global study of the American "mythology" in the European consciousness would reveal, most certainly, topical components that are shared by different nations, just as a diachronic study would show, without the slightest doubt, the very long period of time in which a network of preconceptions and prejudices about America is embedded in a given country. However, each nation includes different materials in the course of the creation of its own "doxological America" depending on the relations that it has maintained with the United States over time and the critical moments that have marked their common history, and it is, similarly, the historical evolution of these relations that influences the slow recomposition of this complex web of images and discourses within a given country. The end of the eighteenth century is one of these privileged moments, and the *Lettres d'un cultivateur américain* played a considerable role in the construction of the meaning of the sign "America" in the French consciousness before its progressive reconfiguration.

As it is recreated in Paris by Crèvecœur, posthumous America is the fruit of this meeting between a collective image and an individual nostalgia inventing a fictitious country whose purely literary existence will nonetheless have direct consequences on reality.[73] Crèvecœur's depiction of a past period in American history, although based on the experience of prolonged contact with the United States, is in fact affected by a discourse constituted prior to this experience and to which it refers to confirm its problematical veracity. Parallel to its commemorative function, which consists in protecting the idealized image of a period prior to the ravages of the war, a period in which harmony reigned between the Native Americans and the settlers as illustrated in the "Anecdote of the Wild Dog," the function assumed by this representation is one of advertising, given that it offers to doxological America the guarantee of an author who refrains from revising it based on the observations that he has made across the Atlantic. It is also a form of advertisement in a complementary sense, since by satisfying the expectations of the contemporary readership, it strived simultaneously to promote itself to the same public and achieve a commercial success that, moreover, it succeeded in doing on a grand scale, the literary product offered to the public having corresponded perfectly to its desires. A complex montage of temporal strata in which the influence of the context of the translation and rewriting bears on the aesthetics and the underlying philosophy of the text, the posthumous America of Crèvecœur is the depiction of a defunct past that pervades in advance the imagination, voyages, and even the narratives of his successors.

The Theodicy of the Bees

The phenomenon of *francisation* of American reality goes hand in hand with that of idealization, as witnessed by numerous choices made by Crèvecœur in the course of the translation. The second letter of the *Letters from an American Farmer* relates, for example, the reflections of the narrator, James, while contemplating the bees that live on his farm: "My bees, more than any other inhabitants of my land, command my attention and my respect. I am astonished to see that nothing exists that has no enemy; one species pursues and lives upon the other."[74] The conception of the world that arises from this spectacle is both neutral and pessimistic: James limits himself to the description of the necessity of the mutual destruction of species; rather than regret or revolt, his observations lead to surprise. Not content to lengthen the English text, the French version radically changes the philosophical lesson: "My bees, more than any other inhabitants of my land, command my attention and my respect. . . . What a shame that in the midst of this harmony, of this differentiation of the species, none can exist independent of the others! All of them have their enemies. The genius of the Creator, perhaps fearing the excessive fertility he had given to matter, found it necessary to temper it by this system of destruction."[75]

The French translation adds to this passage a Latin erudition absent from the original: the celebration of the industriousness of the bees is a theme that is indissociable from pastoral literature and in particular the works of Virgil.[76] Without it being even necessary to explain the Virgilian allusion, the mention of these industrious bees alone signals to the reader that he has just entered the bucolic universe of the *Georgics*. For what reasons did Crèvecœur include in the French text a Virgilian intertext that is not found in the original?

In the "Preliminary Discourse" of *Les Saisons* (1769), Saint-Lambert admits that he has borrowed themes explored by the author of the *Aeneid* and tried to imitate his style.[77] Before giving his opinion of *Les Saisons*, Diderot reread the *Georgics* on the suggestion of his friend Jacques-André Naigeon: the comparison was not favorable to the academician.[78] In all probability, the reading of Saint-Lambert (if not the advice of this man who was part of Crèvecœur's immediate entourage during his stay in Paris) was one of the direct sources of the pastoral tone that permeates the *Lettres d'un cultivateur américain*, which depict primitive American nature as a bucolic garden and do not spare references to Roman antiquity.[79] This propensity for idealization is confirmed later in the same missive: while the text of *Letters* refers directly to the fight to the death between species ("one species pursues and lives upon the other"), that of *Lettres* bemoans their lack of "independence," disguising with this abstract term the necessary destruction of the ones by the others. What the French text strives to guarantee above all is the "harmony" of the American creation. This term, present in this passage, is its key.

The French translation introduces two philosophical systems that are absent from the original: deist thought and a theodicy. The text refers to a "Creator's genius," a circumlocution that belongs to the deist tradition. This "genius" guarantees the perdurability of His work, since the principle of destruction that He introduces into it is intended to contain the exuberance of nature, the excessive "fertility" that would risk, in the long run, compromising its fine scheme. Through the reflection on bees, it is thus the question of evil in the world that is implicitly posed, the animal kingdom playing here the role of a metaphor for the human race. In the English text, the brief development on the struggle between the animal species has a proleptic function: it predicts the war between the loyalists and the patriots in the American Revolution, another example of the destructive instinct that drives living creatures. For its part, the French text is quick to disperse the shadow of violence cast over the American Eden by surreptitiously introducing the notion of theodicy. Far from leading to chaos, the destruction of the species is a principle established by the "great Watchmaker" to guarantee the smooth functioning of His creation. The posthumous America of Crèvecœur is not only the recovery of a lost paradise; it represents the best of all possible worlds.

Memories Reproduced by Memories

Crèvecœur's posthumous America is thus the result of an a posteriori reconstruction that leans toward idealization. It is likewise the result of a double memorial reconstitution that increases still more the gap between this representation and its object. The genesis of the *Lettres* of 1784 was marked by an unforeseen circumstance: the necessity of a rewriting. In the *Mercure* of January 1783, Lacretelle announced the imminent publication of the work of his friend: "Around the same time, M. de Néville of the bookseller's staff sent the manuscript to the minister Vergennes for his approval, or at least he thought he had sent it, but when he requested it three months later, he learned that Vergennes had never received it. They ascertained that the manuscript had been removed from M. Néville's office, an unforeseen mishap that was to delay the publication."[80]

Crèvecœur is forced to produce a new manuscript that isn't published until the end of 1784. It is difficult to determine how much work he was condemned to do by this unfortunate event. In a letter addressed to the editor of the *Courrier de l'Europe*, Crèvecœur stated that he was in the process of retranscribing the 320 pages that were stolen from him and that "the fruit of this theft isn't even half of the whole that is to be published very soon."[81] There is no way of knowing if he had rough drafts to work from during his labor; however, it is certain that this misadventure forced him to undertake a new attempt at recollection, since not only did he have to recall his past but also try to remember the written pages that had disappeared and in which this same work had already been accomplished a first time. The resulting text is therefore, at least in part, the fruit of a second genesis during which Crèvecœur had to rewrite the original version that had been stolen from him, which turned this work, as Chateaubriand has written about another book, into a collection of "memories reproduced by memories."[82] Thus the posthumous America reinvented in the *Lettres* of 1784 may be described as the image of an image representing an idealized and Frenchified version of the New World.

LETTERS FROM BEYOND THE GRAVE

Imagining the Loss
Following the death of his father, discontented with his life of labor and dreaming of changing it, the narrator of the "Pensées d'un cultivateur américain sur son sort et ses plaisirs" ("Thoughts of an American Farmer on His Fate and Pleasures")[83] imagines what would become of him if he decided to sell his property:

> I saw myself wandering; it seemed to me that I would lose all my weight and importance, as well as the esteem of my friends; . . . *and then my land, my house, my fields, and my meadows appeared suddenly in my imagination, in the dearest and most cheerful colors*; the idea of a home, stability, and civil rights, the idea of property, finally, that up to now I hadn't considered seriously, appeared in my imagination in the most attractive colors; and what I formerly believed to be chimerical became for me a genuine source of satisfaction and pride.[84]

The imagined departure from his plantation embellishes the image of the latter and of its existence in the eyes of the narrator: suddenly his domain appeared to him as the foundation of his respectability, his pride, and his happiness. If the very idea of the loss of his property alone provoked a metamorphosis of the image Crèvecœur had of his own condition, one can just imagine to what extent the dispossession he experienced during the War of Independence must have changed his image of prerevolutionary America![85] From the moment that the supposed loss became a reality, the reevaluation of his fate by the American farmer could not lead to an increased enjoyment of his current possessions, nor to a renewed satisfaction at the idea of the position he still enjoyed in this world, but to an impression of irremediable loss accompanied by regrets whose pangs could only be alleviated by writing. "As far as I can tell, there is little nostalgia on either side of the Atlantic for the time when England's thirteen American colonies were part of Great Britain," states Jim Cullen in the work that he devotes to the origin and development of the ideology of the American dream.[86] The *Lettres d'un cultivateur américain* are nonetheless saturated with a nostalgia that is given free rein when the author depicts the bucolic scenes of his existence before the war and develops the posthumous representation of the colonial period.

Temporal Strata

Just like Chateaubriand's *Mémoires*, Crèvecœur's *Lettres* had multiple starting points. In the margins of his chapters, Chateaubriand indicated both the time of the first writing of the text and the moment when he returned to it years later. Book VI of the *Mémoires* is, for example, written in "London, from April to September 1822" and "revised in December 1846." Whereas Chateaubriand displays these two strata of writings, Crèvecœur conceals them. The paratext of his letters regularly presents them as missives written before the American Revolution: the first in the volume is, for example, sent from "Carlisle County" on "August 18, 1770"[87] while the "[l]etter written by Ivan Al-Z, a Russian nobleman, to one of his friends in Europe" is dated October 12, 1769.[88] Other letters have no explicit temporal reference but nonetheless reveal, by certain details in the text, that they were written from the viewpoint of a writer who in no way foresees the imminence of the war. This is the case of the "Second Letter," in which the narrator attributes the rapid population growth of the colonies to the "blessings of peace."[89]

However, these texts are not what they pretend to be, that is, documents that have miraculously escaped the wreckage of the American Revolution and bear the echo of voices now extinct. While the *Lettres* of 1784 are based on previous texts and on contemporary impressions of the facts they describe, they are nonetheless translated, revised, enriched, organized into a volume, and published in a period in which Crèvecœur is no longer the "self" he was before the Revolution, but this "second self" that he struggled to reconstruct after the war.[90] The documentary effect that they produce is thus a matter of art and not of sincerity. Crèvecœur offers the reader a representation of colonial America supposedly written before its disappearance, whereas he transmits to his narrator the idealized vision he developed following his inner fracture. His letter writer had, however, never witnessed the period he depicts; it is Crèvecœur who attributes to him the idyllic description of an America that only exists in his memory. Thus, the representation of the colonial era that he wishes us to accept as contemporary of the facts related is on the contrary a posthumous representation that reinvents a past age of American history as it appears to him retrospectively. In Crèvecœur's *Lettres*, the term "America" does not designate a country located on the other side of the Atlantic; it refers to an imaginary space that the author has recreated in the light of his nostalgia and in which he can only travel by means of memory and writing. Crèvecœur manages to dispel this confusion of the present and the posthumous, of a faithful description and a nostalgic reinvention, in the mind of Brissot, who saw in emigration to the United States a possible alternative to the constraints of prerevolutionary France:

As a man of letters, I did not wish to bow down to the idols of the day, and nonetheless I could only manage to exist through this type of servility. I preferred [I said to Crèvecœur], plying some difficult trade in the United States, but perhaps I could hope that my talents might one day bring me some affluence there.... Such were my ideas each day, such was the theme of my conversations. *Crèvecœur constantly tried to discourage me, to combat my plan, to emphasize the injustices of my enemies, to exhort me to stop attacking them, to choose another genre for my writing.*[91]

Crèvecœur's behavior toward his friend consisted of an effort to moderate the enthusiasm he had himself inspired and is an indication of the ambivalence of his thought, which oscillates between retrospective idealization within a commemorative representation and the growing disappointment he felt toward the real country of which the former is supposedly the image, an ambivalence that was to become even more difficult to assume when his official functions in New York prevented him from publicly expressing all the concerns he had about present-day America when he compared it to his posthumous version.[92]

Harmony and Discord

This process of retrospective idealization is not only an implicit development in the *Lettres d'un cultivateur américain*; Crèvecœur regularly contrasts in the same text the harmony of colonial America and the current agitation of the war. Crèvecœur writes certain letters from the viewpoint of a contemporary of the American Revolution who recalls an earlier era while in the midst of the turmoil of war. The passages in which the vision of an idyllic past and the intolerable reality of the conflict are collapsed together indicate the therapeutic effect of the writing on a narrator who is explicitly identified with the author. This effect is suggested in the conclusion of the "Anecdote of the Sassafras and the Wild Vine," a charming and bucolic text in which Crèvecœur describes the planting of a tree that he hopes will remain, after his own disappearance, the living proof of his love for his daughter. He finishes it with these remarks, which project a retrospective shadow on the luminous memory he is recounting: "I forget for a moment, in repeating these pleasant details, the misfortunes the war inflicted on me.—This sweet memory still swells and stirs my heart. In the middle of the storm that surrounds me, *I have no other consolation than drawing for you a weak sketch of the happy days I've lived.*"[93] This comment indicates the role played by literary writing for Crèvecœur, which helped him escape the present impression of the misfortunes caused by the war by recalling the memory of "days" made all the more "happy" by the fact that they are forever gone. When he declares that his descriptions are only a "weak sketch," the reader must see in this statement more than the affected modesty of a writer admitting his inability to depict satisfactorily the memories he has retained. It is precisely in the impossible superimposition of the memorial scene and the text charged with expressing it that resides, for Crèvecœur, the drive to write, a constantly renewed drive, as is demonstrated by the resumption and progressive augmentation of his *Lettres*. The feeling that literary writing is incapable of representing the past in a manner that conforms to the internal image lodged in the memory of the author constantly refuels his work, and it would be tempting to compare Crèvecœur to Sade based on their comparable practice of rewriting and of textual expansion if the thirst for experimentation and desire for exhaustiveness, if not "the obsessional force of a character, scenario, and argument"[94]—rather than the nostalgia and tragic consciousness of a destructive temporality—were at the source of a process of amplification whose only possible interruption is that imposed by the death of the author.[95]

It is, however, in the work of Marcel Proust that may be found the most fertile point of comparison with the attempt at reinventing lost days undertaken by Crèvecœur. In *En lisant en écrivant* (*Reading Writing*), Julien Gracq describes the typical principle of development in *A la recherche du temps perdu* (*In Search of Lost Time*): "The genetic imperative of proliferation and enrichment takes precedence over the principle of organization every time in the book."[96] Initially conceived as a diptych, then as a triptych, Proust's novel underwent a rapid expansion that was only terminated by the writer's disappearance.[97] This other attempt to recreate the past that is seen in Crèvecœur's *Lettres* exhibits a similar potentially exponential dynamic of augmentation. The twelve texts that compose the thin volume of *Letters from an American Farmer* are succeeded in 1784 by the two volumes of the *Lettres d'un cultivateur américain*, which are joined by a third in 1787 to reach a total of around fifteen hundred pages. Crèvecœur intended to add a fourth volume that eventually became a fully autonomous work, the *Voyage dans la Haute Pensylvanie et dans l'État de New York*, a tome of thirteen hundred pages on the New World whose encyclopedic ambition is demonstrated by the abundance of historical notes that accompany this travel narrative.[98] His writing, however, can never exhaust the subject of America: whether the latter has changed between the time of its discovery and that of its appearance in his texts (in accordance with the first paradox of the New World), or it embodied for the writer an Eden whose disappearance will ever remain the subject of infinite and inexpressible regret, it occasioned the constant resumption of a literary labor that was incapable of expressing its subject in a satisfactory manner.

The "Anecdote of the Sassafras and of the Wild Vine" gave free rein to reminiscence before emphasizing at the end of the text the destruction of an age whose memory it was commemorating. Crèvecœur also occasionally interrupted the temporal continuity in a letter to highlight the historical and personal fracture that the War of Independence represented. In a text dated January 17, 1774,

Crèvecœur depicted the work and the general life of his family in wintertime. Hospitality was the rule during this period in which the harshness of the season was compensated by a "keen, pure joy" in the domestic space. Nevertheless, this description is interrupted by a question put to the addressee:

> You once enjoyed these winter diversions . . . tell me, doesn't the feeble image that I'm offering here still give you pleasure? That is how I spent the happiest moments of my life, in the bosom of liberty, material comforts, gentle familiarity, and friendship. . . . Delightful moments, when will I see you again! Alas! the union, harmony, and fraternity that we enjoyed at that time are replaced today by deep distress, tears, jealousy, and the war with all its murders and flames. I wish to forget them and soothe my heart by turning my thoughts to sweeter memories.[99]

This commentary by the narrator on his own narrative betrays the subterfuge of the writing: the letter cannot have been written on "January 17, 1774," as the paratext asserts; it was necessarily written after the beginning of the American Revolution, since it alludes to its terrible consequences. While the present tense used in the text seems to express the contemporaneous character of the discourse and of its object, it indicates in fact the subjective topicality of the reminiscence: writing is a way to forget momentarily the suffering caused by the war and to return to a yet earlier period when happiness was supposedly felt in all its fullness. The posthumous representation of America thus allows the double updating of the past that it recalls: it commemorates for the reader the defunct age that it undertakes to describe, but it also permits the author to live a past reconstituted in an affective mode in which time is briefly abolished. Whether he is describing colonial America from the viewpoint of a colonist oblivious to the impending war or from that of a contemporary of the conflict, Crèvecœur adorns it with all the characteristics of a Golden Age: the comparison of this epoch of American history to a mythical period is the clearest sign of the retrospective idealization that plays out in posthumous representation.[100]

Portrayal of the Golden Age

In *More Letters from the American Farmer*, Crèvecœur was already comparing colonial America to the Golden Age by identifying it with the tradition inherited from Hesiod and Ovid.[101] According to him, the realization of an ideal of insularity is a necessary condition for the reproduction of this ideal state of history. The family unit presents a first form of self-sufficiency: its members are isolated on the farm like Robinson on his desert island, their autonomy guaranteeing their prosperity and felicity.[102] This unit is characterized by the harmony that reigns there: the American farmer is overwhelmed with emotion to the point of shedding tears when he contemplates, in their abode, his wife cradling their child on her breast.[103] In the *Lettres* of 1784, the themes of family and paternity appear several times. Crèvecœur describes the revolutionary effect on him of the birth of his child and declares that the power of paternal sentiment is inconceivable for someone who has never experienced it.[104] The recurrence of this theme is a new sign of the therapeutic function that Crèvecœur attributed to the writing of his *Lettres d'un cultivateur américain*, since at the time he composed the first two volumes, he had no knowledge of the fate of his wife and two children who remained at Pine Hill, a fate that he would only learn of upon his return to the United States in 1783. The descriptions of domestic bliss that are found in the *Lettres* can be read as a literary compensation for the anguish he experienced in the period when he was finishing his book, in the form of an attempt to commune with the time when such harmony was still possible.

Crèvecœur's American Golden Age is characterized moreover by the political autonomy of communities, as proved by his remarks on the founding of Connecticut: "During the first years, each family lived isolated on its land, occupied solely with its work, with no coercive bonds and with no laws, and they were happy.—*This period was the Golden Age of this province*; they were bound solely by the principles of benevolence, by the need of mutual assistance, by the desire to live in peace."[105] The resurrection of this age of innocence, prosperity, and justice can, however, only be effected if the characteristic insularity of the family unit is reproduced on a broader scope. Ideally, this larger community is subject to an exterior power that imposes as few constraints as possible, a legislative code reduced to its simplest expression being, according to Crèvecœur, the best guarantee of public felicity. Crèvecœur sets in opposition to the legislative constraint put into effect by a political authority the self-regulation of the communities by the reciprocal benevolence of their members and the need for mutual assistance. In the letter titled "Story of André l'Hébridéen," he emphasizes the custom of *trolique*, an instance of mutual aid by the inhabitants of a township when one of them is confronted by a job that exceeds his strength. The praise of this tradition by Crèvecœur illustrates his predilection for the autonomy of small communities and his rejection of an excessive intervention on the part of the state. This political choice explains in part his initial sympathy for the loyalists during the War of Independence: before this event, the distance from the city guaranteed the blessed isolation of the colonies deep in the American forests. Crèvecœur's imagined Golden Age turns the American continent, under the distant *dominion* of the British Iles, into an archipelago that owed only the slightest tribute in money and obedience to the English crown. This inversion prepares the fusion between the tropes of the Golden Age and utopia, the utopian societies being traditionally located in an inaccessible elsewhere. In the *Lettres*, the American colonies are isolated in time as well as in the vast area of the American solitudes.

Characteristic of the Golden Age of Antiquity, the prosperity that reigns in America in the colonial period is praised by Crèvecœur as the result of economic and social conditions that make what one would call today the "American Dream" available to everyone.[106] Crèvecœur repeats it incessantly: the hardworking, the sober, and the enterprising individuals will discover on the other side of the Atlantic inexpensive lands that will allow them to rise to the dignity of citizen and achieve the prosperity of an honest man. Over and over again, he relates the archetypal story of impoverished Europeans who discover in America the reward for the wager of emigration. Like an empirical philosopher following the development of a child, he follows the steps of André l'Hébridéen, who is for him what Émile is for Rousseau: an experimental subject whose development serves as an example. "This feeble description will be sufficient," Crèvecœur hopes, "to convince you that any poor, wise, hard-working and grateful European cannot fail to obtain here, if not riches at least the ownership of some land, work and good wages, happy affluence, and the protection of the laws."[107] Crèvecœur is diffusing a dream of prosperity that was considered at the time to be an invitation to emigration for which Benjamin Franklin himself expressed gratitude.[108] However, it would be nonsense to turn Crèvecœur's *Lettres* into one of the founding texts of the ideology of the American Dream. If the conditions that favored the realization of such a dream may have existed, in the eyes of the author they had already disappeared at the time of the first publication of his work in 1784. The domestic harmony, the independence of the communities, and the prosperity collapsed in a "general shipwreck" so violent that the author could not bring himself to describe it: "How could a man with all my limitations describe for you the progression that led us from the respect of the laws to disorder, insults, anarchy, the spilling of blood? . . . Alas! You would only see powerfully shaken clouds, burning meteors, horrible flashes, threatening lightning bolts, the convulsions of a great continent, a general debacle: such is the image of our situation."[109]

In 1784, Crèvecœur is no longer like those Americans on a never-ending quest for greater prosperity of which a British governor said, ten years earlier, that they would desert paradise itself if they heard of another Eden located farther to the west.[110] The American Dream is already dead in the *Lettres*, and Crèvecœur writes in the present the posthumous representation of a reinvented Golden Age: this paradox escaped those of his readers who crossed the ocean with the hope of finding in the New World the idyllic society that his works depict.[111]

THE *LETTRES* OF 1787: FROM A POSTHUMOUS AMERICA TO A POSSIBLE AMERICA

Nostalgic Paradigm, Progressive Paradigm

In the definitive study he devotes to the images of America in French thought, Echeverria distinguishes between two interpretive paradigms of the New World in the works of the *philosophes* of the eighteenth century: the first characterizes America by the return of a distant past, while the second, turned toward the future, emphasizes the notion of progress.[112] In this study, the first paradigm will be called "nostalgic," since it conceives America as a space in which a past age is revived, and the second "progressive," America serving as the model for a better society made possible by the spreading of Enlightenment thought. According to Echeverria, the 1784 version of the *Lettres d'un cultivateur américain* is representative of the first interpretive current.[113] The critic nonetheless observes a significant inflection in the 1787 version, since this edition belongs more to the current of the second paradigm that is illustrated in particular by the political writings of Condorcet:[114] "In the augmented 1787 edition of his *Lettres*, Crèvecœur added two letters which indicated that he too was shifting to this progressive line. He claims that political and intellectual freedom allowed the American to make a maximum contribution to the material well-being of the community, and at the same time permitted him to develop fully his natural talents and to add to the store of useful knowledge, to the enlightenment of mankind, and to the general progress of civilization."[115]

In the third volume of the *Lettres d'un cultivateur américain*, a gap thus appears between the two interpretive paradigms of the New World, and the reader sees the beginning of a redefinition of the idea of America in French thought, a major reinterpretation that attempts to reformulate a sign defined by the resurgence of an ideal past as a synonym for the promises of the future. While this reconceptualization keeps France in a median position—as a reference point—on the temporal axis, it effects the translation of America in relation to the former by placing it in the far reaches of a future that may possibly be achieved in Europe after having offered to it a mirror in which it may contemplate its origins. When all is said and done, it is in the ambiguity of the characterization of America as a "New World" that are rooted the two contradictory paradigms used to interpret it for the French: "new" both in the sense that it is still in its infancy compared to the ancient civilization of the latter, and because it is still the idea of newness that it projects to the Old World by embodying the future that is going to be realized universally—if not "transmitted," as some would say in order to identify American civilization with an epidemic being spread to the rest of the Western world.[116] An analysis of the *Lettres* of 1787 will demonstrate the coexistence of the progressive and the nostalgic paradigms within a third volume that announces the birth of a possible America after having invented the posthumous representation of a defunct America.

A Tendency Toward Allegorization

The evolution of the image of America between the first and second editions of Crèvecœur's *Lettres* is immediately indicated by their respective illustrations.

LETTRES
D'UN
CULTIVATEUR
AMÉRICAIN,
ÉCRITES A W. S. ÉCUYER ;
Depuis l'année 1770, jusqu'à 1781.

Traduites de l'Anglois par ***.

TOME PREMIER.

A PARIS,

Chez CUCHET, Libraire, rue & hôtel Serpente.

M. DCC. LXXXIV.

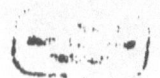

FIG. 1
Title page of *Lettres d'un cultivateur américain*, 1784 edition.

The illustration on the first page of the 1784 edition plays a simple ornamental role: it suggests the ideas of exoticism and travel by means of a globe without having the slightest allegorical function (see fig. 1). Conversely, the 1787 edition of the *Lettres d'un cultivateur américain* is accompanied by illustrations that are more complex visually and that invite the reader to a hermeneutic activity bearing both on the allegorical motifs they introduce at the beginning of the book and the relation of these motifs to the whole volume.

These two illustrations are the work of the painter Claude Bornet and the illustrator Pietro-Antonio Martini. The first serves as a frontispiece to the first volume of the *Lettres* of 1787: Rice describes it as an "allegorical representation of America"[117] (see fig. 2). The children embody, according to him, the idea of abundance, while the Native American woman personifies America. In *Beyond Ethnicity*, Werner Sollors criticizes Rice's reading because it employs

FIG. 2
Frontispiece for *Lettres d'un cultivateur américain*, 1787 edition. Photo courtesy Université de Montréal Library.

two hermeneutic approaches that seem at odds: certain motifs are interpreted figuratively (the woman and the *putti*), whereas others (the Quakers and the immigrants) are assigned a literal meaning. Sollors suggests the application of a single reading grid to this image and to interpret it as the symbolic representation of a process of naturalization: "Seen this way, the engraving symbolizes the rebirth of immigrants as American infants, sequentially shown in the stages of the transatlantic journey, arrival, dance in a magical circle which leads to the unrepresented transformation itself, the new birth through a nourishing Indianized mother figure, and the prosperous settlement in smoke-stacked houses."[118] The woman in the foreground on the left is an abstract representation of the New World according to Sollors, who calls her an "Indianized and female allegory of America" and identifies her with the historical figure of Pocahontas.[119] She gives a new birth to the immigrants as American citizens by offering them a

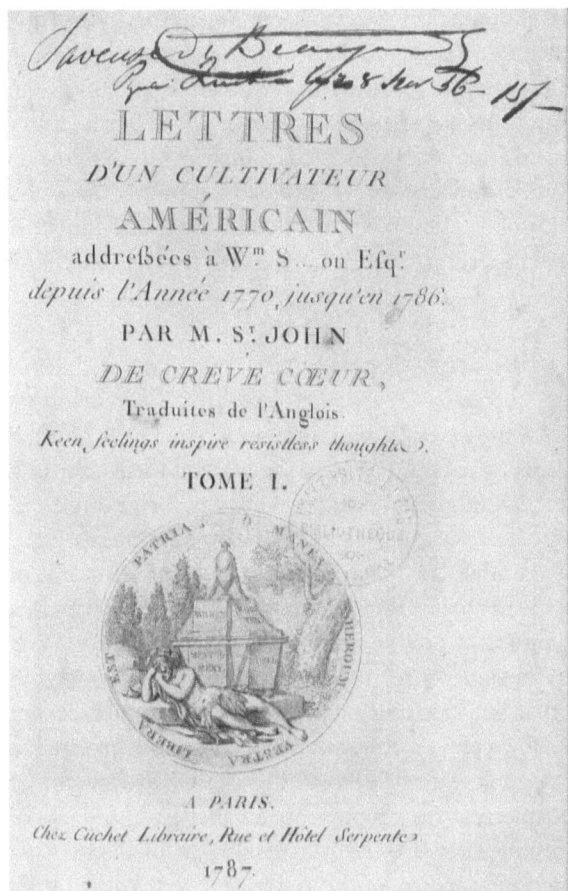

FIG. 3
Title page of *Lettres d'un cultivateur américain*, 1787 edition. Photo courtesy Université de Montréal Library.

nourishing breast, in accordance with the process described in the Latin maxim beneath the image: "Ubi panis, et libertas, ibi Patria" ("Where bread and liberty are found, there lies the motherland"). This maxim had already been quoted by Crèvecœur in the third missive of the *Letters from an American Farmer* ("What is an American?"), although in an abbreviated form.[120] The phrase placed beneath the allegory therefore adds the idea of liberty, which is absent from the 1782 text.

In the medallion decorating the first volume of the 1787 edition, America is represented, allegorically, by the figure of a Native American princess, weeping next to a grave on which are inscribed the names of generals fallen during the War of Independence (see fig. 3). A Latin inscription surrounds the medallion: "O manes heroum vestra libera est patria" (Oh spirits of the heroes, your motherland is free).

By depicting America as a woman moved to tears by the death of those who gave their life for hers, this image expresses the political position of the author in favor of the patriots, whereas the allegiance of the author of the *Letters from an American Farmer* was much more ambiguous.[121] As for the frontispiece of the 1787 edition, it represents the American continent as a space of regeneration: the nourishing breast of America turns out to be a Fountain of Youth for the Europeans, who return to childhood after being suckled. Simultaneously, it offers us a metaphorical representation of the "melting pot," since the immigrants who have come from different European countries are transformed into identical creatures who have been given a virginal nudity that equates their arrival in the New World to a second birth.

Liberty and Cultural Homogeneity
Absent from the Latin maxim quoted by Crèvecœur in 1782, the idea of liberty is added under the frontispiece of 1787 (see fig. 2). In order for America to become the new motherland for European immigrants and the place of their rebirth, it must offer more than material resources and the opportunity for a more comfortable existence; it must also hold out the possibility of freedom. Interestingly, in a letter written only a few months after the publication of the third volume of his *Lettres*, it is precisely for the misuse of their liberty that Crèvecœur criticizes the Americans: "How can you subject to the rule of law a people that for such a long time has not known its salutary restraints, that confuses Liberty with unlimited licentiousness, that believes one can be free without government and rich without industry? How can you control a people that inhabits such a vast, unlimited continent, a people whose behavior has changed so much?"[122] In addition, while the frontispiece of 1787 represents an allegorical process of naturalization of the immigrants, Crèvecœur expresses doubts, in a letter written in the same period, about the capacity of the Americans to become in the near future a united people: "Many years will pass before the Americans have become a nation; *it will even take more than a century before we may observe among them the moral and physical traits of homogeneity that produce those characteristic national nuances*; for, as you know, what we see today is only a conglomerate of Europeans set on different soils and climate, all coming from equally different countries, who cannot yet have any other bonds than those of their needs and their petty local ambitions."[123]

This letter helps us to imagine an alternative illustration to the edition of 1787 of the *Lettres* in which, instead of nearly identical cherubs, a crowd of Europeans distinctly different in appearance would leave a ship and go wherever their fancy takes them to found a multiplicity of communities that are culturally homogeneous but devoid of any ties between them. Consequently, the 1787 frontispiece represents, in an allegorical mode, the process of naturalization that depends on one condition (liberty) and leads to a result (cultural homogeneity) that calls precisely into question the correspondence carried on by the author during the same period. Is this contradiction between the allegorical discourse of the frontispiece and the private letters of Crèvecœur an indication of the difficulty the author met in expressing publicly the concerns he had about the American Republic during his consular appointment? More broadly, is such an opposition discernable between the third tome of the *Lettres d'un cultivateur américain* and the thoughts shared by Crèvecœur in the private letters he sent at the time of its writing? To answer these questions and show that, contrary to the nostalgic paradigm (that glosses over shadowy zones in the depiction of an ideal age), the progressive paradigm of the interpretation of America is inseparable from anxiety and threat, it will be necessary to return to the origin of the edition of 1787.

Two Contradictory Discourses
Thanks to the intervention of Madame d'Houdetot, Crèvecœur began working in the spring of 1783 for the Minister of the Navy, Maréchal de Castries, who wished to know more about the population, geography, and industries of the United States.[124] Crèvecœur drew maps and wrote a report on the young republic, as well as an essay on the establishment of regular postal links between France and the United States, works that he submitted to Benjamin Franklin for comment. Combined with the unfailing support of the comtesse d'Houdetot and that of the Beauvau and La Rochefoucauld families, Crèvecœur's energy is rewarded with the prestigious and newly created position of French Consul in New York.[125] The competition, however, had been ferocious: "I learned later," wrote Crèvecœur, "that nothing less than the combined influence of these great families had been necessary to obtain a consulate that seventeen strongly backed individuals were seeking."[126]

Once he had become an official representative in the United States, he was no longer free to criticize it. He was all the more inclined to play the role of apostle of the young Republic since the memory of his vacillating attitude during the War of Independence had not faded away: the literary panegyric is Crèvecœur's way of making amends for his political inconstancy. In addition, he frequents George Washington, Benjamin Franklin, and Thomas Jefferson, tutelary figures of the new nation who would have taken umbrage had the French Consul written diatribes against their newly founded country.[127] Crèvecœur also counts among his friends the marquis de Lafayette, to whom he dedicated the *Lettres d'un cultivateur américain*.[128] Crowned with glory after his brilliant contribution to the War of Independence, Lafayette is honored by the friendship of Washington himself.[129] While the *Letters from an American Farmer* were dedicated to the abbé de Raynal and celebrated "belonging to a common and universal humanity," their French rewriting is concerned solely with the community of victors, out of fear that the author be confused with the partisans of England; he congratulated Lafayette for throwing off the "yoke" and punishing the "hubris" of the former rulers.[130]

Led to frequent the elites of the American republic, Crèvecœur multiplied his declarations of optimism about the future of the United States in the third volume of the *Lettres*: "This progress is independent and shielded from all the revolutions that may afflict the rest of the universe. There are no places on earth in which the same number of years could produce a series of events so important and useful to humanity as will the populating, clearing, and embellishment of the fertile and vast region that is traversed by the Ohio River and by the rivers that empty their waters into it."[131] However, just as it was instructive to compare the *Letters from an American Farmer* to the texts in *More Letters from an American Farmer*, it is revealing to confront the 1787 *Lettres* to Crèvecœur's private correspondence in the same period. A missive written to Brissot in December 1787 suggests a very different discourse on the United States. It reproaches the Americans, in fact, for being less worthy of a free government than they were at the end of the War of Independence:

> I can assure you that there is almost no virtue or honor any longer, at least among those who are involved in public affairs. That is harsh, but it is true, and I'm beginning to believe that man is not made to enjoy as great a degree of liberty as I thought in 1776. I'm ashamed of all my former dreams.... The spectacle that the Americans have been giving for twelve years is very instructive: the first part was beautiful to see, the second is a process of trial and error, *a heap of errors* mostly, which will plunge them back into disunity, anarchy, and a host of calamities that it is useless to warn them about.[132]

As Chevignard writes, "[O]ne discovers between Crèvecœur and his narrator St. John the same gap that we saw formerly between J. Hector St. John and Farmer James: on the concrete America that the colonist or the consul analyzes with a merciless lucidity is superimposed an imaginary America that his literary double rolls out with an untiring poetic verve."[133] Witness to a troubled age in the history of the United States, Crèvecœur expresses bitter concerns in his private correspondence while creating an imaginary America in his *Lettres* of 1787, in which the posthumous representation of an idealized past cohabits with the promise of a glorious future, in which the nostalgic paradigm of representation of the New World does not prevent the development of the progressive paradigm. This duality of the 1787 *Lettres* becomes clear in the analysis of their underlying structure.

Fragmentation and Structure
Heterogeneity is one of the major characteristics of Crèvecœur's *Lettres*, which treat a variety of themes and move forward by temporal leaps and bounds,

disorienting a reader who values the indications of place and time at the beginning of letters between which he expects, to no avail, a chronological progression, since the author passes, arbitrarily it seems, from the end of the war to its horrors, from the colonial period to the tale of events that occurred after the independence of the United States. While Lezay-Marnésia's *Letters Written from the Banks of the Ohio* accompany the trip toward the west, then the retreat of their author, the *Lettres d'un cultivateur américain* practice a constant historical back-and-forth and include, in addition to the letters signed by Saint-John, tales whose source is not specified, the translation of speeches and newspaper articles as summaries of the progress of the United States since peacetime, so that the proliferation of the discourses and the overlapping of periods recall far more the Harlequin suit that is Chateaubriand's *Voyage en Amérique*: battered by misfortunes and embodied in his work, Crèvecœur's memory resembles a shore the day after a shipwreck, where one seeks the fragments of scattered reminiscences.

Nonetheless, without claiming to discover in the 1787 *Lettres* a rigorous structure so artistically hidden that it is invisible to a superficial gaze, it is possible to discern a conscious organization that governs the apparently aleatory succession of the texts. The reader will remember Julien Gracq's comment, earlier, on Proust's *In Search of Lost Time*: "The genetic imperative of proliferation and enrichment takes precedence over the principle of organization every time in the book."[134] Beside the imperative of "proliferation" that dominates Crèvecœur's work as well, that of "organization" asserts itself in order to structure his opus: in the same way as the *Recherche*, the *Lettres* demonstrate an effort to manage and contain the proliferation of the text, itself engendered by the nostalgia for a past that the author strives to reinvent. To determine the principles dictating the organization of the third volume of the *Lettres*, it is useful to study Crèvecœur's manuscripts conserved by the Beinecke Library of Yale University, and especially a handwritten manuscript titled "Les Treise [sic] Chapitres du Troisième Volume du Cultivateur Américain" (The Thirteen Chapters of the Third Volume of the American Farmer).[135] One observation is imperative in comparing this manuscript and the third volume of the *Lettres d'un cultivateur américain* as Crèvecœur published it in 1787: the distribution of the texts in a different order evinces a well-thought-out intent to organize the volume according to criteria that remain to be identified.

Placed second in the manuscript, the text devoted to the establishment of "Socialbourg" slips to fifth place in the final version. Initially followed by a letter "Sent August 24," it precedes the first of the "Forty-Nine Anecdotes" in the printed version. Likewise, the letters devoted to the postwar period ("Triumphant Entrance of General Washington," "Progress of Things Since the Peace," and "Dismissal of the American Army") are found at the end of the volume in the 1787 version, whereas they were located in the first half of the manuscript. These changes in the order of the texts in the volume thus obey a principle of regrouping: on the one hand, the letters that address the postwar period are sent to the end of the volume while, on the other hand, Crèvecœur alternates, in the first part of the book, the letters on the colonial period and those on the War of Independence, so that they shed light on each other.

The letter allotted to Socialbourg describes the foundation of an imaginary city in the northwest section of Albany County. It relates a dialogue between five men from five different European countries,[136] a miniature drama in which each describes the tribulations he had to endure in his motherland and the dreams he pursued in crossing the Atlantic. Soon these foreigners resolve to join forces to found a settlement in the New York colony; then they endeavor to define the principles that will guide the community, in the area of religion in particular, since the specter of dogmatic quarrels could just as well arise between them as it so often did among their countrymen in the Old World. These individuals, all of different faiths, resolve to combat this eventuality in every way possible and to revere the "Supreme Being" within a "Christian Church,"[137] an appellation chosen in an ecumenical spirit.

Religion is not the only aspect of community life that they decide to organize. By mutual consent, they establish an "agreement" that will determine the details of their association: "The following day, this agreement consisting of seventeen articles written by the vice president was ratified and signed by all. In time, this settlement flourished."[138] Clearly attached to the utopian tradition by the adoption of a large number of characteristic traits—built on a "parallelogram of three thousand acres,"[139] Socialbourg belongs to the tradition of utopian cities whose geometric form expresses the dominion of reason over community life and establishes the order that reigns in a society frozen in the eternal present of an inalterable happiness—the letter contains nonetheless subtle differences by not establishing a sole legislator, as in the originary texts of the genre, but rather five men who determine by a democratic process the political principles on which their association will rest. Edward White rightfully sees therein a new variation on the famous "What is an American?" in the third missive in the *Letters from an American Farmer*, since it proposes the renunciation of each individual's original sense of identity and the creation of a social pact that results in a new identity for each person.[140] But it is also the depiction of an age in which harmony between peoples was possible, an idyllic period whose disappearance the reader is suddenly made to feel by the withering conclusion he gives to this letter: "N.B. [This settlement] was nearly completely destroyed during the last war."[141] The irremediable character of this loss is underlined ever more by the organization of the tome, which places immediately after the description of the circumstances of the founding of Socialbourg—a text filled with optimism until the hammer blow at the end—a series of forty-nine tales related to the War of Independence. The latter describe the various events of the Revolution with a striking tendency to praise American virtues and denounce the cruelty of the British.[142] By means of the passage from the description of a blessed city to the spectacle of its ruins, Crèvecœur shows to the reader how the utopian project of Socialbourg—a project infused with deism and the Enlightenment faith in the power of reason to prevent violence from breaking out—was wrecked on the reefs of the war with the British.

Two other letters, separated in the manuscript, follow one another in the final version and obey the same logic of confrontation between the posthumous representation of colonial America and the depiction of the horrors that followed. Dated October 28, 1774, the letter titled "Sketch of a Journey by Ménéssink on the Delaware to the Wyoming Valley"[143] precedes, in the printed version, a missive written on November 15, 1778, "Sketch of the Destruction of the Settlements That the Inhabitants of Connecticut had Founded on the Eastern Branch of the Susquehanna River in 1766."[144] Contrary to a large number of letters that follow one another with no thematic link and very often no chronological continuity, the one on "November 15, 1778," is explicitly linked to the preceding letter: "After having enjoyed the pleasure of contemplating this long chain of settlements of which I spoke to you four years ago, after having followed with the keenest interest the development of these young societies, the wonderful progress of so much effort and enterprise: was it really necessary for my personal situation to nearly make me a witness of their destruction?"[145]

Once again, the brutal transition from one text to another expresses the shock of the destruction of the settlements founded during the colonial period. The brief silence between these texts is the literary equivalent of Crèvecœur's internal fracture: the organization of the volume is intended to sensitize the reader to the end of the Golden Age by means of the surprising leap from the idyllic representation of the past to the American Revolution, whose injustices are amply described in the book. Following these letters, however, another tale is begun by Crèvecœur: no longer that of the destruction of the New World but that of its progressive reconstruction.[146] The posthumous representation of a past destroyed by war is succeeded by the evocation of a period that is contemporary with the writing, in which one may read all the hopes but also all the fears of the future.

Visions of a Possible America

Crèvecœur devotes the end of the third volume to the first steps of the American republic. The last seven letters cover a period that goes from the departure of the British from New York City in 1783 to the month of December 1786. Significantly, the volume concludes with the translation of a form letter from

Washington whose concerns echo those expressed by Crèvecœur in his private correspondence at the end of the 1780s. This missive celebrates the opportunity offered to Americans to become happy and prosperous but nonetheless describes the beginnings of the Republic as a crucial period that will decide its future.[147] An "indissoluble union of the States"[148] must be adopted as quickly as possible, Washington concludes in the text quoted by Crèvecœur.

The opposition between the federalists and the antifederalists was raging at the time of the publication of the *Lettres* of 1787. Ten years earlier, the Second Continental Congress (composed of the thirteen original states) had proposed "Articles of Confederation" that, signed in 1781, favored the sovereignty of each state over any centralized federal authority. It was not until December 17, 1787, that a convention in Philadelphia accepted the Constitution of the United States of America, which still would not be ratified before March 4, 1789. The correspondence of Crèvecœur demonstrates unambiguously his political antipathies, in particular toward Patrick Henry, who, after having been the first governor of Virginia (1776–79), refused to take a seat at the 1787 convention, owing to his commitment to the sovereignty of the states: "Mr. P. Henry is in my eyes a very guilty man, for I abhor Antifederalists and cannot help considering them as people who want to sacrifice the glory, the prosperity of this country to their selfish, or rather hellish, views."[149] The antifederalist tendency of the southern states provokes most particularly Crèvecœur's anxiety: "The southern States, whose interests are so different, who are so jealous and fear so much the energy, activity, and enterprise of the inhabitants of the North, will form alliances in Europe; then, everything will be irremediably lost. That may well be the consequence of all these democratic ideas, so fine on paper but which will turn out to be so many noxious and deceptive dreams."[150]

The private epistles of Crèvecœur and those that he published under his name exhibit some important similarities, since the reader meets again, in the 1787 *Lettres*, the expression of the same fears: "The hopes of the United States," he wrote in his volume of letters, "will be fulfilled for the greater good of humanity, unless the evil genius of our race nips in the bud such beautiful, comforting hopes; unless, inspiring in Americans the spirit of disunity and delusion, it plunges them into anarchy and leads them to regret that so many efforts have been made and so much blood spilled."[151] According to Crèvecœur, this "spirit of disunity and delusion" was propagated by two types of antifederalists. The first were the partisans of independence and the sovereignty of their state, resolved to defend their economic interests and unwilling to follow the customs system implemented by the federal government.[152] Crèvecœur described the second as evil creatures, driven by the corruption of human nature and ready to plunge America into civil war out of love for anarchy.[153] In his grievances against the antifederalists, Crèvecœur betrayed the anguish he felt before the hidden recesses of human nature, a fear that had never left him since his sojourn in the New York jails.[154] The specter of a corrupt humanity relentlessly determined to do evil for its own sake appears once again in its enigmatic substance at the time of his appointment in New York and causes him to fear for the future of his second motherland.

The *Lettres* simmer with both the hopes and fears that obsessed Crèvecœur regarding the future of the United States. On the one hand, they emphasize the progressive reconstruction of the country[155] and the still-fragile recovery of maritime commerce and agriculture.[156] However, the promises of prosperity will only be fulfilled if the "redoubtable enemies" are vanquished: "[L]uxury and squandering; the business and deceptive lure of credit, such are the redoubtable enemies that the *Americans* have to combat, especially in the *Southern States*; much less frugality and enterprise than before the war, a false idea of liberty that has just cost them so dearly, an idea that it is so easy and so dangerous to abuse, a jealous suspicion of the representatives and leaders that they choose themselves, such are the great pitfalls to which the inhabitants of the *North* are exposed."[157]

This suspicion toward money and credit is typical of the physiocratic discourse for which Turgot (1727–1781) was one of the most famous theoreticians.[158] His brother, Étienne-François Turgot, was Crèvecœur's protector upon his return to France in 1781; he encouraged him to write the *Traité de la culture des pommes de terre* (1782) and received him in his mansion on the Île Saint-Louis. In the tradition of physiocratic principles, Crèvecœur considered land as the primary source of wealth of a nation and warned against money and credit that corrupted its products.[159] On the foundation of these economic principles, the period before the war is again set up as a model by Crèvecœur: the frugal and laborious customs common at that time gave way to the "sentiment of self-interest" that a countryman had already noticed in the United States,[160] as well as that "commercial spirit" whose development Chateaubriand was to observe a few years later during his own journey in America.[161]

Ultimately, the third volume of the *Lettres d'un cultivateur américain* proves to be structured by the two interpretive paradigms of America that Echeverria distinguished. The first part of the volume is organized around the nostalgic paradigm, reviving various scenes from the colonial period that are then opposed to scenes taken from the war: no shadow darkens the posthumous representation of an idealized period, since it is the fratricidal conflict of the loyalists and the patriots that plays the contrapuntal role. Conversely, the second part is marked by the hope for prosperity that is inseparable from the progressive paradigm, but also by severe anguish: this felicity promised to the Americans can only be achieved if they embrace political union instead of an antifederalism that would lead them to ruin, and, likewise, only if they resist the penchant for violence, represented by a metaphor that Crèvecœur placed at the beginning of his volume. Titled "Combat Between Two Snakes," the fourth of the 1787 *Lettres* may indeed be read as a meditation on the penchant for destruction in the natural world and by extension in the human sphere. The fierce struggle between the two reptiles, without our ever learning which one is the winner, serves as a warning: although America is described as a new Eden, it is nonetheless already corrupted.

"The flip side to the sense of hope that goes to the core of the Declaration and the Dream," writes Cullen, "is a sense of fear that its promises are on the verge of being, or actually have been, lost."[162] This paradoxical union of hope and anxiety is also found in the *Lettres* of 1787, which contain both the prediction of a glorious future and the simultaneous fear that this will never come to pass, as well as the last trace of a posthumous America and the uncertain vision of a possible America.

Return to America: Journey in Upper Pennsylvania and the State of New York (1801)

DISPLACEMENT OF THE GOLDEN AGE

In Space and in Time

In the last pages of *L'Étudiant étranger* (*The Foreign Student*, 1986), Philippe Labro relates his return to Paris in the 1950s, after his studies at Washington and Lee University in Virginia. Over the next months and years, the young man observed his countrymen adopting the modes of dress and musical tastes that he had observed during his stay in the United States. Owing to the slow seepage of the "American way of life" into France, the country lags perpetually behind in its imitation of the American model, just as there is often a gap, emphasized by many novelists, between the fashions of the French capital and those of the provinces. To leave Paris is to discover what was in style months earlier, so one has the impression that this geographic move is a journey back in time: the difference between France and the United States in *L'Etudiant étranger* is similar to that between Angoulême and the French capital in Balzac's *Illusions perdues* (*Lost Illusions*, 1837–43). However, America has not always represented the future on the symbolic axis connecting it to France. The *Voyage dans la Haute Pensylvanie et dans l'État de New York depuis l'année 1785 jusqu'en 1798* plunges us back into a time when the roles were reversed, France embodying the possible future of the United States, whereas the latter country represented the mythical past of the former. The following section is devoted to the establishment of this symbolic relationship between the two countries, as well as to the manner in which the posthumous representation of America plays a specular function in the narrative published by Crèvecœur in 1801.

Shipwrecked America

In the guise of a translator, Crèvecœur begins the *Voyage* by a preface in which he recounts the destiny of the *Morning-Star*, a ship from Philadelphia that wrecked on November 12, 1798, on the coast of Denmark. Among the objects strewn on the beach were the manuscripts of a tale of travel in the United States, unfortunately so damaged by the salt water that they had become nearly illegible.[163] The translator deems it possible, nonetheless, to put them in a satisfactory order and make them available to the public. Some of his friends advise him against it: the French will never be interested in them, having just survived the horrors of the Revolution.[164] However, others encourage him to publish them, using an argument that renders explicit the metaphorical dimension of the storm during which the *Morning-Star* had sunk: "At what happier time could this work appear than during the return to calm, justice, and true liberty, *after so many years spent in the grip of the violent unrest, spasmodic storms, and volcanic shocks of the Revolution?*"[165] A land of storms and revolutions, France cannot be approached without the risk of a shipwreck that serves as a warning for the United States.

Crèvecœur was not the only one to describe France as a turbulent zone to be avoided. On the point of returning to his homeland, Lezay-Marnésia expressed a similar anxiety: "This France formerly so fortunate and so beautiful has become a land of fire that is very dangerous to approach."[166] Chateaubriand established, for his part, an analogy between the raging natural elements and the political storm ravaging his country, describing in the *Mémoires d'outre-tombe* a "riot of waves"[167] foreshadowing the revolt of the people that he was preparing to find in his country. According to the "translator" of the *Voyage*, the political upheaval in France increases the urgency of the publication of a book devoted to the United States. This text will play both a pedagogical and a therapeutic role for its readers, who will find in it tableaus that are "at the same time instructive, enjoyable, and comforting."[168] Although Crèvecœur describes henceforth the aftermath of the War of Independence, the celebration of America in this preface has a familiar ring for the readers of *Lettres d'un cultivateur américain*.

The Republican Golden Age

Indeed, what Crèvecœur said about colonial America in the *Lettres*, he now, in 1801, asserts about the American Republic. What, exactly, does he state about the government? Crèvecœur described it as "just and equitable" at the time of British domination,[169] but when he speaks of the young Republic, the description has hardly changed, since he now refers to it as "fatherly."[170] And what about taxes? "Our taxes are light and fairly assessed," an American farmer declared before 1776,[171] whereas similar praise is offered under the Republic, the colonists paying "no other levies to the government than affection and gratitude."[172] Likewise, in the *Lettres*, as in the *Voyage*, Crèvecœur compares America and

Europe to the detriment of the latter. Published in the 1784 *Lettres*, the "Esquisse" ("Sketch") contrasted an overpopulated Europe with a "here" where the immigrants finally have the opportunity to take their destiny in hand: "[I]n Europe, I heard that the excessive population of society stifles the most outstanding talents. Here, the broad range of things allows them to flourish and grow: this is how Europeans become Americans."[173] It is no different in the *Voyage*, where a Scottish officer exclaims, after 1783: "What was I in Scotland . . . , where I had a position that was so easily filled by another? . . . Here, being a member of a rising society, property, laws, and local circumstances have lent me a certain ascendancy and given me a certain weight on the social scale."[174] All in all, nothing has changed in Crèvecœur's discourse on America; nothing other than the date of its production and the period it describes.

From the *Lettres* to the *Voyage*, there is a homology between the American and the French Revolutions. It is created in particular by the use of an identical metaphor: that of the storm.[175] The French Revolution embodies in the *Voyage* the historical fracture that inaugurates the posthumous representation of America, the role formerly assumed by the American Revolution in the *Lettres*. While Crèvecœur, in the latter, contrasts the colonial period with that of the War of Independence, the narrator of the *Voyage* compares the happiness of the young United States to the turmoil of his country since the summer of 1789. Alternatively, the War of Independence is completely absent from the *Voyage*. To be sure, the long voyage that this text relates occurs after the conflict, since it is supposed to take place between 1785 and 1789: that the American Revolution is less present in the *Voyage* than in the *Lettres*, since the narrator was its contemporary and one of its victims, is hardly surprising. Nonetheless, the heroes of the *Voyage* meet men and women who were actors in a war that had just been brought to an end. Questioned by the travelers, certain Americans remember the war but only touch on the subject lightly and move on to others more in line with the praises of America being sung by Crèvecœur: "After having shared with my new countrymen the dangers of the Revolution that emancipated this great country, I took great pleasure in the interesting spectacle of the prodigious growth of its population and that of the ultramontane colonies," states a Dutchman who had settled in Indiana after many travels. Now it is France that appears to be the repository of the human malice that seems to be spared the New World for the moment.

The War in the Background

Chapter 13 of volume 2 is nonetheless an exception to the extent that it is devoted to an episode of the American Revolution: the flight of a family into the Appalachian Mountains. While the *Lettres* relate the anguish of a narrator who fears for his life and that of the members of his family,[176] the character at the center of the "Tale of a Flight into the Appalachians During the War of Independence" chooses to abandon his plantation in South Carolina. In order to escape from the English, he takes refuge with his family and servants in the forest, where four years go by with no misfortunes of any kind. The flight of the family of the "patriarch of Orangebourg County"[177] resembles a pleasant hike: the trek through the forests poses no greater difficulty than stepping over small streams, the milk and butter produced on the banks of the Pacolet are superior to those back home, and even the harsh weather is less a problem than one might have feared. In the shelter of a "spacious and comfortable" cabin,[178] the daughters of the patriarch give him two grandchildren. While many characters in the *Lettres* counted their dead at the end of the war,[179] the community led by the patriarch was increased by "seven children, two white and five black" (201). The members of the expedition are referred to as "family," whether they were free or slaves before the war. The highly unusual situation created by the war permits not only the integration of the slaves into the family of the patriarch on a sentimental level but also introduces a short-lived apprenticeship of democracy that excludes no one. The planter abandons in effect the autocratic functioning that he had adopted in Carolina in favor of an infinitely more liberal system: "Back home, I was the absolute authority, but *as soon as I became a forest dweller, I established a democratic government: each individual had his vote, the Blacks just like the Whites*. I was only the executor of the will of the majority, and each person, by submitting to it, felt that it was his own will. But, I confess, if my family had been larger, I would have modified a little this system, having often had occasion to observe that wisdom does not always result from a greater number of opinions" (200; emphasis added).

The renewal of the social relations within the group hiding in the forest goes further than the welcoming of the slaves into the planter's family, already a rather remarkable phenomenon in itself: the blacks are considered to be the whites' peers and participate with them on an equal footing during community deliberations. Alas, the following text does not say if, upon returning to Carolina, the patriarch kept in place the social contract adopted in the forest; in all likelihood, on the contrary, the old man became again the autocratic figure he was before the war. Of the horrors of this conflict, obsessively present in the *Lettres*, Crèvecœur says nothing in this bizarre chapter. They are off-camera, outside the story as they are out of the sight of the members of this itinerant family; only when they return home do they learn that they had been surrounded by multiple dangers during their journey, dangers that had never even existed for them since they had not even suspected them, and that have now disappeared for good (2:245).

Crèvecœur thus slipped into the *Voyage*, with regard to the American Revolution that represented in the *Lettres* a counterpoint to the colonial period, the "yang" of the dreadful memories systematically opposed to the "yin" of the happy times. The deep structure of the narrative has changed. The *Lettres* obeyed a logic of temporal alternation: the colonial period was opposed to the era of the American Revolution, in the explicit comparisons in the text as well as in the sequencing of its parts. The *Voyage*, for its part, is structured by a system of spatial oppositions in which each term has an axiological value: Europe embodies the negative Other of America, the latter being the idyllic flip side of the former. This symbolic value of one country in relation to the other overlaps with an opposition regarding their respective places on the temporal axis. The representations of the United States and of France have a specular function in that each country may recognize in the other a reverse image of itself. On the one hand, France embodies the disquieting yet possible future that awaits the United States: "Will the distance that, fortunately, [separates us from the Old World] preserve us from its storms? . . . Would the demon of human nature return to exercise its formidable empire on the world? Would it be possible that there are men here who . . . , to spread among us the new European opinions, have resolved to plunge us into the horrors of chaos and to deliver us to the gory fury of anarchy?" (1:83–84).

Confined for the moment to the Old World, this spirit of discord could very well spread to the United States if Americans allowed themselves to be persuaded by the "European opinions" that have sowed chaos in the Old World (1:84). In its turn, America offers France a reflection of its own past: "What a great distance there is between our state of infancy and the nations of Europe that have reached the fullness of things: surrounded by fortifications, possessing all the means of warfare, in a state of perfection through centuries of experience, and countries on which we depend, unfortunately, for a multitude of objects that we could easily produce ourselves if we were more numerous!" (151). Still struggling in a "state of infancy," the United States certainly does not have Europe's sophistication, but what it lacks in conveniences and comfort it amply compensates for with the social equality and public tranquility that its people enjoy (143). In this society that has reached a lesser degree of technical and demographic development, the Europeans can recognize the image of an earlier stage of development of their own civilization, a stage that, if it may be described as inferior in terms of progress, is perceived as superior in terms of felicity. Serving as mutual mirrors, the United States and France recognize in each other, respectively, their future and their past.

While the *Letters* reserved the use of the pastoral tone for the depiction of the colonial period, the *Voyage* sees the flowering of a postrevolutionary Golden Age with similar characteristics. After having halted it at the American Revolution in the *Lettres*, Crèvecœur advances the frontier of the Golden Age here to the end of the eighteenth century. The redefinition of posthumous America in the *Voyage* in relation to the *Lettres* is therefore considerable by its implications, although limited in its means of expression: it is the signifier that changes (colonial America is replaced by the Republic) and not the signified, since the two periods are the object of identical praise. No matter that Crèvecœur's narrative attempts to root itself in its period of production by alluding to the most significant events of the end of the century—beginning with the French Revolution and the rise to power of Napoléon Bonaparte—he still continues to idealize a defunct America whose characteristics are identical to those of the colonial age. This era remains, in Crèvecœur's eyes, the only veritable period of bliss he has known: in the posthumous representation of this age is played out the painful and stubborn quest for a happiness that has vanished. More broadly, a relationship of symbolic equivalence between the United States and France is established in the *Voyage*, such that the depiction of one of these countries always contains an implicit commentary on the situation of the other. The posthumous representation of America thus never has the sole function of preserving the memory of a past period or serving as an outlet for the author's nostalgia: it puts in place an implicit discourse on France as the symbolic double of the United States and permits the former country to see itself as it is perceived from the other side of the Atlantic.

A MIRAGE IN THE PAST

A Tableau Composed of Memory
In describing the evolution of America between the end of the sixteenth century and the end of the eighteenth century, a prominent New Yorker that the heroes of the *Voyage* encounter describes the literary project of Crèvecœur: "What an interesting tableau a clever writer could make of this long series of events, efforts, and adventures, more or less happy or unhappy, from the first colonists that Sir Walter Raleigh led to Roanoke in 1577 . . . to the . . . founding of the interior states of Vermont, Kentucky, and Tennessee! I know of no other subject that is more worthy of the brush of a great painter" (339). The *Voyage in Upper Pennsylvania and the State of New York* embodies the "tableau" suggested by this character: in this vast canvas, the intercalated stories take us back to the origin of the colonization of the American continent, while the peregrinations of the two main characters help us to embrace the shifting totality of a country in constant mutation. Contrary to the *Lettres*, however, this work is not composed by an artist placed before his model.

The *Lettres* of 1784 were based on literary material produced at the time of the author's stay in America—"Frenchified" and "idealized," it is true, in the course of the translation as well as enriched by later additions. Likewise, the *Lettres* of 1787 gathered the translation of texts predating the War of Independence as well as new passages, written during the period when Crèvecœur was the French Consul in New York. Conversely, the *Voyage* was written between 1794 and 1800, that is, after the author's definitive return to Europe: Crèvecœur does not take America as a model as he sees it at the time of his writing but as he remembers it. In addition, it is an imaginary journey that takes place in this country remembered. Contrary to the *Lettres*, which include a majority of letters signed "Saint-John," the *Voyage* relates the roaming of fictitious people.[180] It is, moreover, the fictional nature of this text that dissuaded several houses from publishing it, at a time when authentic travel narratives, rather than fictitious works, were in favor among the public.[181]

Thus, the work and existence of Crèvecœur came to form a surprising chiasmus: whereas he, for his part, moved away from the United States, ashamed of "all [his] former dreams," extending his stay in France, and the concomitant leave of absence from his consular position in New York, so long that he eventually lost his post, his writings constantly return to the America he desired and missed so much.[182] This paradox is resolved when we take into account the silence of Crèvecœur when Brissot suggested to him, as a remedy for the hassles of consular life, a return to rural living: "You will be happier as a simple farmer than as a slave of the great. The shake of his head and the silence of Crèvecœur proved to me that this moralistic advice, good in books, was not at all to his taste."[183] The discourse that Crèvecœur met with silence was none other than his own, found in the mouth of a friend who rivals the narrator of the *Lettres* in enthusiasm. It is in a book, and in a book alone, that Crèvecœur had the luxury of rediscovering *his* America.

"It would seem that America became for Crèvecœur something less and less real, almost a dream world in which he was traveling by memory, a refuge where he could escape from the realities that were troubling him," muses Rice.[184] If America embodies, in the French mind, this "mirage to the West" analyzed by Echeverria, for Crèvecœur it is above all a mirage in the past. While the *Voyage* is striking primarily by the magnitude of its erudition and the abundance of notes that offer an encyclopedic knowledge of the geography and history of the American continent, America is still the object of a posthumous re-creation that reinvents it as an imaginary country.

Carnal Reminiscences

In 1792, the French Republic revoked the eulogist of the American Republic, and the Revolution of 1789 widens the internal fracture caused by its counterpart in 1776: "*Victim of the events in the two Republics* that are to change the face of the earth and affect everyone everywhere, I will finish my career like so many others by carrying with me to the grave the fears and worries that are unavoidably provoked by the state of things, a turbulent and military government that sooner or later will render extremely precarious our life, pleasures, personal security, and property," states Crèvecœur.[185] Violently shaken by the War of Independence, he underwent another political convulsion that confirmed this pacifist all the more firmly in his horror of bloodshed. If we are to believe Rice, Crèvecœur spent the Revolutionary period in "the greatest darkness."[186] Mitchell agrees: "Crèvecœur . . . occupied himself during those dark days with his notes and memoranda, and fell to writing energetically eight hours a day."[187] This dedication to writing, which seems to be an attempt to substitute for historical reality a personal "reality," the memory of a past idealized by nostalgia, recalls the literary enterprise of Giacomo Casanova, who, during the period in which Crèvecœur was writing the *Voyage*, was busy writing "thirteen hours a day," in the solitude of Dux in Bohemia, the *Histoire de ma vie (Story of My Life)*.[188] For both men, the remembering of the past is a way to commune with a bygone happiness: the former sensations return to the writer's body when he strives to describe them.

In *Histoire de ma vie*, Casanova relates the failed reunion with Henriette, a woman he had left in Geneva in 1749 after sharing with her "the greatest romance of his chequered career."[189] Their new meeting occurs in 1763, when the Venetian adventurer asks for hospitality in a Provençal house without knowing that Henriette is the owner. She avoids being recognized by her former lover but gets a letter to him that he only opens after his departure. Upon learning the identity of his hostess the night before, Casanova sinks into reflections in which times melt together:

> Dear Henriette whom I loved so dearly and whom I felt I still loved with the same passion. You saw me, and you did not want me to see you?—Perhaps you thought your charms may have lost the power with which they enslaved my soul sixteen years ago, and you did not want me to see that I had only loved a mortal woman. Ah, cruel Henriette, unjust Henriette! You saw me, and you did not want to know if I still loved you. I didn't see you, and I was unable to learn from your beautiful mouth if you are happy.[190]

Several stylistic characteristics of this text convey the feelings that the act of remembering produced in its author: the agitated writing expresses the emotion of the memorialist and shines through the reiteration of the direct addresses as it does through the repeated variations on the use of the verb "see" ("You saw me, and you did not want me to see you?"; "You saw me, and you did not want to know if I still loved you"). The direct address of the narrator to Henriette—as in a real exchange between two individuals—expresses for its part the emotion of a man who has before his eyes the very object of his thoughts. As for the use of deictics in the rest of the passage, it conveys the emotion of an author who has reached the twilight of his existence, and who, through writing, transports himself back into the very situation of the person he was at the time he lived the event he is recalling several decades later.[191] For Casanova, writing involves the whole being; it is not a simple remembering freely aroused in the mind but, instead, an emotional reiteration of a past experience. "Rather than a lament consolidating a sense of loss flowing from a juxtaposition of then and now, of memory and reality," observes Kavanagh regarding this scene, "Casanova strives for a discourse retrieving the lost beloved as a presence so intense that it recreates the past as present."[192]

The *Voyage* of Crèvecœur is also the theater of curious overlappings of temporal strata. During their stay in Connecticut, the two heroes visit a colonist living a few miles from New Haven. This individual tells how the difficulties of farming are offset by the pleasures offered by the winters:

> As for me, if I were a poet, I would take pleasure in singing about the peace that we enjoy when these numerous enemies are buried beneath the winter snows; the rest and leisure of this season when, like us, the hard-working ox recovers, in his warm stable, from his long, patient weariness. . . . I would not forget the pipe, leading sometimes to dozing off, sometimes to meditation, but always to calm, nor the can of cider mixed with ginger, nor the heat of a good fire around which one sees his wife, children, and often his neighbors.[193]

Although this passage is written from the viewpoint of a fictitious settler who lived in the period he is describing, it is inspired by the memories of the author, who, already in *More Letters from the American Farmer*, spoke of the snowfalls and comforting pipe smoked next to the hearth.[194] Thus, behind the imaginary character making this speech we can detect the voice of Crèvecœur as he strives to recall a time to which he no longer belongs. Although he affects, with his customary modesty, not to fulfill the condition necessary to the undertaking he conceives ("if I were a poet"), Crèvecœur exhibits an undeniable poetic talent in bringing back to life from an unfathomable abyss the multitude of reminiscences he contemplates from the balcony of his memory. It is a form of poetic paralipsis declaring an inability to express something that is contradicted at the very moment of its expression. This retrospective evocation of a period that is dear to him resuscitates not only a flood of images but a range of sensory impressions involving both taste and smell, leading to the nearly total re-creation of the past as he proceeds to describe it. The use of the conditional betrays both the limits of the person who feels incapable of recovering in their fullness the memories he is seeking and, by the anaphoric use of the verbs employed in this mode, each provoking the rise of additional memories, the will to attempt at any cost to revive a past experienced again as if it were the present.

Manipulation and Invention of Sources

Not content to represent contemporary America in the light of memories that are twenty years old, Crèvecœur resorts in the *Voyage* to borrowed erudition. He describes spaces that he never personally visited, initiating a practice often reproached to Chateaubriand at the same time since he draws from the same literary sources as the latter, both men having carefully perused the *Travels Through North and South Carolina* . . . by William Bartram.[195] Crèvecœur includes in his travel narrative multiple annotations that use the simple mention of a name or place to justify a learned disquisition about them. Despite this apparent concern for exactitude and completeness, he displays a surprising casualness in the treatment of his sources: "First, facts supposed to be original are sometimes not facts and sometimes not original; second, facts said to be from one source are usually from another."[196]

Adams bases his revelation of Crèvecœur's deliberate liberties with the truth on his observations on chapter 2 of the first volume. In this passage, Crèvecœur claims to have traveled to Lancaster on June 6, 1787, to attend the inauguration of Franklin College along with Benjamin Franklin. In the course of the ceremony, the famous inventor supposedly gave a speech on the origin of the North American natives, the probability of their common ancestry with the inhabitants of the Western Hemisphere, and the recent discovery of tombs and former fortifications—but neither Crèvecœur nor Franklin were present at this event. The former was somewhere between France and America, where he was traveling to assume his functions as French Consul in New York, while the latter was dining at the table of George Washington. As for the speech that Franklin is supposed to have given, it turns out that it is a compilation of facts gleaned in various works devoted to North America and particularly in the *Notes on the State of Virginia* by Thomas Jefferson.[197] Not satisfied with attributing to Franklin the paternity of a speech composed of textual fragments from a variety of sources, Crèvecœur invented the very circumstances in which it was supposed to have been given. What is the role of this fictitious anecdote? It allowed him first of all to emphasize his acquaintance with Benjamin Franklin: by exaggerating his relationship with this iconic figure, famous in both the Old and New Worlds, Crèvecœur presented himself as the author of a reference book that should be preferred by readers to any other work devoted to the United States.[198] It is likewise a way to introduce a discourse on the future of the Amerindians that belongs to the recurrent themes of the narrative and serves to unify the patchwork that composes the *Voyage*, a veritable Harlequin's coat whose many snags and tears are clearly visible.

The posthumous representation of America in this narrative is thus the result of a double process of fictionalization: the phenomenon of retrospective idealization is completed by deliberate fabrication for purely commercial reasons. Paradoxically, while the journey of Crèvecœur's hero is a narrative pretext to share with the reader the state of the most recent knowledge of America, the liberties the author takes with the facts contribute to the creation of a fictitious image of the United States.

A Fragmentary Narrative

Another characteristic of the narrative adds to the imaginary dimension of this tableau of the United States: its fragmentation. The *Voyage* offers a scenario that justifies the nonlinear nature of the text, that is, the deterioration of the manuscript during the wreck of the *Morning-Star*. The reader finds himself immersed in a work in which the actors are unknown to him and that begins *in medias res* with an exuberant declaration of the interest of the study of the former and the new inhabitants of North America.[199] The chapters regularly finish with notes by the translator in which he points out a lacuna.[200] Although Crèvecœur reproduced maps that demonstrated his wish to create an objective representation of America, the *Voyage* establishes a very unreliable geography, traversed according to the whims of an inner journey whose itinerary is just as fuzzy as the chronology. The passage from one episode to the next exhibits the capriciousness typical of the chronology of a dream: the reader drifts along with the wandering of the characters, overdetermined by the wandering of the manuscript on the waves of the Baltic Sea. The uncertainty that presides over the connection between the different parts is observable, notably, in chapter 11 of volume 2, when the two travelers are the guests of a certain M. E., whose home is located near Niagara Falls. This chapter ends with silence and a rumor: "The two following chapters were so badly stained that the translator couldn't read them. It appears that the travelers boarded a ship on Lake Erie to go to Detroit and Michillimakinack."[201] Despite this declaration by the translator, in the following chapter we are again at M. E.'s home with no way of knowing if this trip really took place. The gaps in the narrative contribute greatly to the destabilization of the reader, who goes from one place to another without the text being oriented toward the resolution of a quest, the reaching of a goal, or the arrival at a specific destination. They are the narrative equivalents of blanks in a memory shot through with forgetfulness and evidence that this America described in such great detail is the product of a posthumous reconstitution, gnawed by time, and interrupted by silences that are impossible to fill.

When all is said and done, this ideal country to which Crèvecœur returned through memory perished completely, like the *Morning-Star*, at the very moment he described it. All that was left for him was to attempt to save what he could by means of his text, which gives a posthumous vision of America. The *Voyage* is posthumous in the primary sense of the term, since it is the work of an author who is supposedly deceased at the time of its publication: "Persuaded that the author was among the unfortunate who had perished within sight of

Hellégaland, this merchant readily granted me permission to take a copy of the manuscript," the translator declares.[202] It is also posthumous if we consider the implications of its date of publication: 1801.

America on the Other Side of the Century

A changing of centuries is not as objective a phenomenon as one might believe, since it depends on a calendar that is not universally accepted and whose use coincides with other religious or traditional calendars throughout the world. The German Protestants, for example, refused the papal calendar until 1700; likewise, Great Britain did not adopt it until 1752 and Russia until 1918. Nonetheless, the closing of one century and the opening of another are endowed with a symbolic dimension that gives rise to meditation on the past decades and those to come, since this break in the calendar, however arbitrary it may be in reality, is no less a significant experience for mankind, which finds therein a reference point in the temporal flow. The fiction of the shipwreck of which the manuscript of the *Voyage* is part of the debris condenses this tension between the end and the beginning, between the fear and the hope that blend together at the turn of a century. The name of this ship is precisely endowed with a symbolic ambivalence: although swallowed up by the sea, the *Morning-Star* still connotes the idea of a rebirth.[203]

Bearing both hopes and warnings, the *Voyage* represents America as if it were a mirage in the past whose example France should follow, placed by its own Revolution in a situation that is similar to that of the United States. The posthumous America of Crèvecœur seeks to be an inspiration for France's future, and perhaps the star that will arise from the revolutionary abyss will be none other than Bonaparte, whom Crèvecœur hopes—before Chateaubriand takes the opposite position in a famous parallel in the *Mémoires d'outre-tombe*[204]—will become for his country what Washington was for the United States.[205] The function of the evocation of the past is not only to conserve the memory of a past period of American history; it is also an opportunity to present to France, through the United States as its symbolic double, the outline of its own future. Alternatively, Crèvecœur embarks on an essentially commemorative description of the Amerindian cultures that exhibits both his empathy for the first inhabitants of America (the feeling of guilt that accompanies the contemplation of their progressive annihilation) and his inability to imagine among these peoples the slightest faculty of durable resistance to the pernicious influence of the white colonists.[206]

A MEMORIAL OF THE AMERINDIAN CIVILIZATIONS

Facing the Power of Time

In chapter 14 of the first volume, one of the heroes of the *Voyage* reveals his predilection for ancient objects going back to his earliest childhood memories and comments on it in these terms: "Everything that has survived the destructive power of time and men attracts and rivets, I know not why, the stream of my thoughts: the further and more uncertain its origin, the more I find it interesting."[207] This passage is certainly autobiographical in nature, as witnessed by a late text by Crèvecœur that describes the taste he developed very young for everything he met that bore the mark of antiquity.[208] Volney and Chateaubriand share his fascination for the "destructive power of time," the former having discovered in "solitary ruins" lessons on the revolutions of empires, while the latter recognized in Crèvecœur's *Voyage* "his own dizziness before the flight of time and the 'debris' of history," before devoting to it two articles, one of which was republished in the *Génie du christianisme* (*The Genius of Christianity*, 1802).[209] What are the congruences and fracture lines between the reflections that Chateaubriand and Crèvecœur devote to the Amerindian civilizations, and to what extent do the posthumous representations that both of them offer describe them as the victims of an inevitable disappearance?

Languages and Posterity
The *Voyage* of Crèvecœur is haunted by the awareness of the ephemeral nature of beings and of their works—of the decline of the Amerindian tribes in particular—and it is because of a similar interest in the vestiges of the past observed in America that Chateaubriand developed his own meditations on the decline of civilizations. Much like an ossuary, Crèvecœur's *Voyage* collects fragments of Amerindian culture in order to preserve them from complete annihilation. In this respect, he once again foreshadows the undertaking of the *Mémoires d'outre-tombe*, an edifice built "with bones and ruins."[210] Nonetheless, there exists between Crèvecœur and Chateaubriand a significant difference: the two men do not have the same degree of confidence in the capacity of writing to preserve what it evokes.

For Crèvecœur, writing is capable of transmitting to posterity the memory of a moribund civilization. Already in the *Letters from an American Farmer*, the translation of the Bible into Natick was considered a "monument"[211] capable of surviving the destruction of the tribe itself. This belief did not abate in the *Voyage*, where the faculty of French to transmit fragments of Amerindian culture to posterity through translation was not put into question in any way. Conversely, Chateaubriand stresses a little more than Crèvecœur the tragic awareness of the omnipotence of time, since, according to him, it does not even spare languages themselves: "The Oranoke tribes no longer exist; all that remains of their tongue is a dozen words pronounced at the crown of trees by parrots turned loose, like Agrippina's thrush cheeping Greek words on the balustrades of Roman palaces. Sooner or later such will be the fate of all our modern dialects, fragments of Greek and Latin."[212]

The inevitable destruction of languages implies the impotence of writing to protect in the long run the memories of men: a literary monument crumbles and disappears when the language in which it was written is no longer intelligible to anyone. Even if the title "*Mémoires d'outre-tombe*" suggests, to its author, the idea of the survival of the text and thus the perspective of a kind of immortality, this discourse will eventually no longer be comprehensible by future generations: thus the vanity of writers who believe they are building for centuries when they are constructing castles of sand. According to Chateaubriand, literature ultimately refuses to grant men of letters the promise of posterity that it dangles before them for a moment. Sooner or later, their existence will disappear from memory when the language in which their talent won them fame is no longer understood by anyone. To the men who seek to accept death by hoping that the memory of their existence will be preserved in a book, or at least associated with the permanence of a text, Chateaubriand responds by pointing out the gulf of time in which fame is inhumed. Before the towering vanity of the literary enterprise, the *Mémoires* show that man can only hope in God, and that posterity is not a slab of marble on which one can engrave one's name for centuries to come but a period of temporary reprieve before the final night into which all of us will plunge sooner or later, the humble and the powerful, the anonymous and the artists. Chateaubriand does not put his final hope in literature but in Christ: "All I can do now is sit down at the edge of my grave; after which I will boldly descend, crucifix in hand, into eternity."[213]

Before the *Mémoires d'outre-tombe* and with more faith in the power of literature to effect passage to the posterity of what it recounts, Crèvecœur's *Voyage* produces a posthumous representation of the Amerindian world, both as a proof of its entry into twilight and as an attempt to safeguard its memory, since the ambition of this work is to collect its vestiges and preserve them in the pages of a book: while Chateaubriand stands before the tomb, Crèvecœur is an herbalist of the past.

The Birth of Ecological Thought

Crèvecœur explains this decline of the Amerindian tribes, for which he sees no solution, by the disastrous influence of white colonists, while accusing the latter of also being responsible for the progressive destruction of the American wilderness. Crèvecœur's perspective on these two phenomena, which he attributes to the same cause, remains nevertheless ambivalent throughout the *Voyage*, in which he seeks moral and practical justifications for the colonization of North America while simultaneously pondering the concrete measures that could be implemented to preserve what it is still possible to save of the virgin New World that was no sooner discovered than lost by the European travelers. The *Voyage* presages by more than seven decades the American ecologist movement and heralds its two principal, and partially conflicting, currents: preservation and conservation.[214]

The preservation movement was at the origin of the creation in 1872 of the first American national park, Yellowstone, and was inspired by the writings of John Muir (1838–1914), whereas the principles of the conservation movement were established by Gifford Pinchot (1865–1946), who defended a planned renewal of the forests. The goals of these two currents are different: while the preservation movement strives to create an aesthetic and sacrosanct territory to glorify the work of the Creator, the conservation movement encourages a rational and moderate use of natural resources to satisfy human needs without damaging nature in a permanent way. To use Pinchot's terms, the goal of the "conservationists" is "producing from the forest whatever it can yield for the service of man."[215] As Figueiredo observes, these two conceptions of protection of the environment are anchored in two philosophical views of nature that are not mutually exclusive and that coexist in Crèvecœur's *Voyage*.

This work emphasizes the ambivalence of the colonization of the American continent, which results in the creation of zones of fertility that, like swarms, spread out into the rest of America (1801, 1:54). However, the farmer is also a destroyer who must cut down trees and burn them, "drain the swamps, plant orchards and enclose them, build roads, houses, and barns" (64). The planning of human territory is done at the expense of vegetable species that Crèvecœur would like to see protected by the colonists. He urges them to destroy only the trees that are harmful and only according to the quantity of wood they will need over the following years to construct and repair their buildings and farms: encouraged for anthropocentric ends, the preservation of nature serves the future interests of mankind (65). In this respect, Crèvecœur's discourse foreshadows that of the conservation movement that advocates the moderate and careful use of natural resources in order to guarantee their survival for future generations. However, these reasons are not the only ones that justify the respect he considers important regarding the vegetable species: "A landowner, after a few years of enjoyment, is instinctively more moved, more flattered, to cross over his forests than his fields. Once cleaned and submitted to the plough, the latter appear to him to be the result of his own work exclusively; here, nothing grows that was not sowed or planted by him; in his forests, however, everything bears the print of grandeur and time, and those feelings unwillingly strike all men, even the most ignorant" (65–66).

While the fields reflect back to man the image of his own power, the forests exhibit a form of transcendence, since their existence is independent of his own will: the impression of grandeur that he experiences when he passes through them is inseparable from the divine of which they are a visible expression. But still more than a sign of the existence of God, it is a form of temporal coalescence that Crèvecœur sees in the trees: they are the incarnation of time, the sign of a duration that infinitely exceeds that which man can ever hope to experience. The ancientness of nature renders it more vulnerable than the works recently produced by the human mind, so its oldest products must be protected: "May future generations preserve with care these beautiful cedars, these gigantic pines, these venerable hemlocks, these oaks more than a centennial, which human industry could never replace and whose crowns, agitated by the winds, sway today on all these summits as well as on the ridges of these coasts!" (2002, 129). It is because they are the link between the present and an age-old past that the forests must be safeguarded, an ideal that relates to the second current in the American ecological movement, preservation, which strives to create "a staging of a 'culturized' nature, archetype of the virgin wilderness, pure, uninhabited, allowing a privileged contact with the divine."[216]

A Paradoxical People
In the *Voyage*, the ideal of preservation of nature has as its corollary the protection of the Amerindian culture, equally threatened. However, just as he exhibits an ambivalent viewpoint on the colonization of the American territory, Crèvecœur produces a finely shaded discourse concerning the tribes of the New World, fluctuating between the empathy he feels for the Amerindians and the unequivocal rejection of the violence they display, between a disparagement of their so-called inferiority to the Europeans and a discreet identification with their cause. He comments explicitly on "the astonishing contradiction" that the first inhabitants of America embody, exhibiting at the same time a great gentleness in their domestic life while treating their prisoners with a terrifying ferocity (2002, 40–41). More than any other circumstance, it is their stubborn rejection of agriculture and a sedentary lifestyle that are most damning in his eyes. One of his characters declares, speaking of the Shawnees: "It is a shame that this nation, one of the largest in the continent, among which you can see so many tall men, whose language is so harmonious and sweet, has always opposed all the efforts that were done in order to inspire its members with the taste of the sedentary and agricultural life!" (271). In addition, Crèvecœur rebels against the Rousseauean writers who praise the Amerindian way of life that he blames, for his part, for the devastating wars (1801, 1:95–96).

The inability of the "savages" to foresee the future is another cause for condemnation in Crèvecœur's narrative. Like an animal "tied to the post of the moment" of the *Second Untimely Meditation* of Nietzsche,[217] the Amerindians pay no attention to the passage of time and only grant importance to plans for war and rampages that divert them from cultivating the land and raising monuments that could prove their existence to future generations: "[T]heir way of living is as empty as an arrow that misses the target," remarks Crèvecœur (2002, 192).

Nonetheless, the representation of the Amerindian world in the *Voyage* cannot be limited to this occasional criticism. The polyphonic character of the text allows Crèvecœur to distribute among several characters the nuanced reflections that the North American tribes inspire in him. Signed by "an adoptive member of the Oneida nation," the *Voyage* exhibits from the outset a strong sympathy that is evidenced many times in the text, especially when he strives to gather traces of the existence of tribes whose survival is threatened. For these both gentle and ferocious peoples are aware of their impending disappearance. If the Europeans assert that the Amerindian nations are heading for annihilation at an astonishing speed (36), the Amerindians themselves share the same conviction: "The race of those who sow the small and marvelous grains must eventually put an end to those who hunt the flesh, unless the hunters choose to sow grains as well" (49). Their resistance to religious education, their dependence on merchandise from the Old World (e.g., powder and lead), as well as their addiction to alcohol—everything points to a rapid annihilation and demonstrates "that their intelligence is less amenable to perfectibility than ours, and that these races are inferior to those of Europe and Asia," according to Crèvecœur (39).

In these circumstances, the implementation of a museographic undertaking becomes urgent. If the annihilation of the debris left by the Amerindians is compared to a sacrilege, their conservation is, conversely, perceived as a religious act. Paradoxically, the protection of the ruins of a civilization judged inferior is presented as a sacred duty: the responsibility of the Europeans in the disappearance of the Amerindians imposes on them the moral obligation to preserve the vestiges of a culture whose ruin they brought about. First of all, Crèvecœur encouraged the preservation of the toponyms:

> It is a precaution I have frequently recommended to the founders of new settlements across the Alleghenies, in Indiana, Washington, in the great Meneamy, in Kentucky, Wabash, Tennessee, etc. This respect for these names should even have been prescribed by law . . . let's transmit to posterity their original names so we will prevent that the memory of these tribes be forever lost in the depths of time and we will make eternal the only proof of gratefulness that we can give and that we certainly owe to the former masters of this continent, whom we have so frequently seduced and abused. (271)

The idea of safeguarding the past is associated by Crèvecœur with that of moral compensation: according to him, the Europeans have the duty to preserve the memory of the Amerindian place names, since their hunger for land took it away from its original occupants. Of course, such compensation may seem very paltry in comparison with the immense territory seized by the white colonists, but Crèvecœur suggests nowhere that the Amerindians should be satisfied with these highly unjust reparations that remain largely symbolic. On the contrary, the encyclopedic ambition of this long travel narrative, in which a considerable proportion of the text and notes is devoted to the patient gathering of linguistic and historical information about the Amerindians, is the indirect expression of an unassuageable guilt whose effect is to constantly strengthen Crèvecœur's resolve to preserve additional cultural fragments for future generations.

Cultural Samples
At the end of *Atala* (1801), Chateaubriand's narrator describes his meeting with some "miserable Indians" who are wandering in the deserts of the New World "with the ashes of [their] ancestors";[218] following the example of the latter, Crèvecœur turned the *Voyage* into a portable ossuary of Amerindian customs. Chapter 5 of volume 1 reproduces, for example, a letter in which a European relates the circumstances during which he wrote down a tale dictated by a young Shawnee warrior. This document is all the more exceptional in that it comes from very far away and that poets are exceptions among these peoples of warriors and hunters. At first glance, the European exhibits a certain condescendence toward the Amerindian's work: "It is the fruit of a wild child, which, helped by a grafting, might have produced something better."[219] Moreover, he denounces the inability of the Algonquin language to express abstract ideas: "Despite my best efforts to translate this little piece as literally as possible, I confess that I had to use some words that do not exist in their language, such as, for example, *soul*, which they replace by *life, animation*; or *shadow*, by *dark form*; *absence*, by *remoteness*. It is because of their incapacity to conceive of the metaphysical ideas attached to some of our words that they have never been able to understand several truths and historical points of our religion."[220]

It would be easy to accuse Crèvecœur of racism toward the Amerindians, given that this statement about their incapacity to understand metaphysical ideas could easily be taken for a denigration of their intellectual capacities. Racism was common among his contemporaries, Volney stating, for example, that the Amerindians are "dirty, alcoholic, lazy, prone to steal, exceedingly proud," and that "nothing is easier than offending their vanity and in this case they are cruel, bloodthirsty, implacable in their hatred and atrocious in their vengeance."[221] However, such a remark from Crèvecœur's pen does not indicate a radical rejection of the peoples of the New World: he expressed many times a predilection for the depiction of emotions that make him a "farmer of feelings,"[222] a brother of these Amerindians for whom imagination was the dominant faculty. For his part, he described his writing as an effort to formulate sensual impressions, and not as the implementation of these "metaphysical ideas" that the Algonquin language was supposedly unable to grasp: "I have no method other than relating, as best I can, the impressions that I receive (for what I have to tell you will concern the sensations I feel rather than my reflections)."[223] The Amerindians display in addition a singular talent in areas where sharing feelings are more important than using discursive thought: Crèvecœur lavishes praise on the speeches of several chiefs that seem, to him, to reach sublime heights.[224] It is thus a characteristic sample of the Amerindian eloquence whose aesthetic is close to that of his own writings that Crèvecœur reproduces, a sample that is accompanied by a direct indictment of the Europeans for having rendered necessary the posthumous representation of a culture whose decline they facilitated:

> *Panima sits under the great Nemenshehela, while the moon is beautiful and glittering, and says to her friend Ganondawé.* Your doorstep has been removed, the ashes of your hearth dispersed, and your fire extinguished, brave Ganondawé! So you have abandoned your wigwam and the village to go to the country of Oans, where White men have made both shadow and freshness disappear! Why do they ignore how to make their living as we do, by hunting and fishing? Why do they ignore how to sleep on the skin of a bear and to drink the water of the stream! They would be less thirsty for our lands, and we would be neighbors and friends.[225]

In this paragraph, Crèvecœur offers a pastiche of the style he attributes to the Amerindians. In accordance with the idea he had of Amerindian languages, the abstract notions are translated by concrete images: the violence that Ganondawé undergoes is expressed by three images that describe the disorder that befalls his abode; his exile is suggested by the abandonment of his wigwam; as for the deforestation and the transformation of the land by the Europeans, they are evoked by a formula describing sensual impressions. The last phrase of the paragraph reveals once again Crèvecœur's ambivalence toward the Amerindians: while he blamed them for their inability to adapt to a sedentary lifestyle and to agriculture, at the same time the Europeans do not know how to be happy with the simple nomadic lifestyle of the natives. Crèvecœur thus proved himself capable of adopting the viewpoint of the Amerindians and of recognizing the legitimacy of their demands to be allowed to adopt the lifestyle of their choice, demonstrating by this fact his desire to reconcile the cultures that shared the American continent.

Since the Amerindian tribes were the new victims of the millenary conflict between nomad and sedentary peoples, Crèvecœur's task was to save through language what could still be saved. The posthumous representation he gives of the Amerindian civilizations thus has a commemorative function; it results both from a sense of responsibility as a European but also from his underlying identification with the cause of a people whose manner of thinking is deeply similar to his own. Nonetheless, it implicitly denies the natives any capacity to resist actively the pernicious influence of a European civilization that he accuses of causing their woes. Crèvecœur, like Chateaubriand, considered the extinction of the Amerindian tribes to be inevitable, and the representation he gave of it expresses precisely the urgency he felt before a decline that its victims were powerless to check. Chateaubriand observed, for example, that the depopulation of the peoples of the New World was imputable to those well-known scourges of alcoholism, diseases, and the wars generated by the Europeans.[226] Facing a situation that they considered unresolvable, Crèvecœur and Chateaubriand turned to writing to preserve and transmit the fruits of their observation of their "savage" hosts before they disappeared. Nevertheless, what Crèvecœur presents as one of the most brilliant successes of this museographic undertaking illustrates simultaneously the distortion suffered by the culture he claims to safeguard through his posthumous representation.

The *Voyage* relates the following tale: "[The missionaries] translated into the Natick language not only the catechism and the prayer books, but also the entire Bible: I saw a copy printed at Harvard University (Cambridge) in 1663. They taught them a few cultural principles, as well as the morality preached in the gospel and whose tenets they had so thoroughly ignored with respect to the natives."[227] Already in the *Letters from an American Farmer*, this translation was referred to as an "extraordinary monument,"[228] directly alluding to the famous lines by Horace: *Exegi monumentum / Perennius acre* (*I finished a monument / More durable than bronze*),[229] and to the ambition to pit the permanence of writing against the destructive forces of time. Although this passage stresses the contradiction between the moral principles spouted by the Europeans and their treatment of the Amerindians, the criticism does not go so far as to denounce a second paradox between an action that purports to be reparative and the assertion of the European universalism that underlies it. Indeed, it is not an Amerindian legend that is preserved by the missionaries but the founding text of their own culture. Thus, the preservation of the Natick language that is presented by Crèvecœur as a form of symbolic compensation offered to moribund tribes only serves to prepare their last members for inclusion into the Christian community, the translation of sacred texts being a precondition of their conversion: "Jesuits maintained the primacy of writing and the centrality of the Holy Scriptures amid an oral culture. They compiled dictionaries and grammars and translated hymns, psalms, and catechisms," notes Sayre.[230]

In *The Writing of History*, Michel de Certeau reflects on the causes of this "primacy of writing" and on the relations of power between written and oral culture: "To writing, which invades space and capitalizes on time, is opposed speech, which neither travels very far nor preserves much of anything. In its first aspect speech never leaves the place of its production. In other words, *the signifier cannot be detached from the individual or collective body."*[231] By separating an utterance from its original context and from the community to which it was first addressed, writing preserves orality intact, while the latter transmits fables whose origin, in the end, is forgotten. But writing is also responsible for the exportation of texts that do not necessarily return to their source of production: the European archivist is like those archeologists at the beginning of the twentieth century who, on the pretext of preserving cultural artifacts, spirited them off to their own countries where they were never again seen by the descendants of the peoples who had produced them. Similarly, the cultural samples frozen and preserved through translation are no longer available to those peoples in the name of whom their safeguarding was effected in the first place. Clements observes, on this subject, that it has become common in our times for the transcription of oral Amerindian legends to be "published in professional journals or museum series that are largely unavailable in the communities where the expressions originally occurred."[232] When he sets out to translate an Amerindian legend, Crèvecœur does not wonder about the social impact of the transcription of the oral culture, since he is convinced of the superiority of the written over the spoken word. By striving to preserve a tale, Crèvecœur disrupts the normal functioning of the Algonquin culture, which is distinguished by the context of a "student-teacher relation" in which the elders play a dominant role in the transmission of knowledge.[233] The following thoughts of McNally bear on the Anishinaabe culture to which the tale translated by Crèvecœur belongs: "The primary orality of the Anishinaabe tradition has secured a certain prestige for the religious and cultural authority of elders who can choose, or not, to relate their knowledge depending on the circumstance and intentions of the student. And that prestige, though local, can still be maintained precisely by not participating in such projects that commit knowledge to posterity through technologies of print, recording, publishing, and the Internet."[234]

Paradoxically, the museographic undertaking of Crèvecœur and Chateaubriand altered precisely what it strived to keep intact: the very effort to transmit cultural artifacts to posterity changes their meaning and, indirectly, the communities that gave them life. The posthumous representation they give of Amerindian civilizations indirectly conveys, at the very moment that it fulfills a commemorative function implying empathy and respect, their underlying conviction of European superiority based on mastery of writing. For neither Crèvecœur nor Chateaubriand assume that the Amerindians have sufficient resilience to protect themselves against a decline for which the two authors agree the Europeans are responsible. Likewise, neither of them sees in the Amerindian culture any monuments capable of passing on to posterity the memory of these dying cultures. While it is true that Crèvecœur mentions buildings raised centuries ago by the Amerindians, edifices that have survived up to his period, the sight of them only raises "doubts and conjectures,"[235] given that the name, origin, degree of development, and the causes of the disappearance of the people who built them remain a permanent mystery. They do not demonstrate the grandeur of a civilization whose memory is perpetuated forever but only leave us to decipher the mute traces of an obliterated existence.[236] Unaware of the capacity of oral cultures to pass on, from generation to generation, a collection of immutable images that relate the origins and history of a tribe "with remarkable consistency," and neglecting to mention the sharing of cultural expertise and expressions during "ceremonial rituals," Crèvecœur and Chateaubriand root in the supposed inability of the Amerindians to resist the destructive power of time an implicit disrespect of their culture that, paradoxically, is accompanied by the desire to safeguard it through its posthumous representation.

An Unforeseeable Causality

This patient collecting of the debris of the past, that the author of the *Voyage* views as the links of "the chain that ties the nebulous past to the fleeting present and will tie the latter to the future,"[237] is an occasion for a melancholy meditation on the passage of time and the causality at work in the world. At the end of the *Voyage*, M. G., a prominent New York citizen, shares the following reflections: "Such are the imperceptible springs of human destinies. And one wishes to foresee, organize future events, as if they weren't necessarily preordained, engendered by those of the past! It was necessary, however, for all of those diverse circumstances to have occurred for my ancestors to be forced to flee their homeland like criminals, and for me to have the pleasure of receiving you under my roof and hearing the interesting tales of your travels in the interior of the continent, which is as foreign to me as if I were born in Europe."[238] The future appears to Crèvecœur as the necessary product of a meeting between causal chains so numerous that it is impossible to foresee their consequences. A new underlying affinity between Crèvecœur and the Amerindians is revealed here, for if he describes them as the perpetual inhabitants of a present in which concern for the past or future have no place, he neither has any illusions as to the capacity of the human spirit to anticipate the future based on knowledge of the past. Provoked by a similar meditation on the sequence of historical events, an identical judgment regarding their unpredictability may be found in Chateaubriand's works: "Memorable example of the sequence of human affairs! A finance bill, passed by the English Parliament in 1765, causes the rise of a new empire in 1782 and the disappearance of one of the oldest kingdoms of Europe in 1789!"[239] Crèvecœur and Chateaubriand share an identical astonishment when they reflect on the causality at work in history. It is the feeling of the profound fragility of men's works that they express, since an uncontrollable causal link proves capable of falling and building empires. Both of them turn toward

America with a feeling of responsibility, for if Chateaubriand presents himself as "the last historian of the peoples of the land of Columbus,"[240] the *Voyage* of Crèvecœur also exhibits the ambition to pass on to posterity fragments of their rhetoric, toponymy, legends, and beliefs, in short, everything language can seize to tear it from the grip of time. Both produce a posthumous representation of the Amerindian world, their works transmitting to posterity the ultimate vision of peoples on the verge of disappearing. In looking toward the West, they are also thinking of the destiny of their fatherland, whose decline is forecast by that of the Native American tribes, proof of the inscription in an erosive and destructive temporality of everything humans produce: the posthumous representation of America is a warning for France. Despite the numerous similarities between their ideas and the subjects that inspired them, however, the works of Crèvecœur and Chateaubriand did not meet the same success.

The *Voyage dans la Haute Pensylvanie et dans l'État de New York* (1801) appeared the same year as a "kind of poem, half descriptive, half dramatic" written "in the desert and in the huts of savages": *Atala*.[241] The exceptional success of this "little work" by Chateaubriand, so rousing that it embarrassed the author,[242] is in stark contrast to the lukewarm, indeed hostile, reception accorded Crèvecœur's book: "Crèvecœur saw everything that Chateaubriand saw and wished to express everything that Chateaubriand expressed. But he didn't possess the genius; his book is bad. Their descriptions are identical with the sole difference that genius makes," states Faÿ.[243] If the author of *Atala* relates a story outside history in an idyllic cadre, Crèvecœur describes, on the contrary, the modifications of the American territory, progressively conquered and developed by an enterprising people: his work is much less inviting than that of his young colleague to a French public more drawn to a dreamy meditation on the Edenic solitudes of the New World. Moreover, its encyclopedic and dense character resembles much more the end-of-the-century travel narratives, whereas *Atala* may be considered to be the harbinger of French Romanticism:[244] Crèvecœur was at the twilight of his life and of the Enlightenment, Chateaubriand at the dawn of his work and of the nineteenth century.

Although their first publication was in 1792, *Les Lettres écrites des rives de l'Ohio* by Claude-François de Lezay-Marnésia, immediately censured by the Girondins, also reappeared at the beginning of the nineteenth century, in 1800, a year before the publication of the *Voyage dans la Haute Pensylvanie* and *Atala*. Ahead of his two colleagues, Lezay-Marnésia reflected on the destiny of France through his depiction of America, but while Crèvecœur and Chateaubriand discovered a possible adumbration of the decline of French civilization in the example of the Amerindian civilizations, Lezay-Marnésia clung to the hope that America still represented the promise of a revival of the Old World in the New.

LEZAY-MARNÉSIA AND NOSTALGIA FOR THE AMERICAN GOLDEN AGE

> If a few French families, with sufficient personal fortunes, were to settle around Fort Pitt, they would discover in this country the charming banks of the Loire and the Seine, but even more favored by nature and with the peace and happiness that have abandoned them.
> —Lezay-Marnésia, *Letters Written from the Banks of the Ohio*

Prologue: Lezay-Marnésia or Wolmar in America

CRÈVECŒUR: A PARADOXICAL DOUBLE

The allusions to Crèvecœur in the *Letters Written from the Banks of the Ohio* reveal the inherent contradictions in the literary project of Claude-François-Adrien de Lezay-Marnésia (1735–1800). Placed at the head of this collection of letters, the "Editor's Foreword" launches an all-out attack against the men of letters who, before Lezay-Marnésia, had ventured to describe North America: "It seems as if they have been in league to deceive us. The ones, extravagant enthusiasts or biased authors, have taken, to paint all of America, the colors that Milton used to paint heaven on earth, presenting its inhabitants like so many perfect Spartans. The others, as unjust as they are excessive, have tried to make us believe that this enormous continent, disavowed by nature, was condemned to an eternal infancy and did not have the strength to produce anything but weak, cowardly, and degenerate animals."[1] The second group of writers includes without a doubt Buffon and Cornelius de Pauw. In several works, Buffon had indeed speculated that the cold and humidity of the climate in America explained the inferior size, weight, vigor, and variety of the American animal species in relation to the European species, as well as the progressive degeneration of the species that originated in Europe and were transported to America. This theory had been espoused and radicalized by

Cornelius de Pauw in his *Recherches philosophiques sur les Américains ou mémoires intéressants pour servir à l'histoire de l'espèce humaine* (*Philosophical Research on the Americans or Interesting Memoirs on the History of the Human Race*, 1768), a work that emphasizes in particular the progressive depopulation of "savage" societies.[2]

Alternatively, it is indeed the author of the *Lettres d'un cultivateur américain* who is the target of the criticism of "extravagant enthusiasts."[3] In his *Recherches historiques et politiques sur les États-Unis* (*Historical and Political Research on the United States*, 1788), Mazzei had already reproached Crèvecœur for giving his readers chimerical ideas about the United States and had attracted thereby the fury of Brissot.[4] According to the editor, the *Letters Written from the Banks of the Ohio* is the first work to blow up the old dichotomy between the panegyrists and the denigrators of America, substituting a discourse that, finally, would tell the full, entire truth about the New World. Nonetheless, one of the main goals of this chapter is to show that, far from having a personal monopoly on truth, Lezay-Marnésia belonged, despite himself, to the first school of authors castigated by the editor in his name: he was not the victorious opponent of Crèvecœur but his reticent double.

If the editor was content to make an implicit allusion to Crèvecœur, Lezay-Marnésia makes a frontal attack in the *Letters Written from the Banks of the Ohio*: "It is common to catch fish that weigh from fifty to sixty pounds, but not eighty to a hundred and even more, as M. de Crèvecœur says. Those who have given credence to the exaggerations of this writer have been completely deceived. Like those painters who, not being capable of capturing the beauty of Helen, represented her as rich and heavily made up, M. de Crèvecœur, not knowing how to render nature how it appears in reality—sublime, magnificent, and often enchanting—made gigantic pictures of it; that was easier."[5] The reference to Crèvecœur plays a catalyzing role by revealing a fundamental contradiction in Lezay-Marnésia's work. While it is in the name of rigorous accuracy that Crèvecœur's ichthyologic approximations are criticized,[6] Lezay-Marnésia is far from producing a completely objective description of the region of Ohio where he wanted to emigrate: he depicts it as he imagined it before traveling there and not as he discovered it to be. If Crèvecœur did in fact exaggerate the fertility of this region of Ohio in a letter of which we will soon speak again, at least he had no personal interest in seeing emigrants move there. On the contrary, by drawing a picture of this region every bit as idyllic as Crèvecœur's, Lezay-Marnésia was seeking to entice his addressees to join him there as quickly as possible. No matter how much the author of the *Letters Written from the Banks of the Ohio* tried to distance himself from his predecessor, posterity has reserved for them the same condemnation, as in the case of Volney, who reproached them for exhibiting a "banal rhetorical talent" whose consequences were disastrous for those who put their faith in the idyllic depiction of the future state of Ohio.[7]

If Crèvecœur appears as a paradoxical double for Lezay-Marnésia, the admiration that the latter professes for Jean-Jacques Rousseau is a thread that not only winds through the *Letters Written from the Banks of the Ohio* but runs throughout his whole work. It is to the influence of the citizen of Geneva on Lezay-Marnésia, as well as to the circumstances of the latter's emigration to America, that the following prologue is devoted.

AT THE SCHOOL OF ROUSSEAU

The admiration that Lezay-Marnésia had for Jean-Jacques Rousseau is abundantly clear in the *Essai sur la nature champêtre* (*Essay on Rural Nature*),[8] as in "Les Lampes" (1788), a text written in honor of Montesquieu, Voltaire, Rousseau, and Buffon.[9] It likewise shines through in *Le Bonheur dans les campagnes* (*Happiness in the Countryside*, 1785), an essay that begins with a declaration—"I saw the ills of the countryside, and I sought remedies"[10] —that rephrases the famous proclamation at the beginning of the preface of *La Nouvelle Héloïse*: "I saw the customs of my time, and I published these letters."[11] Formed at the school of Rousseau, the thought, sensitivity, and imagination of Lezay-Marnésia were brutally confronted with the rigors of life in America when he went into exile on the banks of the Ohio River at the beginning of the French Revolution. Why did this aristocrat decide to emigrate when he was part of the representatives of the nobility who rallied to the Third Estate at the Estates General on June 25, 1789? Why did he choose the untamed lands of the Northwest Territory to establish a colony instead of acquiring property in one of the states that was already an integral part of the American Union—an option that was chosen, moreover, by a large number of his countrymen?[12] Before traveling with Lezay-Marnésia to these dangerous lands, let us retrace the path that led this aristocrat from his native Franche-Comté to the solitudes of the American Northwest.

THE PEN AND THE SWORD

Lezay-Marnésia joined the king's army at the age of twelve with the rank of lieutenant. He served for twenty-two years, rising through the ranks of the military hierarchy. Ensign at twenty and captain at twenty-four, he was forced to leave the service in 1769 with the rank of brigadier (sergeant) after expressing his hostility to the military reforms of Choiseul that widened the social base for the recruitment of officers, whereas Lezay-Marnésia saw in military careers a privilege reserved for the nobility. This first part of his life could have given him experience in bravery and fear and helped him to develop organizational qualities that, during his venture in the New World, would have been of great use to him. Unfortunately, "the marquis is a soldier who never went to war; his physical courage was never put to the test," as Moreau-Zanelli observes.[13]

In 1766, Lezay-Marnésia wrote *L'Heureuse Famille* (*The Happy Family*), a tale considered "quite insipid" by Grimm,[14] in which he adopted a moralizing tone to sing the benefits of country life. The following year, he was admitted into the Royal Society of Belles-Lettres of Nancy, where his first speech announced one of the major themes of his work to come: the study of "rural man."[15] In 1769, he moved into his château de Moutonne with his wife, Marie-Claudine de Nettancourt-Vaubécourt. Among the table companions were the chevalier de Boufflers (to whom Lezay-Marnésia would address the first of the *Letters Written from the Banks of the Ohio*) and Saint-Lambert, a close friend of Crèvecœur—but also Palissot, Cerutti, Chamfort, Dupaty, and Voltaire, whose Ferney property was close to the marquis's estate. This prestigious circle of friends was completed, from the end of the 1770s, by Louis de Fontanes, who was going to become a close friend of Chateaubriand's at the dawn of the Revolution, before the two men found themselves together in exile in London in 1798.

In 1784, Lezay-Marnésia published a *Plan de lecture pour une jeune dame* (*Reading Program for a Young Lady*), which exhibits the breadth of his erudition. Although he denies women the right to scientific instruction, he nonetheless recommends that they acquire a vast culture through historical works and the reading of the illustrious authors of the past. He shows himself to be eclectic, practicing poetry and mineralogy.[16] Lezay-Marnésia contributed likewise to Diderot and d'Alembert's *Encyclopédie*, for which he wrote alone the article "Manstupration" (Masturbation) and, in collaboration with Jaucourt and Montlovier, the article "Voleur" (Thief). He is also the author of *Le Bonheur dans les campagnes* (*Happiness in the Countryside*), published in 1785. This work is particularly important, regarding the thought of the author, for it announces the plans that he later attempted to bring to fruition in America and thus requires a closer look.

LEZAY-MARNÉSIA AND RURAL HAPPINESS

"This little treatise of around three hundred pages contains virtually all of the moral ideas that crystallize around the myth of the good feudal lord, the good farmer, and the idyllic countryside," remarks Moreau-Zanelli.[17] Following the example of Rousseau and Bernardin de Saint-Pierre, Lezay-Marnésia encourages noblemen to return to the countryside. The questioning of the attractions of urban life, as opposed to the supposed purity of country life, is a theme that Rousseau popularizes in *Julie ou la Nouvelle Héloïse* (1761), a novel in which the corrupting influence of Paris on the upright Saint-Preux is described. An elegiac tone permeates this work, in which Lezay-Marnésia foretells the development of an "emulation" in the practice of charity among the nobles, the priests, and the most affluent inhabitants.[18] In describing the practice of philanthropy by the local elites as a means of regenerating country life, Lezay-Marnésia ties into a current of thought dating back to the last third of the eighteenth century, for which charity is no longer viewed as a simple social practice and comes to embody a "vast plan of renewal of customs, social relations, and laws."[19] As Bonnel has demonstrated, Lezay-Marnésia considered charity as the source of a sentimental bond between the aristocrats and their vassals, whose institution was capable of repelling the looming specter of unrest he foresaw scarcely four years before the Revolution.[20]

The paternalism that Lezay-Marnésia advocates in this text is inspired by the functioning of Clarens in *Julie*. Sent by Saint-Preux to Milord Edouard, Letter 10 of the fourth part describes the creation of affective bonds between Madame de Wolmar and her estate staff. Although Rousseau emphasizes the compassion exhibited by the latter toward her workers and servants, it is nonetheless clear that the status of "children"[21] that she attributes to them establishes a radical inequality between her and them that is entirely incompatible, as critics have not failed to point out, with the political thought developed elsewhere by Rousseau, and particularly in the *Contrat social*.[22] Despite his reformist ambitions—Lezay-Marnésia abolished the *corvée* and *mortmain* on his lands[23] and demanded, with other noblemen, equality of taxation between the classes—it is precisely the principle of inequality between men that he will never agree to call into question. In his *Pensées littéraires, morales et religieuses*, published in 1800, the observation of a disparity between levels of intelligence appears to him to demonstrate the necessity of an autocratic government: "[Men] have less need of bread than they need to be led; and the worst government by one person or by a small number is better for them than independence. This truth demonstrates that the idea of pure Democracy is nothing but a chimerical abstraction, impossible to attain."[24] Reformist but convinced that the nobility had a dominant political role to play, indignant at the selfishness of the elite but hostile to democracy, this is the man who was preparing to plunge into the Revolution.

LEZAY-MARNÉSIA IN REVOLUTION

In 1789, Lezay-Marnésia was elected to represent the nobility of the bailiwick of Aval, and he sat beside the Chevalier de Boufflers at the Estates General. He placed in this gathering his hope for the return of the "feudal aristocracy" that preceded the absolute monarchy.[25] A reader of Montesquieu and subscribing to his arguments in favor of the establishment of intermediate bodies between the king and the people, Lezay-Marnésia favored the organization of provincial states, as well as the development of the political role of the nobility, which he considered to be a link between the people and the monarch.[26]

Despite an initial enthusiasm for the reformist character of the Revolution that led him to join the group of forty-seven deputies of the Second Estate who rallied to the Third Estate on June 25, 1789, Lezay-Marnésia was soon devastated by the abolition of privileges on the night of August 4 and shocked by the decree of November 2, 1789, transferring the ownership of the church's property to the nation. The violent rhythm of changes, which went far beyond the simple reforms he and the Monarchists were advocating at the Constituent Assembly, soon turned him into a ferocious adversary of the Revolution. The following excerpt from a letter sent from Paris on November 9, 1789, and addressed to his wife, presents exile in America as the last chance of the nobility: "How, especially, when one has the misfortune of having been noble, can one become accustomed to being nothing but a fallen being who is constantly insulted and debased? I confess that I do not possess this shameful courage. It seems to me that one must reject this kind of 'courage' and rather seek a homeland where he is certain to find rest, safety, and the security that can only be found today in one country, in New England, where good laws and customs make men truly free and as happy as they can be on earth."[27]

The praise Lezay-Marnésia lavishes on New England betrays the inconsistency of his political thought. Indignant at the abolition of privileges and the disappearance of the nobility, he nonetheless chooses to settle in a region where the equality of social classes reigns. This paradox reveals his view of the political and geographical spaces of the United States: he considered them to be a clean slate on which he could establish the utopia of his choice. According to him, the greatest virtue of the American nation consisted in authorizing the creation of settlements whose political form was, however, distinct from his own. The praise of liberty is thus purely rhetorical in the marquis's mouth: liberty is only praiseworthy, in his view, to the extent that it allows him to invent a society in which a patriarchal system will set the parameters and whose members will only be equal if they do not belong to the working class. Similarly, the trans-Appalachian geographical space appeared to him as empty as the American government seemed accommodating: he believed it was a territory where the state of nature still reigned and where disciples of Rousseau were, consequently, the best people to play colonist. Created in 1789, the Scioto Company offered him the opportunity to bring his project to fruition in the region of the Ohio River.

THE SCIOTO COMPANY

The Scioto Company was founded in Paris on August 3, 1789. Bringing together an American poet, Joel Barlow; a Scottish engineer, William Playfair; and six Frenchmen,[28] its goal was to buy from the American Congress an area of around three million acres of land located between the Ohio and Scioto Rivers, over which the Ohio Company—an American business whose interests were represented by Joel Barlow in Europe—held the sole preemptive rights. The documents in question were, however, presented as titles of property and marketed as such by the Parisian partners beginning in autumn 1789. The intention of the Scioto Company was to use the funds invested by its clients to buy the lands from the American Congress and to convert its preemption rights into legal property titles. While the buyers only received at first worthless pieces of paper, the company intended, eventually, to give them ownership of the land that they thought they had purchased. The success of this commercial operation thus rested on two essential elements: the constitution of sufficient capital for the Scioto Company to transfer to the Ohio Company the funds necessary to purchase from Congress the lands that were up for sale[29] and the broad circulation of favorable testimony from the first emigrants to America, who, by expressing their satisfaction with their situation in letters addressed to their close acquaintances, would encourage them to buy land in their turn.

In order to stimulate the sale of land that it was offering for six tournois pounds an acre, the Scioto Company disseminated in the autumn of 1789 two advertisements that described an idyllic alternative to France: the *Prospectus for the Colony on the Ohio and Scioto Rivers in America* and the *Description of the Soil and the Productivity of this Portion of the United States, Situated Between Pennsylvania, the Ohio and Scioto Rivers, and Lake Erie*.[30] Written no doubt by William Playfair, the *Prospectus* proved to be fallacious on two main points. On the one hand, the author failed to mention that the lands being sold were inhabited by Amerindian tribes whose hostility toward the settlers would soon become evident.[31] On the other hand, he jumped the gun when he claimed that the colony was located at the heart of a territory that had been cleared and was already settled: it was as if he considered the optimistic predictions of Crèvecœur on the future prosperity of the region of the Ohio River to have already been fulfilled.

Published in 1787, an excerpt of the *Lettres d'un cultivateur américain* completed the documentation presented by the Scioto Company to its potential clients. Although it has been impossible to locate the exact passage that was distributed in 1789 by the company, there is every reason to believe that it was a fragment of "L'Esquisse du Fleuve Ohyo et du Pays de Kentuckey" ("Sketch of the Ohio River and of the Kentucky Region") in which Crèvecœur describes the area where the lands put up for sale by the Scioto Company are located.[32] Quoted in this text, General Richard Butler promises rapid prosperity for the future colonists of the Scioto and declares that they will be able to enjoy the pleasures of fishing and hunting during the long periods of leisure left to them by the farming of a marvelously fertile land.[33] Written two years before the creation of the Scioto Company, Crèvecœur's text could not have been intended to serve its interests. On the contrary, it is the *Prospectus* and the *Description* that imitate the bombast of the "Esquisse" and, as the latter does, pass off the hope for future prosperity as the promise of a guaranteed fortune for anyone who would just go to the trouble of crossing the Atlantic.[34] Lezay-Marnésia, along with five hundred of his countrymen—aristocrats and commoners, was taken in by these promises.

THE SOCIETY OF THE TWENTY-FOUR

At the beginning of 1790, Lezay-Marnésia was working on the creation of an association of landowners known as the "Société des Vingt-Quatre" (Society of the Twenty-Four). The goal of this organization was to "found a city and colony on the banks of the Ohio . . . under the sovereignty and laws of the United States."[35] The twenty-four partners agreed to purchase one thousand acres each from the Scioto Company, contiguous properties that would form the basis for a community where their city would be built.[36] As Albert, the youngest son of Lezay-Marnésia, remarks: "[His associates] left to my father *the mission of the dove leaving the ark*, which was to go in search of land, and the glory that would accrue to the founder if his endeavor was crowned with success."[37]

The biblical metaphor employed by Albert de Lezay-Marnésia reveals the religious character of the undertaking of his father at the time of the Revolution—which is indirectly compared to the flood sent to men to punish them for their depravity. In the biblical narrative, Noah is elected to survive and continue his lineage owing to his moral integrity and respect for the Creator. Likewise, Lezay-Marnésia based on purity the selection of people who would be saved from the revolutionary "flood": "[W]e will not be indulgent in our choices,"[38] he warns in a letter to his wife. This religious dimension of Lezay-Marnésia's project becomes explicit by his intention to create a bishopric on the Scioto lands at a time when the revolutionaries were attacking the prerogatives of the clergy.[39] Lezay-Marnésia was following in the tracks of the puritans who gained the Promised Land of the New World in the seventeenth century, leading a people unified by its moral values and religious beliefs to a territory where it would strive to keep them intact.[40]

To carry out this program, the Society of the Twenty-Four held nine meetings between January 24 and February 10, 1790, during which the members tended to the most minute details of the organization of the future city. Elitist principles were adopted by the partners in the determination of the conditions of membership in their community: "No persons can be admitted into the society and the city unless they have been introduced by a partner and approved by a plurality of the members—with the exception of relatives of those members."[41] Lezay-Marnésia and his partners intended to control the social composition of their city, as well as the political convictions of its inhabitants.[42]

In addition, they were determined to keep for themselves the real power, to the detriment of the mass of the colonists. The social segregation that they intended to maintain was expressed in geographical terms, since the Twenty-Four foresaw the construction of two cities. The first, named Gallipolis, would provide homes for the workers and would have farming as its primary vocation. Its exact location was established as early as the end of 1789: it would be built on the west bank of the Ohio. The second, the one that the Twenty-Four were resolved to build for themselves and their families, did not yet have a definitive location at the time of these meetings; it was agreed that the landowners would make that determination when they had arrived at their lands. In the mind of Lezay-Marnésia, this second city was to include the essential administrative and religious edifices of the future colony: the church, the courthouse, and a hospital would be built there; there would even be a university where the French language would be taught, as well as a Philosophical Society on the model of those that existed in France at that time. The distribution of the various institutions between the two cities and the ascendancy of the second over the first had not, however, been discussed and agreed to by the applicants to the venture: it was a foregone conclusion for Lezay-Marnésia, while it is probable that the "other emigrants were not informed of his projects, and that they would have been aghast if they had learned of it," surmises Moreau-Zanelli.[43]

SCIOTOPHOBES AND SCIOTOPHILES

The activities of the Society of the Twenty-Four provoked an intense controversy in France as it began its Revolution. The *Chronique de Paris* published an article by Anacharsis Cloots that mocks with a biting irony the "delicate ladies who condemn themselves to this exile as if in the grips of a burning fever" and warns them that it "will be too late to listen to reason when their tresses have become a trophy for the savages who swoop in and take off the pericranium of the peaceful workers."[44] A few days later, Camille Desmoulins goes even further in an article in *Révolutions de France et de Brabant*, in which he promises, with a black humor worthy of the marquis de Sade, an unenviable fate for the wife of Monsieur Duval d'Eprémesnil after the taking of her husband's scalp: "I see her amid the forests with nobody to turn to for help—using her noble muscles to carve out a refuge in a tree trunk, remembering halcyon days with Monsieur Thilorier, the boudoir of her youth, her allowance of 20,000 livres and the sweet nothings of Monsieur de Cluny's ministry. Her own servants will abandon her . . . and around her Monsieur d'Eprémesnil's widow will see only orangutans fighting each other for her third wedding night."[45]

Described as libertines, dupes, and reactionaries, the aristocrats leaving for the Scioto were also compared to the slave traders of the West Indies. Before embarking, the purchasers of land in America recruited workers whom they had sign contracts similar to those of indentured servants in use by English landowners at the time of colonial America, and that were still in force in the western United States. In exchange for their passage to the New World, their upkeep, and a few acres of land at the end of their commitment, the workers sold their labor for four to five years. Likened to slavery by the French patriots, this practice was denounced in pamphlets circulated at the beginning of the Revolution.[46] At the time of Lezay-Marnésia's stay in America (1790–92), slavery still existed in the French colonies (the first abolition was not voted until 1792), as well as in eight American states, including New York. A French emigrant in the revolutionary period, the Marquise de La Tour du Pin, had slaves at her service; her *Mémoires* describe the members of her "black household."[47] The "Northwest Ordinance" of 1787, however, had prohibited slavery in the Northwest Territory, to which the region of the Ohio River belonged. Even if Lezay-Marnésia had anticipated the patriarchal and slave plans of Balzac's Vautrin, it would have been impossible for him to implement them, since the Ohio River marked the frontier between the free and the slave states.

FACT-PROOF UTOPIA

Despite the violent anti-Scioto campaign in the press of the period, Lezay-Marnésia was determined more than ever to reach the United States, and it was in the spring of 1790, from Le Havre, where he embarked on May 26, that he wrote to his friend Duval d'Eprémesnil to direct him to follow his example: "You should prefer the township in America that is calling you to this disastrous land of Europe that is only good any more to serve as an example to the world by uniting in itself everything that is the most debasing in shame and everything that is the most deadly in calamity."[48] After a grueling crossing, Lezay-Marnésia visited Philadelphia and New York, where he met the most influential personalities of the Republic: he was received by Adams, Hamilton, Jefferson, Madison, and General Washington himself. "What he was experiencing for a month corresponded in every respect to the idyllic image he had formed of the New World: the simplicity of Washington, the farmer soldier, the Cincinnatus, and his peers, all the signs of the greatest prosperity and liberty in an enlightened republic were confirmed in the course of this voyage," observes Moreau-Zanelli.[49] The following adventures of Lezay-Marnésia proved, however, to be less pleasant. He reached Virginia, then the city of Pittsburgh. From there, he wished to travel to the lands that he had purchased in the Scioto region, but he had to stop at Marietta (in present-day Ohio): the Amerindian tribes, rulers of the region, prevented him from going any farther.

The terror that the natives aroused in the settlers reached its height when a community north of Marietta, Big Bottom, was attacked on the night of January 2,

1791, by the Wyandots and Delawares, tribes that had heretofore been considered peaceful: only four people survived a massacre that killed fourteen, with three missing. At the beginning of the month of May 1791, a large contingent of troops led by General Saint Clair set off. Its goal was to put an end to the marauding of the Amerindians in the region: they were launching murderous raids against the convoys of pioneers heading for Cincinnati and targeting recently established settlements in Kentucky. But at the Battle of the Wabash, the army of Saint Clair was crushed by a coalition of Amerindian tribes.[50] By an irony of fate, while he was praising the tranquility of the banks of the Scioto in the text of Crèvecœur quoted previously, Richard Butler was among the American victims at Wabash.[51]

Like the other members of the Society of the Twenty-Four, Lezay-Marnésia did not know if he would ever be able to take possession of his lands: located at the center of the military operations, they were more inaccessible than ever during the winter of 1790. He attempted to recuperate his losses from the Scioto Company, but no member of the Twenty-Four ever received the slightest compensation. Nonetheless, the marquis would soon form new illusions.

Followed by his son and several servants, he went to Pittsburgh, where he acquired four hundred acres of land in Pennsylvania. With the letters of his name, he created an anagram and baptized his new propriety "Azile." In his *Souvenirs*, Albert de Lezay-Marnésia asserts that his father could have stayed there to observe from a distance the evolution of the political situation in his homeland.[52] But the marquis soon grew tired of the pleasures of bucolic life and began to regret the good French society that he had deserted to come to the United States. After having just barely escaped prison, where his debts would have led him if his son had not succeeded in obtaining a providential loan, Lezay-Marnésia embarked in Philadelphia. Two years after his departure for the United States, he found himself back in France, in May 1792, dejected and ruined.

THE RETURN AND THE RUIN

"We had left France in order to escape the disasters revolution threatened to bring upon the country; we returned at the very moment that revolution made good upon its darkest promises," writes Adrien de Lezay-Marnésia, summarizing thus the paradox of his emigration.[53] It is the very day of the invasion of the Tuileries, June 20, 1792, that he returned to Paris with his father. In September 1792, the two men obtained the passport that permitted them to leave the capital. Before leaving, however, Lezay-Marnésia gave to Prault the manuscript of his *Letters Written from the Banks of the Ohio*: they would be printed in 1792 but immediately banned.

In a letter from 1800, Lezay-Marnésia alludes to the responsibility of the Girondins in the censuring of his work, without specifying the exact reasons for their opposition.⁵⁴ At first glance, it may seem surprising that the Girondins would be opposed to the publication of a text advocating emigration to America insofar as, in the same period, Brissot saw on the borders of the United States a territory where French domination could be exercised. Brissot had sent Edmond-Charles Genêt across the Atlantic with orders to raise troops and provoke war with Spain and the United Kingdom in Louisiana, Florida, and Canada. The dream of the Girondins was to create "sister republics that shared 'political and commercial interests' with France and the U.S."⁵⁵ Genêt proved, however, incapable of achieving these goals after having failed either to obtain the support of the United States or to raise the necessary funds.⁵⁶

Just like Lezay-Marnésia, the Girondins considered the territory beyond the Appalachians to be a vague geopolitical space where they could contest the domination not only of other European powers but also of the Americans and the Amerindian tribes. Nonetheless, the similarities between Brissot's "sister republics" and the community planned by Lezay-Marnésia prove to be superficial when subjected to a more thorough examination. Lezay-Marnésia designed a plan that, unlike Brissot's, implies no economic or political collaboration between the American colony and mainland France. On the contrary, the cities he dreams of are supposed to unite opponents of the Revolution who would choose to abandon France to its turmoil. Moreover, despite his interest in the creation of French colonies in the west of the United States, Brissot is careful to distinguish his plans from those of the clients of the Scioto Company, whom he describes as aristocrats eager to implant in America the social hierarchies of the Old Regime and maintain there the privileges that the Revolution had just taken away from them.⁵⁷ If he criticizes the reactionary program he ascribes to the noblemen leaving for the Northwest Territory, Brissot does not question the legitimacy of the project initiated by the Scioto Company, in which certain historians think he may have been personally involved.⁵⁸ The creation of a French colony in America would be, he said, useful to both France and the United States, since it would allow them to intensify commerce between the two countries. Rather than aristocrats nostalgic for the Old Regime, however, it is the neediest of the French that should, in his opinion, be transported to the other side of the Atlantic.⁵⁹ These divergences, as well as the hostility expressed toward the revolutionary movement in the *Letters Written from the Banks of the Ohio*, explain the ban Lezay-Marnésia's book suffered under the Girondin government. They reappeared, nonetheless, in 1800, bringing together three letters written by the marquis at the time of his stay in the United States.

Once they had arrived in Saint-Julien at the end of 1792, the marquis and his son rested from their travels there until the enforcement of the "law of suspects" on September 17 of the same year gave them new cause for alarm. Noble and an emigrant, Lezay-Marnésia was arrested in March 1794 before being released in

October of the same year thanks to a certificate of civic spirit submitted in his favor by the commune of Saint-Julien and the revolutionary committee of Orgelet. But the coup d'état of 18 Fructidor Year V (September 4, 1797) and the new wave of repression against the royalists and emigrants that followed interrupted this moment of respite in the ordeals of his life by forcing him to leave France. Necker sheltered him in Switzerland, in his castle at Coppet. The marquis's exile there wore on: struck from the list of expatriates by the Jura department, he was not granted the same exemption in the Haute-Saône, where he still owned land. Having finally received the authorization to return to France, he settled in Besançon, where he began a final work, *L'Action des principes de la religion et de la véritable philosophie*. Less than a year after his return, on December 9, 1800, he passed away, his formerly considerable fortune reduced to debts and the Saint-Julien castle.

A SCATTERED CORPUS

Before leaving this biographical prologue to begin the study of the American letters of Lezay-Marnésia, it is necessary to present the corpus studied in this chapter. The *Letters Written from the Banks of the Ohio* is composed of three letters. The editor presents them as samples of a much broader correspondence: "The author of these letters put in our keeping a manuscript that contains a large number of them. We are presenting only three of them to gauge if they are to the taste of the public."[60] Lezay-Marnésia declares elsewhere that he wrote in America a vast corpus of letters that the "revolutionary events"[61] had destroyed for the most part. Nonetheless, the number of texts he still possessed were sufficient to contemplate the publication of a second, augmented edition, if the public were to give a favorable reception to the first one. This enlarged version never saw the light of day, Lezay-Marnésia having passed away the year of the republication of the *Letters Written from the Banks of the Ohio* in 1800.

Along with the aforementioned three letters, four additional texts that appeared in the *Nouveau prospectus*[62] and the *Reading Program for a Young Lady* will be examined. In October 1790, a month before the writing of the first of the *Letters*, Lezay-Marnésia wrote three missives that foreshadow the idyllic representation of the New World that is found in the volume. Excerpts have survived thanks to the Scioto Company, which placed them at the end of the *Nouveau prospectus*, self-published in December 1790. Following a "Notice" given to potential purchasers of lands in Ohio, the three excerpts of letters written by Lezay-Marnésia provide a resounding confirmation of the most optimistic and deceptive statements of the Scioto Company.

If the texts published in the *Nouveau prospectus* precede the *Letters*, the one that Lezay-Marnésia adds to the second edition of the *Reading Program* serves as an epilogue. Published for the first time in 1784, the *Plan de lecture* was republished by Louis in Paris in 1800 with some texts that were not in the original edition. Among these new texts is a "Letter to Monsieur Audrain, Merchant in Pittsburg,"[63] which provides further commentary on the marquis's American adventure and completes the three texts that form the volume of the *Letters Written from the Banks of the Ohio*. Since Lezay-Marnésia's missives in the *Nouveau prospectus*, those of the 1792 volume, and the letter published in the *Plan de lecture* all reflect the same period and treat the same experience, they must be studied as a coherent ensemble despite their appearance in three different sources.

Of the three texts circulated in the *Nouveau prospectus*, only the first bears a date (October 12, 1790). The two others can only have been written a few days later at most, the *Nouveau prospectus* being published in December 1790—and it took considerable time for Lezay-Marnésia's letters to travel from the East Coast of the United States to the French capital. Written on November 15, 1790; November 2, 1791; and December 15, 1791, respectively, the three texts included in the *Letters* constitute a diary that accompanied the various stages of the marquis's journey (Marietta, Pittsburg, Philadelphia), a veritable rout that inexorably brings the traveler back to his point of departure: like Ulysses, Lezay-Marnésia returns home, but while constantly looking back toward the west, the territory of his unfulfilled dreams. Addressed to M. Audrain, the last letter, written after Lezay-Marnésia's return to France in 1792, was published for the first time in 1800.

Thanks to the geopolitical indecisiveness of the trans-Appalachian space at the end of the eighteenth century, and to the poor reliability of the knowledge about it in Europe,[64] Lezay-Marnésia imagined a Golden Age in the Ohio region and seemed to expect other French emigrants to the United States to join him there. This second chapter is devoted to the fictional construction of a posthumous America in his American letters,[65] the literary models that it appropriates, the political principles on which it is founded, and the effect that it has on revolutionary France, as well as to the tenuous boundary in these texts between lies to others and to himself, and between visionary enthusiasm and madness.

The American Letters of Lezay-Marnésia or the Persistence of Utopia

"THE PROMISED LAND IS THE ONE WE ARE GOING TO INHABIT"

Refutations of the First Prospectus

The posthumous construction of America is begun by Lezay-Marnésia in the winter of 1790 with three short texts published in the *Nouveau prospectus*. Circulated in 1790 by the Scioto Company, the goal of the *Nouveau prospectus* was to reassure candidates for exile who were becoming privy to alarming testimony from their predecessors in the United States. The letters written by the latter contained warnings and complaints that contradicted the idyllic perspectives that the Scioto Company had been dangling before the public since the autumn of 1789. These publicly expressed grievances were all the more inimical to the interests of the company as its leaders knew the importance of the first reports sent back from America: they alone could encourage new departures and foster sales without which, we remember, it could not convert into titles of property the rights of preemption that they held on the Scioto lands.[66] Among those sounding the alarm, the most eloquent is certainly the author of the *Lettre écrite par un Français émigrant sur les terres de la Compagnie du Scioto à son ami à Paris* (*Letter Written by a Frenchman Immigrating to the Lands of the Scioto Company to his Friend in Paris*).[67]

Fiercely determined to discourage potential clients of the Scioto Company, he relates the hardships he had suffered on the *Recovery*, a ship stocked for fifty people that had carried eighty-six passengers to the New World, and which, taking on water everywhere, eventually sank. Having arrived in New York on a second ship that had saved in extremis the *Recovery*'s passengers, the author declares that the Scioto Company had deceived their clients on a number of accounts and, in particular, on the location of the lands they had sold them. The *Prospectus* claims that the territory in question is located "approximately in the center of the United States," in a "commercial area" endowed with "all the conveniences one could hope for," such that in a short time the "capital of the American government" would undoubtedly be established there.[68]

The author of the *Lettre* presents, however, a quite different map:

> To the west of the Scioto, you have to go 160 miles, to the confluence of the Miami and Ohio Rivers, before you come to a colony that is under way. To the east of the Scioto you have to go 220 miles and to the confluence of the Muskingum and the Ohio before finding another colony. . . . In the 380 miles between them, and immediately behind each fort, there are vast forests that extend to the Great Lakes, filled with implacable savages who constantly harass the Americans and destroy pitilessly all the parties they come across. What a charming neighborhood! You must admit that one could not be less *isolated*.[69]

Throughout the twenty-eight pages of his letter, the author contradicts point by point the claims of the *Prospectus*. While it asserts that the settlers will be able to exploit quickly a fertile land, the Scioto emigrant replies that the hostility of the "savages" will seriously compromise the fulfillment of such a fine prospect.[70] While the company claims that the Mississippi will permit the exportation of the colony's products, our emigrant answers that such a promise could only be kept if they went to war with Spain, which controlled New Orleans.[71] A victim of too many disappointments, the author of this letter eventually made an irrevocable decision: he chose to sacrifice his investment in the property in the Northwest Territory and return to France. This negative publicity was disastrous for the Scioto Company, which attempted to respond by publishing the *Nouveau prospectus*.

To achieve its purposes, the company first resorted to an effort to undermine the credibility of its detractors. The author of the *Nouveau prospectus* attributes to partisan motives, personal interest, and jealousy the criticism to which the company has been subjected.[72] He also relies on several authorities who confirm the truthfulness of the first *Prospectus*. On the one hand, he twice cites Crèvecœur, who has praised the quality of the soil and the mildness of the climate in the region of the Ohio River.[73] On the other hand, he offers testimony from emigrants who, contrary to the author of the *Lettre*, confirm the rebirth of the Golden Age west of the Appalachians. Among these testimonies, the most eloquent comes from Lezay-Marnésia.

Exaggerations and Lies

Five excerpts from letters are included at the end of the *Nouveau prospectus*. Three of them were written by Lezay-Marnésia, the two others by a certain M. Baillet and by Dom Didier—the Benedictine chosen by the Society of the Twenty-Four to lead the spiritual life of the future community.[74] The fact that the company only found three people of the hundreds of French who had already gone to America to confirm its claims should have raised questions for the readers of the *Nouveau prospectus*. Moreover, these letters lack the basic information necessary to avoid suspicion: the first does not name the addressee, while the fifth is undated.[75] Among these letters, those of Lezay-Marnésia combine exaggeratedly optimistic predictions with blatantly false declarations in order to offer a representation of a posthumous America that serves as an advertisement, since the marquis is striving to attract new emigrants to his undertaking.

It is true that in the first of his epistles, Lezay-Marnésia pledges to tell the truth on his soul and conscience.[76] Nonetheless, the paragraph following this commitment turns out to be a prospective text and not a faithful description of the Scioto region:

> The lands sold to Frenchmen by the agents of the Scioto Company are *the richest of all those that are under the dominion of the United States.* The neighboring lands, whose clearing only began three years ago, are proof that they are so fertile that you could hardly find any comparable land anywhere else on earth. Cultivated by Frenchmen who are far more active, work far harder, and are much better farmers than the Americans, who have not yet

progressed very far in the art of agriculture or in the other arts, they will yield much more than the fields of their neighbors.[77]

When he wrote this letter, Lezay-Marnésia had not yet reached Marietta, where he would not arrive until the end of October 1790. His expectations regarding the fertility of the land in the Scioto region were consequently simple speculations that just repeat the promises of the Scioto Company that he had heard in Paris. Although it has no objective foundation, the marquis's confidence also shines through this passage: "We will have accomplished all the hard work, and all the difficulties will have been mitigated for those who follow us. They will discover in us brothers who are well settled in attractive, clean, and comfortable houses with abundant and good provisions and very happy to share everything with them."[78] Lezay-Marnésia projects himself into a future in which new emigrants will already have joined his settlement: in a temporal leap betraying his characteristic impatience, as well as his lack of interest in the practical problems of building a city that he was busy legislating before setting the first stone, the colonization of the Scioto was presented to the readers of the *Nouveau prospectus* as an enterprise already completed. By depicting a future where the entire task will have been completed, Lezay-Marnésia gave a prematurely retrospective portrayal of the conquering of the difficulties he had not yet met and of the comparatively easier situation of the new arrivals that, at the time of writing, was likewise hypothetical. He also contributes to an illusion of certainty concerning the prospects of the colony by using the future tense in the ensuing lines of his text as well: while the marquis's readers may have interpreted it as a simple future describing a possible event with a high probability, the tense is loaded here with a predictive value insofar as the circumstances necessary for its realization were still far from being in place. In October 1790, no Frenchman was as comfortably settled in Ohio as the marquis foresaw, and still less blessed with abundant provisions. In other words, Lezay-Marnésia wrote a prophetic text whose fulfillment depended on circumstances that were not yet in existence—but this was not how it was perceived by its readers, who interpreted it as a genuine promise, which became the basis of numerous departures for the United States.[79]

Invitation to the Promised Land

The two excerpts from his correspondence reproduced in the *Nouveau prospectus* not only confirm the predictions of the Scioto Company but blatantly lie about the current situation of the French emigrants in the Northwest Territory. In a letter addressed to his lawyer, Lezay-Marnésia abandons himself to his typical enthusiasm: "It is certain that the lands that they sold me are in the most fertile place of the two worlds, in the mildest temperature, in the most healthy climate, and that each acre of land produces at least forty to sixty bushels of grain and that the sales are so hardy that corn and wheat fetch on the average six pounds a bushel."[80] Of course, Lezay-Marnésia could no more justify such assurances in this moment than he could before his departure from France, since at the time he wrote these lines, he hadn't yet even seen the lands occasioning the use of so many superlatives and was never to set eyes on them.

The last letter is even more optimistic than the preceding ones. While the first one feigns objectivity by informing the potential emigrants that indigo could not be grown on the banks of the Ohio, contrary to what the *Prospectus* had announced, the third, very brief, resorts to a biblical image to describe the Scioto lands: "All the testimonies concur, all the accounts agree, and all assure us that the land we are going to live on is the Promised Land."[81] The image alone summarizes, without Lezay-Marnésia being able to foresee it at the time of writing, the whole American adventure: like Moses, the marquis wanted to lead a threatened people to a place where it could live under its own law and customs; and just as the patriarch, who embraced from Mount Nebo the Promised Land upon which he never set foot, Lezay-Marnésia was not able to go beyond Marietta and never saw the Scioto for which he had undertaken such a long journey.

In the organization of these various epistolary excerpts, the author of the *Nouveau prospectus* exhibits a fine mastery of advertising rhetoric: he is careful to place at the end the text most likely to convince readers to head for the "Promised Land." It still remains to be explained why Lezay-Marnésia was willing to collaborate with the "public relations" campaign undertaken by the Scioto Company. Why did he support this company that had sold to him and others worthless documents?

At the time he was writing these letters, Lezay-Marnésia still believed in his plans for a colony, given that his access to his propriety had not yet been blocked by winter, the war with the Amerindians, and the defeat of Saint Clair at the Battle of the Wabash.[82] Consequently, it was contrary to his interests to mitigate the enthusiasm for exile in France when only people making this choice could give his colony a chance for success. As the author of the *Letter Written by a Frenchman Immigrating to the Lands of the Scioto Company* remarks, the reinforcement of new emigrants was essential to the security of those who had preceded them in America: "It is clear that our security depends on the large number of recruits we will have, that you must expect to see a proliferation of illusions in Paris and the whole kingdom."[83] Despite his efforts to denounce the fabrications of the Scioto Company, the author of this pamphlet confesses that he too is prone to wishing for the arrival of countrymen: "I feel that I am weak and calculating like the other men; I am sometimes surprised to find myself wishing for the company to succeed in attracting many of my countrymen to the Scioto—provided that they are not among my acquaintances!"[84]

This self-centered desire was shared by Lezay-Marnésia, who had sacrificed a considerable fortune to acquire 22,100 acres of land from the Scioto Company, and who was risking his life by preceding the other members of the Society of Twenty-Four into the Northwest Territory. As it turns out, the letters published in the *Nouveau prospectus* played precisely the role intended by its author, provoking a new wave of emigration on the strength of the promises it contained: "The following June, Vandenbemden, one of the colonists who had arrived on board the last ship, was in Philadelphia. He reported to Duer the arrival of a new boat, the *Pennsylvanie*, with around one hundred and twenty people who had 'left France confidently owing to a letter written by the marquis de Marnésia and sent from the Scioto; he depicted this region as a garden of delights.'"[85]

By means of the letters inserted at the end of the *Nouveau prospectus*, Lezay-Marnésia directly influenced the departure of additional Frenchmen for a "garden of delights" that they were going to find bristling with thorns. His missives confirmed the existence of a doxological America for a readership already fascinated by the American mirage, playing therefore a direct role in reality through the description of an imaginary land. Following these three epistolary fragments, the *Letters Written from the Banks of the Ohio* continued the posthumous representation of America begun in the winter of 1790 by Lezay-Marnésia, a representation that, instead of honoring his commitment to speak only the "truth" concerning a country directly observed by the author, made it correspond systematically to the expectations preceding his voyage.

TAMING THE SAVAGERY

The Error of Christopher Columbus

In an article devoted to the concept of "America" in European political thought, Levine describes the fabulous bestiary assembled in the writings of Christopher Columbus:[86] "He claimed to discover cannibals, Cyclops, Amazons, Sirens, dog-faced peoples, people with no hair, and people with tails. These bizarre claims were suggested to him by centuries of fanciful tales passed on through medieval times by supposedly reliable authorities. Essentially, Columbus already knew what he would find, and he found what he thought he would. This self-fulfilling discovery began a pattern of preformed opinions dictating what is supposedly found in America."[87]

The famous error of Christopher Columbus, who was convinced until his last breath that he had discovered a new passage to India, had much deeper consequences than the creation of the term "Indians" to designate, improperly, the first inhabitants of the American continent.[88] For Christopher Columbus did not discover America as a true New World that he had perceived in its individuality without casting upon it the slightest preconception. On the contrary, the certainty he had that he was setting foot on Asia inclined him to transfer to America all of the images that were circulating in European thought about the Far East and to seek in this space what he believed had, perforce, to be there: "He thus identifies the agouti rat as the Pharaoh's rat seen by [Marco Polo] among the Tartars, laments the fact that he doesn't recognize certain kinds of trees, searches desperately for parrots and imagines he has found aloe where it cannot exist because this plant and these animals are proof that he has reached the goal he had set for himself," observes Guyot about the famous explorer.[89] The original error of Christopher Columbus is more than a historical detail: it is a missed opportunity for the human mind to conceive of something as utterly new. Since its entrance into the European consciousness, America has remained a space into which the traveler has transferred images he believes true before he has actually been there. After the first discovery of Christopher Columbus and the prodigious rash of texts it gave rise to, each journey completed by his successors was accompanied by an effort to verify the truthfulness of a discourse biased from the outset and by an approach that consisted in comparing it to their empirical experience, with the result that the American continent remained to be rediscovered beneath this ocean of words.

Much like Christopher Columbus, Lezay-Marnésia knew before arriving what he was going to discover in an improperly named "New World." However, the preconceptions he brought with him were different from those of his predecessors of the sixteenth century: it was no longer half-mythical creatures that he was prepared to find but good, welcoming savages, reassuringly noble, consistent with the new expectations created by Montaigne and reinforced by Lahontan and Rousseau.[90] The transfer and confirmation of the French ideas about the Amerindians play a political role in his work, since its goal was to encourage those who were disappointed by the French Revolution to emigrate by enticing them with the image of a world in which their rule of law would be accepted by the natives. This political objective is at the center of the redefinition of posthumous America in the *Letters Written from the Banks of the Ohio*, unlike the *Lettres d'un cultivateur américain*. Crèvecœur reinvents a past that he lived through personally, following the historical breaks that the American and French Revolutions represented. In the work of Lezay-Marnésia, on the contrary, the posthumous representation of America consists less in recreating a past period of American history than in reproducing and confirming the discourse that the author considered to be true before arriving there. This is the advertising function of posthumous America announced in the introduction, that is, the attempt to promote the existence of a doxological America whose falseness is already apparent for the author at the very moment at which he is working on its construction.[91] Here, Lezay-Marnésia strives to recreate an ideal that has nonetheless disappeared at the time of his writing: driven by nostalgia, he seeks to reinvent the period preceding the evaporation of his own illusions. The author of *Letters Written from the Banks of the Ohio* puts the advertising function into effect from the first letter of the volume, written during his stay in Marietta.

A Threatening Context
At the end of October 1790, Lezay-Marnésia and his travel companions stopped at Marietta, a settlement founded two years earlier in the Northwest Territory, and which had only five hundred inhabitants. Accompanied by the comte de Barth, he awaited there the clearing of the lands acquired by the Society of Twenty-Four, 160 miles downstream on the Ohio River and located at the mouth of the Scioto—the very lands whose fertility he praised in the *Nouveau prospectus* without ever having seen them. The wait was long, for the Amerindian tribes in the region prevented them from leaving Marietta. In his *Souvenirs* (*My Memories*), Albert de Lezay-Marnésia describes the difficult living conditions of the inhabitants of the little city and summarizes the situation of their guests: "[We were] reduced to live, so to speak, the same life as these savages amid the sparse population of Americans, true savages themselves who, with no life or resources elsewhere, had pushed forward into these regions like lost sentinels of civilization who were seeking to make a life in this wilderness."[92]

On November 5, 1790, General Putnam returned to Marietta.[93] During the same period as the first of the *Letters Written from the Banks of the Ohio*, an exchange of letters began between him, Lezay-Marnésia, and the comte de Barth. In a letter of November 9, Putnam invites them to travel to their lands in order to determine the exact place where they wanted to build their colony—which they refused to do. On November 15, Putnam urged them again to join this expedition. He tried to "explain to these pioneer apprentices, devoid of any common sense, and who have just refused once again his offer of an expedition to the Scioto, that before building the slightest structure and mobilizing workers that are so rare in the region, they first have to choose the site of their settlement."[94] Despite these commonsense arguments, Lezay-Marnésia continued to oppose the trip: "The marquis had never expected to have to be on the front lines, physically exposed to the rigors of an expedition in the wilderness or to an Indian attack."[95] His fear of the Amerindian tribes was the cause of his resistance to Putnam's proposals. It tormented him at the precise period in which he wrote the first of the *Letters*, since this one was dated November 15, 1790, the very day when the general pressed him a second time to go to the mouth of the Scioto.[96] However, far from sharing with his readers the worries caused by the Amerindians, Lezay-Marnésia instead relates, in the introductory letter of the volume, a peaceful visit by a little group of Huron warriors and their queen.

Portrait of the Savage as a Colonial Subject

Addressed to the chevalier de Boufflers, this letter begins with an ironic denunciation of the living conditions in Marietta. At first glance, it seems that the program announced by the editor's note—to tell the truth and nothing but—was being rigorously followed:

> Living in the finest house of Marietta, surrounded by generals, majors, and colonels, and by a distinguished throng of knights of the Order of Cincinnatus, *that is to say*, living in a shack as humble as the humblest cottages of Europe, and having for neighbors titled plowmen who drive their own plows, cultivate their fields quite poorly, are dressed in a shabby woolen blanket six days of the week, and blow their noses in their fingers—something that even our peasants in France do not do—I had an unexpected visit, just as I was sitting down to dinner, from the queen of the Hurons, accompanied by her daughter, two ladies of the court, and a nobleman, apparently her head equerry. (47; emphasis added)

The "that is to say" in this sentence plays the role of an unveiling. This adverbial expression reveals the reality hidden beneath the gilding of the discourse and implicates the linguistic abuses by the revelation of the misery he is struggling to cover up. Nevertheless, what begins as a witty work whose Voltairian irony promises a vigorous attack against the Scioto Company soon takes a different turn. Lezay-Marnésia describes the table manners of his Amerindian guests, judging them superior to those of the Americans, which is a way of suggesting that the countrymen of Washington were more savage than the "savages" themselves: the condescendence of Lezay-Marnésia toward the Americans is one of the unifying themes of his three letters. Throughout the meal, the Hurons exhibit a remarkable talent to adapt. While the custom of being served by people who are standing and not eating is foreign to them, they adopt it with no difficulty (48). Scarcely sketched out, the cultural differences separating Lezay-Marnésia and the Hurons are canceled out by the goodwill the latter demonstrate in conforming to the habits of their host. Implicitly, their pliancy regarding French customs indicates their ability to obey the property owners who will reign over the future colony of the Scioto: far from embodying an inflexible otherness, the Amerindians will easily become colonized subjects. In other words, this deceptively innocent depiction of the table manners of his guests indicates the feasibility of the colonial project of the marquis—as it demonstrates at the same time the universality of French norms. Although he is a guest of America, he presents himself as the host of the Amerindians, that is, as someone whose law is being applied in his own residence, and it is precisely toward the extension of his zone of authority that Lezay-Marnésia is working, he who has come to the Northwest Territory to take possession of the 22,100 acres of land bought in Paris.

The following paragraph pursues this attempt to culturally assimilate the Hurons by comparing them to the table companions the marquis used to entertain at Saint-Julien: "You have noticed, Monsieur le chevalier, that there is no company that is not more pleasant after dinner than before." The Amerindians are no exception: "By the end of the meal we were well acquainted and almost on intimate terms" (48). Lezay-Marnésia behaves toward his "savage" guests as he did in France with his vassals: he calls them "my good Indians," with a condescendence tinged with paternalism that recalls the principles enunciated in *Le Bonheur dans les campagnes*.[97] Generous lord, philanthropic aristocrat, he gives them modest offerings that delight them: "They were impressed by my grandness when I presented small tokens of knives, ribbons, mirrors, and needles. Quite rightly, they seemed very grateful. They took hold of my hands, shook them affectionately, and held them up to their hearts with great feeling" (48). This scene depicts the Hurons as being in debt to the marquis, from whom they accept gifts without offering him the slightest one in return, contrary to the customs of the Amerindians for whom an act of generosity required a response of proportionate value.[98] By refusing to mention the reciprocity of gifts during this true account, a reciprocity that would have established a relationship of equals between the participants, Lezay-Marnésia describes an asymmetrical exchange in which the person who exhibits generosity asserts his power over those who receive the presents. Implicitly, Lezay-Marnésia presents himself as the lord of this court for the simple reason that he is French, and it is only composed of "savages." He thus in no way espouses the perspective of the aristocratic Europeans who recognized in the Amerindians a reflection of their own social condition. Liebersohn devotes a study to the nobles of France and Germany who observed "a peculiar affinity between the destiny of warrior elites from two worlds."[99] For the aristocrats from Europe shared with the Amerindians not only a comparable disdain for agricultural work and an identical devotion to the warrior functions within their social organization but also considered themselves to be victims of the growing greed in democratic societies and the custodians of threatened age-old traditions, such that, in the end, they projected onto the Amerindians the anguish they felt regarding their own situation at the end of the eighteenth century. This identification was foreign to Lezay-Marnésia: in his eyes, his superiority to the Hurons derived implicitly from the privileges of birth—the very privileges whose abolition he had been horrified to observe on the night of August 4, 1789—and it did not even occur to him that it could be the result of an arbitrary social convention, not even in the far-off Ohio wilderness. Instead of describing this scene as it, in fact, occurred—the account given by his son is far more plausible than his—Lezay-Marnésia rewrote it, giving himself the dominant place that he wished to occupy. The writing of the *Letters* thus allowed him to correct an experience that did not go as he wished, providing the means to establish the victory of the imaginary over the real by substituting for a disappointing experience a representation organized to confer on the author a superiority in accordance with his fantasies.

However, the personal role played by the letter is coupled with a political function. In the course of a single paragraph, the Hurons made considerable progress in the mastery of French customs: while they were just beginning to learn table manners, suddenly they were reproducing the expressions and gestures with which the marquis's countrymen would have received his gifts in Franche-Comté. Not content with being inoffensive, Lezay-Marnésia's guests are ideal colonial subjects: they behave in the manner the master expects of them, but without speaking his language, which would elevate them to a position of equality from which they could contest his authority.

The Negation of Alterity

The remainder of the letter reduces ever further the cultural distance between the marquis and his guests. Lezay-Marnésia describes the unusual gallantries that he showers on the queen of the Hurons:

> Sitting next to young Paulée (the name of the royal princess), I attempted, with my gestures, to communicate sweet nothings—truly the saddest way to express gallantry is to do so by interpreter—which the good-natured princess did not dismiss. She clearly understood the message in my gaze, which boldly praised her charms. I understood just as well her response, which came in the form of an endearing smile. Emboldened, I took her hand and squeezed it softly in mine. She gently squeezed mine in return. Encouraged further, I kissed Paulée. (49)

This seduction scene is all the more improbable in that it borrows from French gallantry its subtle progression—from the gaze to the hand and from the hand to the kiss—and unites participants who have in common neither age, nor culture, nor even language. In the course of the text, the queen of the Hurons herself becomes a fictional character, Lezay-Marnésia comparing her to the heroine invented by the chevalier de Boufflers, *Aline, reine de Golconde* (*Aline, Queen of Golconde*) (47).[100] As in the "Avis de l'éditeur" (45–46), the concept of truth is at the heart of this passage: the very real individual that Lezay-Marnésia met corresponds to the fictitious creature of Boufflers. This correspondence is, however, made clearer by the marquis, who declares that the queen of the Hurons resembles the queen of Golconde "not when she was on the throne but when she was the young Aline, still rich with her jar of milk and her innocence" (49).[101]

This distinction between two periods in the life of Aline is more significant than it may seem at first, for Boufflers's tale describes the loss of innocence of a charming peasant girl who has numerous amorous adventures and, in the end, becomes the sovereign of the imaginary kingdom of Golconde. Paradoxically, the queen of the Hurons resembles the first Aline, the one who has not yet ascended the throne but who shares with her both youth and purity. Through this comparison, Lezay-Marnésia's guest is inscribed in a literary lineage that includes, among others, Charlotte of Molière's *Dom Juan* (1665) and Fanchette of Beaumarchais's *Mariage de Figaro* (1784). An inexperienced young lady vulnerable to the first seducer who comes along, she loses, under the pen of the marquis, the disturbing strangeness that we later discern in the *Souvenirs* of his son. In short, she is presented as an *ingénue*, a feminine double for the fanciful Huron that Voltaire depicts in his philosophical tale in 1767. The parallel with Voltaire's *L'Ingénu* appears all the more intentional in Lezay-Marnésia's text as, if we are to believe his son, it was not the Hurons but the Chickasaws who paid them a visit in Marietta in November 1790. The author of the *Letters* lied about the identity of his guests' tribe in order to draw them more easily into the realm of fiction and to assimilate them into what he knew of America before arriving there, instead of presenting new images, no doubt more threatening, in the collection of representations he was sharing with his readership.

Portrait of the Amerindian as a Frenchwoman

The physical description of Paulée is a continuation of the attempt to fictionalize the guests of the marquis. It resorts to the canons of French aesthetics and contributes to her assimilation into Lezay-Marnésia's culture of reference: "Her hair is long, free-flowing, and a beautiful black color. Her figure is what you would expect, resembling one of Diane's nymphs. Her legs and charming feet are encased in attractive buckskin boots that reveal their pretty shape" (49). With the exception of the reference to the "buckskin boots," this prosopography could be that of any European woman and does not focus on any specifically Amerindian characteristics in Paulée. Comparing her with one of Diane's nymphs is a cliché of encomiastic poetry that allows the marquis to include a reference to classical culture in this blason of an Amerindian body. Evoking the skin color of his guest, Lezay-Marnésia associates it with oriental exoticism by means of a comparison: "Her skin is swarthy, almost olive, rather like Algerians, Tunisians, or even the Spanish" (49). Far from emphasizing her otherness by her color, Paulée is, on the contrary, made immediately familiar to the French reader, who is invited to imagine her as a Spanish woman. Even her outfit proves to be strangely European: she wears "a little black hat with a large colored ribbon" and "a blouse made of very fine silk." In addition, "a thin silver cross" (50) indicates that she has converted to Catholicism: if the Catholic Church was being violently attacked in this same period in France, at least it still had faithful members in America thanks to the long, hard work of the missionaries. Conversely, the description of the young Amerindian given by Albert de Lezay-Marnésia includes details that would have been much more difficult for his father to relate to French culture: "Her pierced earlobes fell in long fleshy rings on her shoulders, which is a general practice among the Indians; the remainder of the ear was trimmed all around with small silver rings."[102]

The queen of the Hurons loses progressively any cultural specificity in the *Letters*: she is the living confirmation of the image of the Amerindians circulated beforehand in the French imagination. This movement consisting in the description of the unknown through a filter employed in advance by the traveler reaches its peak in the reference to the theater: "If the French theater still exists . . . , do the actresses who play young Indian princesses a great favor by telling them how Paulée is dressed. Alzire, the lover of Manco-Capac, as well as that of the hero of *The Tragedy of the Illinois*, should not cover themselves with feathers like parrots; they should rather adopt Paulée's attire, which is so comely and would, I believe, be a sensation on stage" (50).

Already observed in the preceding chapter, the phenomenon of circularity in the representation of America is repeated here once again. The queen becomes the paradoxical model of a supposedly authentic representation that is, in fact, a reproduction of the imaginary America as it existed in France at the end of the eighteenth century, a model, moreover, that is supposed to rectify the idea that French playwrights have of young Amerindian women. What Saint-John de Crèvecœur accomplishes in his *Lettres* through translation—that is, a confirmation of the ideas of his readership whose truth was guaranteed by his long experience across the Atlantic—Lezay-Marnésia does in his turn by passing off the copy of a preconceived idea as the representation of a scene from life. Of course, Paulée would not be out of place in the *Lettres d'un cultivateur américain*, where one could imagine her amid the natives in the "Anecdote of a Wild Dog," a text that Lezay-Marnésia indeed praises (70).[103] Nonetheless, the portrayal of America by Lezay-Marnésia is fundamentally different from Crèvecœur's depiction on one essential point: they are based on very different models.

Painting the Doxological America
As the aforementioned study of the *Voyage dans la Haute Pensylvanie et dans l'Etat de New York* demonstrates, Crèvecœur relied on memories preceding by far the moment of writing in order to produce the posthumous representation of a lost America. On the contrary, Lezay-Marnésia wrote at the very time of his experience in America letters whose first publication followed immediately his return to France in 1792: the gap between the experience, the writing of the narrative, and the publication was thus minimal, with the notable exception

of the "Lettre à M. Audrain," to which we shall return. Still, Lezay-Marnésia insisted on pairing the discourse he produced in his *Letters Written from the Banks of the Ohio* with doxological America, this collective representation that he had taken, mistakenly, for a faithful description of reality before traveling himself to the country across the Atlantic. The first of the *Letters* finishes with this declaration: "Pleasures, arts, and good taste are not to be found in North America, and especially at the frontiers of the United States. I believe that they will never come here if you do not bring them yourself; but there is tranquility, liberty, and peace here, so I would lack nothing if I had with me my family and one or two friends like you" (51).

Sent in the middle of the Revolution to an aristocrat, this letter boasts deliberately of the tranquility of America, where at least no one risks the guillotine for being a *ci-devant* (former aristocrat). However, a study of the circumstances in which this text was produced revealed that there was absolutely no liberty of movement in Marietta—which one could not leave without the risk of being killed and scalped—and that neither peace nor tranquility reigned, since the hostility between the colonists and the natives was matched in the city by the conflicts between Lezay-Marnésia and his American and French associates. The marquis thus describes the hierarchical and paternalistic relations that he hoped to have with the Amerindians when he was in Paris, and not those that he had, in fact, observed between the settlers and the first inhabitants of North America. Compared to those of Crèvecœur, his letters construct a new type of posthumous America: a literary representation of America expressing the implicit regret that it did not conform to the imaginary version pervasive in France. This regret was, however, dispelled by means of writing, which reproduced the imagined space rather than consenting to see it invalidated by reality. In giving substance to the hopes of a readership inclined to see in the New World a place where one could escape the turmoil of the old one, the posthumous America of Lezay-Marnésia was ultimately given a political function: it tended to prove that it was possible to recreate in the western United States a France that had ceased to exist.

The Politics of Posthumous America
The function of the intertextual relationship established by Lezay-Marnésia between the first of the *Letters* and *Aline, reine de Golconde* is not simply to portray Paulée as an ingénue incapable of resisting the advances of a seducer and, a fortiori, the colonizing designs of the marquis's countrymen. Boufflers's tale describes the reunion of the two principal protagonists in the imaginary kingdom of Golconde. Having become queen, Aline recreates in the gardens of her oriental palace the French countryside where she met the knight during her already distant youth. Led to her, the latter exclaims: "How surprised I was when, having arrived at the edge of the woods, I found myself in a place that

resembled perfectly the one where I had, long ago, met for the first time Aline and found love! It was the same prairie, the same hills, the same plain, the same village, the same stream, the same plank, the same path; all that was missing was a milkmaid, whom I soon saw appear in the same clothes as Aline and with the same pot of milk."[104]

The repetition of the adjective "same" emphasizes the complete similarity between the knight's memory of the place where he met Aline and the artificial spectacle that he has before his eyes: the image of a France belonging to the past reappears in an identical form in a foreign space. Lezay-Marnésia attempted to effect a similar translation in the Northwest Territory, his goal being to recreate there the ideal France that first monarchical absolutism, then the revolutionary movement had prevented from being reborn in metropolitan France. This France that conformed to his desires is the one that he prays for in *Le Bonheur dans les campagnes*, a country where the aristocracy would again play a prominent political role, that of an essential intermediary between the king and the people, and would see its social function enhanced with new prestige by giving rise to an economic and moral regeneration outside the major cities. Just like the imaginary, faraway India, the land west of the Appalachians was a space sufficiently foreign to his countrymen that their fantasies could be freely transposed there. As Desan remarks, "[The] Ohio River Valley held all the moral and expansive possibilities of that moment most idealized by Rousseau: the moment when humanity emerged, still uncorrupted, from the state of nature into the first flush of society."[105] By describing America as his contemporaries imagined it, by depicting the Amerindians in the guise of good savages eager to embrace colonization, Lezay-Marnésia attempted to attract his countrymen to cross the Atlantic and help him rebuild there a France that had not only disappeared, but had never truly existed in the first place. Although it had a therapeutic function for the author who was reinventing the country that had disappointed his expectations, the posthumous representation of America was not only turned toward the past; it also served as an imaginary experiment with a possible future for his homeland.

THE NOSTALGIA FOR BETHLEHEM

The Pennsylvanian Model

In a study devoted to texts written by Voltaire, Raynal, and Diderot about colonial America, Ansart emphasizes the role played by Pennsylvania in the arguments for new liberties presented by these authors: "Pennsylvania thus provided the *philosophes* with a rare example illustrating the practical applicability in a contemporary society of a central tenet of their political credo. In their eyes it demonstrated the falsity of an objection all too often presented to them by their opponents: that religious and civil liberties would be destructive of social order and harmony and lead to chaos. Quite the opposite, the *philosophes* could argue, just consider the peace and prosperity of Pennsylvania!"[106]

Serving as a de facto argument in the debate on tolerance and equality, Pennsylvania allowed these authors to demonstrate that it was possible to apply their theses without toppling the social structure. In his turn, Lezay-Marnésia used the example of Pennsylvania when he described the Moravians of Bethlehem at the beginning of the second of the *Letters*. By its simple existence, the society that they created demonstrated that his own utopian plans were all the more feasible, since they had, in fact, already been put into practice.

However, the evocation of Bethlehem is the result of a retrospective reconstruction and is not a description that was contemporary with the author's stay in this city. Like Crèvecœur, who reimagined colonial America following the War of Independence, Lezay-Marnésia reconstituted the memory of this community after the failure of his ambitions in the Northwest Territory. In Bethlehem, he pretends to discover a model for a society that might possibly come to be, while he was, in fact, speaking of the space on which he was projecting his dashed dreams for a settlement that was already a failure when he took up the pen. The depiction of this city is at the heart of what posthumous America is for Lezay-Marnésia, namely a reinvention of America that, at the same time that it revives a mythical past, is presented as the model for future utopian projects.

An Intact Colonial Project

Written on November 2, 1791, the second of the *Letters Written from the Banks of the Ohio* was addressed to Bernardin de Saint-Pierre, although Lezay-Marnésia admits that he had never met him (86). To what end does Lezay-Marnésia appeal to the author of *Paul et Virginie* (1787)? In 1778, Saint-Pierre had conceived the idea of a settlement under the auspices of France that he wished to establish to the west of the English colonies. This refuge was to take in destitute Frenchmen who would receive land to cultivate. To present the guidelines for this project, Bernardin de Saint-Pierre wrote a memorandum to the Secretary of State for Foreign Affairs, Charles Gravier de Vergennes, that produced, however, no results.[107] A decade later, in 1789, Saint-Pierre was again involved in a similar enterprise: Carré suggests that the comte d'Antraigues and Duval d'Éprémesnil sought to persuade him to help them found a colony in the United States.[108] Lezay-Marnésia was thus not the first person to see in Bernardin de Saint-Pierre a precursor and a possible supporter of colonial enterprises across the Atlantic when he addresses the famous man of letters in these terms: "Gather together, Sir, the debris of Europe, which no longer exists, enrich America with it, the America that does not yet exist and perhaps never will if this great opportunity escapes" (64).

At the time of the sending of this letter, nearly a year had passed since the meal shared by Lezay-Marnésia and his Huron guests in Marietta. In the meantime, Arthur Saint Clair had been defeated at the Battle of the Wabash, and the marquis had taken refuge at Fort Pitt. Just as the first missive began with a brief disclosure of the real living conditions of the French emigrants at Marietta, this one begins with a direct attack on the Scioto Company: "[T]his company, which proposed the creation of a new state within the United States composed of the most energetic, experienced Frenchmen, tempered in the midst of the storm and rich through their industriousness, their sciences, their arts, their fortitude, their courage, and their sociability; this company, after having conceived such a grandiose and beautiful idea, did not display the slightest ability to put it into practice" (53).

The tone has changed considerably since the letters published in the *Nouveau prospectus*, in which Lezay-Marnésia declared: "As regards the Scioto Company, the only thing I have had to defend myself against is the excessive benefits it has accorded me; I have only had to struggle with its lavishness" (131). For the first time, Lezay-Marnésia called into question the Scioto Company. However, while the company may have been guilty in his eyes of not keeping its commitments, he does not accuse it of not mentioning the presence of hostile Amerindians in the area, nor of having ardently promoted a colonial project that could appear, after the numerous setbacks he had just suffered, absolutely insane to him. Far from showing any real acrimony against the Scioto Company, Lezay-Marnésia exhibited despite himself a great deal of consideration for it, since the essential part of the paragraph quoted previously was devoted to praise for the plan it had conceived and commercialized, although it was not successful. It is this plan that remained intact in his eyes and that the rest of the letter strives to validate by moving it from the Northwest Territory to the eastern borders of Pennsylvania. While the letters of the *Nouveau prospectus* and the first of the *Letters Written from the Banks of the Ohio* deliberately hid the truth of the American expedition from the reader in order to convince him to emigrate also, beginning with the second letter of the volume, Lezay-Marnésia tried to persuade his audience, as well as himself, that it was still possible to make his colonial project a reality. As the corpus of his American letters developed, lying to others was gradually replaced by lying to himself and voluntary fantasizing by autosuggestion: the posthumous representation of America was endowed with an advertising function at the same time as it became an imaginary refuge for the author in which he pretended to believe in the future fulfillment of his vanished dreams.

Renaissance of the Golden Age

While Lezay-Marnésia began by recognizing the wrongs for which he was responsible, very quickly, in a gradual slippage that revealed his obsessiveness, he returned to his visions of utopian cities: "Never has such a favorable opportunity presented itself to the virtuous genius who has the courage and the will to gather together men capable of great resolution and place them in the wilderness of the New World to lead peaceful, pure lives in the comfort of a patriarchal community, in the charms of a fraternal existence" (54). Lezay-Marnésia found in the society created by the Moravians of Bethlehem the proof that it is possible to lead to an isolated place individuals committed to "adoring God and practicing the virtues taught, ordered, and rewarded by religion, even in this life" (54). During his trip from New York to Marietta, he had made a stop in this little community that, he tells us, is located "near the Pennsylvania border" (54). This detail is erroneous, because Bethlehem is located equidistant from the northern and southern limits of this state, to the west of New York and Philadelphia. It permitted Lezay-Marnésia, however, to emphasize the isolation of this community, characteristic of the utopian space, while mentioning the name "Pennsylvania," which gave rise to positive associations in the mind of the French reader.

In 1734, Voltaire's *Lettres philosophiques* had contributed to the constitution of the gilded legend of William Penn and its dissemination throughout French culture. After painting an ironic portrait of the enthusiast he was in his youth, the fourth letter reserves for him this splendid praise: "William Penn might well have boasted that he brought back the Golden Age of which so much is spoken and which in fact never really existed save in Pennsylvania."[109] Voltaire never misses an opportunity to cite the Quakers as models in his following works. The *Essai sur les mœurs et l'esprit des nations* (*Essay on the Manners and Spirit of Nations*, 1756), the *Traité sur la tolérance* (*Treatise on Tolerance*, 1763), and the *Dictionnaire philosophique* (1764) all express a keen admiration for the numerous qualities exhibited by the descendants of William Penn: virtue, simplicity, dedication to social equality, and above all, religious tolerance. Like Voltaire, Lezay-Marnésia asserts in the second of the *Letters* that the Golden Age has survived in Pennsylvania, adding that it even has an exact address: the town of Bethlehem.

Founded in 1740, the Moravian community of Bethlehem was given an autarkic organization that made it appear as a utopian city. In the article "Moraves ou frères unis" ("Moravians or United Brothers") in Diderot and d'Alembert's *Encyclopédie*, Joachim Faiguet de Villeneuve (1703–1781) describes with great admiration the way of life of the members of this little society: "Never has equality been so complete as among the Moravians; if the property is held in common between the brothers, esteem and consideration are no less so. . . . Their gentle and innocent life attracts converts and generally earns them the respect of everyone who judges things without prejudice." Bethlehem had already hosted famous guests from France: La Fayette had stayed there in 1777 long enough to recover from a wound received in the Battle of Brandywine, and the marquis de Chastellux had stopped there at the beginning of the 1780s. In his travel narrative, Chastellux describes Bethlehem as an austere society: "As for policing or discipline, there is something monastic about it, since it recommends celibacy, without imposing it, and separates the men from the women."[110] Contrary to the Quakers, whose unflattering portrait in his work will provoke the anger of Brissot, the Moravian community receives from him neither criticism nor any particular praise: Chastellux even confesses, twice, that he has had trouble satisfying his curiosity on the origin, opinions, and the manners of this society.[111] He is interested both in the separation of the unmarried members of the two sexes and in the matrimonial customs of the Moravians, in which he sees an explication for the weak demographic growth of their colony.[112]

For his part, Lezay-Marnésia expresses a far greater enthusiasm for this community that he describes as a "kingdom of peace, wisdom, and tranquil happiness" (54). In his sales pitch, which consists of proving the viability and, even more, the urgency of the creation of a colony of French emigrants in the New World, the Moravians have a prominent place. Their example shows that it is possible for Europeans to emigrate to America and to prosper there, since they left the swamps of Germany for the mountains of Pennsylvania, where they succeeded in creating a flourishing community. It likewise proves the viability of the patriarchal ideas of Lezay-Marnésia as guidelines for an entire society. Finally, Bethlehem attests to the existence of a Golden Age to be found in America, since Lezay-Marnésia resuscitates the memory of this ideal era when he describes the city's water mills: "The constant noise, which has the variety and modulations of these varied sources, is one of the characteristic colors of this tableau, which is not restricted to our sight; but who could put it to use, this invisible color? Homer, Tasso, Virgil, you, Sir" (57).

What the authors grouped together by Lezay-Marnésia have in common is that they each contributed to the development of an imaginary Golden Age in Western culture. In Book 18 of the *Iliad*, Homer evokes the marriage of the nymph Thetis and the mortal Peleus, characteristic of this mythical period in which men and gods were intermingled. Virgile develops the notion of the Golden Age in the fourth eclogue of *The Bucolics* as well as in book II of *The Georgics*, before Le Tasse picks up the same theme in *Aminta*.[113] As for Bernardin de Saint-Pierre, his novel *Paul et Virginie* describes a little virtuous community located in the charming setting of the island now known as Mauritius. The second of the *Letters Written from the Banks of the Ohio* joins this line of famous texts by describing a self-sufficient society whose members live in close contact with nature. Lezay-Marnésia begins by praising the orderliness and cleanliness that reigns among the Moravians: "The first thing I saw was a wide, clean, straight avenue bordered by stone houses, each separated from the others, with no sign of luxury or any exterior decorations but spacious, comfortable, and quite pleasant by their very simplicity" (55). This high praise is to be compared with the far more severe judgment that Chastellux renders on one of their farms: "I was curious to see the farm; I found it well laid out, but the house was less clean and less well kept than the English farms; this is because the manners of the Moravians are still Teutonic, as is their language."[114] The mention of order and simplicity by Lezay-Marnésia resonates like a discreet reminder of the distinctive characteristics of any ideal society since the seminal work of Sir Thomas More, *Utopia* (1516).

If the description of Bethlehem is a catalog of accolades, it is because this community put into practice numerous measures advocated by Lezay-Marnésia when he was living in France, so that the praise he heaps on the Moravians is indirectly intended for himself. He expresses, for example, his admiration for the schoolteachers of Bethlehem who dispense to the young ladies an education whose role is to perpetuate the domination of the patriarchy by training them exclusively for their future domestic activities: "They learn to do all the work that is suitable to their sex. . . . They are prepared for all of the duties that they will need to assume later, and every effort is made to raise them in a manner that will make them good mothers" (56–57). These principles recall those that the marquis defended in his *Reading Program for a Young Lady*, in which he distinguished radically the studies suitable for men from those for women and discouraged the latter, notably, from devoting themselves to the sciences.[115] Lezay-Marnésia likewise praises the prosperity of the Moravians: "It is a beautiful sight for both the eyes and the mind, this mixture of waters rushing onto the wheels and endowing them with their perpetual motion; . . . flocks in the abundant and rich pastures; and the patriarch who directs and commands, and who, his soul at peace, submits everything around him to his intelligence" (57). This tableau is familiar to the readers of the *Essay on Rural Nature*, in whose verse we see similar images employed to sing the praises of joyous rustic work.[116] When all is said and done, this society so close to the dreams the marquis cultivated in France must serve as a model "for all those who wish to reach a state of perfection and wisdom and enjoy all the felicity of which men are capable" (58).

Where Is the Equality?
The ideal city that he was readying himself to describe in detail in the second half of the letter borrows numerous characteristics from the Moravian community. Saint-Pierre—the name that its inhabitants will give it to honor the author of *Paul et Virginie*—will also have its factories, and its women will likewise be raised to become good housewives (56–57). However, a fundamental dimension of Bethlehem disappears in Saint-Pierre: equality. Lezay-Marnésia declares, concerning the Moravians: "What do they lack? The honors that flatter pride, which are for but a small minority that always abuses them; this inequality of means that makes the disfavored dependent on the others, who are all too often

corrupted by their fortune and use it more to humiliate their fellow men than to help them" (58). Although he feigns admiration of the equality of social condition and fortune that reigns among the Moravians, the marquis prefers not to use it as a model when he plans the organization of Saint-Pierre. Indeed, the colony will be founded on hierarchical principles: the workers and the property owners will not be intermingled. The latter will treat the former as Lezay-Marnésia did his workers on his estate in France—as generous and charitable lords—whereas the former will be expected to be content with the subordinate position that is attributed to them in the division of work and administrative and political responsibilities.

According to the indications given by Lezay-Marnésia, it appears that this social inequality is built into the very spatial organization of the future city. Two spaces are separated by a wall: the first, dedicated to the production of goods and foodstuffs, is located outside and is intended for the farmers and artisans; the second, reserved for the landowners, is protected by a wall forming a half circle, enclosing the administrative, educative, and religious buildings. The separation of the two populations is the sign of a hierarchical organization. Although the landowners are substituted, in Lezay-Marnésia's project, for the nobles of the Old Regime, they constitute a new dominant class that is impossible for the working classes to join.[117] No matter that the privilege of birth has been replaced by property, the social classes that result from this new organization are just as impenetrable as those of prerevolutionary France and are a de facto contradiction of the principle of equality to which Lezay-Marnésia proclaimed his adherence. As Albert de Lezay-Marnésia observed about his father, whose contradictions he did not hesitate to point out with a ferociousness that revealed a certain rancor: "My father belonged to that school of philosophers whose philanthropy embraced the whole human race, but too often with the exception of those most close to them."[118] This inconsistency is notable in this particular case, for although the Moravian society provided a model for Saint-Pierre, it was nonetheless only admirable from a distance. In America, Lezay-Marnésia did not seek to experiment with an original social paradigm; he only dreamed of transposing there the superficially reformed double of a period that was brutally interrupted by the Revolution.[119]

Bethlehem in the Mirror of Memory

The model embodied by the Moravian society was recreated from memory by Lezay-Marnésia. In fact, the second letter was not sent from Bethlehem in Pennsylvania but from Fort Pitt, around sixteen months after the marquis's visit to this community whose functioning he admired so much.[120] Although it was not very long, this period had been fraught with difficulties for Lezay-Marnésia, who had been forced to abandon the lands he had acquired in the Scioto region. It had weighed heavily enough on his mind, no doubt, that he was led to recall with some nostalgia the days spent with the Moravians: "The mind rests so gently, the soul is so contented among the Moravian Brothers, that it is not surprising that mine have wandered in their midst, and that for a long while I have neglected my principal subject" (60). Written in the present, this sentence does not reflect the moment when Lezay-Marnésia was among the Moravians but, instead, the time when he recalled, from Fort Pitt, the days he lived in their company, lost in the mellowness of his reminiscences. Thus, the evocation of Bethlehem is the result of an a posteriori reconstruction during which Lezay-Marnésia was moved to idealize the community that had briefly hosted him, and to paint it in idyllic colors that we can assume to be suspicious when we compare them with the far more neutral testimony of Chastellux. The reversal of perspective observable in the last of his American letters, the one sent to Monsieur Audrain after his return to France, has already begun: America is no longer only a space in which a utopian dream can be fulfilled in the future; it already embodies the lost country that the author calls back to mind with a wave of nostalgia, and of which he gives a posthumous representation that turns it into fiction. In other words, the advertising role of posthumous America coexists with a commemorative function, facilitating the preservation of an imaginary period that has been substituted in the author's memory for the one he actually experienced.

SAINT-PIERRE OR UCHRONOTOPIA

A Bipolar Writing

The description of the utopian project for which Lezay-Marnésia solicited Bernardin de Saint-Pierre's collaboration constantly wavered between two poles: the impatience to build a colony whose viability, necessity, and urgency he strived to prove; and the paradoxical confession of the imaginary and compensatory character of his plans. The marquis vigorously asserts his desire to move from words to action: "Will we never make anything but books? Shall we be contented with providing entertainment, with stimulating vivid, gentle, and sensitive imaginations, with giving them pleasure followed by regrets by continually offering them what are indeed often enchanting visions that we only see, unfortunately, in works of genius with no hope that they will ever be realized?" (63).

However, Lezay-Marnésia regularly contradicts his own pitch by revealing that he was only defending this project so relentlessly because of the ephemeral moral escape that it offers him: "Reduced to hopes, I like to indulge them" (98). Do these two contradictory discourses reflect the bipolar condition of an author going from euphoria to depression in the course of his writing? What is the relationship between his undertaking and the concurrent claims of France, England, the United States, and the Amerindian nations of the Ohio region? To what extent, finally, is this project, which is apparently turned toward the future, the product of a posthumous representation, recording far more what it could have been than what it remains to become?

A New, New France

Lezay-Marnésia's ambition was to construct the city of Saint-Pierre on the western fringes of Pennsylvania, on the spot where he bought land after fleeing Marietta. He imagined, however, that the inhabitants of Saint-Pierre would soon found other cities in their turn, which would proliferate in the Northwest Territory and beyond (85). This region was, unfortunately, far from being as vacant as Lezay-Marnésia seemed to believe, characterizing it a little too quickly as a "wilderness of the New World" (54). After being explored at the beginning of the eighteenth century by the French, who developed the fur trade there, this part of the American continent was ceded to England by France in the Treaty of Paris in 1763. It changed hands again at the end of the War of Independence, when the United States took control of the area located to the north of the Ohio River and to the west of the Appalachians. Four years later, on July 13, 1787, the Northwest Ordinance was adopted by the American Congress, creating the Northwest Territory. This region was administered by the federal government until the population grew to at least sixty thousand, at which time its inhabitants were allowed to apply for statehood: Ohio became the seventeenth state of the United of States of America in 1803.

In 1791, however, this territory administered by the United States was occupied both by Amerindian tribes and scattered British outposts that hindered the expansion of the Americans to the west.[121] It was close to a zone of severe geopolitical friction that Lezay-Marnésia planned to create Saint-Pierre, followed by the founding of its "daughter" colonies there one after the other. His project was in direct competition with the growth of the United States and outlined a sort of new New France whose territory would no longer be oriented on the north–south axis, going from Quebec to Lower Louisiana, but on the east–west axis, between Pennsylvania and the Pacific coast.

Utopia or Uchronia?

At the center of this future expanding colony would be located the city of Saint-Pierre. Its primary vocation would be to welcome opponents of the Revolution: "French people who are still truly Roman Catholics" (61), the former nobles, judges, soldiers still faithful to the crown, and even artists deprived of their former patrons would form the first contingent of emigrants—or at least the marquis feigns to be convinced of this. If we were to believe him, Bernardin de Saint-Pierre would have no trouble recruiting a large contingent: "[Y]our only problem will be to choose from the multitude of those who will accompany you" (63).

Imbued with the nostalgia of a largely idealized feudal past, the Marnésian utopian project embodies at the same time a form of "uchronia" before the term existed.[122] Literally, uchronia is an imaginary construct that consists of representing the possible development of a real society following a disruptive incident whose occurrence gradually modifies, through a chain of events, the general physiognomy of the world.[123] Obeying what we might call the "logic of the past conditional" ("What would have happened if . . ."), the author writes an alternative history in the course of which this hypothetical society, initially familiar, becomes more and more alien and eventually gives rise to a reality that is distinct from the one with which we are familiar. Lezay-Marnésia adopted a similar approach with Saint-Pierre, whose conception derived from a criticism of the history of France as it developed from the beginning of the Revolution—differing only in that he rewrote the history of France in another space: the fringes of the United States. The city of Saint-Pierre is both a utopia and a uchronia, because it embodies in America the ideal society that France could have become if its history had unwound differently. We might call it, in fact, a *uchronotopia*, a neologism that denotes the merging of utopia and uchronia in the same project.

What is the disruptive event that prompted Lezay-Marnésia to choose to rewrite the history of France in America? It is the moment when the actors in the revolutionary movement abandoned the goal of amending the absolute monarchy and began a systematic challenge to the very principles on which it was founded. Lezay-Marnésia deplored precisely the fact that the Revolution had sunk into what he considered to be an anarchical drift and declared that the patriots had rendered the people of France ferocious after having turned it away from the wisdom that would have consisted in restricting itself to selected reforms (63). The idea that the Revolution had exceeded the limits it should have respected is also articulated by Lezay-Marnésia's fictitious double as he is presented in the satirical work by Hugh Henry Brackenridge, *Modern Chivalry* (1792).

Brackenridge had met Lezay-Marnésia in 1791 in Pittsburgh before turning him into a character in his novel. He attributes to the marquis reflections that correspond to those that the latter formulates in the *Letters Written from the Banks of the Ohio*: "[T]here never was a people more generally disposed to a degree of reform, than the people of France, at the commencement of the revolution. . . . But a reform once begun, it was found impossible to arrest it at a middle point. It may be resolved into a thousand causes, but the great cause was, the insatiable nature of the human mind, that will not be contented with what is moderate."[124]

According to Lezay-Marnésia, what had begun as a reformist movement whose ambitions were perfectly praiseworthy had fallen into unfortunate excesses, the very ones that had prompted his friend Duval d'Éprémesnil to say, "And I too, Monsieur, trusted in the people; I was severely mistaken; the king that I was cursing is an angel; the people I was invoking is a fury."[125] The uchronotopia of Lezay-Marnésia is a mental experiment involving the imagining of a world in which the Revolution would not have plunged French society into what he sees as an anarchical drift, but in which it would have instead wisely confined itself to the reforms advocated by him and his friends in the Club des Impartiaux (Club of the Impartials).[126] In short, Saint-Pierre is an attempt by Lezay-Marnésia to revive a defunct France, a France whose rebirth seemed possible at the dawn of the Revolution and that, failing to be born in metropolitan France, could be born anew in the fringes of the United States.

France: A Veritable Scioto
If America is described by Lezay-Marnésia as a space in which a past France can be recreated, France is presented by the Parisian revolutionaries, conversely, as the true Scioto. Indeed, among the adversaries of the Scioto Company, numerous were those who borrowed from America the values that are most frequently attributed to it in the works of the *philosophes*—liberty, equality, authenticity, virtue, tolerance—in order to associate them hereafter with France as it embarked upon the Revolution. This transfer is observed by Desan in a multitude of pamphlets and satirical articles published between 1789 and 1790: "Once the nation no longer 'trembled under an oppressive regime,' remaking France took precedence over colonizing the New World. Transatlantic cultural exchange fortified nationalist sentiment: the self-dubbed Patriots sought to steal the mantle of authenticity and liberty from l'Amérique and drape it around the new French nation instead."[127] While Lezay-Marnésia portrayed himself as a patriarch leading a persecuted people in the New World, it was France henceforth that was featured as the Promised Land in the discourse of the patriots. The abolition of privileges and the sale of the church's property gave them new reasons to criticize the emigration of Frenchmen to the United States: if these people were really seeking equality, liberty, and land to cultivate, France could henceforth offer it all to them while sparing them the dangers presented by a risky transatlantic crossing and the American "savages," not to speak of the dishonor attached to the desertion of your motherland.

Titled "The French on the Banks of the Scioto, Epistle to an Emigrant to Kentucky" (1790), a poem by François Andrieux (1759–1833) reveals the new meaning that is assigned to America in the writings of the patriots.[128] This text features a philosopher who, after being imprisoned in the Bastille, decides to take up residence on the banks of the Scioto. The news of the French Revolution is brought to him by aristocrats hostile to the Revolution. When he learns that the values of liberty and equality, formerly identified with America, are now alive in his country, he hastens to return there, abandoning the New World to the *ci-devant* who are preparing to recreate there the abuses of the Old Regime.

In Lezay-Marnésia's discourse, as in that of the Parisian patriots, "France" and "America" are less neutral toponyms than concepts laden with political, moral, and polemical connotations whose meaning changes according to the person who employs them. Before being geographical spaces, America and France are ideas whose definitions are so closely connected that their characteristic elements spread from one concept to the other according to the viewpoint the speaker is defending.

However, if the Marnésian utopia is indeed a reactionary political construction, it is not necessarily counterrevolutionary in the sense generally given to this expression. Unlike the aristocrats who gathered around the comtes de Provence and d'Artois in Coblence, from whence they organized the struggle against the Revolution, the inhabitants of Saint-Pierre do not assemble with the intention of returning to France brandishing their weapons. Lezay-Marnésia foresees far more peaceful relations between the colony and the former country of its members: "I believe that good people should leave France in this time of willful disorder and misfortune; but I also believe that, forced by their sensitivity and their principles to abandon her, they should conserve a tender and painful memory of her and try to share with her all the good things they will have found in a more peaceful world" (74). For the citizens of the American colony, France will not be a country to conquer: there will only subsist a sentimental bond between it and Saint-Pierre, illustrated by the offering of "a wealth of plants" (74) to add new charms to the gardens of France. The peaceful character of the future colony is expressed, in addition, by its method of expansion. Lezay-Marnésia is convinced that happiness can only exist in cities of moderate size, recalling those of ancient Greece. When the population of Saint-Pierre has reached a maximum, the surplus colonists will leave to found other cities that, while independent of each other, will nonetheless remain united by an annual meeting of representatives charged with discussing their common interests (85). In short, Saint-Pierre will serve as the capital of an empire whose growth will be accomplished by demographic, and not military, means. But how does the ambitious marquis conceive the relations between Saint-Pierre and the government of the United States?

Birth of the "Salad Bowl" Theory
Lezay-Marnésia intends to build Saint-Pierre between the Allegheny and Monongahela Rivers, not far from Pittsburgh. His text diverges from the utopian genre by anticipating the creation of a new society within a preexisting political entity, instead of situating it, as Sade does, for example, with the Tamoé utopia in *Aline et Valcour* (1793), in an unexplored region of the world, in this case in the middle of the Pacific Ocean. The marquis clarifies that Saint-Pierre will submit to the established power: "I know that it cannot be a state in a state. It will be under the

authority of the state of Pennsylvania and will not be a power in and of itself" (90). However, the future society will still preserve its own characteristics: "Like the Moravian Brothers or, if you prefer, like the Jews, it would have particular usages and customs that, far from being contrary to the laws of the state, would only impose a stricter duty to conform to them" (90). The comparison of the citizens of Saint-Pierre to the Jewish people is useful to the marquis in imagining ways to preserve the identity of a particular people living within a larger community. By what means, therefore, does the marquis intend to safeguard the "usages" of his countrymen? Lezay-Marnésia recommends that the people of Saint-Pierre keep themselves at a distance from the rest of the United States. According to him, its isolation amid the American population will allow it to maintain its identity intact, a goal that will also be furthered by its refusal to participate in public affairs:

> Passive citizens, enjoying the protection and benefits of a free and moderate government, your good Frenchmen will restrict themselves to paying their taxes and will levy none themselves unless it be at the request of the administration. The seats of representatives and senators, and especially the portfolios of ministers, would only distract them from fonder concerns and more precious interests. They will be far above these offices, which their sense of duty will always lead them to respect, but which their good sense will prevent them from ever occupying. (92)

In Lezay-Marnésia's view, the inhabitants of Saint-Pierre will turn away from American political life owing to their attachment to their original language and culture, considered to be defining elements of an identity that they will need to guard all the more jealously as it could easily be contaminated. Conversely, the United States will only ever be for them a simple host country and not a superior community in which they would wish to dissolve their differences along with those of immigrants from other countries. If critics have credited Saint-John de Crèvecœur with having offered in the third of the *Letters from an American Farmer* the original formulation of the concept of the melting pot, Lezay-Marnésia is a partisan, before its time, of the idea of the salad bowl, according to which the different components of the American nation are juxtaposed rather than mixed together, each preserving its own characteristics within the United States.[129] While it is true that the image of the "salad bowl" does not flow as such from Lezay-Marnésia's pen (just as Crèvecœur develops the idea of melting without employing the term "melting pot"), it is no doubt a prefiguration of multiculturalism that is conceptualized by this French aristocrat for whom communities of distinct origins can coexist on American soil without having to adopt the goal of melting their differences into a homogenous identity.

If the expression "salad bowl" (to which the Canadians prefer "cultural mosaic") did not take on its current sociological import until the 1950s, the concept for which it serves as a metaphor had indeed been imagined as early as 1791 by Lezay-Marnésia.

The marquis is absolutely determined to demonstrate that the city that he describes at length to Bernardin de Saint-Pierre is feasible. His rationale rests in particular on precise economic calculations: "We said, Sir, that each family of property owners would possess 1,500 acres of land. With such an expanse of remarkably fertile land, how easy will it not be for them to furnish the workshops with all the hemp, flax, and wool they will need, as well as the wheat, potatoes, vegetables, and meat necessary to feed the workers? Each one of them will contribute a hundredth of the cost of the above" (82).

The recourse to precise calculations, to flattering expectations that are nonetheless wrapped in the mantle of prudence, was familiar to the readers of the *Prospectus* that the Scioto Company had distributed in the autumn of 1789. This document shared, notably, the following prediction: "Let's suppose moreover that the settlers arrive here next March. The first harvest, that of autumn 1790, will be 1,500,000 bushels: a third will go to the farmers, another sixth will be put aside to donate to people who arrive on their own from Europe to settle in this country or who may arrive from some other part of America, and there will still remain 700,000 bushels to send to Europe."[130] It is paradoxical that Lezay-Marnésia borrows from the Scioto Company a mendacious rhetoric of which he was himself a victim, and that he uses it to persuade his countrymen to come share a fate that, as he knows better than anyone, is far from idyllic. On paper, the lands are claimed, divided up, farmed, and produce profits in scarcely a few years: Crèvecœur, whose *Voyage* may be read in many respects as publicity for America, had nevertheless the honesty to warn candidates for emigration of the numerous challenges that awaited them at the beginning of their undertaking.[131] With more experience in gardening and in the laying out of property than in the clearing of lands and draining of swamps, Lezay-Marnésia passed willingly over difficulties that he had never personally faced.

A Paper Castle
However, as detailed as Lezay-Marnésia's uchronotopic project is, it is nonetheless haunted by the specter of its own negation. Although the author predicts that Saint-Pierre will subsist a great number of centuries, certain passages of the letter clearly betray misgivings. Lezay-Marnésia presents the different stages of construction of the future city: "Whether of wood or bricks, the houses are quickly erected" (76); "In the second year, the Lord's house will be built. . . . In the third year, the buildings designed to render justice and to hold assemblies will rise" (83–84). The succinct character of these notations reveals the minimal

interest the author has in the practical conditions of the construction of the future settlement: everything happens as if the buildings were going to rise on their own, with the swiftness and ease of an opera set. This comparison is, in fact, used by Lezay-Marnésia to insist that it is an inappropriate manner of describing his writing: "Do not think, Sir, that driven by the pleasure of imagining and describing I am using my pen as if it were the whistle at the opera used to produce new decorations in the blink of an eye. Nothing is so rigorously true as everything that I have the honor of telling you" (76).

We are dealing here with a veritable denial in the Freudian sense of the term, that is, a statement by which a subject reveals the very truth that he is in the process of denying.[132] The opera image that Lezay-Marnésia only uses to assert that it in no way characterizes his writing is, paradoxically, the best metaphor for it: despite himself, he reveals to the reader that his forecasts do not rest on anything tangible, and that his colony will have no more reality than a cardboard decor. After the out-and-out lies contained in his letters in the *Nouveau prospectus* and the first missive of the *Letters Written from the Banks of the Ohio*, Lezay-Marnésia turned to a subtler form of fabrication in which he proves to be a victim of his own rhetoric and only awakens so brutally from his own illusions because he had deluded himself with them for so long a time. He also interrupts the thread of his discourse to comment on the writing of the letter: "Excuse me, Sir, for these innumerable details, perhaps useless and boring to you but quite attractive to me. When the whole face of the earth is battered by dreadful storm winds, the idea of your republic gives me repose, consoles me, and charms me; it grips me, and I caress it lovingly. I am like a passenger surrounded by dangers in a furious sea, threatened by lightning, terrified by waves, who discovers, by the bright, fleeting, sinister light of the flashes, one of the Islands of the Blessed" (87).

This passage contradicts the dominant discourse of the letter. In order to promote the idea of emigration, Lezay-Marnésia multiplied the promises of peace and happiness to the future inhabitants of Saint-Pierre. However, this paragraph dispels the dreams that the rest of the text had painted in such glowing colors by hinting at the unenviable fate of its author. Moreover, the comparison of Saint-Pierre to the Islands of the Blessed further undermines his arguments. At first glance, the rural tranquility that reigns, according to Pindar, on these mythical islands could justify the parallel Lezay-Marnésia draws with the banks of the Monongahela.[133] Nonetheless, in Greek mythology these islands are located in hell: that is where virtuous souls find their repose after death. "Utopia" is a term whose meaning is rendered ambiguous by its Greek root: is it the "place of happiness" or the "place that exists nowhere"?[134] The fundamental ambiguity of the utopian plan is at the very heart of the society imagined by Lezay-Marnésia: while he pretends to believe that Saint-Pierre embodies the promise of happiness on earth, he is led to admit that it represents especially the hope of a postmortem felicity that helps him, albeit with great difficulty, to bear his current misfortunes. Lezay-Marnésia is nowhere so clear about the true object of the letter, however, than in the concluding paragraph:

> Finally, Sir, I've reached the end of this enormous letter, which I have just as much trouble tearing myself away from as you will have reading it, if you have the energy to read it to the end. *Reduced to hopes, I like to indulge them.* Deceived in my expectations both by the people I fled and by the one I came looking for, I thought that the latter would take justice and reason as guides in seeking liberty, and that the former, who seemed to have become wiser, would be able to benefit from the liberty that both circumstances and the innumerable mistakes of its former masters gave to it. (98; emphasis added)

By admitting the difficulty he experienced in putting an end to his letter, Lezay-Marnésia recognized the therapeutic character of an exercise in writing of which he was, ultimately, the true addressee, since it was highly unlikely that he would receive a response from a famous writer whom he had never met (and no sign of a response has, indeed, ever been found). The length of the letter, which represents by itself more than three-quarters of the volume, suggests that the time devoted to the writing gave him a brief respite from his oppressive personal difficulties. Saint-Pierre was already playing a compensatory role in relation to the initial plan for a settlement on the banks of the Scioto. In the end, it is the writing of this letter that mitigates the pain of the failure of Saint-Pierre by permitting the author to savor in his imagination a city that he senses will never be born: "May the man of genius, the good man I am asking to assemble them, accept this honorable mission and become the benefactor of a society of true wise men and of their descendants! At the very least, may my ideas, so pure, not be dismissed as pleasant pipe dreams!" (98). The repetition of the formula "May . . ." turns this letter into a kind of supplication and reveals the chimerical character of a paper castle he has strived in vain to build in America. While it was being presented as a project to be realized in the near future, the uchronotopic city of Saint-Pierre was described when it was already defunct. Not being able to actually bring it into existence, Lezay-Marnésia gives it a consistency in language through its posthumous representation.

LETTERS FROM THE MONONGAHELA: FROM A POSSIBLE AMERICA TO A POSTHUMOUS AMERICA

A French America

In many respects, the last letter of the volume is the most interesting by what it does not say rather than by what it does. It is addressed by Lezay-Marnésia to his eldest son, Adrien, and begins by speaking of "Azile," the four-hundred-acre plantation the marquis had acquired in Pennsylvania after the collapse of his plans in the Northwest Territory: "I have left, my dear Adrien, this *Azile* that I have praised so much without going too far. In all likelihood I will never see it again; however, I wish to speak to you about it once again, or rather I want to acquaint you with the neighbors I left there. I need to do this to soothe my heart. This little picture, worthy of ancient times, may interest you, although to paint it well a common brush would not suffice; one would need Greuze's delicate strokes" (99; emphasis original).

It is essential to note this "or rather," which effects a change of theme in the course of a sentence, in order to understand the stakes hidden in this letter. Lezay-Marnésia announces the elegiac description of a lost paradise before modifying the object of the text by introducing into it Monsieur and Madame des Pintreaux, his neighbors. Why does he immediately leave the property on which he had spent the last remnants of his fortune? And to what extent does the story of his countrymen allow him to gloss over the pathetic outcome of his grand projects in the New World?

Lezay-Marnésia takes numerous liberties with the biography of a Frenchman whom he had indeed met in Pittsburgh in 1791, Jean-Baptiste-Charles Lucas des Pintreaux.[135] The story narrated in the third of the *Letters Written from the Banks of the Ohio* may be read as a rewriting of the life of Lucas des Pintreaux, heavily influenced by the memory of a moral tale published by Lezay-Marnésia in 1766, *L'Heureuse Famille* (*The Happy Family*).[136] The marquis relates to his son the love between Monsieur des Pintreaux and Élise, opposed, alas, by their families because of the disparity of their social conditions. After receiving letters of recommendation from Benjamin Franklin, Monsieur des Pintreaux and his beloved embark for America, where they are married before acquiring property not far from Fort Pitt.

In scarcely five years, Monsieur and Madame des Pintreaux achieve prosperity: "Their flocks had grown and their fields expanded; their orchard was already producing an abundance of fruit, and three charming children added a new interest to their days, doubling their happiness" (109). Just as in the second of the *Letters*, the grammatical constructions used by the author illustrate his lack of concern for the practical dimension of life in the New World: in reading him, one would be led to believe that the flocks multiply without any help from the farmers, that the fields increase in size by virtue of a natural disposition to grow, and that the fruit fall on their own accord into the baskets of the farmers.

This letter presents a remarkable chiasmus between the path of Monsieur des Pintreaux and that of Lezay-Marnésia himself. Whereas the marquis went to America by choice and decided to return to France at the beginning of 1792, Monsieur and Madame des Pintreaux were forced to emigrate by their families and prefer to stay in the United States when the opportunity to return to their motherland presents itself. Indeed, Lezay-Marnésia tells us that years after her departure, Madame des Pintreaux returns alone to France to collect the money from an inheritance. Repenting, her family greets her with open arms and urges her to stay with them and send for her husband and their children back in the United States. But the courageous Élise leaves as quickly as possible, eager to find again the "peace of mind" and the "pure pleasure" (109) that one only enjoys in the New World. By staging the refusal of Élise, Lezay-Marnésia was suggesting that even if an emigration to America is initially the result of exterior constraints, it may ultimately become a matter of personal choice. This crossing of Lezay-Marnésia's path and the discourse in his *Letters*, in opposite directions, reproduces the same phenomenon we saw in Crèvecœur's letters, since the latter writer decided to prolong his leave from his consular position in New York until he lost it, while continuing to praise the United States in the *Voyage dans la Haute Pensylvanie et dans l'État de New York*.[37] After portraying America as a land of milk and honey, the two authors preferred to contradict their works by their acts rather than publicly repudiating their declarations in favor of French emigration across the Atlantic. Lezay-Marnésia concludes the story of Monsieur and Madame des Pintreaux with this statement: "If a few French families, with sufficient personal fortunes, were to settle around Fort Pitt, they would discover in this country the charming banks of the Loire and the Seine, but even more favored by nature and with the peace and happiness that have abandoned them" (112). This fascinating utterance implies that the American territory is another France where immigrants can rediscover the most pleasant things that they left behind in their country while liberating themselves from the evils, injustices, and violence that rendered life in their motherland unbearable.

The Art of Denial

In a movement of self-contradiction that is typical of Lezay-Marnésia, however, he does not close his letter with this reassuring and paradoxical image, comparing emigration to America to a trip to France. The letter finishes with a declaration of gratitude to M. Audrain, "a Frenchman living in Fort Pitt for five or six years": "He brought enchantment to my solitude with the most interesting conversations, guided me through the most difficult circumstances, consoled me in my distress, and prevented me from falling into total despair. He helped me with his time, his work, his intelligence, and all the resources of his mind, and ultimately rescued me from a horrible predicament, from the misery in which the dishonest actions of the disastrous Scioto Company had plunged me" (112).

"Most difficult circumstances," "total despair": the reader will learn no more than that, for the letter is soon closed, once Lezay-Marnésia has recommended M. Audrain and his children to his elder son. One notes the strange structure of this text, which begins, as noted previously, on an elegiac note in order to evoke the loss of a property of which, ultimately, the author says nothing, before speaking of a couple that he proposes as a model for potential emigrants although he reinvents their story, and then speaking in veiled terms of his return to France for reasons that he does not divulge. These literary obfuscations are the reflection of contradictions by Lezay-Marnésia, who has turned denial into a fine art: while still dreaming of promoting the colonial project to which he sacrificed two years of his life and most of his fortune, a project that was the conclusion of an existence devoted to reading and political meditations, he knew very well that he was the victim of his own illusions and of the Scioto Company. The story of Monsieur and Madame des Pintreaux is only a diversion that allowed Lezay-Marnésia to pass over the failure of his grandiose dreams in America.

"The Kind Illusions of the Golden Age"

A text published in 1800 by Lezay-Marnésia in the second edition of the "Reading Program for a Young Lady" is complementary to the third of the *Letters* in that it continues the elegiac discourse that this letter only sketched out. Titled "Letter to M. Audrain, merchant in Pittsburg," this missive suggests how greatly he misses the country that he was only too happy to leave eight years before: "Beautiful Monongahela, wide and clear Allegheny, my happiness has remained on your delightful banks; I shall not find it on the shores of the rivers in France where peace will surely not return anytime soon" (139–40). Although he had promised the Frenchmen who would settle in America that they would rediscover there the banks of the Loire and the Seine, he declares himself incapable of feeling in France the delightful emotions that suffused him on the banks of the New World: "However, I had scarcely left it when my heart leapt back toward this tranquil America. . . . Yes, my friend, on these happy shores one is always young at heart, always at peace because he desires nothing more than the facile perfection of the beautiful, superb sites that are so easily rendered fertile by his spade. It calls out to settlers from all reaches of the universe, inviting them to come and *bring to life the pleasant illusions of the golden age on the soil where it should exist, if it is still possible for it to exist anywhere*" (142–43; emphasis added).

In appearance, nothing has changed between this letter and the *Letters Written from the Banks of the Ohio*: the reader finds the same latent influence of Crèvecœur's *Lettres*, the same celebration of a felicity available to the reader if only he will consent to cross the ocean. And nonetheless, something has clearly changed beneath the surface. While the *Lettres d'un cultivateur américain* moved from the description of a posthumous America to that of a potential America, the progression goes in the opposite direction in Lezay-Marnésia's writings, which end up commemorating the memory of a retrospectively idealized country after having depicted it as a place in which one could revive a France that had disappeared. Despite the fact that the *Letters Written from the Banks of the Ohio* sometimes sound like an advertisement, touting the advantages of emigration and the profits awaiting Frenchmen in America, they still betray now and then the uncertainties of the author—allowing a complaint about the Scioto Company to escape him or sharing a detail that revealed how much more difficult his situation was than he wanted to admit. In the end, if Lezay-Marnésia presented himself as a contemporary of an American Golden Age, it was especially to get his revenge, through language, on a reality that resisted his desires.

Conversely, his letter to M. Audrain represents a different exercise. If we are to believe him, the America that he hurried to leave, at the risk of losing his life in his own country, was still the home of the Golden Age that is constantly evoked in both his and Crèvecœur's texts. Of course, this ideal period has not completely vanished at the time of his writing: "There, for many long years to come, the people will enjoy few of the pleasures that luxury and the arts bring, but they will be rich with the gifts offered by a fertile, inexhaustible, magnificent nature and happy with the absence of uncontrollable passions and the vices that corrupt, ravish, and destroy many peoples who used to be civilized" (139–40). However, it was now impossible for Lezay-Marnésia to return there, and it was with many regrets that he described a country that appeared to him, henceforth, with the deceptive allure of an increasingly distant past. The advertising function of the posthumous representation, which reproduced the fruits of a collective imagination that preceded the journey, thus gave way, once the trip itself was over, to a commemorative function that idealized an expired America at the time of the writing. It was in this country now doubly distant (since both space and time now separate the author from it) and in this country alone that a perfect felicity was possible: "Farewell, my friend, my heart is heavy; I glimpsed happiness, and it is with the fondest regret that I recall it; tears are coming to my eyes. Farewell" (143). This was, of course, a retrospective illusion. Just as Crèvecœur recalled sentimentally the life he had led in the New York colony, a life that entailed numerous difficulties, Lezay-Marnésia was embellishing the memory of the existence he knew near Pittsburgh, the very existence that displeased him so much that he sold his paradise dirt cheap and left Eden at the risk of meeting the guillotine at the end of his journey. For Lezay-Marnésia and Crèvecœur, not only is happiness elsewhere, but it is also before. The conjunction of American exoticism and the nostalgia for a past age, this convergence that we call "posthumous America," is at the heart of their respective works. It is a special case of the manner in which men deceive themselves on the nature of happiness; that is, by setting it in a time and place that they can only access by memory. The nostalgia provoked by an America that has radically changed in the interval between the journey and the writing is likewise the source of the literary venture that will be studied next: that of Chateaubriand.

3

CHATEAUBRIAND AND NOSTALGIA
FOR FRENCH AMERICA

> France once possessed, in North America, a vast empire that stretched from Labrador to Florida, and from the shores of the Atlantic to the most remote lakes of Upper Canada.
> —Chateaubriand, *Atala*

Prologue: Chateaubriand and the Metamorphosis of Fictions

CHATEAUBRIAND AND THE SHARKS

Édouard de Mondésir, who crossed the Atlantic in the company of François-René de Chateaubriand, left an intriguing account of an episode that is less anecdotal than it may appear at first glance:

> The chevalier, I would almost say the Don Quixote, who often liked to take risks, wanted to go swimming in the ocean. Although the sailors asked him if he had ever done that before, and when he answered in the negative tried to dissuade him from this dangerous caprice, they had to let him have his way. They had us all, priests and Levites, go below. The bather undressed completely, they passed straps and ropes beneath his armpits, and he was lowered thus into the water. Scarcely had his feet touched the surface than he fainted, and they hurried to pull him back up for fear that a shark might cut him in half.[1]

Can we believe Mondésir's tale when we know that he found the eccentric behavior of the young Chateaubriand intolerable?[2] The memorialist gives, in fact, a radically different account of this same scene. After diving gracefully from the bowsprit of the ship, followed by other passengers, the bold swimmer found himself in great peril:

> Sharks showed up in the waters around the ship, and shots were fired to scare them off. The swell was so large that it slowed my return to the boat and exhausted my strength. I had an abyss beneath me, and the sharks could bite off an arm or leg at any time. . . . I was able to grab the rope, but my bold companions were already hanging on it; so when they pulled us to the side of the ship, I was at the end of the rope, and the others all pressed down on me with all their weight. . . . They pulled me up onto the deck half dead; if I had drowned, what a good riddance it would have been for me and for the others![3]

While it is the simple idea of a shark that frightens the young man in Mondésir's text, it is a whole shoal of sharks that almost devoured Chateaubriand, if we are to believe the latter. Which of these two versions is closest to the truth? In the study he devotes to Chateaubriand's America, Bazin notes the striking similarity between the perilous swim of the young chevalier and the painting of John Singleton Copley titled *Watson and the Shark*.[4]

During his exile in London between 1793 and 1800, Chateaubriand would have been able to see this canvas, which had been on display at the Royal Academy since 1778. In addition to this source of inspiration for the scene he describes, there is a possible literary influence. In the *Lettres d'un cultivateur américain* (1787), Crèvecœur relates a little story illustrating the bravery of the Americans. The "5th Anecdote" tells of the death of a sailor whose thigh was devoured by a shark before one of the comrades avenged him by diving into the water to gut the predator. The dramatic circumstances of the attack are emphasized by Crèvecœur: "The voracious monster, seeing his prey flee, cuts through the waves in a flash and arrives at the very moment when the body of the last swimmer, seized by his comrades, was already in the lifeboat: he bites off his thigh. A second sooner and this unfortunate fellow would have been saved."[5]

In Crèvecœur's anecdote, the last swimmer makes it into the lifeboat at the very moment that the monster attacks him, a detail that emphasizes the horrible misfortune that befalls him. If we except the attack itself, Chateaubriand describes a similar situation in the *Voyage en Amérique*, then again in the *Mémoires d'outre-tombe*. It is therefore entirely possible that, having read Crèvecœur's tale shortly before his departure, he remembered it when he was swimming in the Atlantic and feared that he was risking a fate similar to that of the sailor. Years later, the memory of Copley's painting and that of Crèvecœur's tale may well have coalesced in his mind in such a way that he related, in the *Voyage* and in the *Mémoires*, not what actually happened but the recreated memory of a scene that, by dint of being described no doubt many times, eventually became regarded as a true version of the events.

Beyond its apparently anecdotal and probably fictitious character, this text allowed Chateaubriand to introduce surreptitiously a central theme throughout his memoir writings: a meditation on alternative destinies. Chateaubriand imagines here the memory he would have left for posterity if a shark's jaws had taken his life at the age of twenty-two, a memory that would have been perfectly nil, since he had not yet accomplished anything that would have preserved any trace of his existence in the memory of mankind. In the introduction to the *Voyage*, we find a similar meditation in the course of which Chateaubriand imagines the consequences that the discovery of the famous Northwest Passage would have had on the rest of his existence, going so far as to suppose that he could have settled in the place he had discovered and die forgotten by everyone (140). This meditation on the nullity of human life and the ultimate insignificance of any worldly glory that might perchance be showered on a person, since he is destined to disappear, is often taken up by Chateaubriand, for whom the *Voyage en Amérique* is a return to the origin of both his person and his apprenticeship as a writer, a return through memory that is accompanied by the dizziness provoked by this question: "[A]nd if my life had finished before beginning?"

Ultimately, this scene of swimming with real or fictitious sharks gives rise to two central questions, both in the criticism devoted to Chateaubriand's American texts and in the present study. The considerable distance between the event related and the moment of writing prompts one to pose the question of the accuracy of the testimony of a writer who may be mixing incomplete memories with pictorial and literary reminiscences that affect the representation he is giving of events that occurred in his past.[6] Moreover, this episode reveals that the goal of Chateaubriand in the *Mémoires* is not only to safeguard memories of himself and his time; they are also a gallery in which he exposes the possible portraits of the various individuals he could have become.[7] Thus, the posthumous voice of the author regarding his existence immortalizes also what did not take place but what could have been; it takes on the task of representing destinies that nearly were his. This immortalizing voice of the memorialist is haunted by the dream of its own negation: it imagines at what moments the conditions might have been such that it would not have had the same events to relate, but it also imagines the events that could have prevented its very existence if, by chance, the author had died before having accomplished anything or if his path in the world had led him to an Arctic solitude reminiscent of that awaiting him in his grave.

Surprisingly, it is not retrospective anguish but rather regrets that Chateaubriand expresses in imagining these definitive impasses, as if writing had been more of a burden for him than a salutary activity. Is this just an artist's coquetry? There is that, of course, in this affectation of scorn for what one loves the most, but, more deeply, perhaps, the lassitude of someone who had the crushing responsibility of saving through writing the memory of his person and of all those he had seen die, one after the other, the tumultuous history of his epoch and his own life, the metamorphosing countries he had crossed and even all these beings distinct from himself that he had very nearly become. In the *Voyage* and in the American books of the *Mémoires*, this responsibility extends to an entire continent, since by virtue of the law illustrated by the first paradox of the New World—one can only write about America at the turn of the eighteenth century at a time when it has ceased to be what it was—the country visited in 1791 by Chateaubriand no longer exists except in his memory. In his mental geography, it is a nodal point to which his memories draw him constantly back, for it is the symbolic locus where his destiny could have been brought to a halt before beginning, the one where he could have taken directions so radically different that his existence and his person would have been changed forever. The rest of this prologue presents the circumstances of a journey whose remembrance allows Chateaubriand to carry out the archeology of his identity and of his literary vocation. He also describes the uncertainties that surround both his exact route and his motivation, for it is in the gap with reality that is written this representation of an imaginary journey in a bygone period of American history: what we call posthumous America.

THE INVESTIGATION OF RENÉ DE MERSENNE AND ITS CRITICAL POSTERITY

What degree of credibility may we lend Chateaubriand's narrative of his journey in America? This question is among those that have caused the most ink to flow in the history of French literary criticism. A certain René de Mersenne posed it, in fact, while the author was still alive. In 1832, he discovered an article in the *American Quarterly Review* (December 1827, 460) whose author judged Chateaubriand's descriptions chimerical and stated that it was impossible he had visited certain places that he had nonetheless described: a man capable of populating the banks of the Mississippi with parrots, monkeys, and pink flamingos could not seriously claim to have seen them with his own eyes. Resolved to determine who was telling the truth, the American journalist or Chateaubriand, Mersenne followed the supposed route of the latter to compare his writings to the spectacle the New World actually offered, initiating a critical tradition marked by suspicion and creating at the same time the method his successors were going to imitate: checking the veracity of Chateaubriand's narrative by following him step by step.[8] The conclusions of his inquiry were published in two letters in 1832 and 1835. They are adamant: Chateaubriand's descriptions are pure "cock-and-bull stories."[9] Sainte-Beuve became aware of Mersenne's writings, which prompted him to write this apparently conciliatory commentary: "The criticisms that were made of the first pages of *Atala*, as regards the lack of faithfulness of the images, show us that Chateaubriand did not seek to produce a precise pictorial reality but rather, after a rapid general view, took the liberty of rearranging his *memories* and employed, following his fancy, the rich images emanating less from his memory than from his imagination."[10]

By pretending to sweep away suspicions, Sainte-Beuve was nonetheless mischievously propagating them. After the publication of his study in 1860, an undercurrent of suspicion persisted among critics: to quote Émile Faguet, Chateaubriand was suspected of "having described a bit more than he had seen."[11] In 1899, Joseph Bédier attempted to put the question to rest by means of three successive articles.[12] He asserted that Chateaubriand did not visit all the places he describes, and that he borrowed copiously from the *Voyages* of Bartram to fill the gaps in his own experience. Numerous critics followed Bédier's example, noting Chateaubriand's borrowings from various authors—notably Charlevoix, Beltrami, and Bartram—and casting doubt on the authenticity of certain episodes of the journey related by "the Enchanter," as Chateaubriand was sometimes called.[13] The second half of Chateaubriand's journey, the part that he claims led him toward the southwest of the United States, has for a long time taken the top prize for skepticism. If it appears indisputable that Chateaubriand, after debarking in Baltimore on July 10, 1791, did indeed go to New York, then to Boston, before going up the Hudson to Albany and then following the Iroquois Trail until Niagara Falls, it seems that the rest of his trip, in the Ohio Valley first, then to Pittsburgh and on into Louisiana, is solely a product of his imagination.

Nonetheless, this questioning of the reliability of Chateaubriand's account belongs to an outmoded phase of criticism, replaced henceforth by another in which the specialists are in agreement regarding the general sincerity of the author. This is the case, notably, of Painter, who shows in his biography that Chateaubriand's narrative is consonant with what we now know about the speed of transportation in America at the time of his stay. More recently, this debate has been taken up by Bassan, who reaches the same conclusions as Painter and Switzer in observing that the travels of Chateaubriand by stagecoach are in agreement with the schedules furnished by the newspapers of the period, whereas the speed of his trips on horseback and by boat is the same as that of his contemporaries on identical routes.[14]

In the recent biography that he devoted to Chateaubriand, Berchet also tends to believe in the sincerity of the writer. In his opinion, Chateaubriand was telling the truth when he asserted that he traveled toward the southwest in following the course of the Ohio River. Conversely, the biographer doubts that Chateaubriand went down as far as the mouth of the Mississippi and tends to believe that he headed for the East Coast after reaching the confluence with the Kentucky River.[15] To support this hypotheses, Berchet quotes a page taken from Chateaubriand's *Mémoires* in which the author recalls the conclusion of his travels in the American southwest: "I was so enchanted with my travels that I no longer thought about the North Pole: the poet had conquered the traveler; I wandered for the sake of wandering with no other goal than dreaming."[16] The end of Chateaubriand's journey became a dreamy meandering whose erratic itinerary could not leave him with precise memories; he thus recreated the memories a posteriori, adding memorial vagabondage to geographical nomadism and dreams of an aging memoir writer to those of the traveler. By declaring that "the poet had conquered the traveler," Chateaubriand reveals the tension that exist between two distinct goals and two possible identities, a tension that is present from the very conception of his travel plans.

THE AMERICAN MUSE AND THE NORTHWEST PASSAGE

Chateaubriand's fascination with the New World was not a recent development. "He had dreamed long before of travelling to America, on All Soul's Eve at Combourg in 1784, when the Capuchin missionaries told of their life among the Red Indians, and again in the spring of 1786, when he announced to his acquiescent father his intention to 'go and clear forests in Canada,'" remarks Painter.[17] The plan for a trip to the United States began to take shape beginning in 1790 when he sketched out the plot of *Les Natchez*. After describing the sojourn of the Amerindian Chactas in Paris, Chateaubriand wanted to relate his adventures in America but quickly discovered that he needed personal experience with this country: "I soon noticed that I was not familiar with the true colors, and that if I wanted to create a faithful image, it was necessary, following Homer's example, to visit the people I wanted to portray."[18] His family's consent was indispensable, and Chateaubriand, who could not obtain from them the necessary sums for his journey by revealing his hopes for literary glory, had to find a plan that was both practical and, if possible, grandiose: he declared that he would go to America in quest of the Northwest Passage.[19]

This undertaking was fashionable: it is evoked, for example, in the last edition of the *Lettres d'un cultivateur américain*.[20] In Chateaubriand's mind, it would combine both geographical exploration and ethnographical research, since the young knight intended to make use of his frequenting of the Amerindians to later portray them in his novels, while at the same time contributing to a better knowledge of the topography of the North American continent. In addition, this quest for knowledge was to serve the geopolitical interests of France: "If I succeed," Chateaubriand declared, "I will have had the honor of imposing French names on new regions, giving my country a colony on the Pacific Ocean, taking the rich fur trade away from a rival power, and preventing this rival from finding a shorter way to India by giving this path to France itself."²¹ The discovery of the Northwest Passage thus also involved a symbolic, economic, and political gain for his country: it was urgent to undertake it.

However, the blessing and financial support that Chateaubriand received from the members of his family cannot be explained solely by their support of this ambitious project: they also saw it as a way for him to escape a political climate that was becoming exceedingly threatening.²² Chateaubriand remarks, "The chaos was growing: it was enough to have an *aristocratic* name to be exposed to persecution: the more conscientious and moderate your opinion was, the more suspect and denigrated it became. I decided to fold my tent: I left my brother and my sisters in Paris and headed for Brittany" (1:417–18; emphasis original).²³ The curiosity to discover a new world was thus reinforced by the threats that were growing in the traveler's motherland: there is a striking parallel between Chateaubriand and this other emigrant, Usbek, of whom the *Lettres persanes* inform us that he is going to France not only to discover this unfamiliar country but also to flee the country of his birth, and it is precisely Montesquieu that Chateaubriand remembers when, in *Les Natchez*, he defamiliarizes France for his reader through the gaze of Chactas the Amerindian.²⁴

During the preparation for his journey, Chateaubriand found an enthusiastic ally in the person of his grandfather-in-law, Chrétien-Guillaume de Lamoignon de Malesherbes.²⁵ Magistrate, botanist, statesman, and "friend of Rousseau" (1:567),²⁶ Malesherbes supported the publication of the *Encyclopédie* and defended Louis XVI during his trial. Keenly interested in geography, he had established a correspondence with Saint-John de Crèvecœur when the latter was French Consul in New York. In 1783, he wrote him to "request a large quantity of tulip tree, wax tree and white cedar seeds."²⁷ In his *Mémoires*, Chateaubriand states that M. de Malesherbes "had gotten him all worked up about the trip" (1:417) and describes the study sessions that they devoted together to the preparation of an expedition that the old man lamented not having the strength to join.

As Painter observes, this expedition was doomed to fail before even beginning, and adventurers more experienced than Chateaubriand explained to him the extent of the difficulties he could not even begin to imagine.²⁸ Sometime after his arrival on the East Coast of the United States, Chateaubriand visited a certain M. Swift, an American who described to him the numerous skills he would have to acquire before being ready even to begin his exploration.²⁹ Chateaubriand claims that this warning in no way diverted him from his plans, but, nonetheless, his expedition project was pushed into the background in the rest of a text that resembles more a tale of wandering than a journey oriented toward a precise goal. After scarcely five months on American soil, Chateaubriand decided to return to France: he relates how this decision was prompted by the discovery of a newspaper reporting the flight of the king to Varennes, and how the voice of honor immediately ordered him to fight in his service.[30] The definitive abandonment of the plan to discover the Northwest Passage was a matter of much ambivalence for Chateaubriand: it was one of the nodal points in the destiny of the memorialist to which he returned in his reflections on the direction his existence took and in his dreams of alternative futures. As Hollier remarks, "Chateaubriand himself often presented his literary career as a consequence of this disappointment. At times, happy about the turn of events that resulted . . . , he was, at other times, longing for the peace of mind this missed opportunity had cost him."[31]

However, it is not only the archeology of his identity and of his literary vocation that his American works permit Chateaubriand to complete but also the exploration of an original period of America corresponding to the discovery of the New World by the first French travelers. The search for the origins of the writer and of America are superimposed in a work where remembrance fosters a journey toward oneself as well as toward a deceased continent of which writing permits a posthumous representation. On what memorial process does the latter depend?

METAMORPHOSIS OF FICTIONS

Four years before his death, Chateaubriand wrote a letter that includes the following reflection: "I've mixed many fictions with real things, and, unfortunately, in time the fictions take on a reality that transforms them."[32] This confession describes how fiction eventually comes to take on the cloak of reality when, repeated over and over again, it opposes imaginary representations to memories of actual events and eventually replaces them. This process is at the heart of the literary creation of posthumous America. Not only does Chateaubriand describe America several decades after traveling there—and the memories that he shares have had time to be transformed according to the aforementioned logic—but among the fictions mixed in with the "real things" was the dream of a journey that would have taken place not at the end of the eighteenth century but at the end of the Renaissance, a dream of meeting a state of nature that the Europeans had not yet degraded and an Amerindian population still unchanged. Here, truth is not opposed to falsehood, and the author does not knowingly deceive his reader, since fiction has become truth at the end of a process that precludes identifying it as the fiction it formerly was. Just like Crèvecœur and Lezay-Marnésia, Chateaubriand progressively reinvented America as he remembered it. The nostalgia for the sixteenth century that is expressed in the *Voyage en Amérique*, as in the *Mémoires d'outre-tombe*, in the explicit references in these works as well as in their formal and stylistic choices, proved to have a political dimension as well, since through the evocation of this epoch it was the ultimate failure of the French colonial venture in America that Chateaubriand was lamenting and its pursuit in other places that he was advocating.

Chateaubriand Cosmographer: *Le Voyage en Amérique* (1827)

EMERGENCE OF A VOICE FROM BEYOND THE GRAVE?

Genesis of the Voyage

"For Chateaubriand, any narrative is 'from Beyond the Grave' and gives voice to the dead."³³ This idea borrowed from Reichler guides this section, devoted to the problems of enunciation in the *Voyage en Amérique*. "Problems" in the plural, because several voices organize this work, and it is necessary to follow the stages of its genesis in order to understand the reasons for their coexistence, as well as those that explain the emergence of a defunct voice that has come to speak of a vanished country and of a mankind in decline. In the absence of the phonograph, whose invention was going to fascinate Villiers de l'Isle-Adam in *L'Ève future* (1886), because for the first time in history a machine could conserve the living trace of a deceased being, the inimitable range of his voice, Chateaubriand stages the return of a persona who was the author and, nonetheless, is no longer that person. How does the appearance of a voice from beyond the grave lead to a commemorative representation of America whose function consists in safeguarding both the memory of what it has ceased to be and of a traveler in whom the author can scarcely be recognized? The genesis of the *Voyage en Amérique* spans three countries and nearly thirty-six years during which the text was produced, lost, and rewritten from memory. It proves to be comparable to the origin of the *Lettres d'un cultivateur américain*, which is likewise the result of a reconstitution after the theft of a first manuscript.³⁴ Nonetheless, the creation of the *Voyage en Amérique* is still more complex, since the manuscript was lost a second time then invented in both senses of the term: both rewritten and recovered like one discovers a treasure. It is thus literally a posthumous America that we are going to discover, the literary representation of a country that was buried for three decades in a trunk before being exhumed. We will accompany the stages of its production by means of the information provided by the paratexts of the *Essai sur les Révolutions*, *Atala*, and the *Voyage en Amérique* itself, whose first edition dates from 1827 and is included in the plans for the *Œuvres complètes*, published between 1826 and 1831 by Ladvocat.³⁵

During his voyage across the Atlantic, Chateaubriand began the *Tableaux de la nature américaine* (*Paintings of American Nature*), *Atala*, and *Les Natchez*. In the *Mémoires*, he relates several tales about the manuscripts that accompanied him during the campaign of the émigrés: "I would sit down, with my rifle, in the middle of the ruins; I would take from my haversack the manuscript of my *Voyage en Amérique*; I would place the separate pages around me on the grass; I would reread and correct the description of a forest, a passage of *Atala*, in the rubble of a Roman amphitheater, getting ready to conquer France" (1:588). Chateaubriand depicts himself at work, setting a creation scene in which two memories collide: those in the pages he was writing at that time and those concerning the circumstances of their composition. To the rubble of this Roman amphitheater, to the ruins that surrounded the author, is opposed the permanence of a work through which the writer himself will ascend to posterity. The manuscript of *Atala*, however, was to guarantee not only the posthumous existence of Chateaubriand but also his survival on earth, since it found itself between his body and a shell fragment during the siege of Thionville (1:608). Alas, the original version of Chateaubriand's American works was lost: "The manuscript of these travels, of which you will find a few excerpts in the work I am offering here to the public, perished, with the rest of my fortune, in the Revolution," bemoans Chateaubriand.[36] What text is he designating, precisely, by the expression "the manuscript of these travels"? A note added in 1826 to the second edition of the *Essai sur les révolutions* offers a clue: "Yes, the *very first* manuscript of these travels, but not the manuscript of *Les Natchez*, written in London, in which a large part of the original manuscript is preserved."[37] If we follow Chateaubriand's successive statements, it becomes apparent that the London manuscript of *Les Natchez* is composed of a considerable part of the original manuscript written in the United States, whereas that of the *Voyage en Amérique* disappeared during the Revolution before being rewritten in England at the time of his exile between 1793 and 1800. Chateaubriand manifests a deep regret over the loss of the original version of his American memories, as if it represented a quintessential state of the text that his later remembering could not equal:

> People were kind enough to grant some praise to my manner of depicting nature; but if they had seen these various writings on my knees, among the savages themselves, in the forests and on the shores of the American lakes, I dare to presume that they would have perhaps found things even more worthy of the public. Of all that, all I have left are a few separate pages, among which the Night, that is included here. I was destined to lose in the Revolution my fortune, relatives, friends, and what one never recovers when it is lost, the fruits of the labors of one's mind, the only thing that really belongs to us.[38]

To the nostalgia he felt for a period of his youth in a country whose intrinsic mutability was often stressed by him—"the United States is growing more quickly than this manuscript"[39]—may be added his nostalgia for the first version of a text that, by dint of having been lost and having the seal of radical authenticity, since it was produced in the heart of the territory he had come to discover in order to be immersed in its colors, is graced with incomparable qualities that cannot be matched by any other later attempt. Even so, the story of the writing of the *Voyage* is far from being finished at this point. The text that we read under this title is not the one that was composed in London during his exile, since Chateaubriand lost the fruits of his labor a second time.

A Manuscript from Beyond the Grave
In 1800, Chateaubriand decided to return to France. He could not bring with him the voluminous manuscript that he had written during his years of exile, for there were no less than 2,393 in-folio pages. Forced to choose from this textual mass, he took out *Atala* and *René* from *Les Natchez* before storing the rest of his manuscripts in a trunk that he put in the keeping of his London hosts (1:746). If *Atala* was designated by Chateaubriand as "his devoted daughter," *Les Natchez* and the *Voyage en Amérique* resembled abandoned orphans, left in the English capital where they would languish with no news from their father for fifteen years. Chateaubriand took his negligence so far that he even forgot where his offspring were awaiting him.

In 1814, when he resumed his communication with England, the memorialist's mind played a dirty trick on him, for he could no longer recall the name of the Englishwoman with whom he had left his texts: "Based on some vague, even contradictory, information" (1:746), some friends of Chateaubriand became clever sleuths for him. Through great perseverance, they managed to unearth his youthful works in the home of the children of the owner of an apartment Chateaubriand had formerly rented in London. From a trunk resembling a coffin arose the works written by Chateaubriand during his London exile when, between 1793 and 1800, he must have remembered the original manuscript that he had lost. The *Voyage* is thus a work produced by memory with successive interlocking versions in the heart of which subsisted a discourse contemporary with a defunct age. This work gives a commemorative representation of America whose function consists in reviving through language a period that no longer existed at the moment that it was described. In order to approach as close as possible this period, Chateaubriand included in the *Voyage* the oldest documents that he could recover.

The Novice Author and the Aged Writer
The temporal distance between the production and the rediscovery of these texts produced a doubling of Chateaubriand's persona that he describes in regard to *Les Natchez* but which is just as true of the *Voyage en Amérique*. "What happened

to me has perhaps never happened to an author before, that is, to read after thirty years a manuscript that I had completely forgotten. I passed judgment on it as if it were the work of a stranger: the aged writer confirmed in his art, the man enlightened by criticism, the man with a calm mind and musty blood corrected the rough drafts of a novice author, abandoned to the whims of his imagination."[40]

We will retain his terminology in the following pages in order to distinguish between Chateaubriand at the moment of the rediscovery of the manuscript in 1827 (the "aged writer") and Chateaubriand during his exile in London ("the novice author"). After the rereading and revision of the manuscript, the final stage of the literary work undertaken by the aged writer consisted of staging the history of his own book. He chose to intermingle the voice of the novice author with his own, inscribing in the text the circumstances of its production in its final form: "This journey bears within itself its own commentary and its history," he warned in the author's notice at the beginning of the *Voyage en Amérique* (75). The *Voyage* contains numerous references to the "manuscript" found in London, the aged writer reminding us that he drew from it the essential matter of his narrative. Doing so, he organized the resurrection of words pronounced long ago by the novice author: "Now I let the manuscript speak: I give it to you as I found it, sometimes in the form of a *narrative*, sometimes in that of a *diary*, sometimes in *letters* or in simple *annotations*" (109; emphasis original). Chateaubriand behaves toward this voice as if he were a necromancer, capable of recalling the dead back into existence, beginning with this former "I" in which he no longer recognizes himself, because youth is really and truly over for him. It seems therefore that the *Voyage* is a space where a voice emerges to speak in the present of a defunct country. For the first time in this study, are we dealing with a commemorative representation that is not the result of an a posteriori reconstruction but an account, unaltered, of the traveler's original vision of America? This voice would thus be contemporary with the age it describes, while at the same time reaching from beyond the grave the aged writer who no longer recognizes it as his own. To the contrary, while the commemorative image of America offered by Chateaubriand seems to preserve the original impression of the novice author, it is, in fact, the reconstructed memory of the aged writer that it offers the reader.

Elaborations of the Past
The enunciative split in the *Voyage en Amérique* is more complex than Chateaubriand suggests. Certain passages that the aged writer attributes to the novice author are not given "as is," despite what he says, but are the result of a reworking at the time of the elaboration of the definitive version of the text. The example of the "Journal sans date" ("Undated Diary") is, in this respect, revealing, for

this section of the *Voyage* is one of those in which the voice of the novice author seems to speak with a particular liveliness, as if it had achieved the miracle of anticipating the recording of sounds and images and was communicating to us a fragment of reality of the New World such as it was perceived in 1791.

The "Journal sans date" is presented by the aged writer as a document rediscovered in the London manuscript following the "Lacs du Canada" (192). This text presents itself as a kind of logbook written by Chateaubriand in 1791 and surmounts the second paradox of the New World described in the introduction. Indeed, the "Journal sans date" seems to have succeeded in its attempt to describe the United States in the present and not when it had ceased to be what the author describes. "Journal sans date": paradoxical title, as Degout points out, for what is a "diary" that makes no mention of the "days" it is recounting and during which it was written?[41] More precisely, Chateaubriand reduces the temporal unity of the diary by isolating segments that are shorter than days: the hours, during four days and three nights. Replacing days with hours as the unit of measurement is a means of bringing together as closely as possible two times that it is impossible to superimpose completely: that of the writing and that of the experience. This nearly perfect coexistence is illustrated in the following passage:

> Midnight.
> The fire is beginning to go out, the circle of light shrinking. I listen: a formidable calm weighs on these forests; it sounds like silence giving way to silence. I seek in vain to hear in this universal tomb any noise that reveals life . . .
> Half-past midnight.
> The repose continues, but the rotted tree breaks and falls. The forests moan; a thousand voices rise up. Soon the noises grow weak: they die in the quasi-imaginary distance: silence again invades the wilderness. (196–97)

The passage from silence to the nocturnal racket of the birds in the trees and back to silence takes place in thirty minutes. Combined with the brief period of time, the use of the present creates for the reader the illusion that Chateaubriand's pen is recording the variations of the sonorous atmosphere of the American forests, as if writing had become a cassette deck capable not only of recording the sounds but, contrary to the *phonautograph*, of playing them back at will.[42] Was America finally being described in real time?

In an article published in 1998, Degout presents a second version of the "Journal sans date."[43] It is called the "copy" to distinguish it from the "Journal sans date" published in the *Voyage*. His study reveals that the copy is not a logbook kept by Chateaubriand in America but a volume of memories written after his return to Europe. Likewise, the "Journal sans date" is not what it claims to be, that is, a fragment torn from time, a gem extracted from the New World and set in the composition of the *Voyage en Amérique*, a work by the novice author that he had written during pauses in the middle of the American forests, surrounded by Amerindian guides and by the presence of a whole world hidden in the trees: noises, birdsongs, muffled cracking.... As we meet it in the *Voyage*, the "Journal sans date" is the result of a later rewriting and enrichment of the copy. As Degout observes, "At no time are we in the presence of raw material, but rather of two very successful 'reworkings.'"[44]

An additional proof supports this hypothesis. When reading the "Journal sans date," one notes numerous borrowings from the *Voyages* of Bartram.[45] Bartram's work was published for the first time in English in 1791 and translated into French in 1798: Chateaubriand's borrowings from this text thus prove definitively that the "Journal sans date" is not the work of the young traveler in America but, in its final form, that of the aged writer. However, Chateaubriand strived to preserve the fiction of a manuscript rediscovered and faithfully transcribed, in particular when he stated, in a note in the "Journal sans date": "I am leaving as is all these things produced by youth; please excuse them" (194). Precisely, these "things" were not produced by youth but were instead the work of the aged writer reconstituting and thus altering a posteriori the impressions he remembered from thirty-six years before. We recognize here the process of the "metamorphosis of fictions" described earlier: the memory presented to the reader as genuine is the result of an elaboration during which fiction is merged with truth and eventually takes its place.

Ultimately, the *Voyage en Amérique* is not a space from which emerges a voice from beyond the grave, miraculously returned from the dead after the wanderings of the manuscript. It is rather a stage play that only announces two characters but in which, in fact, three voices can be heard. The first two, we already know them, are those of the aged writer and of the novice author. The third is the one produced by Chateaubriand when he attempted to revive in the present a past experience, which, he asserted, was being offered to the reader in its original purity, whereas it is in fact being relived in the manner of a fleeting reminiscence and an irreparable loss. For Chateaubriand, time is simultaneously found and lost: his consciousness of time is a tragic consciousness that is not brightened by the hope of a victory of writing over death. Thus, the posthumous America created by Chateaubriand is a retrospective literary construction signed by a writer who was trying to describe the New World as he perceived it thirty-six years earlier but whose literary incarnation is imbued with the experience of loss and disappearance. The "Journal sans date" thus reveals a painful awareness of the passage of time, when it evokes those "generations of trees" that cover each other over and that the traveler steps over as so many lifeless corpses (196). Breaking with the Rousseauian tradition in which the silence of nature is associated with the idea of tranquility, plenitude, and rest, Chateaubriand identifies the silence of the forests with the calm of the grave: "Let me rest a moment in this double solitude of death and nature: is there any other refuge where I would prefer to sleep forever?" (196). There is the suffering of bereavement at the heart of this recollection of a distant age. This diffuse suffering allows us to distinguish the commemorative writing of America in the works of Crèvecœur, Lezay-Marnésia, and Chateaubriand. In the *Lettres d'un cultivateur américain,* the recalling of memories of a retrospectively idealized period invested the present by opposing a luminous vision to an unbearable present. The memory of the past was more radiant than the experience itself had been, and it was still more radiant than the period of its reemergence. Concerning the final Lezay-Marnésia, the one whose castles in America had definitively collapsed, a similar conclusion is warranted: for him too, when he was working in the solitude of Saint-Julien, immersed in the anguish of the Revolution, the posthumous representation of the New World provided a moral escape, a kind of erasure of time. If the Golden Age will never return, at least it is still possible to reinvent it. To the contrary, the commemorative representation of America in Chateaubriand's works may be distinguished from that of his two compatriots by the spectral nature of the apparition that it invokes. The past arises from beyond the grave, but it does not announce the victory of writing over the time that has destroyed what it is trying to save: America is resuscitated, but not like Lazarus leaving his tomb—rather like a phantom that has preserved its ectoplasmic nature in coming back to life.

A WEB OF ANACHRONISMS

Reenactment

The posthumous representation of America in Chateaubriand's *Voyage* is characterized by the adoption of an anachronistic aesthetic: that of the period that the text strives to resuscitate. Chateaubriand undertook a work of total recreation that safeguards the memory of the past by using his own language. If we tried to find an equivalent for it in the museographic domain, it would not be a collection in which the artifacts of the past are exposed behind glass or on mannequins. Chateaubriand's work is comparable rather to the city of Williamsburg in Virginia, where flesh-and-blood individuals in period costumes stroll down streets that have been preserved in their original colonial state. English has a term that is lacking in French: "reenactment," for which the term "reconstitution" is only an imperfect translation. If the works of Crèvecœur and Lezay-Marnésia reconstitute the past by producing a discourse on it, those of Chateaubriand attempt to *bring it back to life,* to *stage it* in a form already outdated at the time of the writing. In order to bring to light the formal uniqueness of the *Voyage en Amérique*, it is first necessary to place it in the context of its production.

Travel Narratives and Tourist Guidebooks

The form of the travel narratives in America was changing at the end of the eighteenth century. The young United States attracted numerous visitors, whether they were infatuated with the supposed grandeur of the American model, like Brissot or Chastellux, crossed the Atlantic to escape the French Revolution, like La Rochefoucauld-Liancourt and Volney, or taken refuge there after the loss of Saint-Domingue, like Moreau de Saint-Méry.[46] The account of their journey was most often organized, as Rossi remarks, "either day by day or by chapters that follow the progress of the trip, with care taken to give as many temporal and spatial indications as possible."[47] These chronicles of personal experiences were accompanied by commentaries on broader questions (the political system, society, manners, religion, slavery, etc.) and lingered on themes that, from narrative to narrative, came to be regarded as obligatory exercises: numerous authors, for example, devoted a passage to the Quakers.[48] In addition, the narrator provided ample information intended for the reader who might one day decide to follow in his footsteps: he indicated, notably, the distance between the cities to help him prepare for his stay.[49]

During his journey in the northeastern United States, La Rochefoucauld-Liancourt informs the reader, for example, that in Lebanon, in the State of New York, it is possible to stop at the tavern of a certain M. Staw, where the boarders get together to drink mineral water.[50] Although the primary purpose of his text is to describe the stages of his own trip, the author also offers practical information to his readers. This informative function turns many travel narratives into virtual tourist guidebooks, a form that is developing and becoming autonomous at the turn of the eighteenth century.

The notion of reproducibility constitutes nonetheless a means of distinguishing the travel narrative from the guidebook. A travel narrative is the tale of a journey that cannot be relived identically, either by the reader or by the author himself. Indeed, it is the adventure of an individual who has completed a trip at a precise moment in history. As such, his experience cannot be repeated by anyone: it is possible to walk in the footsteps of a traveler, but as years go by, the successor perceives as a sentimental pilgrimage what was originally lived as an intimate initiative experience. Reading only serves to revive the experience of the journey and to *bring to the present*, each time the account is read, the travels that it relates; but it is like a past relived in the mind, and not like an experience equivalent to that of the traveler, that the journey is reproduced.

On the contrary, the role of a guidebook is to describe an itinerary that the traveler can complete as it is described, which is illustrated by the regular updating of the information that it provides so that it reflects as closely as possible a changing reality: the revision of the guidebook is critical to the repetition of the experience of its author. Of course, it was necessary for an individual to travel at a given time in the past in order to be able to describe the places mentioned in his guidebook; nonetheless, this past moment is destined to be integrated into someone else's future. All the reader has to do is go to the place indicated, and the past of the author of the guide will become his present: he will discover the places described by his predecessor, since they will not have had time to change significantly since the publication of his work.

Contrary to the majority of the travel narratives devoted to North America at the turn of the eighteenth century, Chateaubriand's *Voyage en Amérique* has no resemblance to a guidebook: that is one of its most important characteristics. The celebration of the uniqueness of the subject is exhibited in the recalling of an experience that is impossible to duplicate. Indeed, Chateaubriand's America is not an America that one can visit: it has been lost, it belongs to the past, and the only way to travel there is by memory and reading. Chateaubriand, therefore, does not bother with details on the means of transportation or the location of inns—that he finds moreover atrocious, often preferring to spend the night in the forest. These details have no sense, since they are already outdated at the time of the publication of the *Voyage* in 1827. Roads have been built, reducing the length of time necessary to travel from one place to another: "If I were to see the United States today, I would no longer recognize it: where I left forests, I would find planted fields, where I beat my way through bushes, I would travel on highways. The Mississippi, the Missouri, and the Ohio Rivers no longer flow by in solitary majesty; large ships with three masts ply them; more than two hundred steamships enliven the shores" (373).

The memorial cartography preserved by the author could not serve as a guide for the travelers of the 1830s; the form of America, alas, has changed more quickly than Chateaubriand's heart.

Chateaubriand and Cosmography

Chateaubriand's narrative stands out as an exception to the travel literature of the period for an additional reason. While he readily describes the *Génie du christianisme* as the first text of the "new literature," Chateaubriand hardly appears as an innovator in the *Voyage*, whose singularity consists rather in the return of an anachronistic discourse: cosmography. "A collage of heterogeneous textual fragments between which 'voids' are going to remain," as Lestringant defines it,[51] cosmography postulates the profound albeit hidden unity of the Creation, the harmony between divine, human, and natural things being the sign of the conformity of essences that it is incumbent upon the scholar to bring to light. The subjectivity of the cosmographer plays a key role in the production of this discourse, since it serves to unify the diverse materials used in the work. If the Creation is a space of hidden correspondences, it is up to the cosmographer to emphasize the secret relations between the spaces he describes. For this purpose, he never limits himself to the description of what he has seen himself—a limit that defines the opposite method, that of the "topographers" that Michel de Montaigne wished for[52]—since the description of the places crossed by the cosmographer is a pretext to enlarge the perspective: his discourse ultimately embraces territories that he only knows through the books of others. While basing the legitimacy of his discourse on the experience of his own travels, the cosmographer does not hesitate to resort to the compilation of ancient and modern sources. He combines ancient authorities and individual testimony, his own writing and that of his collaborators, motivated by a totalizing ambition that nonetheless entails the risk of the discourse crumbling into a series of digressive notations assumed by a polyphonic enunciation.[53]

Although it was written well after cosmography had died out, Chateaubriand's travel narrative revived this form of discourse at the beginning of the nineteenth century.[54] The heterogeneousness of the subjects treated in the *Voyage* is a first trait it has in common with the cosmographers of the sixteenth century. Chateaubriand relates a series of personal experiences that took place during what he calls his "Itinéraire" (130): his crossing of the Atlantic, his meeting with Washington, his accident at Niagara Falls, and so forth. Furthermore, he devotes an entire chapter to the fauna and flora ("Histoire naturelle"), before producing a series of chapters whose ambition—typical of the cosmographic discourse—is to conduct an inventory of the particular facts known about America in order to produce an exhaustive knowledge of it. The markedly diverse character of his work is demonstrated likewise in the conclusion, in which Chateaubriand turns away from North America to bring his attention to bear on the Spanish colonies of the New World, whose history he compares to that of the former English colonies: after putting on the garb of a traveler and of a specialist in natural science, now he was adopting the discourse of a historian and a political thinker.

The fragmentation of the *Voyage* into diverse discourses is not the only characteristic of cosmographic literature that this work exhibits: the integration of borrowed erudition is another.[55] Chateaubriand readily admits that he has drawn part of his information from his readings: "Immediately after the description of Louisiana, the manuscript gives a few excerpts of the travels of Bartram that I had translated rather carefully. Mixed in with these excerpts are my own rectifications, observations, reflections, additions, and my descriptions. . . . But in my work everything is so much more entangled that it is almost impossible to separate what is from me and what is from Bartram, nor even to recognize it" (218).

This confession is liable to be interpreted both as a proof of intellectual integrity (Chateaubriand recognizing what he owes to Bartram) and as a strategy intended to counter from the outset any accusations of plagiarism—that he had good reason to fear. Even if borrowing information from one's predecessors is a common practice in travel literature, Chateaubriand did not confess the full extent of the debts he owed his precursors, as is proved, especially, by his tense relationship with Giacomo Costantino Beltrami (1779–1855). Chateaubriand made this Italian traveler and man of letters quite bitter by not acknowledging (as he was wont to do) the borrowing of a certain number of texts from the latter's work titled *Découverte des sources du Mississippi et de la Rivière sanglante* (*Discovery of the Sources of the Mississippi and of the Bloody River*, 1828).[56] A modern cosmographer, Chateaubriand compiled information taken from works of his traveling colleagues to fill the gaps in the London manuscript, numerous at the time of its providential recovery.

Chateaubriand's borrowings often came from ancient sources. James Fenimore Cooper was one of the first to observe that Chateaubriand had consulted documents composed five decades earlier: "The book speaks plainly for itself, and if Mr. Chateaubriand has painted them [the Sioux] materially different from what I have he has been led into an error. . . . *He probably gained his information from the old French writers, half a century old,* while I have consulted our own means of intelligence, and my own observation."[57] Cooper opposes two types of representations of the Amerindian world: one taken from life—his—the other the result of a bookish compilation, the reliability of the sources being inversely proportional to their ancientness. The debate between Cooper and Chateaubriand evokes the terms of the one that, long ago, pitted Jean de Léry against André Thevet, the first presenting himself as the champion of "autopsy"—a method that guarantees the truth of a discourse by a direct confrontation between the author and object he is treating—and the second being considered a representative of cosmography, a method whose partisans did not hesitate to resort to the authority of ancient sources.[58]

However, at the end of the "Itinéraire," Chateaubriand announces his desire to update the information contained in his book: "The thirty-six years that have gone by since my journey have shed much light and changed many things in the Old and the New World; those years modified and corrected the judgments of the writer" (230). This passage suggests that the work of the "aged writer" consisted in updating the views of the "novice author" by completing its information by means of more recent works.[59] It is true that Chateaubriand very often proves to be well informed: the chapter "État actuel des sauvages de l'Amérique septentrionale" ("Current State of the Savages of North America"), for instance, contains information on the population of the Amerindian tribes, the surface of the territory that they have been granted, and the relations that they maintained with the American authorities. Many of these facts were unknown in France at the time of the preparation of the *Voyage en Amérique,* and Chateaubriand very likely obtained them from his contacts among the French diplomats.[60] Nonetheless, to complete the information he offers on various subjects that he treats after the "Itinerary" itself, Chateaubriand does not restrict himself to the most recent works he has at his disposal: he exhibits a curious interest in "totally different sources, older, foreign, seeming to show a certain disdain for the American writings of his contemporary countrymen," as Rossi observes in his presentation of the book.[61] The Enchanter disdains, for example, the *Tableau du climat et du sol des États-Unis d'Amérique (Chart of the Climate and Soil of the United States of America,* 1803) by Volney, but he borrows widely from William Bartram and Jonathan Carver, as well as from Le Page du Pratz and Charlevoix.[62]

The analysis of these borrowings allows us to glimpse a whole network of intertextual connections: sometimes Chateaubriand takes information from authors who have themselves found it in the works of their own predecessors. Such is the case of this detail on beavers—"he uses this tail as a trowel and sled"—that he finds in Beltrami, who had discovered this fact in Lahontan (234, note 3). By the meshing of these interwoven intertextual references, Chateaubriand's narrative includes knowledge that comes from the beginning of the seventeenth century—which is at the very least paradoxical for an author who is unambiguous about his wish to update the information presented in his text. For what reasons would he cultivate anachronism by drawing his information from texts that are not only old but sometimes even precede the tale of a journey he claims to be bringing up to date?

"Geometrical Truths" and "Truths of the Imagination"
The article devoted by Chateaubriand to the *Voyage* of Mackenzie helps us to attempt a response to this question. "When the first Frenchmen who set foot on the shores of *Canada* speak of lakes that resemble seas, of waterfalls that plunge down from the sky, of forests of unfathomable depth, the spirit is far more moved than when an English merchant, or a modern scholar, informs you that he has reached the Pacific Ocean and that Niagara Falls is only one hundred and forty-four feet high. What we gain in knowledge, we lose in feeling. The geometrical truths have killed certain truths of the imagination that are far more important to morality than one might think."[63]

Chateaubriand sets up here an opposition between two types of representations of America: that of the first travelers and that of modern scientists. The first did not have at their disposal precise scientific instruments. To help their readers imagine the New World, they resorted to analogy ("lakes that resemble seas") and to hyperbole ("waterfalls that plunge down from the sky"; "forests of unfathomable depth"). Their descriptions produce what Chateaubriand calls a "truth of the imagination." By this expression, he designates information that conveys to us not what the object is in itself but the manner in which it strikes the imagination of the person who is contemplating it: in short, and to paraphrase Mallarmé, the first travelers chose to depict not "the thing" but "the effect that it produces," which is another way of saying that they produced a poetic representation rather than a scientific discourse.[64] The image that they gave of America provokes strong emotions in the reader, allowing him to travel at their sides in his mind, since "tired of the society in which we live, and of the sorrows that surround us, we like to lose ourselves in thought in faraway countries and among unknown peoples."[65] In the example of the first travelers, Chateaubriand finds a source of aesthetic inspiration, since they knew the secret of painting an enchanting picture of the New World.

For their part, the modern scientists produce an opposite type of representation of America, spreading what Chateaubriand refers to as "geometric truths."[66] They generate scientific knowledge for their readers, using units of measure that rigorously characterize the objects that they describe. Measuring, however, puts an end to reverie; it determines the nature but also the limit of an object: "Niagara Falls is only one hundred and forty-feet high," we say, and suddenly an objective fact replaces the deep feeling that a subject experiences before what he considers less as a quantifiable physical phenomenon than as a grandiose phenomenon, a marvel that he thanks God or nature for creating. In addition, modern scientists are distinguished from the first travelers by their practice of naming: "the Pacific Ocean" is a labeled space, whereas the first travelers do not speak either of Lake Michigan, or of the forests of the Catskills, or of Niagara Falls but of "lakes," "forests," and "waterfalls," bathing them in a poetic vagueness that is preserved by both their anonymity and the use of the plural. As in the magical stories in fairytales, these elements of the natural décor can be found on no map, and while they are indeed real since they have been seen by the traveler, they belong, for the reader, to the realm of the imaginary. The first travelers and the modern scientists are opposed, finally, by the time of their respective reigns: if the time of the first is now past, we have entered, Chateaubriand tells us, into a period that has inherited from the Enlightenment an encyclopedic ambition whose goal is to generate an exhaustive inventory of knowledge about the world and therefore to erase inexorably from the maps the very mention of the *Terra Incognita* that, in yesteryear, still gave rise to dreams and the desire for adventure.

Although Chateaubriand's birthdate placed him in the age of the modern scientists, he judged severely the sacrifice of imagination in favor of the accumulation of objective knowledge that seemed to characterize his period. The readers of the nineteenth century, grown blasé through the proliferation of travel narratives, were only beguiled by descriptions of faraway countries under certain conditions. As Chateaubriand asked, with a dose of melancholy: "In the past, when one had left his home like Ulysses, that person was an object of curiosity: today, other than a half-dozen individuals distinguished by their unusual personal merit, who can get anyone interested in the tale of his travels?" (137). To appeal to one's readers, it is no longer enough to have traveled the world over: it is still necessary to have corrected a map or otherwise contributed to the exhaustiveness of geographic knowledge.

Well, Chateaubriand's *Voyage* reveals nothing to the readers of the nineteenth century that they could not already have learned by reading the works of his precursors. On the one hand, Chateaubriand completed a journey that was, all in all, rather classical, the description of Niagara Falls appearing, for example, in a large number of previous accounts.[67] On the other hand, his American adventure did not result in any discovery, since he had quickly given up any plans to discover the Northwest Passage in favor of wandering around the forests of the New World.[68] Consequently, how does Chateaubriand intend to "get anyone interested in the tale of his travels" if he cannot take credit for the slightest find? He goes against the "modern scientists" and adopts the aesthetic of the travel narratives of the first French explorers of the New World. In his effort to write in the manner of his predecessors, the very imprecision of his itinerary plays a key role whose value has gone unrecognized by a whole critical tradition.[69] For a long time now, the inaccuracies of Chateaubriand concerning his journey in North America have been interpreted as more or less clever attempts to dissimulate the modest distances that he had in fact traversed. The presupposition of these works criticizing Chateaubriand's contradictions and geographical approximations consisted in the certainty that he wanted to pass himself off, for posterity, as a much more adventuresome traveler than he was in reality. But this accusation cannot be valid, considering the fact that Chateaubriand readily admitted that he belonged to the "crowd of obscure travelers who only saw what everyone else saw, who contributed nothing to the furthering of scientific progress, and who added nothing to the store of human knowledge" (137). In recognizing the scientific insignificance of his journey, its relative banality, Chateaubriand turned an apparent weakness into a poetic force that allowed him to embrace the charm of those old narratives, in which the spaces were blurred and the places unnamed, in which the traveler had no idea exactly where he was in the vastness of the New World. In the end, the imprecision of his itinerary was an aesthetic choice rather than a ruse employed to fantasize about his journey.

We recall that René de Mersenne compared the descriptions of *Atala* to their models in the New World.[70] In concluding that Chateaubriand had lied, is he not revealing the lack of comprehension of a modern scientist in regard to the descriptions of a traveler at the turn of the eighteenth century who is trying to write like the "first Frenchmen" of the sixteenth century? The absence of certain "geometrical truths" in the *Voyage*, denounced by a whole critical tradition, may be explained by Chateaubriand's resolve to cultivate in their place those truths of the imagination that abound in the texts of his predecessors.[71] Ultimately, the posthumous representation that Chateaubriand offers of his American journey has an analeptic function, recreating a past trip as if it had taken place in an even earlier period.[72] Chateaubriand recreated his journey of 1791 by adopting the anachronistic approach of the former cosmographers and the literary techniques of the first French travelers in America in order to bring back the charm of a country whose power of fascination was progressively reduced as it was explored, and in order also to endow with an aesthetic interest a journey that, judged according to the standards of modern scientists, could have appeared insignificant. The America of Chateaubriand is an imaginary continent, combining the nostalgia for the period of his own trip with that for an earlier period whose disappearance he deplores.[73]

MOURNING FOR (NEW) FRANCE

Vestiges of New France

"Both the idealization and the criticism of America were to some extent a projection of French and English aspirations and anxieties and an attempt to account for—and come to terms with—Europe's progressive loss of status and influence," observe Craiutu and Isaac.[74] Like the French and English authors referred to by these two scholars, Chateaubriand is preoccupied with the decline of his country, and it is vestiges of its former power in the New World that he discovers with regret as he crosses through the wilderness. In the *Voyage*, the posthumous representation of America has a specular function: through the recalling of the disappearance of New France and the decline of the Amerindian tribes, it reflects the loss of vitality of French civilization in the course of the last years of the Restoration.

Following the Iroquois Trail to Niagara Falls, the young Chateaubriand comes up against an invisible border that is defended by the Amerindians: "The savages of Niagara Falls, under the command of the English, were put in charge of guarding the border of Upper Canada on this side. They confronted us armed with bows and arrows and prevented us from passing. I had to send the Dutchman to Fort Niagara to ask permission from the commandant to enter the territory that was under British control; I did so with a heavy heart, because I remembered that France had once held dominion over this region" (180). Chateaubriand had hastened to leave the American cities of which he speaks in the *Voyage* just as he had visited them: as quickly as possible. Plunging into the woods allowed him to keep as close as possible to an ancestral past, the object of his fascination, and this blessed immersion in the forests of the New World afforded him moments of enthusiasm bordering on delirium, one of which he relates, with a certain humor, in the *Voyage* (167). However, the encounter with this administrative constraint in the middle of the forest reminded him of a painful political defeat: that of the French colonial empire in North America. This chagrin at the idea that his country no longer dominated immense regions of the New World pervades the sumptuous beginning of *Atala*: "France once possessed, in North America, a vast empire that stretched from Labrador to Florida, and from the shores of the Atlantic to the most remote lakes of Upper Canada."[75]

With this "once," whose tone and placement at the beginning of the sentence recall the "Once upon a time" that introduces fairytales, the narrator evokes the New France that, like the magical universe with which it is associated, henceforth belongs to a past so distant that it seems to be a figment of his imagination.[76] Nonetheless, at the time of the publication of *Atala* in 1801, Chateaubriand had not entirely given up hope of seeing the French empire rise once again in America: "[I]f, by a strategy at the highest political level, the French government decided one day to ask England for the return of Canada, my description of New France would take on a new interest."[77] His viewpoint is typical of a segment of French public opinion for which the signing of the Treaty of Paris did not constitute a definitive abandonment of French ambitions on the other side of the Atlantic: "From the perspective of Paris, it was unclear that France had been permanently chased from North America in 1763. Only in retrospect does the year emerge as a defining moment, and even then it can appear as one of those turning points at which history failed to turn," Furstenberg observes in this regard.[78] Despite these hopes, Canada was never returned to France, and Bonaparte disappointed all those who, like Chateaubriand, would have liked to see a revival of the French adventure in the New World.

In 1827, when Chateaubriand published the *Voyage en Amérique*, he had nothing left to express, regarding this episode, other than "regrets" and the lack of "hope": New France was indeed dead.[79] He tried to put his grieving behind him, haunted by the disappearance of an empire whose causes remained at the center of his reflections, and to imagine what it could have become, what profit and glory it could have brought to France if she had been able to keep it. However, the goal of the posthumous representation of this empire is not just to celebrate its memory: it allows us to imagine what could have been its alternate destiny.

The Logic of the Past Conditional
In rereading the London manuscript,[80] and in adding to it some reflections on the "Current State of the Savages of North America," Chateaubriand is faced with the memory of New France and its past glory: "In tracing this tableau of a primitive world, in speaking constantly of Canada and of Louisiana, in studying

on old maps the vast area of the former French colonies in America, I was plagued by a painful idea; I wondered how the government of my country had managed to allow to perish these colonies that would be today an inexhaustible source of prosperity for us" (370). Once this problem was clearly stated, Chateaubriand invites his reader to imagine and traverse, as if he had a map beneath his eyes, the vastness of a territory equivalent to "more than two-thirds of North America" (371). He then asks a series of questions that amount to nothing less than speculations on an alternate future: "What would have happened if said colonies were still in our hands at the time of the liberation of the United States? Would this liberation have taken place? Would our presence on the American soil have facilitated or hindered it?" (371). Just like Lezay-Marnésia, Chateaubriand found in the history of the relations between France and the United States a source of inspiration for uchronic scenarios.[81] Lezay-Marnésia indeed saw in America the last chance to build the reformed French society that could have been achieved in France itself if only the Revolution had not become so radical. Chateaubriand, in his turn, wonders what influence a New France that had remained in the hands of metropolitan France would have had on the progress of the American Revolution. For these two authors, the destinies of America and France could not be conceived separately. Their recourse to uchronia may be explained by the need to understand the successive historical upheavals that occurred at the end of the eighteenth century and to find in imaginary constructs a compensation for the territorial losses and political changes that followed on each other's heels at such an unbridled rhythm.

In *The Spectacular Past*, Samuels describes the need of men and women at the beginning of the nineteenth century to grasp, through the consumption of historical spectacles (wax museums, panoramas, dioramas, etc.) and narratives on the past (novels, short stories, plays) the role played by recent history in the transformation of their identity: "Through the consumption of popular and visually realistic forms of history, bourgeois spectators were able to envision the process of historical change that had created their new subject positions."[82] The uchronic discourse may be conceived as another expression of this need to analyze retrospectively, given that it focuses on the identification of key moments in history that hung by a thread but resulted in incalculable consequences by the chain of events that they precipitated. More than classical historical representation, however, uchronic reflection constitutes a revolt against history as it came to be written; it is a meditation on the past, not to understand the manner in which it informs the present but to understand how it could or should have been written differently to bring about a reality considered to be preferable. Chateaubriand pursued this uchronic reflection when he sought to imagine the future that would have awaited New France if France had not ratified the Treaty of Paris in 1763: would it not have become, in the end, an independent state?

This question had been asked in 1803, in the course of deliberations on the fate of French Louisiana. In a work from 1829, with which he hoped to dispel the regrets still felt over the sale of this colony nearly thirty years after the fact, Barbé-Marbois recounts one of the arguments advanced by the partisans of this transaction: "If, having become a French colony, [Louisiana] grows and becomes important, there will be in its very prosperity a seed of independence that will soon grow. But the more it blossoms, the less chance there is that we could hold onto it."[83] Chateaubriand too envisioned the possibility of independent French colonies in North America. However, contrary to Barbé-Marbois, for whom this eventuality was a good reason to get rid of a territory destined to escape sooner or later the control of metropolitan France, he considered it as an event that would still have been advantageous to his country: "Would New France itself become free? Why not? What problem would it be for the motherland to see the flowering of an immense empire sprung from its bosom, an empire that would spread the glory of our name and of our language in another hemisphere?"[84] Here, Chateaubriand was perpetuating the traditional perversion of the maternal metaphor, used so often to describe the relations between metropolitan France and its colonies: far from imitating the mother who nourishes her child, it was, on the contrary, France who was drawing new strength from the exploitation of the colonies.[85] In fact, he insisted on the numerous material advantages that the liberated colonies could have offered to his country, which could have exploited the vast market that it would have retained in America (371). Nevertheless, if Chateaubriand is in disagreement with Barbé-Marbois, while basing his rationale on an identical postulate, that is, the inevitability of the independence of the French colonies in North America, it is because he grants a supreme importance to immaterial interests: those of "glory" and of "language."

Chateaubriand is particularly defensive regarding the glory of France when it concerns the role played by his countrymen in the colonization of North America. He claims to disabuse those who would tend to minimize the participation of the French in this immense endeavor: "The national pride of the Americans leads them to attribute to themselves the merit of most of the discoveries in the western part of the United States, but one should not forget that the French of Canada and Louisiana, arriving from the north and the south, had traveled through these regions long before the Americans" (210). However, Chateaubriand recognizes with thinly concealed bitterness that this considerable accomplishment was far more the result of individual initiatives than of a national policy advocated by France (140); perhaps he was thinking of his own attempt to discover the Northwest Passage, for which he had received no official support.[86] Glory—a concept inherited from the Old Regime by Napoleon, who turned it into one of the foundations of a "policy of fusion" uniting revolutionary and egalitarian principles with aristocratic and traditional values[87]—proved to be at the center of Chateaubriand's political reflections as well, owing to their nationalist character. Like Napoleon, for whom war was the only way to earn glory, and for whom the extent of its empire was the measure of the grandeur of a nation, Chateaubriand was favorable to the pursuit of the prestige of military conquests in foreign countries: after the sale of Louisiana, he expressed his hope that France would build a new empire around the Mediterranean.[88] In this respect, Chateaubriand subordinated the national interests of foreign countries to those of his homeland and placed the rights of his countrymen before those of their colonial subjects. Throughout his writings devoted to colonization, the glory of France is his primary criterion for any decisions.

The interests of the French language are likewise a constant preoccupation, haunted as he is by the specter of its impending disappearance. The question of the fragility of languages is omnipresent in the *Voyage*.[89] Those spoken by the Amerindian tribes were of particular interest to Chateaubriand, who devoted an entire chapter to them (283–90). Although he declared that the indigenous peoples of North America have preserved nothing of their ancestral culture but their languages (369), even certain of these have eventually disappeared, as in the case of Natchez, that was only "a softer dialect of Chickasaw" (283). A similar destiny threatened the other Amerindian languages, that risked being lost like the mislaid volume referred to by Chateaubriand: "We also have the manuscript of an Iroquois-English dictionary; unfortunately, the first volume, from the letters A to L, has been lost" (290). In this general meditation on the mortality of languages, French is no exception: if Chateaubriand asserts that, everything considered, the independence of New France would have been an advantage for metropolitan France, it is because this enlarged Francophone world would have covered a much greater surface than it did in his time. Chateaubriand's discourse on the French colonies of the New World stems from the same past conditional logic as Lezay-Marnésia's earlier description of Saint-Pierre, given that the two men both imagine what French America could have become if other historical circumstances had prevailed.[90] Thus, the posthumous representation of America, at the same time that it commemorates a bygone age, is accompanied by a meditation on a future that very nearly came to be. For just as we imagine what a person *would have wanted*, what she *would have said*, or, still better, what *should have happened* to avoid her premature demise, the author of a posthumous representation of America, when he notes the disappearance of a period of its history, likewise seeks to imagine the events that could have prevented it. The posthumous representation of America is similar to the image that Chateaubriand gives of himself in the *Voyage*: it is a portrait of both what was and what could have been in other circumstances, for this recreation of the past underscores the fragility of the present by recalling that it could have been written in a different manner.

Politics of the French Language

After citing several economic and strategic advantages that the preservation of New France could have brought to metropolitan France, Chateaubriand returned to the question of the French language. He was saddened by the place that it had been assigned in the world: "We are excluded from the new universe where the human race is being reborn. The English and Spanish languages are used in Africa, Asia, in the islands of the South Sea, and on the continent of the two Americas to interpret the thought of several million people, while we, dispossessed of the conquests of our courage and genius, scarcely hear the language of Racine, Colbert, and Louis XIV spoken in a few villages of Louisiana and Canada, which are under foreign domination; it only exists there as a witness of our reversals of fortune and our political errors" (290).

At first glance, Chateaubriand was only concerned with a linguistic problem. He deplored the weak international influence of French, especially when he compared the fate of his mother tongue with that of Spanish and English, languages that, by dint of being supported by more effective colonial policies, were practiced in 1827 in a far wider territory and by a much larger number of speakers. Nonetheless, it was not only the fate of the French language that concerned him but more exactly the role that it could have played in a successful colonial policy. The short enumeration at the end of the aforementioned excerpt illustrates this position. The "language of Racine" is a well-known expression referring to an author who used the French language so brilliantly that his idiom became a metaphor for it. Conversely, the locutions "language of Colbert" and "language of Louis XIV" are not expressions that can be used innocently as synonyms of "language of Molière." Chateaubriand employs them to connect the French language explicitly to the creation of the colonial empire.

If Colbert has remained famous in the history of his country, it is not for signing works that expressed the quintessence of the French language. It is for contributing to the construction of the power of his master as Secretary of State of the King's House and of the Navy, but also by creating commercial companies—the Compagnie française des Indes Orientales (1664), the Compagnie française des Indes Occidentales (1664), and the Compagnie du Levant (1670). Colbert was also the originator of the first version of the Code Noir (Black Code) (implemented two years after his death in 1685) and of the institutionalization of slavery and slave trade by France.[91] In the colonial domain, moreover, he furthered the development of the colony in Canada by contributing to the constitution of its "demographic and economic base."[92] The expression "language of Colbert" may thus be read as a synonym for "language of the individual who worked for the glory of France through the construction of its colonial empire."

Likewise, to use the expression "language of Louis XIV" allowed Chateaubriand to adopt a conception of the Great Century that saw it as the time of a double apotheosis, that of both France and of its national language.[93] This thesis was developed by numerous authors in the seventeenth century, and notably by Father Bouhours (1628–1702). The power of France and the spreading of French go together, if we are to believe this writer: "They already speak French in all the courts of Europe. All enlightened foreigners pride themselves on knowing French; even those who hate our nation the most love its language . . . ; the people themselves, even though they are only commoners, share in that respect the good taste of respectable people: they learn our language nearly as soon as their own, as if by a secret instinct that informs them, in spite of themselves, that they will one day have to obey the king of France as they would their legitimate master."[94] The expression "language of Louis XIV" as used by Chateaubriand refers therefore to a time when the diffusion of French was both a means of cultural domination by France in Europe and the result of the military prestige of the Sun King. However, the use of this term is imbued with a dark irony.

Chateaubriand published the *Voyage* at a time when the "language of Louis XIV" was spoken in a country that no longer had anything in common with the one that Father Bouhours was praising. While the monarchy he exalted "[had not] changed since its establishment,"[95] the one that Chateaubriand had under his eyes at the time of the publication of the *Voyage* had been restored following the Revolution and the Empire. Moreover, far from sowing its "lilies" throughout the world, it had seen the vast empire built by Louis XIV and Colbert shrink progressively. If Chateaubriand was also convinced that there was a community of interests between France and its language, it did not lead him to believe, as did Father Bouhours, in the incorruptibility of the second on the basis of the supposed inalterability of the first: it was, on the contrary, because he recognized the probability of a degeneration of France when he meditated on the decline of French in the world. To reflect on the ruins of New France as Chateaubriand did was not only to adopt an elegiac posture and apply the "logic of the past conditional," an action with no impact on the present, since the French colonial empire in America was already definitively eliminated when the *Voyage* was published. This meditation also allowed the author to hold out to the inhabitants of metropolitan France a mirror in which they could contemplate a possible future for their country. The posthumous representation of America thus never serves solely to preserve the memory of a past period in order to embalm it in a book; the commemoration also stands as a warning. This specular relationship between New France and metropolitan France was reinforced by Chateaubriand through the homology he established between his countrymen and the Amerindians.

Portrait of the Frenchman as an Amerindian
According to Chateaubriand, human civilizations are subjected to an ineluctable historical law that dictates their progressive degeneration and leads eventually to

their disappearance. "Every society, he believes, including the Indian societies of America, is built on the ruins of a preceding human civilization that possessed its own rules and development, often remarkably complete," observes Reichler.[96] Chateaubriand finds the proof of the decline of the Amerindian tribes in the shrinking of their population and in a general corruption for which he blames the pernicious influence of the Europeans: "Thus, their civilization, in penetrating by commercial means into the Amerindian tribes, instead of developing their intelligence resulted in their degradation" (367). However, this phenomenon of degradation does not concern solely Amerindian civilization, since, several times in the *Voyage*, the fate of the French colonial empire in America and that of the Amerindian tribes are paired: "Thus, France disappeared from North America, like those Indian tribes with which they got on so well, and of which I observed a few remnants," Chateaubriand laments (372).

The good relations between the Amerindians and the French is a commonplace of colonial discourse on North America. Presented by Chateaubriand as the result of an affinity between the temperament of the Amerindians and that of his countrymen (363), it was in reality a consequence of the fragility of the first settlements in the New World, the French forming with the natives alliances that were essential to their survival. After noting the inability of the French to reduce to slavery a very large number of Amerindians, Miller concludes, "French settlements in the early years were small, male, seasonal, and incomplete, requiring reliance on and intermingling with native peoples. The colonial encounter in New France nativized the French perhaps as much as it Frenchified the Indians."[97]

This identification between the fate of the French empire in America and that of the Amerindian tribes has, however, a broader significance: it announces in its turn the decline of France, as if a historical chain linked the Amerindians to New France and New France to its metropolitan parent. In this respect, Chateaubriand reverses the meaning traditionally lent to the good relations between the Amerindians and the French. Whereas this so-called affinity between the two peoples was used to justify the integration of the Amerindians into the French empire, Chateaubriand turned it into a warning to his countrymen, concerned that they risked meeting a fate similar to that of those tribes whose members in times past called the king of France "our father." Chateaubriand emphasized, therefore, the existence of an irresistible historical process that had already affected the Amerindian tribes and which, soon, would finish its work in France itself, so that this country could very well become, in the not too distant future, the theater of a narrative in which a young traveler would describe the ruins of the Louvre and the demolished towers of Notre-Dame and would meditate on the progressive decline of French civilization while murmuring French words whose meaning had been long forgotten. The progressive decadence of the Amerindian tribes was thus far more than a simple example to which the situation of France could be compared: it was a reflection of the decline of France after the first empire.

Published three years before the end of the Restoration, the *Voyage en Amérique* proposed a veiled reflection on the history of France during the first half of the nineteenth century and, especially, on its ability to survive the break caused by the Revolution: "Between the lines, there is indeed an account of France's present state in 1826 that we need to read, a state that could constitute a stage in a definitive degeneration," observes Rossi.[98] In this history, Chateaubriand played a prominent role: after having been the French Minister in Berlin, then ambassador to London (1821), the representative of France at the Congress of Vienna (1822), and Minister of Foreign Affairs, he was dismissed on June 6, 1824, by the president of the Council of Ministers, Joseph de Villèle.[99] It was then that he undertook the publication of his *Œuvres complètes*, of which the *Voyage en Amérique* is a part. The recovery and rewriting of this text came therefore at a time when Chateaubriand was harboring particularly severe doubts about the future of the Restoration: "Caught between a new very republican world and an old very military empire, which suddenly shivered in the embrace of peace, Europe more than ever needs to understand its position in order to save itself. If we add exterior political errors to our internal political errors, the *decomposition* will occur more quickly: the cannon that we sometimes refuse to fire for a just cause, sooner or later we are forced to fire it for a deplorable one."[100]

"Decomposition": the term is typical of political thought according to which societies are like men and head imperceptibly toward their disappearance. Chateaubriand's faith in the future of the French monarchy weakened even more during the years following the publication of the *Voyage*. Lefort remarks that after 1830, the author of *Atala* was one of the rare writers of his time to become aware that the monarchy was just as incapable of coinciding with what it was before the Revolution as to continue on in the present.[101] Already in *Les Natchez*, Chateaubriand's distant horizon was "the fall of European civilization into a decadence that the Revolution was destined to consummate," as Fumaroli remarks.[102] The horizon is no less dark in the *Voyage*, where the example of the loss of New France serves as an omen for the mainland.

The use of the specular function in the *Voyage* is an additional point in common with the works of Crèvecœur and Lezay-Marnésia, in which the description of America is always associated with a depiction of France, whether it is to set it up as a model, as Crèvecœur does, or to present it as a refuge for the French fleeing the Revolution, as Lezay-Marnésia proposes. For France, America is a figure of otherness in which it is nonetheless possible to recognize itself, a double through which it can pass to return to itself.[103] This double has, in fact, a fundamental point in common with France: it shares the same future. In the chapter titled "Present State of the Savages of North America," Chateaubriand recalls the name that the Iroquois had given themselves: "Driven by the European populations toward the northwest of North America, the savage peoples come to die, by a strange destiny, on the very shore on which they disembarked centuries ago to take possession of America. In the Iroquois language, the Indians called themselves *men of forever*, ONGOUE-ONOUE: these *men of forever* no longer exist, and the foreigners will soon leave only the soil of their tomb to the legitimate heirs of a whole world" (359).

The shore of North America is both a point of departure and of arrival, the place of birth of a civilization and the place it puts in its final appearance. Similarly, do the peoples of Europe who cross the Atlantic not have to fear, in several centuries or in a shorter period of time, the extinction that has struck their predecessors in North America? The earth is covered with civilizations that aspire to immortality and nonetheless perish one after the other. Of course, the decline of the Amerindian tribes had an exterior cause—the conquest of their territory by the colonists—whose equivalent is not to be found in the Restoration. Nevertheless, Chateaubriand observes in the *Itinéraire de Paris à Jérusalem* (1811) that the destruction of great civilizations may have a variety of origins: "Athens and Sparta did not fall for the same reasons that led to the downfall of Rome."[104] Following in the footsteps of Montesquieu, who had studied the roots of the decadence of Rome,[105] Chateaubriand reflected on the progressive decline of Greece, which he explained by internal factors, in particular its moral corruption and lack of political ambition after the victory of Sparta over Athens: "In its turn, triumphant Lacedaemon, like Athens, found in its own institutions the first cause of its ruin."[106] Likewise, the decline of France during the Restoration also had causes inherent to its own social organization, in particular the development of what Chateaubriand calls, in a text from 1818, "the principle of self-interest."[107] Variable, diverse, this shortsighted principal "can only be the shifting base of an edifice of a few days," whereas the one he opposes to it, "the principle of duty," is the most stable foundation on which a political regime can be built, since it encourages individuals to devote themselves to the general good. In Chateaubriand's opinion, the victory of "the principle of self-interest" over "the principle of duty" is a regrettable novelty introduced into French political life by the Restoration, since the French Revolution—despite the numerous atrocities that occurred during that period—saw many examples of noble sacrifices ("these horrible times are also the occasion for acts of great dedication").[108] Alternatively, the first Empire—which Chateaubriand disparaged mercilessly—partially redeemed itself by inspiring in the French an unquenchable thirst for glory and by keeping alive the aristocratic tradition of honor ("Buonaparte charmed people by the prestige of his glory; and everything that is great bears within itself the principle of a law").[109] On the contrary, the rapid proliferation of the "principle of self-interest" during the first years of the Restoration was responsible for an increase in moral corruption that risked bringing it down: "[T]his principle of self-interest, upon which they want to base our government, corrupted the people more in the space of three years than the whole Revolution in a quarter century."[110] Whether it has internal or external causes, the decadence of societies is an inevitable historical phenomenon, and if it can no doubt be slowed down, Chateaubriand believes it impossible to stop or reverse it: all civilizations degenerate and their last vestige—the national language—will disappear in its turn. Amerindians, Americans, and Frenchmen of France and America form, in spite of their differences, a group united by a common destiny: in the *Voyage*, they all intone the common requiem of their ineluctable disappearance.

Ultimately, Chateaubriand's discourse on America allows us to deconstruct the meanings suggested by the expression "New World." This formula presupposes, in fact, that America is second in relation to Europe, since the latter "discovered" it: more recent, it is also less civilized, as bears witness the vastness of the forests that cover it. For Chateaubriand, the predominance of nature in America does not indicate a lesser degree of civilization in relation to Europe: it is, on the contrary, the sign that time has accomplished its destructive work for a longer length of time, permitting the forests to grow and cover the remnants of forgotten cultures. Such is the conclusion he is led to by the discovery of some Amerindian ruins on an island: "What people had lived on this island? Its name, race, the time of its existence, everything is unknown; it lived perhaps when this particular world that was hiding it in its bosom was still unknown to the three other quarters of the earth. The silence of this people is perhaps contemporary with the noise made by great European nations fallen silent in their turn, leaving nothing of themselves but ruins."[111]

By reversing the order of temporal precedence traditionally established between Europe and America, Chateaubriand nonetheless established an underlying continuity between the peoples of these two continents. The silence of the Amerindian tribes foreshadows that of the European nations who, after having been in the spotlight, will disappear in their turn from the memory of mankind: in the mirror of America may be read the future of France, and Chateaubriand will give a yet darker illustration of this specular relationship in the *Mémoires d'outre-tombe*.

The Reenchantment of America: The *Mémoires d'outre-tombe* (1848)

AESTHETICS AND POLITICS OF CONVERGENCE: FROM AMERICA TO THE ORIENT

Farewells to Analogy
In completing the books VI to VIII of the *Mémoires d'outre-tombe*, Chateaubriand brought to the surface a new island in the archipelago of his American texts.[112]

The *Voyage en Amérique* exhibited a curious survival of cosmography, a discourse combining heterogeneous textual fragments in order to show the harmony of divine creation based on correspondences hidden from the uninitiated.[113] The American books of the *Mémoires*, for their part, throw off the vestiges of cosmographic thought by producing an original form of representation of the New World. Chateaubriand dismissed the analogical approach at the beginning of the relation of his journey to the United States, developing in its place an aesthetic of convergence of America and the Orient. How is the farewell to analogy effected in the *Mémoires*? And to what extent does the posthumous representation of America allow us to reflect on the future of the French colonial empire?

Analogy is an effective, albeit dangerous, means of evoking what has not yet been seen or thought. Dangerous, indeed, because the inherent risk of analogy consists in identifying the unknown to the known in order to ward off the distress provoked by the confrontation with otherness. Let us return a moment to the period of André Thevet that was referred to earlier, when European travelers brought back to their countries the first notion of plants and animals foreign to their countrymen. Thevet described the tapir to his French readers in the following terms: "Its fur is reddish like that of certain mules or cows over here; and that is why Christians over there [in Brazil] call such animals cows, since they only differ from cows in that they do not have horns; but, in fact, it seems to me that they resemble donkeys as much as cows."[114] This passage demonstrates the difficulty facing a traveler when he attempts to give his contemporaries an initial notion of an unfamiliar object. Among the devices at his disposal, analogy enables him to introduce an unknown object by comparing it to another with which the reader is already familiar. However, a new object is not only the counterpart of an object that is familiar to the reader, with the exception of a few obvious differences; a whole series of comparisons is required to describe it. The hybridization of the new object is the first consequence of the analogical method: the tapir is only conceivable in the form of a composite image, combining fragments of reality borrowed from a variety of sources. Moreover, a second consequence of analogy is to "reduce otherness to resemblance."[115] The series of comparisons required to familiarize the reader with the new object eventually blurs its specificity: its difference is progressively obliterated as similarities with familiar objects enable the mind to grasp it.

In the American books of the *Mémoires d'outre-tombe*, Chateaubriand distanced himself from the practice of analogy, a device that was omnipresent in his travel narratives, and particularly in the *Itinéraire de Paris à Jérusalem* (1811).[116] This symbolic dismissal is expressed implicitly in the tale of his crossing of the Atlantic. Chateaubriand recalls a certain Pierre Villeneuve and the conversations they had. Villeneuve was a man of considerable experience and "had served in India under the Bailli de Suffren and in America under the comte d'Estaing; he was involved in myriad matters."[117] He answers the chevalier de Chateaubriand's questions as an heir to the cosmographers of the sixteenth century:

> I asked him how the people were dressed, the form of the trees, the color of the earth and the sky, the taste of the fruit; if the pineapples were better than the peaches, the palm trees more beautiful than the oaks. *He explained all of that to me by comparisons with things that I knew*: the palm tree *was* a large cabbage, an Indian's dress that of my grandmother; the camels resembled donkeys with a hump; all the peoples of the Orient, and especially the Chinese, *were* cowards and thieves. Villeneuve was from Brittany, and *we never failed to finish* with praise for the incomparable beauty of our motherland. (1:436; emphasis added)

This summary of their conversations is both an implementation and an implicit questioning of the analogical approach. The European points of reference identified with the unfamiliar realities of the New World have an intentionally grotesque quality ("large cabbage," "my grandmother's dress," "donkey with a hump"). To demonstrate the weakness of the analogical method that establishes correspondences between unconnected realities on the sole basis of a superficial resemblance, Chateaubriand eschewed the use of the logical element of comparisons, the adverb "like," repeated many times by Thevet in the excerpt quoted previously. He lays bare the latent logic of analogy, which consists in concluding that two things are indissociable on the basis of an apparent similarity by identifying the European referent with the American object by the use of the auxiliary "to be." By asserting that the palm tree *is* a large cabbage, he demonstrates by a reductio ad absurdum the inability of analogy to introduce adequately an object absent from the reader's own universe. In addition, we recognize in Chateaubriand's "donkey with humps" a distant descendant of Thevet's "donkey-cow," unless the author of the *Mémoires d'outre-tombe* was recalling here the *tapiroussou*, an animal "half cow half donkey" according to Jean de Léry, or of the Egyptian hippopotamus that Herodotus described as a cross between an ox and a horse.[118]

This implementation of the analogical approach leads to its questioning, because Chateaubriand was suggesting that it gave a pseudoscientific basis for the ethnocentrism of the person who was using it. The conversation with Pierre Villeneuve finishes, in fact, with generalizations that we would not hesitate today to call xenophobic: "all the peoples of the Orient, and especially the Chinese, were cowards and thieves." Thus, the result of the analogical approach is to compare peoples and produce conclusions that, far from astutely analyzing their differences, shows how they are supposedly similar. When he finishes his generalizations, the conclusion of Chateaubriand's travel companion is not surprising:

"Villeneuve was from Brittany, and we never failed to finish with praise for the incomparable beauty of our motherland." The expression "we never failed to finish" denotes the mechanical character of an ethnocentric judgment derived from a reasoning based on analogy. The travelers—who had not even yet arrived at their destination at this point in the narrative—have already decreed the superiority of their own country over those that one of them had not even yet visited. With consummate art, Chateaubriand demonstrated the inability of analogical discourse to portray its object adequately and, without making a single comment on the conversations he has just summarized, suggests through irony his critical reservations.

It would be regrettable to only see in this brief exchange an example of the author's humor. Its placement at the juncture between the travel narrative and the arrival in America endows it with a programmatic function. Chateaubriand announces here, indirectly, that he will not use analogy as a means of description of the New World: the posthumous representation of America in books VI to VIII of the *Mémoires d'outre-tombe* features rather an aesthetic of convergence.

Spatial and Temporal Convergence

In the *Mémoires d'outre-tombe*, Chateaubriand adopts a synoptic vision on landscapes as on the panorama of his life.[119] An explorer of his own memory, Chateaubriand assumes this perspective when he seeks to account for his individual history in order to emphasize the secret relationship between the apparently unconnected events of his life: looking down from the summit of his life, advanced in age and approaching death, the author is able to establish parallels that he could not perceive when, younger and playing the role of his own life, he only had the limited perspective of a traveler tracing his path as best he could. Critics have already emphasized the existence of the parallels that abound in Chateaubriand's work, not only between individuals (himself and Napoleon, Napoleon and Washington) and countries (France and Greece) but also between different moments of his existence.[120] In a phrase that has remained famous, the author presents thus his typical bent of mind: "My memory constantly opposes my journeys to my journeys, mountains to mountains, rivers to rivers, forests to forests, and my life destroys my life" (4:157).

The first view of America was the pretext for one of these overlaps, sudden convergences of two distinct moments and places provoked by an experience of the author: "Two days after this accident, we sighted land. My heart leapt when the captain pointed it out to me: America! It was just barely discernable in the top of a few maples sticking up from the water. The palm trees at the mouth of the Nile beckoned to me from the shore of Egypt in the same manner" (1:454–55). This is the narrator of the *Mémoires*, writing after the journey to the Orient related in the *Itinéraire de Paris à Jérusalem*, offering a comparison that the traveler was incapable of in 1791, since he was not to travel to Egypt until October 1806; reciprocally, Egypt reflects in its turn America, as also witnessed in the *Itinéraire*.[121] One of the most revealing examples of this memorial operation by collision of memories takes place in another travel narrative by Chateaubriand, the *Voyage au Mont-Blanc* (1805):

> Finally, the odor of pine is aromatic and agreeable; it has a particular charm for me, especially since I smelled it from the sea, twenty leagues from the Virginia coast. It therefore always awakens in my mind the idea of this New World that was announced to me by a perfumed breath, this beautiful sky, these brilliant seas where the perfume from the forests was wafted to me on the morning breeze; and as everything is linked in my memory, it calls also back to mind the feelings of regret and hope that occupied me when, leaning on the railing of the ship, I was dreaming of the motherland I had lost and of this wilderness I was going to find."[122]

To achieve the juncture between two memories, a common term is necessary. In the *Voyage au Mont-Blanc*, it is the odor of the pine tree; in the *Mémoires* and the *Itinéraire*, the sight of trees and pyramids. This common term calls forth, uncontrollably, a memory of the past in the present moment. The verb "to awaken" used in the passage just quoted suggests that an individual moves forward in time, bringing with him buried memories that are just waiting for an event that will trigger their arousal, intact. However, it is not just a question of confronting two memories, the odor of pine in the Pyrenees recalling that which perfumed the coasts of Virginia, and this scent only. Through this memory, a whole past affective universe rushes back into mind, the perfume only being a trigger: Proust was not mistaken in recognizing in the *Mémoires* the intuition of the phenomenon of "involuntary memory," whose complexity would be explored in *In Search of Lost Time*.[123] In the excerpt of the *Voyage au Mont-Blanc*, the "feelings of regret and hope" that Chateaubriand experienced upon the discovery of America come rushing back to him; the *Itinéraire*, instead, indicates the return of his "frame of mind" at the moment of his discovery of the pyramids of Egypt.[124] When the conjunction of two memories occurs, a former attitude arises to color the present frame of mind of the author, producing an affective simultaneity of discrete moments in the past and the opportunity to meditate on what, in his life and in the general course of the world, has changed between the remembered moment and the instant of its later recollection.

The Logic of Convergence

At first glance, a purely personal logic presides over the chain of memories in the mind of the author. If the odor of the pine trees in Virginia and that of the pine trees in the Pyrenees are intrinsically comparable, the maple of the New World has no objective similarities with the palm trees of the Nile, any more than the ruins in Ohio resemble the pyramids in Egypt. This detail shows an essential difference between analogy and convergence. Analogy is based on apparent similarities on which people in general can agree: to return to the example found in the work by André Thevet, the morphology of the tapir presents objective resemblances with that of the donkey and the cow that are borne out upon close examination. Contrary to analogy, spatial and temporal convergences do not result from the revelation of points in common that can be confirmed by simple observation. Indeed, convergence is rendered possible by an object that plays the role of an intermediary: the odor of the pine tree links the present moment and the memory of the Virginia coast. However, it is for Chateaubriand alone that this scent brings together two periods of his life, since he associates it with memories that are uniquely his. While analogy can be generalized, convergence remains a personal phenomenon. Moreover, analogy is a device at the service of dissemination of knowledge: it serves to introduce to others an unfamiliar object—at the cost, it is true, of an omission of subtle differences between the objects compared in order to emphasize their similarities. Alternatively, convergence remains restricted to the awareness of an individual in whom periods of life meet and merge. A brief detour in the thought of Spinoza will help us to further clarify the logic it obeys.

In proposition XLIV of the second part of his *Ethics*, Spinoza studies the mechanism by which two distinct objects appear simultaneously in the mind of an individual.[125] The "soul" of the subject—to use Spinoza's vocabulary—conceives of the existence of a necessary relationship between two objects while the establishment of this connection results from the repetition of a situation ruled by chance. In the course of proposition XLIV, Spinoza gives the example of a child who saw Pierre in the morning, Paul at noon, Simeon in the evening, and Pierre again the next morning. The child, he says, will ultimately associate each of these three men with the respective moments of the day when he had met them. However, although he conceives of it as a necessary relationship, this relationship established between Pierre and the beginning of the day only exists for the child. Likewise, the link that unites Ohio and the pyramids of Egypt, the shores of the Nile and those of Virginia, the forests of the New World and the desert of Sabba is contingent, for it is only for Chateaubriand that there is a connection between these spaces, a connection established by a common term (pyramids, trees, horses, etc.). These secret springs that govern the memory of Chateaubriand suggest to Riffaterre a typology of memories: "There are thus two types of recollections in Chateaubriand: the memory that is related to general truths of philosophical meditation, and the memory that, on the contrary, focuses on the authenticity of personal experience. The latter, which we could call affective memory, is nothing other than the Proustian memory: its mechanism is the sudden superimposition of a current sensation and an old recollection."[126]

Nonetheless, the distinction established by Riffaterre between "philosophical memories" and "affective memories" minimizes the collective significance that his personal "recollections" hold for him. In fact, the spatial and temporal convergences observed in the *Mémoires d'outre-tombe* do not obey solely an affective logic that would permit us to oppose them to memories related to "general truths of philosophical meditation." In the *Mémoires*, the singular is not opposed to the collective, given that the personal memories of the author are endowed with historical and political dimensions. What is the collective value of the convergences in the American books of the *Mémoires*? What political role do they confer on the commemorative representation of an America foundering at the turn of the eighteenth century?

From America to the Middle East

Before conceiving the project of the *Mémoires d'outre-tombe*, Chateaubriand had begun the *Mémoires de ma vie*, whose ambition was to "account for oneself to oneself," to explain his "inexplicable heart," in which "most of the sentiments have remained buried."[127] The *Mémoires d'outre-tombe* distinguish themselves from this original autobiographical project inspired by Montaigne by establishing a homological relationship between the history of the author and that of his epoch: "If I were destined to live on, I would represent in my person, represented in my memoirs, the principles, ideas, events, and catastrophes, in short, the epic of my time, especially since I saw a world begin and finish, and the opposing characteristics of this ending and this beginning are mingled with my opinions."[128] The specificity of the autobiographical enterprise of Chateaubriand consists in this voluntary superimposition of the history of the hero of the *Mémoires* and that of his time, such that the evolution of one embodies metaphorically that of the other.[129] The hero of the *Mémoires* is more than the contemporary of a historical evolution that he can report on for posterity: his destiny is described as the symbolic incarnation of a period of the history of the world. As Cavallin phrases it, "Not only the action of the historical person, but also the character, official identity, personal biography, childhood, adulthood, and old age, the history and personal identity of the man of the *Mémoires* are historical . . . , that is, capable of representing or symbolizing the history of human destinies in the age when he lived."[130] Interpreting his own life as if it were a myth before writing it as such, Chateaubriand did not attribute to chance the coincidences he discovered in the various events of his existence but interpreted them as signs of a global journey. This symbolic dimension of the experiences of the hero of the *Mémoires* is revealed, in particular, in the analysis of the following passage, whose earlier version in the *Voyage* was briefly referred to above:

> I had to send the Dutchman to Fort Niagara to seek a permit to enter the territory that was under British control; I did so with a heavy heart, because I remembered that France had once dominated both Upper and Lower Canada. My guide returned with the permit: I still have it; it is signed "*Captain Gordon*." Is it not peculiar that I found the same English name on the door of my cell in Jerusalem? "Thirteen pilgrims had written their names on the door inside the room: the first was named Charles Lombard, and he was in Jerusalem in 1669; the last is John Gordon, and the date of his passage is 1804." (1:487; emphasis original)

A recollection of Jerusalem arises during a retrospective narration devoted to the region of Niagara Falls. The convergence between these two periods is provoked by the mention of the English name "Gordon." In his memory of America, as in the one left by Jerusalem, this name is associated with an obstacle: it designates the captain of whom Chateaubriand is obligated to request the authorization to continue his journey on a land that formerly belonged to France; it then appears to him on the door of a cell. In the second case, the name "Gordon" is the last one on a list that begins with a French surname: just as the French preceded the English in Canada, the Jerusalem list suggests that they were also the first to reach the holy city where the English have now succeeded them. The spatial and temporal convergence in this excerpt allowed Chateaubriand to indicate a direction of the history of his time: he points out the continuity between the French colonial enterprise in the New World and in the Orient and designates the English as the adversaries who posed an obstacle to French expansion in the Mediterranean basin as they had already done in America. More broadly, if we accept the idea that the *Mémoires* relate, through the destiny of their hero, the epic of a passage between two centuries or, as Cavallin says, "the myth of this palingenetic passage from an old abolished world to a new world to come," it becomes necessary to reevaluate the recurrent convergences in books VI to VIII. These sudden convergences between discrete places and periods are endowed with a value that is less strictly subjective than the associations of ideas in Spinozan philosophy: they have a collective and political significance.

The story of captain Gordon is far from being the only example of a correlation between the two great journeys that Chateaubriand related in the American books of the *Mémoires* and in the *Itinéraire*. These two works evoke frequent parallels between America and the Orient, and allow Chateaubriand, as Dobie remarks, to "create an imaginary comparison between his own subjectivity and the world, such that the circular completeness of his studies and of his life cycle correspond to that of the history of the world."[131] As we saw in the course of our study of the *Voyage en Amérique*, Chateaubriand deplores the disappearance of the French colonies of North America, for they would not only have represented a considerable economic advantage for metropolitan France but would also have facilitated the expansion of the French language overseas.[132] French colonial ambitions, however, after suffering major setbacks in North America and Haiti, turned at the beginning of the nineteenth century toward a new space: Africa and, in particular, North Africa. Between 1798 and 1801, France undertook the Egyptian campaign under the command of Bonaparte, followed by that of his successors. After the assassination of Jean-Baptiste Kléber on June 14, 1800, and the Turkish offensive of August 31, 1801, the French expeditionary corps returned home. The colonial projects of France in North Africa were, however, far from being abandoned at this time, as the beginning of the colonization of Algeria in 1830 clearly proves.

In the course of his political career, Chateaubriand was an ardent partisan of French expansion in the Orient. In a speech given before the Chamber of Peers in 1816, he declared himself in favor of a new "crusade" in order to terminate the enslavement of Christians by the "Barbary powers."[133] Since the slave trade had just been abolished by the English Parliament, it was urgent, Chateaubriand claimed, to lead a Christian-inspired initiative to "put an end to white slavery."[134] Like Alexis de Tocqueville, Chateaubriand would also applaud with great enthusiasm the Algiers expedition (3:449) and consider the conquest of Algeria as one of the major accomplishments of the restored monarchy (4:310).[135] The French colonial project thus received his unconditional support, whether it took place across the Atlantic or in the region of the Mediterranean basin. Dobie observes, in this respect, the superimposition of the evolution of the French colonial enterprise and the personal experience of the author: "It goes without saying that the travels of Chateaubriand correspond to the migrations of French colonization; France had lost her American colonies in 1763, with the exception of Louisiana, but prompted by Talleyrand, it began to establish itself in the Levant, a region that promised to be just as receptive."[136] The goal of these "correspondences" between the journeys of Chateaubriand and the displacement of French ambitions was to emphasize the continuity of the colonial enterprise from one space to the next and to announce through the portrayal of the past the potential of the future. The bond uniting these two colonial projects, however, is not only expressed metaphorically in the *Mémoires*. When he describes Niagara Falls, Chateaubriand compares explicitly the French missionaries in America to Napoleon's soldiers in the Orient: "Our priests embraced the beautiful vistas of America and consecrated them with their blood; our soldiers applauded the ruins of Thebes and presented arms in Andalusia: all the genius of France is in the joint militia of our camps and our altars" (1:490). In this passage, we find a pairing of two projects of conquest (spiritual and military) on two spaces (America and the Levant) for the greater glory of a single nation: France. By embodying in his personal journey the future destinies of his country, Chateaubriand designated the Orient as the new area of legitimate expansion of France after the disappearance of its empire in North America. In doing so, he mixed inextricably the commemorative representation of a past America and a programmatic political discourse. The convergence aesthetics developed in the *Mémoires d'outre-tombe* presents the Orient as the compensation offered to France for the loss of its North American empire. It compares discrete spaces in order to underline the extension of French ambition from America to Algeria and only evokes the colors and fragrances of the Orient in the middle of the landscapes of the New World to balance the loss of an empire with the promise of another that France would need to take control of and preserve in a more sustained manner. By emphasizing the void that the disappearance of its empire across the Atlantic had left in the history of France, the posthumous representation of America designated the Orient as a second chance for it to cover itself with glory and shine throughout the world.

THE DISSEMINATION OF THE SIXTEENTH CENTURY

The End of the Concordance
Claude Lévi-Strauss was an attentive reader of Chateaubriand. If he readily recognized the debt he owed to Rousseau, the shadow of the author of *Atala* also hovers over *Tristes tropiques*.[137] The elegiac style and sumptuous sentences, the twilight vision of an Amerindian humanity in its final gleaming before a clearly irremediable decadence, the inclusion by the older author of textual fragments written by the person he was at the time of his travels, and even the functioning of his memory by sudden temporal convergences—there are numerous characteristics of the unclassifiable work signed by Lévi-Strauss in 1955 that recall the writing of Chateaubriand.[138] Among the multiple echoes between their works, none can be heard so clearly as that of the regret concerning an original experience of alterity, an epiphany that never occurs twice and after which the modern ethnographer pines in viewing his travels as pale copies of those that had been accomplished centuries before: "I would have liked to have lived in the time of *real* journeys, when one could see in all of its splendor a spectacle not yet spoiled, contaminated, damned; not having crossed this area myself but like Bernier, Tavernier, Manucci...."[139] However, Lévi-Strauss was not frozen in a melancholic posture, observing that the innumerable losses that the ethnographer is justified in regretting—these customs, celebrations, and beliefs of which nothing remains other than the fragmentary testimony of their predecessors—are to some extent

compensated for by the knowledge and curiosity with which the modern traveler is armed when he observes so-called primitive societies. Losses and gains balance out in this alternative that the ethnographer cannot escape: "sometimes an ancient traveler, confronted with a prodigious spectacle of which he understood nearly nothing—or still worse, that moved him to mockery and disgust; other times a modern traveler, seeking the remnants of a world that has disappeared."[140] These reflections were capable of dispelling some of the regrets felt by the most recent visitor of the New World, since his predecessors could only contemplate with the most rudimentary optical equipment the most shimmering and diverse spectacle that was offered to them. *Tristes tropiques* is marked both by a strong melancholy for a mythical time, that of the beginnings, but seeks nevertheless to eschew nostalgic lamentation by assigning to ethnography a new object, "the study of modes of organization of the sentient experience—and that is what Lévi-Strauss will explore in *La Pensée sauvage* and *Mythologiques*."[141]

More than a century earlier, Chateaubriand was also turning toward the period of the first contact between Europe and the New World, both to lament not having been its contemporary and to seek the means of reviving it: "The Canadians are no longer how they were depicted by Cartier, Champlain, Lahontan, Lescarbot, Laffiteau, Charlevoix, and the *Lettres édifiantes*: the sixteenth century and the beginning of the seventeenth were still the time of outsized imagination and naïve mores; the marvel of the one reflected a virgin nature, and the candor of the others reproduced the simplicity of the savage" (1:495). The verb "reflect" underscores the harmony that formerly existed between the European imagination and American nature. In the sixteenth century, the imagination of the travelers was capable of fictions whose marvels equaled those that nature still offered, in this period when human activity had not yet altered it. Likewise, the simplicity of Chateaubriand's predecessors in America was just like that of the first inhabitants of the New World: the traveler was scarcely different from the Amerindian, for both of them were inclined to believe in the existence of monsters that would not have been out of place in the *Odyssey* (495). The fragile miracle of this harmony between the observer and the observed, still possible in the sixteenth and at the beginning of the seventeenth centuries, had definitively dissipated at the time of the writing of the *Mémoires*. Henceforth, the traveler could no longer escape the second paradox of the New World: he always comes too late when he arrives in America in search of a virgin nature and a new world—in which he discovers a society whose advanced state of civilization reminds him painfully of Europe.

Chateaubriand explained the disappointment that awaited the Europeans in America by the considerable increase of knowledge available on its subject: "[T]he interest in travel narratives diminishes each day, as the number of travelers increases; the philosophical spirit has put an end to the marvels of the wilderness," he observed in the article devoted to the explorer Alexander Mackenzie.[142]

The "philosophical spirit" that accumulates and organizes knowledge on the American continent was directly opposed to the "outsized imagination" of the sixteenth century, just as the "modern scholars" and the first European travelers in America were set in opposition.[143] While the spirit of the Enlightenment considered the increase of knowledge to be one of the instruments of human progress, Chateaubriand felt that it accomplished simultaneously a work of destruction, since it promoted a rational mundaneness by reducing the place left to dreaming and imagination. He directly foreshadowed the analyses of Max Weber in his studies of religious sociology and Marcel Gauchet in *Le Désenchantement du monde (The Disenchantment of the World)*.[144]

The term "disenchanted," precisely, was used by Chateaubriand when he cited in his article devoted to the discovery of the Northwest Passage an alexandrine by his friend Fontanes: "The disenchanted woods have lost their miracles."[145] It is to this disenchantment that Chateaubriand opposed the charms of his writing in books VI to VIII of the *Mémoires d'outre-tombe*. Indeed, the problem that he met consisted in representing the New World as he would have liked to discover it and consistent with the image bequeathed by the European travelers of the sixteenth century, instead of representing it as he had seen it, that is, as a country whose reality disappointed one's desires and deceived one's expectations. In other words, it was incumbent upon him to provide an analeptic representation of the United States.

An analeptic representation of North America accomplishes a double flashback: the narrator remembers both his journey and an earlier period whose recollection allows him to reenchant the America that he formerly knew. In the case of Chateaubriand, the analeptic representation of the New World permitted him to merge together the memories of his journey in 1791 with the unsatiated dream of a trip that would have taken place during the Renaissance. The alternative evoked by Lévi-Strauss—between the travelers of yore partially blind to the prodigious spectacle before them and their successors who, better able to appreciate it, discover it nonetheless after its contamination by the emissaries of their own culture—was overcome by Chateaubriand, who dreamed that he was a modern traveler transported through the magic of literature to the very heart of this bygone age. Thus, the analeptic representation of America in the *Mémoires d'outre-tombe* presupposes an aesthetic operation in which the choice of vocabulary is a critical dimension: it is in the choice of the signifiers, in the materiality of the writing, that Chateaubriand's effort to reenchant his tardy voyage was expressed.

The Logic of the Signifiers
In books VI to VIII of the *Mémoires*, Chateaubriand uses a vocabulary belonging to the sixteenth century and provides, at key moments of his narrative, quotes borrowed from French authors of the Renaissance. His posthumous

America represents an attempt to revive this past period: because he had not belonged to those naive and brave Frenchmen who tread upon a continent unknown to their countrymen, Chateaubriand availed himself of the aesthetic of the sixteenth century to resuscitate, as Lévi-Strauss calls it, a "crucial moment of modern thought," the moment when, "thanks to the great discoveries, a mankind that believed itself complete and perfect suddenly received, like a counter-revelation, the announcement that it wasn't alone."[146] Described as "the supreme reward" by Lévi-Strauss, the original experience that the ethnographer tries to reproduce in being "the first white man to enter an indigenous community"[147] remains inaccessible to Chateaubriand, who had not journeyed very far into the American wilderness and had only met tribes that had been in contact with European colonists for ages. While the direct experience of a journey back in time remains possible—although it is infinitely rare and always threatened—for the enterprising ethnographer who discovers a village "still intact," for Chateaubriand this ideal experience was necessarily mediated by the literary reinvention of a journey completed long ago and that he wished still more distant. It was thus to writing that he entrusted the task of implementing a brief abolition of time in order to transport himself to the period of the first French gaze upon America.

The use of a vocabulary belonging to a past state of the French language is relatively rare in the *Mémoires d'outre-tombe*: "If we consider the whole work, the total number of rare words, archaisms, technical terms, and out-and-out neologisms is modest: a little more than a hundred; and for the most part this batch appears *in toto* in the twelve first books and in the sections of the 4th part written between 1830 and 1833," observes Mourot.[148] These anachronistic terms are virtually absent from the *Voyage en Amérique*. A comparison of certain passages of this narrative with their rewriting in the *Mémoires* reveals distinct and significant vocabulary choices.

In order to describe the movement of a sign hung on a branch, Chateaubriand uses the verb "to swing" (*balancer*) in the *Voyage*.[149] However, he prefers the verb "to shake" or "to wave" (*brandiller*)—an old term that Maurice Scève uses in "Le Microcosme"—to depict the same scene in the *Mémoires*: "Since English manners follow the English everywhere, after crossing countries where there was no sign of inhabitants, I noticed the sign of an inn that was shaking [*brandillait*] on the branch of a tree" (1:484).[150] What is the logic that dictates this use of terms belonging to the language of the sixteenth century? Chateaubriand himself answered this question: "Through a bizarre assembly, there are two men in me, the man of earlier times and the man of the present: it happens that the old French language and the modern French language are both natural to me; lacking one of them, a part of my ideas was lacking as well; I therefore created a few words and rejuvenated a few others;

but there is no affectation, and I was careful to only use the expression that came to me spontaneously."[151]

This passage reveals that the use of anachronistic words and neologisms depended on what came into the author's mind naturally. If there is any pastiche of the "old French language," it is not the result of a deliberate choice: following a long immersion in works from the Renaissance, Chateaubriand acquired a perfect mastery of their lexicon, whose terms came to mind of their own accord when he tried to express a specific nuance of his thought. In books VI to VIII of the *Mémoires*, he uses terms from the sixteenth century when he strives to portray the New World, indicating by this fact the incompleteness of a representation of America that would make no reference to this period.

In large part devoted to the story of the crossing, book VI displays a specific vocabulary: it unites maritime and technical terms, as well as a certain number of Latinisms. Conversely, terms belonging to the vocabulary of the sixteenth century appear in Chateaubriand's writing when he relates his journey by land in America, and, revealingly, beginning with the chapter that follows the depiction of the cities that he hastened to leave. Chateaubriand uses, notably, terms that are characteristic of the poetry of the Renaissance: "We camped in prairies adorned [*peinturées*] with butterflies and flowers" (485). This "peinturées" that is found in the poetry of Ronsard's contemporaries, adds a light sixteenth-century sheen to a scene of nature from the end of the eighteenth century, sorely needed to restore it to its original splendor and enhance its colors.[152] Following the same logic, the verb "s'enguirlander" ("to embellish") and the substantive "affiquets" ("jewels," "ornaments"), employed a little further on (509), contribute to the Renaissance ornamentation of a landscape, increasing its attractiveness at a time when civilization had already disfigured it.

Elsewhere, Chateaubriand seeks to recapture a past psychological state through the use of an anachronistic term. Such is the function of the substantive "vastitude" ("vastness") in the following sentence: "Mackenzie, and after him several others, to the benefit of the United States and Great Britain, made conquests over the "vastitude" of America that I had dreamed of to expand my native land" (469). This word was used in the translation of the *Sermons de Guerricus* (1540) by Jean de Gaigny and was hardly seen again before its reappearance in the dictionaries of the nineteenth century.[153] The form is based on the term "vastité," which we find in Du Bellay in the *Défense et illustration de la langue française* and in Montaigne in the *Essais*.[154] While we would have expected the term "immensité" in the *Mémoires*, "vastitude" expresses more intensely the idea of a limitless space. Indeed, the similarity of the words "vastitude" and "vastité" adds the connotation of "desert," since "vastité" comes from the Latin word *vastitas*, which carries this meaning. Its use allowed Chateaubriand to offer an echo of the old French language spoken by the contemporaries of Michel de Montaigne, who is evoked, precisely, in the seventh book of the *Mémoires*. Through this anachronistic term, he attempted to revive the voice and psychological state of the first French travelers, fascinated by the mysterious depths of the American spaces in which they sought a passage to China, while recalling simultaneously the irremediable disappearance of the New World as they had known it.

The use of the verb "s'énaser" ("to bump into"; literally, "to hit one's nose against") plays a similar role in the following sentence: "Alas! I imagined I was alone in this forest where I walked so proudly; suddenly "je viens m'énaser contre" [I bumped into] a shed!" (1:473). Chateaubriand uses it during a crucial scene in the story of his journey. After escaping the American cities, here he is, finally, in the forests where he thinks he has found the state of nature evoked by Rousseau. Well, the young chevalier soon finds himself confronted with a stupefying scene: he meets a Frenchman playing a violin and giving dancing lessons to some Amerindians. Chateaubriand concludes the chapter with this statement: "Wasn't this a crushing blow for a disciple of Rousseau, this introduction to primitive life by a ball given by the former kitchen boy of General Rochambeau to some Iroquois? I had a great urge to laugh, but I was in fact sorely humiliated" (1:474).

As Berchet notes, however, in his edition of the *Mémoires* (1:474), Rousseau had experienced a similar misadventure himself: Chateaubriand was, in fact, well within the lineage of Rousseau that he thought he was refuting when he met a disappointment in which could be read, between the lines, as the decline of "primitive life." Indeed, Rousseau relates in the seventh walk of the *Rêveries du promeneur solitaire* (*Reveries of the Solitary Walker*, 1782) his euphoria at the idea of having found "a refuge unknown to the whole universe"—before discovering, not far from the place where he was standing, a stocking factory. In Chateaubriand's text, the use of the term "s'énaser" connects the dream of a virgin nature such as the travelers of the sixteenth century knew it and the brutal discovery of a mark of civilization demonstrating that the state of nature was only an illusion.

This hiatus between dream and reality, between an imagination nourished by books and a period that no longer permits its blooming, recalls irresistibly the figure of Don Quixote, briefly mentioned by Chateaubriand in the *Mémoires* (1:377–78) and a parodic double to which he was maliciously compared.[155] Like Cervantes's hero, his brain stuffed with books on chivalry and battling windmills, Chateaubriand set out for America, his mind ablaze with grandiose visions drawn from travel narratives, only to collide—in both the physical and metaphorical senses of the term in the aforementioned example—with a reality that bitterly disappointed his expectations. But just as Cervantes presents a Don Quixote who persists in harboring chivalrous hopes in a world devoid of magic, Chateaubriand describes himself as another Knight of La Mancha in

America, chasing the evanescent dream of a New World remained intact since the sixteenth century. When everything contradicted the illusion in which they were absorbed, the traveler—and years later the author—continued to favor what they had desired to see instead of what they did in fact observe, and only the subtle irony of Chateaubriand leads us to understand that he was not a dupe of his own dream. Ultimately, the effect of the anachronistic terms that flow from Chateaubriand's pen was to unite the sixteenth century (the time of the quotations), the eighteenth century (the time of the action), and the nineteenth century (the time of the narration) within the *Mémoires d'outre-tombe*. The search for lost time undertaken by Chateaubriand thus goes beyond the period of his youth: it also attempts to conquer a period that he deplored not having known.

The Logic of Quotations

The use of an anachronistic vocabulary is not the only literary means implemented to accomplish the flashback that the analeptic representation of the United States presupposes. The quotations used by Chateaubriand also facilitate the cohabitation in the same text of different ages and the merging in the same posthumous representation of the dream of a distant sixteenth century and the memory of a vanished eighteenth century.

In particular, the memory of Montaigne's *Essais* arises in the *Mémoires* when Chateaubriand speaks of the song of a young Amerindian named Mila: "Wasn't this the couplet quoted by Montaigne? 'Grass snake, stop; stop, grass snake, so that my sister may draw from the pattern of your painting the manner and the fine work of a rich cord, so that I may give it to my mistress; thus may your beauty and disposition be forever preferred to all other snakes.' The author of the *Essais* saw in Rouen some Iroquois who, according to him, were very reasonable people: 'But all the same,' he added, 'they aren't wearing breeches!'" (1:494).

The parallel between the Amerindians observed by Chateaubriand and those that Montaigne met in Rouen is rather surprising. Contrary to what Chateaubriand claims, Montaigne did not meet Iroquois but Tupinambás from Brazil.[156] It is therefore impossible that the Iroquois of Chateaubriand sang in 1791 the same song as the "Brazilians" with whom Montaigne chatted in 1562. As absurd as it seems, this parallel reveals in Chateaubriand the dream to abolish time. To compensate for not having had the opportunity to see the Amerindians in a state of nature, this repentant disciple of Rousseau takes pleasure in believing that he heard a voice that, by means of oral transmission linking the generations together, was the very voice of the Amerindians met by Montaigne. Although he had come too late to America, at least the traveler could console himself with the illusion of having been linked with the sixteenth century momentarily, the time of a song. Thus, the presence of both the sixteenth and eighteenth centuries does not only occur in the posthumous representation of America: the traveler briefly experienced it—at least, the author feigns to believe he did—upon hearing from beyond the grave the voice that resonated in the ears of Montaigne, a predecessor whose autobiographical project originally influenced his own.[157]

The quotation from Ronsard in the eighth book of the *Mémoires* seems still less motivated by the context than that from Montaigne. It comes after one of the most frequently commented scenes of the whole American section of the *Mémoires*. Chateaubriand recalls his meeting with "two Floridian ladies" whom he describes in an amorously poetic way: "They lived in an atmosphere of perfume emanating from them, as do orange trees and flowers in the pure exhalations of their leaves and calyces" (1:514). Alas, the two young women were forcibly taken from him by a "*Bois-brûlé*" ("mixed race") and a Seminole warrior (1:518; emphasis original). After their abduction, Chateaubriand quotes the poem by Ronsard dedicated to Mary, Queen of Scots, on the eve of her departure for Scotland:

> *In such robes were you dressed,*
> *Leaving alas! the beautiful country*
> *(whose scepter you held in your hand)*
> *When pensive and bathing your bosom*
> *With the fine crystal of your tears rolling down,*
> *Sad, you walked down the long paths*
> *Of the great garden of this royal castle*
> *That takes its name from a spring of water.*

Chateaubriand accompanied this verse with the following commentary: "Did I resemble Marie Stuart strolling at Fontainebleau when I walked in my savannah after my widowhood? What is certain is that my mind, if not my person, was wrapped in a *crespe, subtil et délié* ["a black crêpe, subtle and delicate"], as Ronsard adds, an old poet of the new school" (519; emphasis original).

Through this parallel, Chateaubriand was feminized and stressed how humiliating it was for him not to have been able to prevent the ravishing of the two ladies by the two warriors. In all respects, this scene was in no sense glorious, since the two young women in question were practicing the oldest trade in the world, and the second one resembled a mosquito (520). Chateaubriand describes his personage here, not without irony, as another Don Quixote, fallen in love with the coarse peasant girl that he names his Dulcinée du Toboso: he saw radiant nymphs where others would have recognized prostitutes. However, Chateaubriand does not compare himself to just any woman but to a famous queen, beginning through the quotation of Ronsard's verse a process of "purification"—to use the term of Béatrice Didier—that helps to glorify the scene.[158] This process was completed by the writing of *Atala* and *Les Natchez*, works in which Chateaubriand recalls the memory of the two Floridians in order to create the characters of Atala and Céluta. Far from being represented there as courtesans, they are transformed by Chateaubriand, who makes of one "a virgin, and of the other a chaste spouse, as a form of expiation" (520). The complete redemption of their models cost their lives to both Atala and Céluta: the first poisons herself rather than break her mother's promise, and the second, inconsolable after René's death, leaps to her death from the top of a waterfall.

Immediately after describing the abduction of the two Floridians, Chateaubriand remarks: "That is how everything fails in my story, since all I have left is images of what passed so quickly: I will walk down the Champs-Élysées with more shadows than any man has ever brought with him" (518). These memorial images preserved by the author cry out to be set and transmitted in the form of literary paintings: those that he offers his readers in the *Mémoires d'outre-tombe* in the form of tableaus worked over to such an extent that one wonders what is owed to dream and what to reality in these compositions in which the human body conveys the essence of a sublimated décor.[159] The analeptic representation of the United States is the means to a double victory over time, since it permits the recreation of both a past period and another that preceded it. It does not reveal a documentary truth on America but the personal truth of an individual who recreated it in remembering it.

However, there arises in the *Mémoires d'outre-tombe*, beside this posthumous America, the representation of another America, contemporary with the writing and whose characteristics are radically different. When Chateaubriand is no longer describing the United States visited in 1791 but what they had become in the years 1835–40, the elegiac tone becomes critical and, paradoxically, the eulogist of the New World, the one who had never completely recovered from the fascination of his American solitudes, participates in the elaboration of French anti-Americanism.

FROM POSTHUMOUS AMERICA TO CHRYSOGENOUS AMERICA

A Growing Pessimism
From *Voyage en Amérique* to *Mémoires d'outre-tombe*, Chateaubriand exhibited a growing concern toward the future of the United States.[160] In the final chapters of *Voyage en Amérique*, published in 1827, Chateaubriand used the following terms to describe the manner in which the American character was being transformed: "Are Americans perfect men? Don't they have their vices like other men? Are they morally superior to the English to whom they owe their origin? Won't the homogeneity of their national character be eventually destroyed by this strange foreign emigration that constantly flows into their population from

all over Europe? Won't their commercial spirit come to dominate them? Isn't financial interest beginning to become the preeminent national failing?"[161]

Although these reasons for concern are quite real, the interrogative form adopted by Chateaubriand tends to reduce the impression of urgency: the "commercial spirit" is only beginning to assert itself, and one may still doubt that it will ever become the principal passion of the Americans. After 1840, such reticence could no longer be justified, and Chateaubriand broadened and toughened the criticism he had timidly suggested in 1827. Before relating his departure from America in the *Mémoires d'outre-tombe*, he made a point of summing up his impressions of the New World when he finished chapter 5 of book VIII, which he developed between 1822 and the 1840s. Berchet observes that the second part of chapter 5 was very likely composed in a later period than the first part: "The subsequent development certainly constituted, in the 1845 version, a separate chapter added later" (1:524, note 2). Composed only three years before Chateaubriand's death, this chapter thus contains the ultimate state of his reflections on the United States, reflections that are striking in their radical pessimism.

Philistine America

The 1845 section begins by creating an unbridgeable gap between the America of yesteryear—whose posthumous representation is preserved in the preceding pages—and the America that exists at the time of the writing of the *Mémoires d'outre-tombe*: "If I were to see the United States today, I would not recognize it. The forests that I knew have been replaced by planted fields; instead of beating my way through bushes, I would travel on highways; in the land of the Natchez, Céluta's hut has given way to a city of around five thousand inhabitants; today Chactas could be a member of the House of Representatives."[162]

It is precisely his conviction that he had visited a country whose character had changed radically that induced the author to memorialize the country that used to be. In a famous passage from the *Préface testamentaire*, Chateaubriand describes his existence as a crossing between two shores: "I found myself between the two centuries as if I were at the confluence of two rivers; I dived into their troubled waters, leaving in the distance the old shore where I was born, and swimming buoyed by hope towards the unknown shore where the new generations are going to land."[163] The America of 1791 sits on the "old shore," whereas the 1840 version awaits it on the "unknown shore," the two separated by a river impassable in the opposite direction. Does the hope that the author previously nursed prove to be justified when he measures it against the evolution of the United States during the first half of the nineteenth century? No: the America he saw before him proved to be disappointing, as was the America of 1791. Now the memoir writer no longer attempted to highlight the experience of the traveler but rather to analyze the reasons for the current decadence that portends even worse for the future. For after having evoked the impressive development of the United States and its growing population, Chateaubriand moved on to a new, more critical, stage in his reflections: "Nonetheless, it is useless to seek in the United States what distinguishes men from other beings on earth, their spark of immortality and the embellishment of their existence: literature and the fine arts are nowhere to be seen in the new Republic" (527). The following passage treats a critical question in the edification of French anti-Americanism: philistinism.

In an article from 1928, Paul Hazard points out the similarity of the fifth chapter of book VIII of the *Mémoires d'outre-tombe* and a work published in 1841 by Eugène A. Vail, *De la littérature et des hommes de lettres des États-Unis* (*On Literature and Literary Figures in the United States*).[164] What does Vail say in this text? That writers are a virtually unknown species in the United States, that Americans prefer by far the practical arts to literature, and that they only design to take up the pen in the "infrequent intervals offered by the various activities of agriculture, commerce, and industry, if it is not the practice of the scientific professions."[165] However, these reservations do not lead him to deviate from his true goal: to prove that despite the short history of their literature, the American writers have already distinguished themselves in numerous genres, such as religious literature, history, and political economy, and that there are good reasons to hope that, in the future, they will also distinguish themselves in works of the imagination. Chateaubriand's reading brings him, however, to the opposite conclusion: "[W]hile Chateaubriand developed the same theme as Vail, he adapted it to his own ends. The ideas are the same, the developments analogous, and the images similar—and in adding it all up, Vail concludes with praise, Chateaubriand with criticism," observes Hazard.[166]

Indeed, Chateaubriand describes disdainfully the state of literary production on the other side of the Atlantic in the first half of the nineteenth century. He chooses to explain the flowering of practical literature by the historical circumstances of the formation of the American people: "The American has replaced intellectual operations with practical ones. Do not attribute to native inferiority his mediocrity in the arts, for these have not been his focus. Thrown by diverse causes into a wilderness, agriculture and commerce were his sole concerns: before developing more elevated modes of thought, one has to live; before planting trees, one has to cut them down in order to plow the fields" (527).

The national genius of the Americans, in this perspective, was thus oriented toward material operations, because the conquest of a hostile land and the need to use their intelligence in the resolution of concrete problems had long been their principal focuses. By emphasizing the feeble development of literature in the United States, Chateaubriand revives, alternatively, an old debate between the Abbé Raynal and Jefferson in the preceding century. While the former ironically expressed surprise that America had not yet given birth to any great talents in the arts and sciences, Jefferson answered with the example of Washington,

Franklin, and Rittenhouse.[167] Chateaubriand is, of course, in no way denying the capacity of the United States to produce exceptional inventors: on the contrary, the sciences appear to him to be an area in which the Americans excel naturally (528). And he certainly does not go so far as to deny the existence of writers in the United States, since he cites Fenimore Cooper and Washington Irving: "Today the American novelists, Cooper and Washington Irving, are forced to take refuge in Europe to find literary reviews and a public" (531). If America has indeed produced authors, they are nonetheless obliged to leave their motherland, since their talent is virtually unrecognized there; worse, it is scorned and considered "childish" (531). It is as if, several years in advance, we are hearing Baudelaire's fulminations against the Americans, guilty of having ignored the genius of his "poor Eddie" (Edgar Allan Poe).[168] As for the American poets, Chateaubriand has only this condescending comment: "[T]hey scarcely rise above the mediocre" (531). Disdaining to cite Bryant, Longfellow, and Sigourney, he nonetheless names a few of their works to which his haughty benevolence awards this compliment: they "deserve a glance" (531). Berchet comments on the weakness of the conclusion of chapter 5, which tries to create an artificial parallel between America and Greece, certain philhellenic American poets having complained about "the lost liberty of the Old World." Is Chateaubriand becoming evasive here, hesitating to formulate a conclusion that, if we follow his train of thought, could only be scathing? Let us suggest, as a pastiche, a version of the conclusion he could have penned: "The Americans offer the sad spectacle of a people whose degenerated language is a reflection of their own decadence."

Indeed, the end of chapter 5 completes the picture of a philistine America by the evocation of a language for which Chateaubriand displays unconcealed scorn: "The language of the great writers of England has been *creolized, provincialized, and barbarized* without having gained any energy in the cradle of virgin nature; it has been necessary to draw up catalogs of American expressions" (531; emphasis original). Nature's glorious spectacle, far from driving the language spoken in America to sublime heights, has been unable to free it from the confinement that renders it less and less intelligible to the rest of the Anglophone world, which is reduced to consulting lists that provide the correct expressions for their "barbaric" equivalents. This stagnating idiom suggests more a colony developing its own particular character than the language of an independent nation—which introduces the judgment pronounced by Chateaubriand a little further on: "In sum, the United States gives the impression of a colony and not a motherland" (536).

The Twilight of the Leaders

This spiral of deterioration likewise threatens the Americans themselves: "But we need to point out one sad thing: the rapid degeneration of talent, from the first men involved in the American turbulence to those of the present time; and nonetheless these men exist in the same era" (528). Such decadence appears to have come too early according to Chateaubriand, who maintains that the American people had no period of youth and has not yet reached old age: this nation in the full bloom of maturity is experiencing a premature debilitation, a judgment that foreshadows that of Baudelaire.[169] In order to evoke the mediocrity of the American statesmen of the mid-nineteenth century, Chateaubriand compares their meager talent to the eloquence of the first American presidents. He cites the farewell speech of General Washington, given on the occasion of his departure from the presidency in 1797, as well as an excerpt of a letter written in 1782 by Jefferson following the death of his daughter. The duo of American presidents is, however, joined by an unexpected guest: Logan, an Amerindian chief who distinguished himself in 1774 in the war between the Virginia colony and the Shawnee and Mingo warriors. Chateaubriand illustrates his eloquence with an excerpt from a famous speech he gave to Lord Dunmore known as "Logan's Lament," which is engraved on the monument raised in his memory in Pickaway County, Ohio. The inclusion of this quote, alongside those by Washington and Jefferson, is rather surprising: Logan fought beside the British during the Revolutionary War, and the reference to him comes in a paragraph that is connected neither to the preceding nor the following one. There is nonetheless an implicit logic in the linking of these three quotes of very diverse origin.

From among a much larger group of quotes found in Vail's *De la littérature et des hommes de lettres des États-Unis,* Chateaubriand only borrowed the short excerpts that he offered in the *Memoirs from Beyond the Grave.* These three excerpts develop the idea of grieving, of disappearance: Washington gives his farewell and begs for the indulgence of posterity; Jefferson grieves the death of his child and Logan that of his whole family. A strong theme thus links together these three examples of eloquence. Chateaubriand implicitly emphasizes the underlying continuity that unites the Amerindian chief with the two American presidents. By putting on the same level three great "chiefs," Logan, Washington, and Jefferson, he suggests that the destiny of the latter two will soon be the same as that of the first: no men of their mettle, of their "race," exist anymore; the great Americans, like the great Amerindians, will have no successors. Chateaubriand, who described the men of the July Monarchy as "mites" (3:22), has no better opinion of the leaders who followed Washington and Jefferson;[170] once again, the degeneration is noted on both sides of the Atlantic. And again, after establishing a parallel between Frenchmen and American Indians,[171] he uses the disappearance of the latter to issue a warning.

Chrysogenous America

In the following chapter, Chateaubriand pursues his analysis of the "degeneration" of the Americans. Chapter 6 of book VIII suggests two explanations: the omnipresence of commercialism and the spread of selfishness in American society. In 1827, Chateaubriand only foresaw the possibility of a triumph of the commercial spirit in the United States.[172] After 1840, there can no longer be any doubt, and he now expresses the same idea firmly: "The mercantile spirit is beginning to invade them; self-interest is becoming the national vice" (534). One of the unexpected consequences of this mentality was the creation of diverse social classes in the United States. If we are to believe Chateaubriand, the fear that equality would disappear from the New World became a reality after 1840: "One imagines that there is one general social level in the United States: that is a complete error. There are social strata that are mutually disdainful and do not frequent each other" (534). To designate the growing aristocracy in the United States, born of capitalist wealth, Chateaubriand uses the neologism "chrysogenous." This term deserves further attention, for it accompanies a reflection on the paradoxes of a gentry founded on money.

During the Old Regime, nobility could be acquired either by birth or by purchasing a title. The dual nature of this system was governed by a hierarchy: given that superiority of rank within the aristocracy was directly proportional to the distance of its origin, a nobility that was acquired more recently and by money was inferior to ancient nobility based on the heroism of a distant ancestor. Since money in France was considered to be a lowly means to attain a higher status, newly minted noblemen attempted to conceal the source of their position by adopting the values and prejudices of the old nobility. Initially the social situation in America appeared different, since there is no hereditary nobility comparable to what is found in Europe. Moreover, if money was the means to reach the pinnacle of society in the United States, anyone was theoretically capable of climbing to the highest ranks by becoming wealthy: this was the source of the ideology of the American Dream and the mythology of the self-made man. However, Chateaubriand showed that in the United States the aristocracy of wealth imitated the manners of the Old World in much the same way as the minor French nobles who attempted to dissimulate the recent origin of their privileged condition. Possessed by "the love of distinctions and the passion for titles" (534), the wealthiest Americans eventually came to disdain their own country and to imitate the European aristocrats: "Suppose an American possesses an income of a million or two. Yankees like this, members of elite society, can no longer live like Franklin; the true 'gentleman,' disgusted by his new country, seeks the old in Europe. You meet him in inns imitating the English—with all their extravagance or spleen—by doing a grand tour of Italy. These prowlers from Carolina or Virginia buy run-down abbeys in France and plant English gardens with American trees in Melun" (535).

The chrysogenous aristocracy in the United States threatened the spirit of equality in the New World, since it adopted the social ethos of the Old World: noble by their money and yet plebian by birth, the American aristocrats were a true paradox. Trying to find roots for their social superiority, they espoused the prejudices of European nobility and behaved with more arrogance than a "German prince with sixteen quarters" (534). In addition, this social class threatened the equality of social status by accumulating such excessive wealth that it provoked hostility from the rest of society: "And what is extraordinary is that while financial inequality flourishes and an aristocracy rises, at the same time there is an egalitarian impulse from the outside that forces the industrial or landed gentry to hide their luxuriance, to dissimulate their opulence for fear of being murdered by their neighbors" (535). Chateaubriand criticized the concentration of wealth in the hands of the few, but contrary to Tocqueville, for whom the following question was paramount, he did not bring up the problem of inheritance.[173] Nevertheless, by asserting that the accumulation of capital by a minority facilitated the birth of a form of aristocracy in the United States, Chateaubriand suggested that the excessive fortunes compromised equality by creating a dominant class that was capable of perpetuating itself.

In *Capital in the Twenty-First Century*, Thomas Piketty analyses the origin of the concentration of wealth in the hands of a minute percentage of the world population and demonstrates that the testamentary transmission of said wealth progressively accentuates the inequalities. The United States is cited as one of the countries where this tendency is particularly evident: the caste of the ultrarich that is currently evolving is the contemporary equivalent of the chrysogenous aristocracy described by Chateaubriand.[174] When Chateaubriand criticized the disproportionate importance of money in America, he sought to highlight the paradox of a society that believed it had guaranteed for everyone the possibility of climbing the social ladder by making this dependent on the accumulation of capital rather than by the possession of a hereditary title. In his opinion, American society had not succeeded in making elevated social positions accessible by everyone; on the contrary, it permitted people with sufficient capital to achieve a position of superiority that they could then preserve by passing their fortune on to their heirs and by creating a separate caste through the adoption of the exclusive social habits and practices of European aristocracy.

Concerned originally with the financial sphere, the criticism of the spectacle given by the United States in the 1835–40 period eventually landed on the moral plane: "A cold, hard selfishness reigns in the cities; piasters and dollars, banknotes and coins, the rise and fall of stocks, that's all they can talk about. It's like being at the stock exchange or at the counter of an enormous shop" (536). By attacking selfishness in the United States, Chateaubriand was at the same time targeting philistinism: hungry for money, Americans had no other topic of conversation or thought about anything else, as was demonstrated by the narrowness of the subjects discussed in their newspapers, which were "filled with business matters or rude cackling" (536).

In the conclusion of chapter 6, Chateaubriand led a final somewhat muddled charge against the Americans: "Are Americans being subjected, unawares, to the law of a climate in which plant nature has thrived at the expense of animal nature, a law combatted by the best minds but whose refutation hasn't been completely successful? One might wonder if Americans weren't too quickly worn down by philosophical liberty, like Russians by enlightened despotism" (536). Juxtaposed in this brief passage, two profoundly different theses arrive at the same conclusion. The first tends to prove that North America's climate has had a beneficial influence on the growth of plant species while it has proven to be harmful to the development of animal species. In other words, the development of the vegetation is inversely proportionate to that of the animals. Supposedly scientific, this "law" purports to demonstrate the progressive dumbing down of Americans, since it applies to men as much as to the other animal species. This implicit conclusion is quite shocking, especially since the rationale on which it is founded itself rests on a theory that was refuted by "the best minds" that Chateaubriand did not bother to identify. He was thinking most likely of Buffon's theory on the degeneration of species in America, which he deformed somewhat, however, by making an arbitrary distinction between "animal nature" and "plant nature," only the former being affected by the debilitating influence of the climate.[175] Far from developing his thoughts in the following sentence, he advanced a new explanation for the so-called intellectual mediocrity of the Americans: the premature abuse of "philosophical liberty." Abandoning the climate theory as soon as he had evoked it, he proceeded to explain the decadence of American mores by the influence of ideas. The expression "to wear down" is revealing here, for it again reveals the nature of the underlying reflections of Chateaubriand on the fate of the United States and its inhabitants: the idea of decline, of progressive degeneration. It hardly matters that Chateaubriand tried to give the appearance of caution in using the interrogative form or careful formulas like "One might wonder if . . . ,"; he was nonetheless suggesting that America was on the road to ruin, and that Americans were becoming decadent, themes that would have considerable longevity.[176]

These pages devoted to the United States by Chateaubriand are striking by the peremptory nature of criticism that is not founded on any personal observation. He had not seen, since a five-month stay in 1791, the America of which he was speaking in the present after 1840, and he nonetheless did not deign to cite the sources that supported his reflections. One senses his bad humor, the gloom of an old man criticizing the evolution of a country in which he no longer recognizes *his* America. If he was indeed the eulogist of a posthumous America, which was not the real America that he had visited in 1791 but another more personal America reinvented in the course of his writing and throughout the years, in the end Chateaubriand showed himself to be, paradoxically, after Talleyrand and La Rochefoucault-Liancourt, between Stendhal and Baudelaire, before Huysmans and Céline, one of the links in the interminable chain of French anti-Americanism.

CONCLUSION

America, a Mobile Sign

America is seen as the purest embodiment of the future because, lacking the entrenched past that impedes the coming of modernity in Europe, America is deemed to be modernity incarnate.
—Levine, "The Idea of America"

A Shifting Significance

America is a mobile sign. The meaning assigned to it at the turn of the eighteenth century was evolving, moving from a critical philo-Americanism to a systematic anti-Americanism,[1] from a fascination with the past to an expression of concern for the future. Accordingly, the statement by Levine at the start of this conclusion does not provide a definition of what America has always been but the meaning that it holds today, at the end of an evolution described in the following manner by Craiutu and Isaac: "America has moved from representing a pastoral Arcadia and Europe's past to symbolizing Europe's future and the land of incessant change, mobility, impersonality, and progress—in short, the apotheosis of modern society."[2] The first meaning historically conferred on the sign "America" may be summarized by the idea of a Golden Age prior to the civilization in which the Europeans recognized the contemporary resurgence of a mythical past. The works analyzed in this study participated broadly in the creation of this definition of America by durably associating the latter to the idea of a distant past that has finally returned, whether it be by describing a pastoral Golden Age, as Crèvecœur does, by resuscitating in the western part of the United States an ideal moment in the history of France as Lezay-Marnésia does, or by seeking for the vestiges of an America unchanged by the European presence, as Chateaubriand does. They are privileged spaces in which to observe both the zenith and the beginning of the decline of the enthusiasm for America in the French mind, since they were produced at the turn of a century that marks the redefinition of America and the progressive obfuscation of the meaning with which it is endowed. Indeed, the meaning of a sign is always capable of evolving, and the connotations gravitating around it, like electrons around the nucleus of an atom, can be replaced progressively by new associations of ideas, more or less flattering, depending on historical events that may lead us to consider it differently or on the propagation of a discourse that attempts to reconceptualize it on new bases. This study will be brought to a close by asking why the redefinition of America in French thought began with the French Revolution and how the hyperbolic philo-Americanism at the end of the eighteenth century became the fierce anti-Americanism of the nineteenth century.

The classic work by Echeverria, *Mirage in the West*, provides the beginning of a response to this question. If the "American Dream" disappears, it is, according to him, because it no longer has any reason to exist after the Revolution: "[The dream] died because it became unnecessary. It had been created, deliberately or not, as a device to prove that certain ideals were universally true and universally practical, that any democratic constitutional republic founded on the principles of political and civil liberty, popular sovereignty, the rights of man, and the enlightenment of the people would produce moral salvation and social and material progress."[3]

Once the French Revolution had begun, the enthusiasm for the American model became useless, since its primary function was to show the viability of political reforms to be implemented in France, while embellishing its model at the expense of the truth. "The moment the first stone was wrenched from the Bastille, the American example became superfluous," observes Echeverria, before adding, "Those who continued to believe in the Revolutionary creed had no longer any need to look across the Atlantic to find justification for their ideals and their actions."[4] However, if this hypothesis explains the decline of the philo-American discourse, it does not help us understand the rise of anti-Americanism in French opinion, since the disappearance of the "American Dream" would not lead automatically to the development of a discourse condemning the imminent spread of American values throughout the world.

America: Figure of Alterity

To explain fully the intensification of French anti-Americanism during the nineteenth century, it is necessary to add that America, after 1794, did not only lose the role of model that it had formerly played; it became a figure of otherness to which France could only relate by noting their differences.[5] Both the mobile and polysemous characteristics of the sign "America" explain this change in status.

Contrary to the linguistic sign whose meaning is determined by convention within a community of speakers, a political sign is endowed with contradictory meanings depending on the person who uses it, since it plays the role of an argument among opposing theses that manipulate it with little regard for its referent. In the eyes of the opponents of 1789, America appeared as the fatal instigator of the Revolution and the noxious justification of those who chose to sever their allegiance to their legitimate sovereign. As for its partisans, they saw America as a cumbersome precedent, given that it minimized the historical uniqueness of the French Revolution and contradicted its pretention to alone carry aloft the torch of universal values. Although the real influence of America on the French Revolution was diversely appreciated by the partisans and adversaries of 1789, they all regarded it as the cradle of a civilization that was radically different from French civilization. If France was regenerated by the Revolution, it was at the same time definitively distinguished from America; and if "true" France was really what it was before 1789, America was still its antithesis. In both cases, America was no longer the double of France but rather a nation that exhibited a conflicting spirit, culture, and values. This is, paradoxically, how the polysemous character of the sign "America" developed into an exclusively condemnatory discourse.

The revolutionary break thus led to a reevaluation of the symbolic function that America was capable of fulfilling in relation to France. Unable to play anything other than the role of a foil, the sign "America" was no longer employed in a discourse attempting to imagine France in comparison to Washington's Republic, to find across the Atlantic the justification for political reforms; it designated an "other" against which the French identity was defined in a critical spirit. This radical change in the meaning bestowed on America, itself inseparable from the development of anti-Americanism in the nineteenth century, was accompanied by a reversal of the respective positions of France and the United States on an imaginary temporal axis. Whereas America was identified by the philo-American discourse with the resurgence of a mythical past, the anti-American discourse emphasized the alterity that it represented, seeing it as what it was not yet but threatened to become, that is to say, the foreshadowing of a disquieting future.

A Paradoxical Philo-Americanism

In fact, what characterizes philo-Americanism is not only the promotion of a eulogistic discourse on the New World but also the postulate of a similarity between

America and France that rested on the principle of anteriority of the former in relation to the latter. The study of the works of Crèvecœur, Lezay-Marnésia, and Chateaubriand has revealed that these authors reinvented America's past in order to imagine the means to a possible regeneration of France. The myth of the Golden Age, whose resurrection in the New World stirred the imagination of Crèvecœur and Lezay-Marnésia, was constructed like a model that was to inspire the French to adapt it to the specific character of their society by promoting reforms such as the return of the aristocracy to the countryside, the limiting of the power of the monarchy, the creation of elites playing the role of intermediaries between the people and the king, as well as the establishment of festivities nurturing affective bonds between the dominant and dominated social classes. In the literal sense, Lezay-Marnésia was calling for the rebirth of a defunct France in the United States, where it would finally discover the circumstances conducive to the implementation of the political and social program of the *Monarchiens* that the Revolution seemed to favor for a moment before crushing it. Likewise, the elegiac portrayal of an extinct New World in *Atala* conceals a pragmatic hidden agenda: Chateaubriand hoped that his description of New France would turn out to be useful, if ever his country decided to reconstitute its lost colonial empire.[6] In the final analysis, philo-Americanism reconstructed America's past in order to conduct experiments there for a possible future for France.

Conversely, anti-Americanism displaces the United States on the temporal axis by reconceptualizing it as a foreshadowing of an undesirable future. It views America as an image of the country that France could become if its inhabitants were not careful. This perspective is adopted notably by Baudelaire, who associated the verbal expression he invented, "to become Americanized" [*s'américaniser*], with the imminence of an apocalyptic future in which the French, like the other peoples on earth, will have become American on the moral plane: "Mechanics will have so Americanized us, progress will have so completely atrophied our spiritual side, that nothing in the murderous, sacrilegious, or unnatural dreams of the utopians could be compared to its results."[7] By describing an ongoing process, the expression "to become Americanized" summarizes by itself the fear at the root of French hostility toward the United States as it developed in the nineteenth century: that France would adopt the values of American civilization and eventually resemble it like a certified copy, a fear whose expression is still found today in the criticism of a supposed "Americanization" of cultural, gastronomic, and fashion norms in France. The title of Georges Duhamel's work *Scènes de la vie future* (*Scenes of Future Life*, 1930) is symptomatic of this representation, both prophetic and reprobative, of the United States.[8] In this text, whose influence was considerable on the intellectuals of its time, Duhamel adopts the position of a Cassandra warning the Old

World of the dangers that the barbaric Americans pose for the great European civilization:

> No nation has yet, more deliberately than the United States of America, abandoned itself to the excesses of the industrial civilization. . . . There can no longer be any doubt that this civilization is capable of, and indeed is in the process of, conquering the Old World. This America thus represents, for us, the Future. Let each of us Occidentals immediately denounce loyally whatever is American in his house, in his manner of dress, in his soul. Our future! Inside twenty years, we will be able to find all of the stigmata of this voracious civilization on the limbs of Europe.[9]

Associated with the memory of the invasions that brought Rome down, the growing cultural domination of America was also compared to a silent epidemic whose inexorable character threatened the very spirit of European civilization, without any apparent recourse capable of confronting the inexorable advance, the devious and corruptive intrusion deep inside people: "There is, on our continent, in France as everywhere else, broad spaces that the spirit of Old Europe has already deserted. The American genius is colonizing, little by little, a given province, city, home, or soul."[10]

The elements that constitute American society, such as they are described by its denigrators, will eventually prevail, they are persuaded, beyond its borders: puritanism, the lure of profits, publicity, mass production and consumption, the paradoxical assertion of the value of the individual associated with a permanent surveillance of each by the others in order to guarantee social conformity. All of these American traits—if we are to believe its detractors—are rapidly proliferating by means of globalization, since this insures the triumphant circulation of material goods that characterizes the economic success of the United States, just as it insures the dissemination of cultural goods promoting the ideals at their base. While philo-Americanism invented a fantasized image of America in order to utilize it in a political debate over the future of France, anti-Americanism redefines it as a radical otherness threatening the specificity of the French identity, a specificity that is itself problematical and that uses hostility toward the United States in its effort to define itself: France is a country whose lifestyle, health system, and social services in general, among many other things, are considered as models to the extent that they differentiate themselves from their equivalents across the Atlantic. In the final analysis, the fundamental nature of anti-Americanism is to see in the United States not only a country but especially an idea, through a process of abstraction that usually is employed by its partisans rather than its detractors. But this idea, as defined by the latter, cannot be summarized as an ideal of equality that the heroes of the American Revolution supposedly announced for the first time in the history of the world—this equality that, according to Tocqueville, is, far more than liberty, the true base on which American civilization resides. On the contrary, this idea is summarized rather by a simpleminded form of hedonism that many observers foresee spreading across the planet. What Régis Debray called, significantly, "the exported America" and others have called "the American cancer" is the "American Way of Life" caricatured as a negation of critical reflection and the expression of a desire for instant and crude gratification, with an underlying darker purpose: an appetite for domination that is now playing out in the political domain after having restricted itself earlier to that of culture and morality.[11]

All the same, philo-Americanism and anti-Americanism are not antithetical discourses, the one opposing systematically the positions of the other, because the paradoxical nature of the first prevents us from viewing it as the strict opposite of the second. Indeed, philo-Americanism reserves its admiration for what no longer exists and, still better, for a largely fictionalized representation of America and not for a real period in its history. By idealizing the past, this current only succeeds in better emphasizing the extent to which the present is inferior to it: French admiration for America undermines its own foundation by recognizing that it can only be provoked by a defunct object. In this respect, the growing pessimism of Chateaubriand regarding the United States is a phenomenon symptomatic of an evolution under way in his time: "Circa 1830, it really was 'in' in Europe to sneer at America," observes Roger in his seminal study on French anti-Americanism.[12]

In a complementary manner, the circulation of the philo-American discourse by Crèvecœur, Lezay-Marnésia, and Chateaubriand prepared the disappointment of travelers who would visit this country hidden behind the ocean and a mountain of books. It was, in fact, when the fictitious past of America was compared with its present state by the people who had traveled there that the philo-American sentiment tended to wane. The French officers, for example, filled with enthusiasm by the myth of the rebirth of the Golden Age in America, went there to defend the cause of the insurgents only to discover a less idyllic reality than they had expected; many were transformed into denigrators of the model that had given rise to their premature admiration.[13] Likewise, the emigrants who took refuge in the United States during the French Revolution, seeking an unadulterated state of nature in which they could reconstruct their country, returned home at the first opportunity.[14] In short, America only ever aroused the enthusiasm of the French if it was first subjected to a reinvention: it could only be loved when it was already lost.

APPENDIX

The manuscript "Les Treise [sic] Chapitres du Troisième Volume du Cultivateur Américain" indicates the organization of the chapters initially planned by Crèvecœur for the third volume of the *Lettres d'un cultivateur américain*. It is preserved at the Beinecke Library of Yale University under the reference "GEN MSS 722, Box I, Folder 6. J. Hector St. John de Crèvecœur papers, Series II, Writings." The chapters are listed here, followed by the table of contents of the third volume as published in 1787. Regarding the differences between this table of contents and the one that Crèvecœur eventually adopted in the final version of his work, see pp. 48–51.

"The Thirteen Chapters of the Third Volume of the American Farmer"

1. My Children Fanny and Louis.
2. Settlement of Socialbourg.
3. August 24 (sent for the first vol.).
4. Triumphant Entrance of General Washington.
5. German Family.
6. Progress of Civilization in America.
7. Progress of Things Since Peace.
8. Dismissal of the American Army.
9. Answer to C. C., Squire.
10. Details on Snakes, Birds, and Flies.
11. Description of the Great Cohos Trail of the Connecticut River.
12. Description of the Settlement of Cherry Valley.
13. Fifty-Eight Anecdotes.
14. Ohyo and Kentucké [Ohio and Kentucky].
15. Trip on the Susquehanna.
16. Destruction of the Settlements of the Susquehanna.
17. Detail of Several . . .

Table of Contents of the Third Volume of *Lettres d'un cultivateur américain* (1787)

1. Boston, March 28, 1784.
2. New York, May 17, 1773. Outline of the Great Cohos Trail of the Connecticut River, Located Two Hundred Miles from Its Mouth.
3. Lancaster, January 15, 1778. The German Woman.
4. Albany, January 26, 1784. Battle of Two Snakes.
5. New York, March 10, 1757. Translated from the Original Manuscript in New York on June 18, 1786. Origin of the Settlement of Socialburg, Located Northeast of Albany County in the New York Colony.
6. New Haven, October 11, 1784. First Anecdote.
7. Philadelphia, May 20, 1764. Circular Letter Addressed to the General Assembly of the Friends of Pennsylvania, All the Churches, and All the Members of Their Society Living in the English Colonies of the Continent.
8. Orange County, October 28, 1774. Outline of a Journey from Minisink on the Delaware River to Wyoming, on the Eastern Branch of the Susquehanna at Warriors Run, to Buffalo Valley, to Shamokin, Wiolucing, and Onaquaga; Return by the Great Portage of Cookhouse at Shohactin and at Mahakamack, Going Down the Delaware Through the Blue Mountains.
9. Orange County, November 15, 1778. Outline of the Destruction of the Settlements That Inhabitants of Connecticut Had Made on the Eastern Branch of the Susquehanna River in 1766.
10. Cherry Valley, October 1784. History of the Settlement Known as Cherry Valley, Located on the River of the Same Name, Six Miles from Lake Otzégé, in Montgomery County, by the Son of One of the First Colonists.

11. New York, July 16, 1784. Detail of Several Interesting Circumstances That Preceded and Followed the Triumphant Entrance of General Washington in the City of New York.—Departure of the English.—Restoration of the American Government.—The General Resigns His Commission to Congress.—His Return to Private Life.
12. New York, September 15, 1784. Dismissal of the American Army.
13. New York, June 30, 1785. Narration of Several Circumstances Relative to the Journey That the Marquis de La Fayette Has Just Completed in America.
14. In Louisville, August 26, 1784. Outline of the Ohio River and of the Kentucky Country.
15. New York, October 12, 1786. Outline of the Civilization in the Thirteen United States.
16. New York, December 28, 1786. Brief Outline of the Most Interesting Things the Americans Have Done Since the Peace.
17. Headquarters, Newburg, June 18, 1783. Circular Letter from General Washington.

NOTES

Introduction

1. On the ambiguity of the term "America," see Isaac, "'America' Between Past and Future," in *America Through European Eyes*, 263–64. In the present study, the term "America" refers exclusively to the thirteen British colonies before the War of Independence and the expanding territory under the jurisdiction of the United States of America following their independence in 1783.

2. Regarding the works written by French travelers in the United States during this period, see especially those by Echeverria and Everett, *The French Image of America*.

3. François Barbé-Marbois, "Mémoire sur le commerce entre la France et les États-Unis," quoted by Chevignard in "D'une révolution à l'autre: les consuls de France aux États-Unis, 1783–1789," 67.

4. Vermont in 1791, Kentucky in 1792, Tennessee in 1796, and Ohio in 1803.

5. These successive stages in the expansion of the American nation include the purchase of Louisiana from France (1803), the annexation of Florida (1819), the entry of Texas into the Union (1845), the relinquishing of the Oregon Country by England (1846), and the acquisition of New Mexico, Nevada, Utah, Arizona, and California following the war with Mexico from 1846 to 1848.

6. The most densely populated of the thirteen colonies at that moment were Virginia, Massachusetts, Pennsylvania, and the Carolinas.

7. The censuses completed in each decade in the United States indicate the following numbers of inhabitants: 12,900,000 (1830), 17,100,000 (1840), 23,200,000 (1850), and 31,400,000 (1860).

8. "An inhabitant of Philadelphia who had only seen three coaches, then two or three ships from London each year and some small boats going to the Colonies, had seen, in the course of his life, three hundred coaches and from twelve to fifteen ships leave for all the ports in the world no matter how far-flung" (Moreau de Saint-Méry, *Voyage aux États-Unis de l'Amérique*, 299).

9. On this question, see Furstenberg, *When the United States Spoke French*.

10. La Rochefoucauld-Liancourt, *Voyages dans les États-Unis d'Amérique, fait en 1795, 1796 et 1797*, 1:81.

11. This inherent challenge to the representation of the United States has continued well after the eighteenth century, owing to its ongoing pursuit of economic and demographic development. Georges Duhamel emphasizes, for example, the city of Chicago, whose rapid growth outstrips any discourse that attempts to characterize it at a given moment: "Chicago stretches along the edge of Lake Michigan for forty-five kilometers. Stretches or rather stretched: before I can finish my sentence, Chicago is a mile longer. Chicago! Tumor City! Cancer City! Where any statistic comes after the battle, where any addition is to be redone before it is finished." Duhamel, *Scènes de la vie future*, 89.

12. Rémond, *Les États-Unis devant l'opinion française*, 3.

13. Rémond, *Les États-Unis devant l'opinion française*, 22.

14. Rémond, *Les États-Unis devant l'opinion française*, 22.

15. On Benjamin Franklin's *Avis*, see Harsanyi, *Lessons from America*, 42–43.

16. Rémond, *Les États-Unis devant l'opinion française*, 24.

17. On this question, see chapter 2, pp. 77–123.

18. The *Oxford English Dictionary* (third edition, December 2006) provides these three definitions of the word "posthumous": "Of an action, reputation, etc.: occurring, arising, or continuing after death," "Of a child: born after the death of its father," "Of a book or writing: published after the death of the author."

19. The impression of having witnessed a major historical rift is expressed primarily by the contemporaries of the Revolutionary War and of the French Revolution through the evocation of multiple catastrophes in the works examined in this study.

20. Chateaubriand, *Mémoires*, 1:429.

21. Riffaterre, *La Production du texte*, 151; emphasis original.

22. Mathy, *Extrême-Occident*, 15.

23. Crèvecœur, *Lettres d'un cultivateur américain*, 1784, 1:32.

24. Tocqueville, *De la démocratie en Amérique*, 1:14.

25. Musset, *Poésies complètes*, 274.

26. Chateaubriand, *Mémoires*, 1:474. On this scene, see chapter 3, p. 170.

27. Jullien, *Récits du Nouveau Monde*, 22.

28. On this question, see my article, "Posthumous Louisiana," 164–81.

29. Tocqueville, *De la démocratie en Amérique*, 2:291.

30. Tocqueville, *De la démocratie en Amérique*, 2:291.

31. Chateaubriand, *Mémoires*, 1:474. On this passage, see chapter 3, p. 170.

32. See the letter of October 2, 1801, from Chateaubriand to Louis de Fontanes in *Correspondance générale*, 150. On October 8, 1801, Chateaubriand published in the *Mercure de France* a "Discussion historique sur les ruines trouvées sur les bords de l'Ohio dans l'Amérique septentrionale et dont il est parlé dans le Voyage en Pennsylvanie de M. de Crèvecœur" ["Historical discussion on the ruins found on the banks of the Ohio in North America of which it is spoken in the *Voyage en Pennsylvanie* by M. de Crèvecœur"]. This text was republished in 1802 in the *Génie du christianisme*, 546–47; 1130–32.

33. The hero of Alain Mabanckou declares: "The religion of the dream is anchored in the consciousness of the youth of the country. . . . I also felt the duty to keep the dream alive" (*Bleu-Blanc-Rouge*, 139).

34. Chateaubriand, *Atala*, 1:16.

35. On this question, see pp. 127–29.

36. On this question, see pp. 124–27.

37. The study of Thomas Philbrick, *St. John de Crèvecœur*, is an exception. It demonstrates the originality of the *Voyage dans la Haute Pensylvanie* compared to *Lettres d'un cultivateur américain*, whereas the first text is often compared negatively to the second. Howard C. Rice refers to it, most notably, as a "mediocre book" (*Le Cultivateur américain*, 104).

38. Passages of Crèvecœur's narrative that weren't included in Plet's edition are quoted from the original edition: *Voyage dans la Haute Pensylvanie et dans l'État de New York, par un membre adoptif de la Nation Onéida, traduit et publié par l'auteur des Lettres d'un cultivateur américain*, 3 vols. (Paris: Édition Marandan, Year IX [1801]).

39. Plet, "Postface," in *Voyage dans la Haute Pensylvanie*, 349.

40. It is, for example, regrettable that chapter 3 of the third volume is absent from Plet's edition. Significantly placed at the end of the first half of the book, this "eighteenth-century version of the journey into 'the heart of darkness'" (Philbrick, *St. John de Crèvecœur*, 155) describes the manner in which the characters bond again with a past that American civilization has forsaken.

41. See our article, "Crèvecœur: The Art of Equivocation," 147–49.

42. Published by Prault in 1792 and reprinted in 1800, the *Letters Written from the Banks of the Ohio* were reedited by Benjamin Hoffmann and translated into English for the first time by Alan J. Singerman in 2017. All the quotations from the text refer to this recent edition (published by Penn State University Press).

Chapter 1

1. Fitzgerald, *The Crack-Up*, 69.
2. Crèvecœur, *Lettres d'un cultivateur américain*, 1787, 1:475.
3. Crèvecœur, *More Letters from the American Farmer*, 154.
4. Chevignard, "Confusion, Fusion, Diffusion," 143.
5. Crèvecœur, *Lettres d'un cultivateur américain* (1784, vol. 2; 1787, vol. 3) is the French version of the *Letters from an American Farmer* (1782, vol. 1). On the differences between these two versions, see pp. 25–35.
6. This term is used by Chevignard in *Au miroir de la mémoire* [*In the Mirror of Memory*], 16.
7. Philbrick, *St. John de Crèvecœur*, 16.
8. On the causes of Chateaubriand's trip to America, see chapter 3, pp. 129–31.
9. Lezay-Marnésia celebrated his fifty-fifth birthday a month after his arrival in the United States, on July 29, 1790.
10. Robert de Crèvecœur, *Saint-John de Crèvecœur*, 8–9.
11. Robert de Crèvecœur, *Saint-John de Crèvecœur*, 14.
12. On these hypotheses, see Chevignard, *Au miroir de la mémoire*, 13.
13. On this question, see the letter from Crèvecœur to Franklin quoted by Gilbert Chinard in *Les Amitiés américaines de Madame d'Houdetot*, 13.
14. Lezay-Marnésia's stay in the United States lasted from July 1790 to May 1792; Chateaubriand's from July to December 1791.
15. See Mitchell, *St. Jean de Crèvecœur*, 307–9.
16. "Au rédacteur du *Mercure de France*, 4 janvier 1783," *Lettres d'un cultivateur américain*, 1784, 1:ix.
17. Lopez, *Mon Cher Papa*, 162. Élisabeth-Françoise-Sophie de La Live de Bellegarde, comtesse d'Houdetot (1730–1813), inspired a violent passion in Jean-Jacques Rousseau, as well as the character of Julie in *La Nouvelle Héloïse*. In 1757, she began a love affair with Jean-François de Saint-Lambert that lasted for half a century. In addition, she enthusiastically supported the cause of the American rebels and became very close to Benjamin Franklin and Thomas Jefferson. The sympathy she felt for the United States, as well as a friendship she had formed years before with the father of Crèvecœur, led her to help the author of the *Letters from an American Farmer*: she hosted him in her home in 1782 and, as the reader shall see, played a decisive role in the literary and diplomatic career of her protégé. On Madame d'Houdetot and Crèvecœur, see Chevignard, "Les Souvenirs de Saint-John de Crèvecœur sur Mme d'Houdetot."
18. Robert de Crèvecœur, *Saint-John de Crèvecœur*, 70; emphasis added.
19. On the relationship between Crèvecœur and Madame d'Houdetot, see Robert de Crèvecœur, *Saint-John de Crèvecœur*, 71.
20. Quoted by Chevignard in *Au miroir de la mémoire*, 20–21.
21. D. H. Lawrence, *Studies in Classic American Literature*, 33.
22. As D. D. Moore remarks, "Such blurring of Crèvecœur and the rustic Farmer James continues to the present moment despite the recent flowering of scholarship on Crèvecœur and his ambitious epistolary fiction, *Letters*." *Letters from an American Farmer*, x.
23. White, "Crèvecœur in Wyoming," 380.
24. Crèvecœur, *Voyage dans la Haute Pensylvanie*, 2002, 26.
25. On this question, see Chevignard, "Saint John de Crèvecœur en Bavière (1808–1809)."
26. The fourth letter in the *Lettres d'un cultivateur américain* is titled "Thoughts of an American Farmer on His Fate and the Pleasures of the Country," 1784, 1:47–80. It is the translation of a rewriting of Letter II of the *Letters from an American Farmer*, 14–27.
27. Crèvecœur, *Letters from an American Farmer*, 15–16.

28. Crèvecœur, *More Letters from the American Farmer*, 273; emphasis added.
29. On this question, see Traister, "Criminal Correspondence," and the introductions of Moore to *More Letters*, xlvii–lvi, and *Letters*, xx–xxiii.
30. Crèvecœur, *Letters from an American Farmer*, 191.
31. Jehlen, "J. Hector St. John de Crèvecœur," 204–22.
32. In "Crèvecœur Revisited," Cunliffe rejects the term "collaborator" to characterize Crèvecœur, preferring "neutralist" or "quietist" (135).
33. Crèvecœur, *Lettres d'un cultivateur américain*, 1784, 1:392–93.
34. Crèvecœur, *Lettres d'un cultivateur américain*, 1784, 1:405.
35. This text is titled "Esquisse de ma vie depuis ma sortie de prison à New York le 17 septembre 1779 jusques à mon retour dans la même ville comme consul de France le 17 novembre 1783" ["Outline of my life from my release from prison in New York on September 17, 1779, until my return to the same city as the French Consul on November 17, 1783"]. It is introduced by Chevignard in "St. John de Crèvecœur à New York en 1779–1780," 161–73.
36. Crèvecœur, "Esquisse de ma vie depuis ma sortie de prison à New York," in "St. John de Crèvecœur à New York," 170.
37. Plato, *The Sophist*, 135.
38. On the metamorphosis of Crèvecœur into a writer from the Revolutionary War on, see Chevignard, "St. John de Crèvecœur in the Looking-Glass," 178.
39. On Brissot and Crèvecœur, see Rice, *Le Cultivateur américain*, 204–13.
40. Brissot, *Examen critique des Voyages dans l'Amérique septentrionale de Monsieur le marquis de Chastellux, ou Lettre à Monsieur le marquis de Chastellux, dans laquelle on réfute principalement son opinion sur les Quakers, sur les Nègres, sur le Peuple et sur l'Homme*, 17.
41. On this society, see Darnton, "The Craze for America: Condorcet and Brissot," in *George Washington's False Teeth*, 127–28.
42. Brissot, *Mémoires sur ses contemporains et la Révolution française*, 2:410.
43. Brissot, *Mémoires sur ses contemporains et la Révolution française*, 2:411.
44. On the French translation and the rewriting of the *Letters*, see pp. 25–35.
45. On Sophie d'Houdetot's circle of acquaintances, see Chinard, *Les Amitiés américaines de Madame d'Houdetot*, and Lopez, *Mon Cher Papa*.
46. Brissot, *Mémoires sur ses contemporains et la Révolution française*, 2:400.
47. Other than "the night of fire at Port-Royal" (from November 23 to November 24, 1654), during which Blaise Pascal had a mystical experience that influenced the rest of his opus, one may also put in this category the experience Rousseau had on the way to visit Diderot at the Vincennes prison that inspired him to treat the question on the arts and sciences proposed by the Académie de Dijon.
48. The first letter of the third volume of the *Lettres d'un cultivateur américain* (1787, 3:1–34) recounts the circumstances in which Crèvecœur learned, upon returning to the United States in 1783, of the destruction of Pine Hill and the death of his wife.
49. Rice, *Le Cultivateur américain*, 75–106.
50. Chevignard, "*Saint-John de Crèvecœur*. Letters from an American farmer *et* Lettres d'un cultivateur américain: Genèse d'une œuvre franco-américaine" (thèse, Université de Lille III, 1989).
51. On this problem, see Aldridge, "Le problème de la traduction, au xviiième siècle et aujourd'hui," 747.
52. Literal translation was defended by those who saw it as a way to learn foreign languages. In *Some Thoughts Concerning Education* (1693), John Locke recommended to novice Latinists to throw away their grammar books and take up the translation of pleasant books.
53. On this question, see Aldridge, "Le problème de la traduction," 754–55.
54. The twelve letters of the *Letters from an American Farmer* (comprising 173 pages in Moore's edition) became the three volumes of the 1787 edition of the *Lettres d'un cultivateur américain*, including, respectively, 478, 437, and 592 pages in the Cuchet edition.
55. On this question, see the prologue of chapter 1, pp. 19–21.

56. On this question, see the letter from Crèvecœur to the comtesse d'Houdetot quoted by R. de Crèvecœur, *Saint-John de Crèvecœur, sa vie et ses ouvrages*, 379–80.

57. See Rice, *Le Cultivateur américain*, 75–76.

58. Named consul in New York in July 1783, Crèvecœur left for America in September of the same year. He had to entrust the publication to Saint-Lambert, Lacretelle, and Target, who assumed the responsibility of negotiating with the publisher, Cuchet, and reading the proofs for him.

59. On this question, see p. 31.

60. For example, Crèvecœur, *Lettres d'un cultivateur américain*, 1784, 1:289.

61. Bernardin de Saint-Pierre alludes to the "Anecdote d'un chien sauvage," in *Paul and Virginia* (1787), 139.

62. Crèvecœur, *Sketches of Eighteenth-Century America*, 132–34.

63. On this question, see Rousseau, *Émile, ou de l'éducation* (1762), in *Œuvres complètes*, 4:598.

64. On the reception of this text, see Rice, *Le Cultivateur américain*, 82–83.

65. On this question, see F. Lestringant, *Cannibals*.

66. Apostolidès, "L'altération du récit," 76.

67. On this topic, see Rousseau, "Discourse on Inequality," 66.

68. Rousseau himself emphasizes the dangers of an excessive use of the concept of state of nature: "Our politicians offer the same sophisms about love of freedom as our philosophers do about the state of nature" ("Discourse on Inequality," 106).

69. The tendency of the French partisans of the independence of the United States to repeat the same set of ideas is emphasized by Echeverria in *Mirage in the West*, 79.

70. This idyllic vision is expressed many times in the *Lettres* and notably in the following excerpt: "Ah! Why, my friend, hadn't I learned to play the lyre? I could perhaps have tried to put into song our American water nymphs, our pastoral Gods, the green of our mountains, the fertility of our valleys, the majesty of our rivers" (1784, 1:73).

71. Rice, *Le Cultivateur américain*, 207.

72. Cunliffe, "European Images of America," 494.

73. On the use of Crèvecœur's *Lettres* by the Scioto Company, see chapter 2, pp. 83–84.

74. Crèvecœur, *Letters from an American Farmer*, 19.

75. Crèvecœur, *Lettres d'un cultivateur américain*, 1784, 1:59–60.

76. Book IV of the *Georgics* is devoted to bees.

77. Saint-Lambert, "Discours préliminaire," in *Les Saisons*, vi.

78. Diderot, *Œuvres complètes*, 5:240.

79. Crèvecœur compares the barns of Ulster County in the New York colony to the "temples of Ceres" (*Lettres d'un cultivateur américain*, 1784, 1:200).

80. Quoted by Rice, *Le Cultivateur américain*, 85.

81. Quoted by Rice, *Le Cultivateur américain*, 86.

82. Chateaubriand declares, concerning the *Mémoires* of Madame de Rémusat: "The author burned them during the Hundred Days, and then wrote them again: they are now only memories reproduced by memories; the color has faded...."

83. Crèvecœur, *Lettres d'un cultivateur américain*, 1784, I:47–80.

84. Crèvecœur, *Lettres d'un cultivateur américain*, 1784, I, 49; emphasis added.

85. The "Pensées d'un cultivateur américain" are signed "St. John." Although one must be careful not to identify the author completely by his alter ego in the *Lettres d'un cultivateur américain*, the choice of this signature nonetheless indicates that the content is autobiographical.

86. Cullen, *The American Dream*, 37.

87. Crèvecœur, *Lettres d'un cultivateur américain*, 1784, 1:1–12.

88. Crèvecœur, *Lettres d'un cultivateur américain*, 1784, 1:137–71.

89. Crèvecœur, *Lettres d'un cultivateur américain*, 1784, 1:23.

90. On this dichotomy, see the prologue to chapter 1, pp. 16–17.
91. Chateaubriand, *Mémoires*, 2:410; emphasis added.
92. On this question, see pp. 47–48.
93. Crèvecœur, *Lettres d'un cultivateur américain*, 1784, 1:228–29; emphasis added. The autobiographical dimension of this text is not only emphasized by the signature—St. John—but by a footnote by the editor, who states: "This scene took place between the author and his daughter" (*Lettres d'un cultivateur américain*, 1784, 1:229).
94. Delon, "Introduction," in *Œuvres de Sade*, 2:xix.
95. The progressive expansion of the *Lettres d'un cultivateur américain* recalls the successive and ever-expanding versions of the story of Justine: *Les Infortunes de la vertu* (1787), *Justine ou les malheurs de la vertu* (1791), and *La Nouvelle Justine ou les malheurs de la vertu* (1797). On the origin of the "myth of Justine," see Delon, "Introduction," in *Œuvres de Sade*, 2:ix–xix.
96. Gracq, *En lisant en écrivant*, 97.
97. On this question, see Compagnon's preface to *Du côté de chez Swann*, 7–45.
98. On the origin of the *Voyage dans la Haute Pensylvanie*, see Rice, *Le Cultivateur américain*, 103.
99. Crèvecœur, *Lettres d'un cultivateur américain*, 1784, 1:281.
100. On this mythical period evoked by Hesiod—who located it in a distant past—see Minois, *L'Âge d'or*.
101. On this question, see Moore's introduction in *More Letters from the American Farmer*, lvii.
102. For a comparison of an American colonist and Robinson Crusoe, see Crèvecœur, *Lettres d'un cultivateur américain*, 1784, 1:126.
103. Crèvecœur, *Lettres d'un cultivateur américain*, 1784, 1:55.
104. The power of paternal sentiment is discussed several times in the *Lettres d'un cultivateur américain* (e.g., 1784, 1:54, 259).
105. Crèvecœur, *Lettres d'un cultivateur américain*, 1784, 2:54–55; emphasis added.
106. On the American Dream, defined as "the first of those great moments of secular mysticism which modern man has been experiencing for the last two hundred years," see Echeverria, *Mirage in the West*, 116.
107. Crèvecœur, *Lettres d'un cultivateur américain*, 1784, 1:105.
108. See the letter of February 16, 1788, from Franklin to Crèvecœur, translated by R. de Crèvecœur, *Saint-John de Crèvecœur*, 372.
109. Crèvecœur, *Lettres d'un cultivateur américain*, 1784, 1:287.
110. Letter from Lord Dunmore to Lord Dartmouth, December 24, 1774, quoted by Miller, *Origins of the American Revolution*, 77.
111. On the readers of Crèvecœur's *Lettres* who decided to emigrate to the United States, see Rice, *Le Cultivateur américain*, 204–13.
112. Echeverria, *Mirage in the West*, 144–61.
113. Echeverria, *Mirage in the West*, 147.
114. On this subject, see Condorcet, *Writings on the United States*.
115. Echeverria, *Mirage in the West*, 155.
116. Trained as a doctor, Georges Duhamel compares the Americans to bearers of the virus of the "material or mechanical civilization" that threatens to contaminate the "moral or genuine civilization" of which Europe is the cradle (*Scènes de la vie future*, 13).
117. Rice, *Le Cultivateur américain*, 96.
118. Sollors, *Beyond Ethnicity*, 76–77.
119. Sollors, *Beyond Ethnicity*, 80.
120. "*Ubi panis ibi patria* is the motto of all emigrants" (*Letters from an American Farmer*, 31). "*Ubi panis ibi patria*": Latin for "Where my bread is, there is my homeland."
121. On this question, see the prologue of chapter 1, pp. 22–24.

122. Letter from Crèvecœur to La Luzerne, New York, May 16, 1788, quoted by Chevignard, "D'une révolution à l'autre: les consuls de France aux États-Unis, 1783–1789," 73.
123. Letter from Crèvecœur to La Rochefoucauld, New York, December 1, 1788, in Chevignard, "D'une révolution à l'autre," 74; emphasis added.
124. On this question, see Lopez, *Mon Cher Papa*, 165–66.
125. On Crèvecœur's supporters, see R. de Crèvecœur, *Saint-John de Crèvecœur*, 78.
126. Chevignard, "Les Souvenirs de Saint-John de Crèvecœur," 260.
127. Jefferson attended the marriage of America-Francès de Crèvecœur with the diplomat Louis-Guillaume Otto on April 13, 1790, in New York.
128. See the "Épître dédicatoire" of the *Lettres d'un cultivateur américain*, 1784, 1:iii–vi.
129. Lafayette recommended Crèvecœur to Washington. See R. de Crèvecœur, *Saint-John de Crèvecœur*, 138.
130. Crèvecœur, *Lettres d'un cultivateur américain*, 1784, 1:v.
131. Crèvecœur, *Lettres d'un cultivateur américain*, 1787, 3:406.
132. Letter from Crèvecœur to Brissot, December 20, 1787, quoted by Chevignard, *Au miroir de la mémoire*, 105–6; emphasis added.
133. Chevignard, *Au miroir de la mémoire*, 102.
134. Gracq, *En lisant en écrivant*, 97.
135. Référence GEN MSS 722, Box 1, Folder 6. J. Hector St. John de Crèvecœur papers, Series II, Writings. The tables of contents of the manuscript and the 1787 volume are reproduced in the appendix, pp. 187–88.
136. There is a German, a Frenchman, an Englishman, a Scot, and an Irishman.
137. Crèvecœur, *Lettres d'un cultivateur américain*, 1787, 3:91.
138. Crèvecœur, *Lettres d'un cultivateur américain*, 1787, 3:96.
139. Crèvecœur, *Lettres d'un cultivateur américain*, 1787, 3:85.
140. White, "Introduction to and Translation of Hector St. John de Crèvecœur's 'Origin of the Settlement at Socialburg,'" 237.
141. Crèvecœur, *Lettres d'un cultivateur américain*, 1787, 3:96.
142. See especially the "Forty-First Anecdote" (*Lettres d'un cultivateur américain*, 1787, 3:139), in which the generosity of the patriots is demonstrated.
143. Crèvecœur, *Lettres d'un cultivateur américain*, 1787, 3:161–208.
144. Crèvecœur, *Lettres d'un cultivateur américain*, 1787, 3:209–15.
145. Crèvecœur, *Lettres d'un cultivateur américain*, 1787, 3:209.
146. Crèvecœur describes the rebirth of New London, Connecticut, after its partial destruction in 1779 (*Lettres d'un cultivateur américain*, 1787, 3:514–15).
147. Crèvecœur, *Lettres d'un cultivateur américain*, 1787, 3:574.
148. Crèvecœur, *Lettres d'un cultivateur américain*, 1787, 3:576.
149. Letter from Crèvecœur to Jefferson, New York, November 9, 1787, in Boyd, *The Papers of Thomas Jefferson*, 332.
150. Letter from Crèvecœur to La Luzerne, New York, May 16, 1788, quoted by Chevignard, "D'une révolution à l'autre," 71.
151. Crèvecœur, *Lettres d'un cultivateur américain*, 1787, 3:499.
152. On this question, see R. de Crèvecœur, *Saint-John de Crèvecœur*, 95.
153. Quoted by Chevignard, *Au miroir de la mémoire*, 103.
154. On this episode in Crèvecœur's life, see pp. 23–24.
155. Crèvecœur, *Lettres d'un cultivateur américain*, 1787, 3:565.
156. Crèvecœur, *Lettres d'un cultivateur américain*, 1787, 3:495.
157. Crèvecœur, *Lettres d'un cultivateur américain*, 1787, 3:497; emphasis original.
158. Anne-Robert-Jacques Turgot is the author of *Réflexions sur la formation et la distribution des richesses* [*Reflections on the Creation and Distribution of Wealth*, 1766], which was a source of inspiration for Adam Smith's *The Wealth of Nations* (1776). Crèvecœur was a distant relative.
159. On the physiocratic school, see Vardi, *The Physiocrats*.

160. "This nation, like all those that are republican and commercially oriented, nearly always puts the sentiment of self-interest before that of honor." Letter from D'Annemours to Castries, Baltimore, March 31, 1783, quoted by Chevignard, "D'une révolution à l'autre," 69.

161. On the criticism of commercialism in the United States by Chateaubriand, see pp. 177–80.

162. Cullen, *The American Dream*, 40.

163. On this question, see Crèvecœur, *Voyage dans la Haute Pensylvanie*, 1801, 1:vii.

164. Crèvecœur, *Voyage dans la Haute Pensylvanie*, 1801, 1:viii.

165. Crèvecœur, *Voyage dans la Haute Pensylvanie*, 1801, 1:xii; emphasis added.

166. Letter from Lezay-Marnésia to his wife, Philadelphia, April 24, 1792, quoted by Bourget-Besnier, *Une famille française sous la Révolution*, 53.

167. Chateaubriand, *Mémoires*, 1:539.

168. Crèvecœur, *Voyage dans la Haute Pensylvanie*, 1801, 1:viii.

169. Crèvecœur, *Lettres d'un cultivateur américain*, 1784, 1:98.

170. Crèvecœur, *Voyage dans la Haute Pensylvanie*, 2002, 185–86.

171. Crèvecœur, *Lettres d'un cultivateur américain*, 1784, 1:25.

172. Crèvecœur, *Voyage dans la Haute Pensylvanie*, 2002, 26.

173. Crèvecœur, *Lettres d'un cultivateur américain*, 1784, 2:309.

174. Crèvecœur, *Voyage dans la Haute Pensylvanie*, 2002, 112.

175. Crèvecœur, *Lettres d'un cultivateur américain*, 1784, 1:229.

176. Crèvecœur, *Lettres d'un cultivateur américain*, 1784, 2:240–67.

177. Crèvecœur, *Voyage dans la Haute Pensylvanie*, 2002, 196.

178. Crèvecœur, *Voyage dans la Haute Pensylvanie*, 2002, 198.

179. See, for example, "Le père infortuné" ["The Unfortunate Father"], in *Lettres*, 1784, 1:356–61.

180. In the *Lettres d'un cultivateur américain*, Crèvecœur establishes no autobiographical pact with his reader, since "Saint-John" is presented as the son of an American colonist, who is a fictitious double for the author and not for Crèvecœur himself. The choice of this name nonetheless indicates that the author recognizes that he was, at least partially, inspired by his own experiences in creating his character, and if it is an interpretive leap to identify Crèvecœur with Saint-John, it would be impossible to assert that the fictional character owes nothing to the biography of the author who purposefully gave him his own surname.

181. On this question, see Mitchell, *St. Jean de Crèvecœur*, 293.

182. On this question, see Rice, *Le Cultivateur américain*, 38.

183. Brissot, *Mémoires*, 2:400.

184. Rice, *Le Cultivateur américain*, 40.

185. Quoted by Chevignard, "St. John de Crèvecœur à New York," 166–67; emphasis added.

186. Rice, *Le Cultivateur américain*, 39.

187. Mitchell, *St. Jean de Crèvecœur*, 293.

188. "I write thirteen hours a day that feel like thirteen minutes." Letter from Casanova to Opiz, January 10, 1791, quoted by Luna, *Casanova mémorialiste*, 55.

189. Childs, *Casanova*, 59.

190. Casanova, *Histoire de ma vie*, 2:1194–95.

191. "You did not want me to know that you existed until I arrived here, because you feared that I would turn around and go back to have the satisfaction of seeing you; but I will see you *tomorrow*. You had me informed that your house would always be open to me. But no. The order you gave to Marcoline shows me that you do not want to see me again *right now*. You have perhaps left *this morning*, God knows to go where" (Casanova, *Histoire de ma vie*, 2:1195; emphasis added).

192. Kavanagh, "Casanova's Autobiography of Chance," 158.

193. Crèvecœur, *Voyage dans la Haute Pensylvanie*, 2002, 238.

194. "A Snow Storm as it Affects the American Farmer," in *More Letters*, 142–45. The letter titled "Description d'une chute de neige" is its translation and rewriting (*Lettres d'un cultivateur américain*, 1784, 1:261–84).
195. On Crèvecœur's borrowings, see Philbrick, *St. John de Crèvecœur*, 149–50.
196. Adams, *Crèvecœur's Eighteenth-Century Travels*, xxxvii.
197. On this episode, see Adams, "Crèvecœur and Franklin," 273–79, and *Travelers and Travel Liars*, 158–61.
198. On Benjamin Franklin and his rise to the rank of "public figure" in the French consciousness in the eighteenth century, see Lilti, *Figures publiques*, 87–95.
199. Crèvecœur, *Voyage dans la Haute Pensylvanie*, 2002, 31.
200. For example: "(The chapter that contained the details of the journey up to this fort was, with the exception of a few lines, so badly damaged that we were unable to translate it)" *Voyage dans la Haute Pensylvanie*, 2002, 82.
201. Crèvecœur, *Voyage dans la Haute Pensylvanie*, 2002, 186.
202. Crèvecœur, *Voyage dans la Haute Pensylvanie*, 1801, 1:vii.
203. On this subject, see Chevignard, "Entre débris et débuts" ["Between Debris and Beginnings"], 124–25.
204. Chateaubriand, *Mémoires*, 1:463-66.
205. Napoléon is described as the "Washington of France" in the *Voyage* (1801, 1:iv).
206. An earlier version of the following section, "A Memorial of the Amerindian Civilizations," has previously been published as "Chateaubriand, Crèvecœur, and the Twilight of Native American Civilizations," in *Loxias* 56 (March 2017): http://revel.unice.fr/loxias/index.html?id=8618.
207. Crèvecœur, *Voyage dans la Haute Pensylvanie*, 1801, 1:204.
208. On the fascination Crèvecœur expressed for the vestiges of the past, see his text written in 1803 and quoted by R. de Crèvecœur, *Saint-John de Crèvecœur*, 5.
209. Volney, *Les Ruines*, xi–xii; regarding Chateaubriand's "vertiges," see Chevignard, "Entre débris et débuts," 122; for the references to the *Voyage* in the *Génie du christianisme*, see p. 190, note 32.
210. Chateaubriand, *Mémoires*, 1:429.
211. Crèvecœur, *Letters from an American Farmer*, 81.
212. For a reflection on this passage, see Hollier, "Incognito," 25–43.
213. Chateaubriand, *Mémoires*, 4:607-08.
214. On these two movements that developed during the second half of the nineteenth century, see Figueiredo, "Aux sources du débat écologique contemporain," 69–82.
215. Chateaubriand, *Mémoires*, 1:498. Pinchot, *The Training of a Forester*, 13.
216. Figueiredo, "Aux sources du débat écologique contemporain," 77.
217. Nietzsche, *Seconde considération intempestive: de l'utilité et de l'inconvénient des études historiques pour la vie*, 75.
218. Chateaubriand, *Atala*, 99.
219. Crèvecœur, *Voyage dans la Haute Pensylvanie*, 1801, 3:106.
220. Crèvecœur, *Voyage dans la Haute Pensylvanie*, 1801, 3:112; emphasis added.
221. Volney, *Tableau du climat et du sol des États-Unis d'Amérique*, 2:370.
222. Crèvecœur, *Letters from an American Farmer*, 17.
223. Crèvecœur, *Lettres d'un cultivateur américain*, 1784, 1:2.
224. Crèvecœur, *Voyage dans la Haute Pensylvanie*, 1801, 3:113.
225. Crèvecœur, *Voyage dans la Haute Pensylvanie*, 1801, 3:118.
226. On this topic, see Chateaubriand, *Voyage en Amérique*, 178.
227. Crèvecœur, *Voyage dans la Haute Pensylvanie*, 1801, 3:390.
228. Crèvecœur, *Letters from an American Farmer*, 81.
229. *Odes*, III, 30. On Horace and the search for immortality through writing, see Jackson, *Those Who Write for Immortality*, 1–23.
230. Sayre, *Les Sauvages Américains*, 204.

231. Certeau, *The Writing of History*, 216; emphasis original.
232. Clements, *Native American Verbal Art*, 8.
233. McNally, *Honoring Elders: Aging, Authority, and Ojibwe Religion*, 271.
234. McNally, *Honoring Elders*, 273.
235. Crèvecœur, *Voyage dans la Haute Pensylvanie*, 2002, 55.
236. Chateaubriand's *Voyage en Amérique* (1827) describes a comparable discovery of ruins whose origin remains unknown (*Voyage*, 221).
237. Crèvecœur, *Voyage dans la Haute Pensylvanie*, 1801, 1:205–6.
238. Crèvecœur, *Voyage dans la Haute Pensylvanie*, 1801, 3:276.
239. *Mémoires*, 1:470. Chateaubriand returns to this idea, that he was already formulating in 1797 in the *Essai historique, politique et moral sur les révolutions anciennes et modernes, considérées dans leurs rapports avec la Révolution française* [*Historical, Political, and Moral Essay on Ancient and Modern Revolutions Considered with Respect to Their Relationship with the French Revolution*], 147.
240. Chateaubriand, *Voyage*, 137.
241. Chateaubriand, *Atala*, 18.
242. On this question, see Chateaubriand, *Mémoires*, 2:44.
243. Faÿ, *L'Esprit révolutionnaire*, 301.
244. For a comparison of the destinies of *Atala* and the *Voyage dans la Haute Pensylvanie*, see also Rice, *Le Cultivateur américain*, 104–5.

Chapter 2

1. Editor's foreword, in *Letters Written from the Banks of the Ohio*, 45–46.
2. The theory of degeneration is presented by Buffon notably in *Animaux de l'ancien continent; Animaux du nouveau monde; Animaux communs aux deux continents* (1761) [*Animals of the Old Continent; Animals of the New World; Animals Common to Both Continents*] and *De la Dégénération des animaux* (1766). On this theory, see Roger, *The American Enemy*, 1–29; Duchet, *Anthropologie et histoire*, 214–57; and Echeverria, *Mirage in the West*, 3–38; 65–66.
3. Behind the allusion to "biased authors" we recognize the Jesuit Joseph-François Lafitau: in his *Moeurs des sauvages américains, comparés aux moeurs des premiers temps* [*Manners of the American Savages Compared to the Manners of Antiquity*, 1724], he establishes a regular parallel between the Amerindians and the peoples of antiquity.
4. See Mazzei, *Recherches historiques et politiques sur les États-Unis de l'Amérique Septentrionale*, 4:100. Concerning the squabble between Brissot and Mazzei, see Rice, *Le Cultivateur américain*, 91–92.
5. Lezay-Marnésia, *Letters*, 70.
6. Lezay-Marnésia misrepresents what Crèvecœur actually stated, since the fish of which the latter speaks weigh between twenty and eighty pounds. See Crèvecœur, *Lettres d'un cultivateur américain*, 1787, 3:408.
7. It is to Lezay-Marnésia that Volney is referring behind the anonymous prophet of the "Empire of Ohio": "We are pretty far from the poetic felicity sung by the *American Farmer* and from the delights of the future capital of the *Empire of Ohio* prophesied by another writer. If the makers of such fictions could hear their own panegyrics, surely they would be disgusted by this banal rhetorical talent that, in the present case, has destroyed the fortune of five hundred families" (*Tableau du climat et du sol*, 2:391).
8. Lezay-Marnésia, *Essai sur la nature champêtre*, 5.
9. The poem "Les Lampes" was published for the first time in the *Journal de Paris* of April 27, 1788, before being reprinted in *Les Paysages, ou essai sur la nature champêtre, poème* [*Landscapes, or Essay on Rural Nature, Poem*, 1800].
10. Lezay-Marnésia, *Le Bonheur dans les campagnes*, vi.
11. Rousseau, *La Nouvelle Héloïse*, 5.

12. The Northwest Territory was a territory created in 1787 by the United States in which slavery was forbidden. It included the present-day states of Ohio, Indiana, Illinois, Michigan, and Wisconsin, and disappeared in 1803 when its southeast section was admitted to the Union as the State of Ohio. The colony of "Asylum" is an example of other options available at this time to French emigrants like Lezay-Marnésia and his followers. Founded in 1793 at the instigation of Antoine-Omer Talon and the vicomte de Noailles, it was situated in the State of Pennsylvania and intended for refugees from France and Saint-Domingue (today the island shared by Haiti and the Dominican Republic). On Asylum, see Furstenberg, *When the United States Spoke French*, 227–45.

13. Moreau-Zanelli, *Gallipolis*, 335–36.

14. Grimm, *Correspondance littéraire*, 7:127.

15. On this question, see Bonnel, *Éthique et esthétique du retour à la campagne au XVIIIEM^e siècle*, 56–67.

16. In 1778, Lezay-Marnésia published an *Essai sur la minéralogie du bailliage d'Orgelet en Franche-Comté* [*Essay on the Mineralogy of the Bailiwick of Orgelet in Franche-Comté*].

17. Moreau-Zanelli, *Gallipolis*, 171.

18. Lezay-Marnésia, *Le Bonheur dans les campagnes*, 188.

19. Duprat, "*Pour l'amour de l'humanité*," 1:xxx.

20. Bonnel, *Éthique et esthétique*, 233–94.

21. Rousseau, *La Nouvelle Héloïse*, 444.

22. On this question, see Knee, "Wolmar comme médiateur politique," 117–27.

23. The *corvée* was unremunerated work that was required of a lord's serfs; *mortmain* was the right of a lord to inherit the property of his vassals.

24. Lezay-Marnésia, *Plan de lecture pour une jeune dame*, 152.

25. Bonnel, *Éthique et esthétique*, 300. On the evolution of the political positions taken openly by Lezay-Marnésia during the revolutionary period, see Bonnel, *Éthique et esthétique*, 297–336.

26. On the question of intermediate bodies, see Carcassonne, *Montesquieu et le problème de la constitution française au XVIIIe siècle*. Regarding the organization of provincial states and the political role of the nobility, see, respectively, Lezay-Marnésia, *Le Bonheur dans les campagnes*, 28 and 88–89.

27. Bourget-Besnier, *Une famille française*, 25.

28. On the composition of the Scioto Company, see Moreau-Zanelli, *Gallipolis*, 91.

29. The contract with the American Congress stipulated that the Ohio Company would make four payments of $500,000 each, and that at the time of each payment, it would take ownership of one-quarter of the total area. Consequently, it had to have a minimum of $500,000 on hand to be able to sell the slightest parcel of land. On this question, see Moreau-Zanelli, *Gallipolis*, 15–38.

30. The first document (Paris: Prault, 1789), twenty-four pages long, is not signed, but everything indicates that its author was William Playfair. The second document is held at the Bibliothèque nationale de France (Pb 1597).

31. On January 9, 1789, two pacts were made between General Arthur Saint Clair and various Amerindian tribes in the Northwest Territory. These pacts were never respected and, as early as the spring of 1789, there was an Amerindian attack on an isolated homestead in the region. The unrest grew increasingly worse until the Battle of the Wabash on November 4, 1791, which was a major victory for the Amerindians. On this battle, see p. 200, note 50.

32. Crèvecœur, *Lettres d'un cultivateur américain*, 1787, 3:387–437.

33. Crèvecœur, *Lettres d'un cultivateur américain*, 1787, 3:415–16.

34. See Moreau-Zanelli, *Gallipolis*, 108.

35. Moreau-Zanelli, *Gallipolis*, 188.

36. Lezay-Marnésia bought more land than the minimum required for inclusion in the Société des Vingt-Quatre: on January 14, 1790, he acquired twenty thousand acres for

himself and one thousand acres for his daughter. On the fifteenth, he bought another one thousand acres, then one hundred more on February 11.

37. Alfred de Lezay-Marnésia, *My Memories* [1851] in *Letters Written from the Banks of the Ohio*, 146; emphasis added.

38. Letter from Lezay-Marnésia to his wife (Paris, November 9, 1789), quoted by Bourget-Besnier, *Une famille française*, 25.

39. Despite their entreaties to Pope Pious VI, the Twenty-Four failed in their attempt to obtain the creation of a new bishopric. On Lezay-Marnésia's plans in the area of religion, see Moreau-Zanelli, *Gallipolis*, 199–208.

40. Lezay-Marnésia remarks, revealingly, "If I had been able to choose my fate, it is that of Abraham or Boaz that I would have preferred" (*Letters*, 75).

41. Moreau-Zanelli, *Gallipolis*, 189.

42. Some of the members of the Society of the Twenty-Four did not belong to the aristocracy: Jean-Paul Guérin, Lezay-Marnésia's secretary, for instance, and Jean-Daniel Smith, a medical doctor, were among the partners.

43. Moreau-Zanelli, *Gallipolis*, 195.

44. March 15, 1790, quoted by Duval in *Écrits révolutionnaires, 1790–1794*, 7. On Cloots, see Soboul, "Anacharsis Cloots," 29–58, and Labbé, *Anacharsis Cloots, le Prussien francophile*.

45. March 22, 1790, quoted by Bonnel, *Éthique et esthétique*, 381.

46. On this question, see Moreau-Zanelli, *Gallipolis*, 195–96.

47. Dillon, *Mémoires*, 205.

48. Bonnel, *Éthique et esthétique*, 381.

49. Moreau-Zanelli, *Gallipolis*, 306.

50. At the beginning of the expedition, General Saint Clair commanded around two thousand men, accompanied by around two hundred civilians. But in the month of November, desertions and illnesses reduced the expedition to 1,120 members, including the civilians. At dawn on November 4, 1791, Saint Clair's men were surprised by a thousand warriors led by Little Turtle, chief of the Miamis, and Blue Jacket, chief of the Shawnees. After several hours of combat, Saint Clair gave the order to retreat. Of his 920 men who fought that day, 631 were killed and 264 wounded. As for the two hundred civilians, they were nearly all massacred. The Amerindian forces only had to grieve twenty-one dead and forty wounded. The rout of Saint Clair at the Battle of the Wabash is the worst defeat ever suffered by the American army while fighting the Amerindians. On this battle, see Eckert, *That Dark and Bloody River*, 558–69.

51. The defeat of Saint Clair had long-term repercussions in the history of the United States. After the House of Representatives began its investigation into the military disaster at the Battle of the Wabash, George Washington established the position that the president has the right to refuse to divulge documents or other materials that contain information that he believes should remain confidential. This decision gave birth to the doctrine of executive privilege that was invoked, notably, by Richard Nixon at the time of the Watergate affair and by Bill Clinton during the Lewinsky affair. On the history of executive privilege, see Garvey and Dolan, "Presidential Claims of Executive Privilege," 1–42.

52. On this topic, see *My Memories*, in *Letters Written from the Banks of the Ohio*, 154. Each time that it is possible, we will quote excerpts from the *Souvenirs* published in the appendices of the *Letters* of Lezay-Marnésia. When we quote passages from the *Souvenirs* that were not reproduced in the *Letters*, we will refer to the original edition.

53. Lezay-Marnésia, *Mes souvenirs*, 22.

54. "Circumstances did not allow three of them to be brought out that were published as essays by Prault in 1792. The Girondins ruled at the time. Other factions followed the Girondins, and the liberty of the press was reduced to the freedom to take immense risks" ("Letter to Monsieur Audrain, Merchant in Pittsburgh," in *Letters*, 139).

55. Desan, "Transatlantic Spaces of Revolution," 502.

56. See Ammon, *The Genêt Mission*, and Furstenberg, *When the United States Spoke French*, 44–53.
57. Brissot, *Nouveau voyage dans les États-Unis*, 2:424–25.
58. On the possible involvement of Brissot in the Scioto Company, see Desan, "Transatlantic Spaces of Revolution," 478–79.
59. Brissot, *Nouveau voyage dans les États-Unis*, 2:426.
60. Editor's foreword, in *Letters Written from the Banks of the Ohio*, 45.
61. Lezay-Marnésia, *Letters*, 139.
62. Anonymous, *Nouveau prospectus de la Compagnie du Scioto* (1790).
63. Lezay-Marnésia, *Plan de lecture*, 1800, 205–23.
64. Brissot comments, in regard to the Northwest Territory, that it is "completely unknown to the Europeans," *Nouveau voyage dans les États-Unis*, 417.
65. The expression "American letters" refers to the corpus of letters by Lezay-Marnésia studied here, including the *Letters Written from the Banks of the Ohio*, the letters of the *Nouveau prospectus*, and the "Letter to M. Audrain."
66. See Moreau-Zanelli, *Gallipolis*, 253.
67. Anonymous text. Whenever possible, we will quote excerpts of this letter reproduced in the *Letters Written from the Banks of the Ohio*.
68. *Prospectus pour l'établissement sur les rivières d'Ohio et de Scioto en Amérique*, 8.
69. *Letter Written by a Frenchman Immigrating to the Lands of the Scioto Company*, in *Letters Written from the Banks of the Ohio*, 125; emphasis original.
70. *Letter Written by a Frenchman Immigrating to the Lands of the Scioto Company*, in *Letters Written from the Banks of the Ohio*, 126.
71. *Letter Written by a Frenchman Immigrating to the Lands of the Scioto Company*, in *Letters Written from the Banks of the Ohio*, 126.
72. The author of the *Nouveau prospectus* was probably William Playfair. On his role in the activities of the Scioto Company, see pp. 82–84.
73. We refer here to the original edition of this text. Whenever possible, we will refer to the excerpts published in the appendices of the *Letters Written from the Banks of the Ohio*.
74. After embarking for the United States in May 1790, Dom Didier went to Gallipolis, where he lived briefly before moving to Missouri. He died there in 1799.
75. Lezay-Marnésia, *Letters*, 129.
76. Lezay-Marnésia, *Letters*, 129; emphasis added.
77. Lezay-Marnésia, *Letters*, 130.
78. The first is an "Excerpt of a Letter from M. de Marnésia, October 12, 1790," in *Letters Written from the Banks of the Ohio*, 128–30; the second is an "Excerpt of a Letter from M. de Marnésia to M. de Beyerley," in *Letters Written from the Banks of the Ohio*, 131–32.
79. The declarations of Lezay-Marnésia appear still more unrealistic when they are considered in the context of the unrest that characterized the Northwest Territory at that time: his letter is dated only eight days before the defeat of Josiah Harmar by Shawnee and Miami warriors at the Battle of Pumpkin Fields on October 22, 1790 (129 dead and 64 wounded on the American side).
80. "M. de Marnésia Writes on September 24 to M. Gréa," in *Letters*, 131.
81. "Excerpt of a Letter from M. de Marnésia to M. de Beyerley," in *Letters*, 131.
82. *Lettre écrite par un Français émigrant sur les terres de la Compagnie du Scioto*, 23.
83. *Lettre écrite par un Français émigrant sur les terres de la Compagnie du Scioto*, 25.
84. On the obstacles to the success of the plans concocted by Lezay-Marnésia and the Society of the Twenty-Four, see pp. 86–87.
85. Moreau-Zanelli, *Gallipolis*, 345.
86. "Letter from Columbus," in the *Journal of Christopher Columbus*, 198–200.
87. Levine, "The Idea of America," in *America Through European Eyes*, 20.
88. Levine, "The Idea of America," in *America Through European Eyes*, 19.
89. Guyot, *Analogie et récit de voyage*, 54.

90. See Levine, "The Idea of America," in *America Through European Eyes*, 24.
91. On the concept of doxological America, see pp. 6–7.
92. Lezay-Marnésia, *My Memories*, in *Letters*, 154.
93. Rufus Putnam (April 9, 1738–May 4, 1824) began his military career during the French and Indian War before winning fame in the War of Independence. In 1786, he created with General Benjamin Tupper the Ohio Company of Associates, whose goal was to acquire and populate lands in the Northwest Territory. Named administrator of the company, Putnam arrived at the mouth of the Muskingum River on April 7, 1788, and founded the first settlement in the Northwest Territory: Marietta.
94. Moreau-Zanelli, *Gallipolis*, 335.
95. Moreau-Zanelli, *Gallipolis*, 335–36.
96. November 15 is also the date at which the break between Lezay-Marnésia and the other members of the Société des Vingt-Quatre is consummated. The marquis announces in a letter his decision to found a settlement on his own lands, independent of Aigle-Lys and Gallipolis, owing to growing disagreements with his associates. On this episode, see Moreau-Zanelli, *Gallipolis*, 338–51.
97. On *Le Bonheur dans les campagnes*, see pp. 80–81.
98. On the importance of reciprocity in the exchange of gifts among the Hurons, see Dickason, *Le Mythe du Sauvage*, 130.
99. Liebersohn, *Aristocratic Encounters*, 1.
100. On *Aline, reine de Golconde*, see Kavanagh, "Bouffler's *La Reine de Golconde*."
101. The tale by Boufflers, *Aline, reine de Golconde* (1761), has been reedited by Carrell in *Le Lit bleu* [*The Blue Bed*], 345–55.
102. Lezay-Marnésia, *My Memories*, in *Letters*, 153.
103. On the "Anecdote of a Wild Dog," see pp. 28–32.
104. Boufflers, *Aline, reine de Golconde*, 350.
105. Desan, "Transatlantic Spaces of Revolution," 474.
106. Ansart, "From Voltaire to Raynal," 79.
107. Letters from Bernardin de Saint-Pierre to M. Hénin (October 2, 6, 20, and 21, 1778) in *Correspondence*, 1:215–36.
108. See Moreau-Zanelli, *Gallipolis*, 69–70, and Carré, "Les émigrés français en Amérique," 4.
109. Voltaire, *Philosophical Letters*, 13.
110. Chastellux, *Voyages de M. le marquis de Chastellux dans l'Amérique septentrionale*, 2:257.
111. Chastellux, *Voyages de M. le marquis de Chastellux dans l'Amérique septentrionale*, 2:252, 256.
112. Chastellux, *Voyages de M. le marquis de Chastellux dans l'Amérique septentrionale*, 2:257–58.
113. In *Aminta* (1581), the first act finishes with a piece by the "Golden Age" chorus, in which love is opposed to the stifling laws of honor.
114. Chastellux, *Voyages de M. le marquis de Chastellux dans l'Amérique septentrionale*, 2:259.
115. Lezay-Marnésia, *Plan de lecture*, 1800, viii–ix.
116. Lezay-Marnésia, *Essai sur la nature champêtre*, 103.
117. On this question, see our article "Bâtir des châteaux en Amérique," 320–21.
118. Lezay-Marnésia, *Mes Souvenirs*, 23.
119. The establishment of Frenchman Bay that Rosalie-Josèphe Bacler de Leval wanted to found in the current State of Maine is another example of a colony whose ideal consisted in the reproduction of the advantages that the aristocracy enjoyed in France. On this question, see Childs, "Fontaine Leval," 187–222.
120. Lezay-Marnésia was in Bethlehem at the end of August 1790.

121. It took the victory of Anthony Wayne over the Amerindian Confederation of the West at the Battle of Fallen Timbers (August 20, 1794) and then the signature of the Treaty of Gand (December 24, 1814) after the War of 1812 with the British to remove the remaining two obstacles to the western expansion of the United States.

122. The term "uchronia" was invented in 1857 by Charles Renouvier when he began a novel titled *Uchronie (l'utopie dans l'histoire)*, first published in 1876. In *Uchronie*, Renouvier imagines an alternative history that would have been born if Christianity had not spread throughout Europe.

123. Louis Geoffroy-Château is considered to be the author of the first uchronic work, *Napoléon et la conquête du monde, 1812–1832* (1836), although the term "uchronie" was invented by Renouvier (see the preceding note). Geoffroy-Château invents a world in which Napoleon seized Saint Petersburg in order to make it his winter quarters during the Russian campaign. The author imagines that this strategy would have permitted Napoleon to avoid the disastrous retreat toward Western Europe and, in the long run, unify all the peoples on earth in a French empire. On this text, see Gallagher, "What Would Napoleon Do?" 315–36.

124. Brackenridge, *Modern Chivalry*, 221.

125. This comment by Duval d'Éprémesnil is quoted by Lescure in the *Mémoires sur les Assemblées parlementaires de la Révolution*, 2:6.

126. Lezay-Marnésia declares his adherence to the political ideas of the Impartials in the *Letters*, 61–62.

127. Desan, "Transatlantic Spaces of Revolution," 493.

128. Written in 1790, this text was published the following year in the *Almanach des Muses*. It is reproduced in the appendices of Lezay-Marnésia's *Letters*, 117–22.

129. On Crèvecœur and the concept of "melting pot," see p. 46. Glazer gives the following definition of the theory of the "salad bowl": "But for most of those who advocate multiculturalism, it is a position-taking stance on the racial and ethnic diversity of the United States. It is a position that rejects assimilation and the 'melting pot' image as an imposition of the dominant culture, and instead prefers such metaphors as the 'salad bowl' or the 'glorious mosaic,' in which each ethnic and racial element in the population maintains its distinctiveness" (*We Are All Multiculturalists Now*, 10).

130. Anonymous, *Prospectus*, 11–12.

131. A character speaks, for instance, of the six months of hard work to "drain a few acres of swamp and to clear seventeen acres," in *Voyage dans la Haute Pensylvanie*, 1801, 1:47. Regarding the question of Crèvecœur's publicity for America, in the *Voyage*, see pp. 63–65.

132. On this concept, see Freud, "Negation" [1925], 235–42.

133. The idyllic character of the Islands of the Blessed is emphasized by Pindar in *Olympian Odes, Pythian Odes*, 71.

134. On the ambiguity of the term "utopia," both "non-existent country" and "country of felicity," see Funke, "L'évolution sémantique de la notion d'*utopie* en français," 20.

135. Des Pintreaux (August 14, 1758, Pont-Audemer–August 17, 1842, Saint Louis, Missouri) was elected to the House of Representatives of the United States by the State of Pennsylvania (1792–98) and became judge in the Pennsylvania jurisdiction (1794). In 1805, he was appointed by Thomas Jefferson as judge of the territory of Louisiana. On des Pintreaux, see Cleland, "John B. C. Lucas, Physiocrat on the Frontier," 1–15; and McDermott, "John B. C. Lucas in Pennsylvania," 209–30.

136. Cleland claims that the documents available on M. des Pintreaux contradict nearly every detail of the narrative of Lezay-Marnésia ("John B. C. Lucas, Physiocrat on the Frontier," 3). McDermott had reached a similar conclusion in his study, stating that the third of the *Letters* was "in the main a literary indulgence on the part of Lezay-Marnésia" ("John B. C. Lucas in Pennsylvania," 211). In *L'Heureuse famille*, Lezay-Marnésia tells the story of Allard, an affluent worker and his wife, Amélie, from a noble but impoverished family. Their child, Basile, falls in love with Lucie, the daughter of poor farmers, and decides to marry her.

Amélie opposes this misalliance, out of pride, before progressively accepting the union of Basile and Lucie.

137. See p. 60.

Chapter 3

1. Mondésir, *Souvenirs d'Édouard de Mondésir*, 22.
2. In his *Souvenirs*, Mondésir describes a scene in which, like Ulysses, Chateaubriand had himself tied to the mast of the ship during a storm. On the reasons for the dissension between Chateaubriand and Mondésir during their journey, see Berchet, *Chateaubriand*, 163–70.
3. Chateaubriand, *Mémoires*, 1:453–54. A slightly different version of the same text appears in the *Voyage en Amérique*, 150.
4. Bazin, *Chateaubriand en Amérique*, 66. The canvas of Copley (1738–1815) was inspired by a true event that occurred in 1749. Brook Watson, a fourteen-year-old orphan who was serving as a sailor on a commercial vessel, was attacked by a shark in the port of Havana where he was swimming alone. His companions, who were waiting on board to escort the captain to shore, sent out a lifeboat to help him. Watson survived the attack but lost his right leg. This painting is conserved at the National Gallery of Art in Washington. It represents the exact moment when, while Watson is on the point of being saved by his comrades, a shark is closing on him with wide-open jaws.
5. Crèvecœur, *Lettres d'un cultivateur américain*, 1787, 3:102–5.
6. On the origin of the *Voyage en Amérique*, see pp. 132–34; on the origin of the American books of the *Mémoires d'outre-tombe*, see pp. 36, and 173–74.
7. See, for example, Chateaubriand, *Mémoires*, 4:208.
8. Readers of the *Itinéraire de Paris à Jérusalem* (1811), such as Alphonse de Lamartine, likewise followed in the steps of Chateaubriand with the intention of refuting his observations and to distance themselves from a cumbersome model. On this question, see Moussa, "Un voyage dans l'*Itinéraire*," 93–102.
9. On these letters by René de Mersenne, see Bédier, "Chateaubriand en Amérique," 504.
10. Sainte-Beuve, *Chateaubriand et son groupe littéraire*, 1:207; emphasis original.
11. Faguet, *Dix-Neuvième Siècle. Études Littéraires*, 3.
12. Bédier, "Chateaubriand en Amérique: Vérité et fiction," later revised and republished in *Études critiques*, 127–94; Bédier, "Chateaubriand en Amérique: Vérité et fiction (Suite)," 59–121; Bédier, "Chateaubriand en Amérique: Réplique à un contradicteur," 80–109.
13. Among the studies that treat this problem, see Dick, "Quelques sources ignorées," 228–45.
14. See Chateaubriand, *Travels in America*, trans. R. Switzer, and Bassan, "Le Vertige du temps," 96–101.
15. Berchet, *Chateaubriand*, 188–89.
16. Chateaubriand quoted by Berchet, *Chateaubriand*, 189.
17. Painter, *Chateaubriand: une biographie*, 189.
18. Chateaubriand, *Atala*, 16.
19. In 1791, the existence of this passage allowing people to travel by sea from Greenland to the Pacific Ocean was still an unresolved problem. George Vancouver concluded, after his expedition from 1791 to 1795, that there was no maritime passage south of the Bering Straits. The explorer Alexander Mackenzie confirmed Vancouver's opinion after his journey by land between 1789 and 1793, whose results were not known until 1801. Chateaubriand published in the *Mercure de France* on August 14 and on September 11, 1802, an account of Mackenzie's voyage before returning to the Northwest Passage in the preface of

Voyage en Amérique, where he notes other expeditions led at the beginning of the nineteenth century. The first successful navigation of this passage was the Gjøa expedition (1903–6), led by Roald Amundsen.

20. Crèvecœur, *Lettres d'un cultivateur américain*, 1787, 3:525.
21. Chateaubriand, *Mémoires*, 1:469.
22. Regarding the financial support granted by Jean-Baptiste de Chateaubriand to his brother, see Berchet, *Chateaubriand*, 159.
23. The fate of people close to Chateaubriand justified, unfortunately, his fears: his brother, Jean-Baptiste de Chateaubriand; his sister-in-law, the comtesse de Chateaubriand; her parents; and M. de Malesherbes were all guillotined on April 22, 1794.
24. In Letter VIII of the *Lettres persanes* (1721), Usbek explains to his friend Rustan that it was the relentless attacks against him by his enemies during his absence from the court that had led him to the decision to leave Persia. Regarding the influence of the *Lettres persanes* on *Les Natchez*, see Yee, *Exotic Subversions*, 28.
25. On Malesherbes, see Grosclaude, *Malesherbes*.
26. On the relationship of Malesherbes to Rousseau, see Fumaroli, "Chateaubriand et Rousseau," 208–9.
27. Bazin, *Chateaubriand en Amérique*, 53.
28. Regarding the obstacles to the discovery of the Northwest Passage by Chateaubriand, see Painter, *Chateaubriand: une biographie*, 208.
29. Chateaubriand, *Voyage*, 165–66.
30. Chateaubriand, *Voyage*, 402.
31. Hollier, "French Customs, Literary Borders," 43.
32. Letter of November 1844, quoted by Lebègue, "Les Avatars du voyage de Chateaubriand en Amérique," 102.
33. Reichler, "Le deuil et l'enchantement," 159.
34. On this question, see pp. 34–35.
35. The publication of the *Œuvres complètes* was necessitated by the fragile financial situation of Chateaubriand after his dismissal from the Villèle ministry on June 24, 1824. On the stages of their marketing, see Levaillant, *Splendeurs, misères et chimères*, 219–32.
36. Chateaubriand, *Essai sur les révolutions*, 53.
37. Chateaubriand, *Essai sur les révolutions*, 53; emphasis original.
38. Chateaubriand, *Essai sur les révolutions*, 443.
39. Chateaubriand, *Mémoires*, 1:470.
40. Chateaubriand, *Les Natchez*, 103.
41. Degout, "De la remémoration d'outre-tombe," 102–8.
42. Scott de Martinville applied in 1857 for the patent of the phonautograph, an apparatus for engraving acoustic vibrations on a sheet of paper. It was not until 1877 that Edison discovered how to conserve the sounds and to reproduce them at will: the phonograph was born.
43. This copy is conserved at the Bibliothèque nationale de France (French manuscript 12454, folios 46–48).
44. Degout, "De la remémoration d'outre-tombe," 105–6.
45. Chateaubriand devotes a section to wild turkeys that turns out to be inspired by Bartram's text, as is clear when one compares *Travels Through North and South Carolina* (58) and *Voyage en Amérique* (194). On this question, see the critical edition of the *Voyage en Amérique* by Switzer (1:135) and the edition published by Regard in *Œuvres romanesques et voyages* (p. 1293, n. 1).
46. On La Rochefoucauld-Liancourt, Volney, and Saint-Méry, see Furstenberg, *When the United States Spoke French*.
47. "Présentation," in *Voyage en Amérique*, 44.
48. See, for example, the narrative of Chastellux, *Voyages de M. le Marquis de Chastellux dans l'Amérique septentrionale*, 1:244.

49. Moreau de Saint-Méry's account offers numerous short notes containing information for potential travelers. See, for example, his *Voyage*, 84.
50. La Rochefoucauld-Liancourt, *Voyages*, 2:336.
51. Lestringant, "Rhétorique et dispositif d'autorité," 3.
52. "Des cannibales," in *Essais*, 211.
53. See Jeanneret, "Léry et Thevet," 240.
54. Regarding the progressive questioning of cosmographic discourse, see Lestringant, "Le déclin d'un savoir."
55. The *Cosmographie universelle* (1575) by André Thevet borrows broadly from the three-volume work by the Venetian, Giovanni Battista Ramusio, *Delle navigationi et viaggi* (1550–1606). On this question, see Lestringant, *L'Atelier du cosmographe*, chap. 2, "Leçons antiques: un Orient livresque," 59–77.
56. See Riberette, "Chateaubriand et Beltrami," 40–47.
57. Cooper, *The Letters and Journals of James Fenimore Cooper*, 1:212; emphasis added.
58. On the concept of "autopsy," see Lestringant, "Le déclin d'un savoir," 252.
59. On this terminology used by Chateaubriand to distinguish two stages of his literary apprenticeship, see pp. 134–35.
60. On this question, see Chateaubriand, *Voyage*, 364–65, note 23.
61. Rossi, "Présentation," in *Voyage en Amérique*, 43.
62. On the travel narratives of these authors, see the bibliography.
63. Chateaubriand, "Alex. Mackenzie," in *Œuvres complètes*, 88.
64. "I invent a language that must necessarily spring from a very new poetics, that I could define with these few words: *to paint not the thing but the effect that it produces*," Stéphane Mallarmé, letter of October 30, 1864, to H. Cazalis, in *Œuvres complètes*, 681; emphasis original.
65. Chateaubriand, "Alex. Mackenzie," 87.
66. On the concept of geometric spirit in the eighteenth century, see Frängsmyr, Heilbron, and Rider, *The Quantifying Spirit of the Eighteenth Century*.
67. The Niagara Falls are described, notably, by La Rochefoucauld-Liancourt (*Voyage*, 2:10–17) and Saint-John de Crèvecœur (*Voyage dans la haute Pensylvanie*, 2:73–87).
68. On the Northwest Passage, see pp. 129–31.
69. See the prologue of chapter 3, pp. 127–29.
70. See the prologue of chapter 3, p. 127.
71. The example of Madison Stathers illustrates the denunciatory intention of certain readers of Chateaubriand. In *Chateaubriand et l'Amérique*, she declares that her ambition is to prove that he never visited the places described in *Atala*, and that his life was "a continual lie toward the world" (112).
72. In the vocabulary of Gérard Genette, an "analepsis" is the relating of an event that preceded the main story being told (*Figures III*, 77–121). Similarly, an analeptic representation of North America constitutes a return to an earlier past: the narrator remembers a period that preceded the time of his actual trip, a reminiscence that allows him to enhance the America that he had, in fact, known.
73. An earlier version of the following section, "Mourning for (New) France," has previously been published as "Chateaubriand and the Mourning of (New) France" in *French Forum*.
74. Craiutu and Isaac, *America Through European Eyes*, 7.
75. Chateaubriand, *Atala*, 33.
76. On the history of New France, see Havard and Vidal, *Histoire de l'Amérique française*.
77. Chateaubriand, "Préface de la première edition (1801)," in *Atala*, 22.
78. Furstenberg, "The Significance of the Trans-Appalachian Frontier," 657.

79. "I have come to say a few words about the destinies of America, of these other peoples, heirs of the unfortunate Indians: *I have no other pretention than to express regrets and hopes*," Chateaubriand, *Voyage*, 137; emphasis added.

80. On the recovery of the manuscript of the *Voyage en Amérique*, see p. 134.

81. On "uchronia," in Lezay-Marnésia's *Letters*, see pp. 112–14.

82. Samuels, *The Spectacular Past*, 270.

83. Barbé-Marbois, *Histoire de la Louisiane*, 289.

84. Chateaubriand, *Voyage*, 371.

85. On Chateaubriand and the colonial ideology in France, see Prasad, *Colonialism, Race, and the French Romantic Imagination*, 72–98.

86. In 1790, Chateaubriand had planned to discover this route between the Sea of Greenland and the Pacific Ocean before quickly abandoning the project. On this subject, see the prologue of chapter 3, pp. 124–32.

87. On the "policy of fusion" established by Napoleon, see Morrissey, *The Economy of Glory*.

88. On this question, see p. 164.

89. This question quickly arises in the preface of the *Voyage* (113), concerning the languages of India.

90. On the question of Lezay-Marnésia's description of Saint-Pierre, see pp. 112–14.

91. On the representations of slavery in French literature and culture, see Miller, *The French Atlantic Triangle*.

92. See Havard and Vidal, *Histoire de l'Amérique française*, 101.

93. See Guion, "Langue et nation," 347–63.

94. Bouhours, *Les Entretiens d'Ariste et d'Eugène*, 163.

95. Bouhours, *Les Entretiens d'Ariste et d'Eugène*, 163.

96. Reichler, "Le deuil et l'enchantement," 157.

97. Miller, "'Slaves' in My Family," 109.

98. Rossi, "Présentation," in *Voyage en Amérique*, 62.

99. Chateaubriand refused to support in the legislature the head of government, Villèle, who was engaged in a controversial plan to convert pensions. Irritated by this lack of political solidarity, Villèle obtained from Louis XVIII the dismissal of Chateaubriand.

100. "Préface générale (edition de 1826)," in *Œuvres complétes*, 1:iv; emphasis added.

101. See Lefort, "Mort de l'immortalité ?" 3:197.

102. Fumaroli, "Chateaubriand et Rousseau," 213.

103. Beginning with the French Revolution, America is less and less described as a double for France but rather as an *other* for it. On this question, see the conclusion, pp. 182–83.

104. Chateaubriand, *Itinéraire*, 904.

105. Montesquieu, *Considérations sur les causes de la grandeur des Romains et de leur décadence* (1734).

106. Chateaubriand, *Itinéraire*, 905.

107. "Polémique (Paris, 5 décembre 1818)," in *Œuvres complètes de M. le Vicomte de Chateaubriand*, 28:191.

108. "Polémique (Paris, 5 décembre 1818)," in *Œuvres complètes de M. le Vicomte de Chateaubriand*, 28:192.

109. "Polémique (Paris, 5 décembre 1818)," in *Œuvres complètes de M. le Vicomte de Chateaubriand*, 28:194.

110. "Polémique (Paris, 5 décembre 1818)," in *Œuvres complètes de M. le Vicomte de Chateaubriand*, 28:191.

111. Chateaubriand, *Voyage*, 221.

112. An inscription indicates the place and date of the composition of books VI to VIII of the *Mémoires d'outre-tombe*: "London, from April to September 1822." Nonetheless, the edition by Berchet highlights events that took place in 1843 (see Chateaubriand, *Mémoires,*

1:427, note 1). The final version of these books was not achieved until three years later, as indicated by the note "Revised in December 1846" placed at the beginning of the books VI, VII, and VIII. The final writing of the *Voyage en Amérique* thus preceded that of books VI to VIII of the *Mémoires*.

113. On the adoption of cosmographic discourse in the *Voyage*, see pp. 140–43.
114. Thevet, *Le Brésil d'André Thevet*, 194.
115. Montalbetti, *Le Voyage, le monde et la bibliothèque*, 177.
116. On analogy in the *Itinéraire*, see Guyot, *Analogie et récit de voyage*, 149–212.
117. Chateaubriand, *Mémoires*, 1:436.
118. See, respectively, Léry's *Histoire d'un voyage faict en la terre du Brésil*, 257, and Herodotus, *Histoires*, 2:114.
119. On this question, see Richard, *Paysages de Chateaubriand*.
120. See Dobie, "La rhétorique du rapprochement," 63–87.
121. Chateaubriand compares the pyramids of Egypt to those he observed on the banks of the Ohio River: "[The Pyramids] reminded me of monuments that were less pompous but that were also tombs; I'm speaking of the sod structures that cover the ashes of the Amerindians on the banks of the Ohio. When I visited them, I was in quite a different *frame of mind* than when I beheld the mausoleums of the Pharaohs: at that time I was beginning the journey, and now I am finishing it. The world, in those two periods of my life, appeared to me precisely as an image of the two deserts where I saw those two kinds of tombs: happy solitudes, arid sands" (*Itinéraire*, 1144, emphasis added).
122. *Voyage au Mont-Blanc*, in Chateaubriand, *Œuvres complètes*, 7:822.
123. See Proust, *Le Temps retrouvé*, 226.
124. See the excerpt of the *Itinéraire* quoted in note 121.
125. "[I]f the human body has been once affected simultaneously by two exterior elements, as soon as the soul later imagines one of them, it will remember also the other, that is, it will consider them as both being present, unless other causes are in play that prevent their presence." Spinoza, *Éthique*, 1:211.
126. Riffaterre, *La Production du texte*, 137.
127. Berchet, "Préface," in *Mémoires d'outre-tombe*, 1:22.
128. Chateaubriand, "Préface testamentaire," in *Mémoires d'outre-tombe*, 1:758.
129. On this question, see the study of Cavallin, *Chateaubriand mythographe*, as well as his article titled "Chateaubriand mythographe," 1087–98.
130. Cavallin, *Chateaubriand mythographe*, 13; emphasis original.
131. Dobie, "La rhétorique du rapprochement," 84.
132. On this question, see pp. 151–52.
133. "Proposition faite à la chambre des pairs," in *Œuvres complètes de M. le Vicomte de Chateaubriand*, 30:42.
134. Chateaubriand, "Proposition faite à la chambre des pairs," in *Œuvres complètes de M. le Vicomte de Chateaubriand*, 30:41.
135. Tocqueville favored the colonization of Algeria in the name of the overriding interests of France. As Nesbitt remarks, "Tocqueville's writings on Algeria consistently subordinated the Rights of Man to those of the French citizen. These texts reveal that in the context of his political functions, Tocqueville placed the rights of the French citizens and the need to shore up an infirm French democratic tradition before the human rights of its colonial subjects. Tocqueville could simultaneously defend the use of violence against Algerian subjects while condemning French slavery because his predominant criterion in all of these writings was not the problem of human rights, but the glory and solidity of the democratic French state" ("On the Political Efficacy of Idealism: Tocqueville, Schoelcher, and the Abolition of Slavery," in *America Through European Eyes*, 95). On Tocqueville and the colonization of Algeria, see likewise Pitts's introduction to her edition, *Alexis de Tocqueville: Writings on Empire and Slavery*.
136. Dobie, "La rhétorique du rapprochement," 85.

137. Regarding Rousseau's influence on Lévi-Strauss, see *Tristes tropiques*, 421.

138. In the part devoted to the Nambikwaras, Lévi-Strauss cites an account written by a fellow ethnographer concerning the members of this tribe (310). In order to counter this "heartbreaking description" with memories of a period ten years earlier that he had spent in the company of the Nambikwaras, Lévi-Strauss included a text composed when he was living with them (310–11). This practice of self-quotation and contextualizing by an older author of notes he had taken during his journey echoes the duality of Chateaubriand in the *Voyage en Amérique* where "the novice author" and the "aged writer" share the paternity of the text (see pp. 134–135). Regarding the functioning of the memory, Lévi-Strauss uses the expression "mental tracking" (143) to designate the passage from Brazil to South Asia in the fourth part of his work. The memory of a hotel in Brazil, for example, recalls that of a trip to Pakistan in 1950 (125).

139. Lévi-Strauss, *Tristes tropiques*, 32–33; emphasis original.

140. Lévi-Strauss, *Tristes tropiques*, 33.

141. See Debaene and Jeannelle, "Où est la littérature?," *Fabula/Les colloques, L'Idée de littérature dans les années 1950*, June 2004 http://www.fabula.org/colloques/document66.php.

142. "Alex. Mackenzie," 88.

143. On this question, see pp. 143–46.

144. According to Weber, the disenchantment of the world consists in breaking away from magic as a means of obtaining salvation. This concept is used in the revised 1920 edition of *The Protestant Ethic and the Spirit of Capitalism*. It was later espoused by Marcel Gauchet in *Le Désenchantement du monde* (1985).

145. "Alex. Mackenzie," 88. The line of verse comes from Fontanes, "La forêt de Navarre," in *Œuvres*, 1:4.

146. Lévi-Strauss, *Tristes tropiques*, 348.

147. Lévi-Strauss, *Tristes tropiques*, 348.

148. Mourot, *Le Génie d'un style*, 170.

149. Chateaubriand, *Voyage*, 178.

150. Scève's "Le Microcosme" (1562), may be found in his *Œuvres poétiques*, 234.

151. Fragment quoted by Berchet in *Mémoires*, 1:48.

152. See, for example, P. Desportes, "Chanson," in *Choix des poésies*, 232.

153. This term was found before in the writings of Pascal (see Jungo, *Le Vocabulaire de Pascal*, 55), of Choiseul in 1762 (see Gohin, *Les Transformations de la langue française*, 273), and of Mercier on the eve of the Revolution (see Mercier, *Mon bonnet de nuit*, 2:127).

154. For Du Bellay, see *Les Regrets*, 205; for Montaigne, the "Apologie de Raimond de Sebond," in *Essais*, 630.

155. As we saw earlier, Édouard de Mondésir compares Chateaubriand to Cervantes's hero: "The chevalier, I would almost say the Don Quixote, who often liked to take risks, wanted to go swimming in the ocean." See his *Souvenirs*, 22.

156. See "Des cannibales," in *Essais*, 208–21.

157. On this question, see p. 162.

158. "Whatever absurdity might be found in this parallel, whose goal, here again, is the purification of the American episode, disappears thanks to the magic of Ronsard's verse," Didier, "Voyages croisés," in *Chateaubriand Mémorialiste*, 65.

159. See Cabanès, "L'encadrement du *Voyage en Amérique*," 61–67.

160. "Chrysogenous" is a neologism invented by Chateaubriand. It refers to an aristocracy "born of capitalist wealth. This neologism, with its Greek etymology, is a humorous reference to Byzantine titles" (Berchet in *Mémoires*, 1:534, note 2). We will comment later on the use of this term by Chateaubriand (pp. 177–80).

161. Chateaubriand, *Voyage*, 381.

162. Chateaubriand, *Mémoires*, 1:524–25. Page numbers in the following text all refer to this volume. In the *Voyage* (373), Chateaubriand evokes in similar terms the radical changes in the United States since his stay there.
163. Chateaubriand, "Préface testamentaire," in *Mémoires*, 1:758.
164. Hazard, "Chateaubriand et la littérature des États-Unis," 46–61.
165. Vail, *De la littérature et des hommes de lettres des États-Unis d'Amérique*, xvi.
166. Hazard, "Chateaubriand et la littérature des États-Unis," 52.
167. Jefferson, *Notes*, 64.
168. Baudelaire, *Edgar Allan Poe, sa vie et ses ouvrages*, in *Œuvres complètes*, 2:249–95.
169. "Both young and old, America chatters and rambles with remarkable glibness" Baudelaire, *Edgar Allan Poe, sa vie et ses ouvrages*, in *Œuvres complètes*, 2:320.
170. Might Chateaubriand be thinking of Presidents Martin Van Buren (1837–41), William Henry Harrison (1841), or John Tyler (1841–45)?
171. On this question, see pp. 146–56.
172. Chateaubriand, *Voyage*, 381.
173. Whereas Chateaubriand announced the formation of an aristocratic class in the United States, Tocqueville asserted that the law on inheritance served the cause of social equality: having adopted the principle of equal shares between heirs, the United States mitigated the bequeathing of entire estates to one person. On this question, see Tocqueville, *De la Démocratie en Amérique*, 1:42.
174. As Paul Krugman observes, "The current generation of the very rich in America may consist largely of executives rather than rentiers, people who live off accumulated capital, but these executives have heirs. And America two decades from now could be a rentier-dominated society even more unequal than Belle Époque Europe" ("Why We're in a New Gilded Age").
175. On Buffon's theory on the degeneration of species in America, see pp. 77–78, and p. 198, note 2.
176. On this question, see Roger, *The American Enemy*.

Conclusion

1. Philo-Americanism is a discourse expressing admiration and enthusiasm first for the English colonies in North America and subsequently for the United States itself (there was a philo-Americanism before and after the War of Independence). America was thus conceived as a model that the French were to imitate as they sought to reform their own political institutions and to promote values that, supposedly, had found their full expression across the Atlantic (in particular, religious tolerance and freedom of speech, as well as equality before the law and of social classes). Philo-Americanism is organized around recurrent themes and based on the same authorities whoever the speaker was, turning it into a coherent and systematic discourse rather than a disparate assortment of pro-American sentiments. Its characteristics will be further developed in the course of this conclusion. In regard to anti-Americanism, Roger, in his benchmark study of the topic, gives the following definition: "Anti-Americanism is an unbridled discourse, not only because it is rife with irrationality and bubbling with humors, but also because it takes an essayistic form, rather than that of a dissertation or a demonstration. (It does not follow 'orders' either; there is no anti-American conspiracy.) Its logic is one of accumulation, accretion—'I'll take that one' or 'give me a little bit more of that'—in short, it is a mad dash that ignores the Aristotelian principle of non-contradiction" (*The American Enemy*, xvi–xvii).
2. "Introduction," in *America Through European Eyes*, 7–8.
3. Echeverria, *Mirage in the West*, 183. By "American Dream," Echeverria is referring to the whole set of opinions favorable to the United States in Old Regime France and not to what this idea evokes today, that is, the myth of guaranteed prosperity for hardworking people

who have come to seek a better life in America. In the rest of this conclusion, the expression is used in the sense given by Echeverria here.

4. Echeverria, *Mirage in the West*, 183.

5. In regard to French anti-Americanism in this period, see Echeverria, *Mirage in the West*, 175.

6. On this question, see Chateaubriand, *Atala*, 22.

7. "Fusées," in *Œuvres complètes*, 1:665–66.

8. Regarding Duhamel and the discourse of French intellectuals on America in the modern period, see Mathy, *Extrême-Occident*, 52–103.

9. Duhamel, *Scènes de la vie future*, 16–17.

10. Duhamel, *Scènes de la vie future*, 217.

11. See, respectively, Debray, *Contretemps*, 104, and Aron and Dandieu, *Le Cancer américain*.

12. Regarding Chateaubriand's pessimism toward the United States, see pp. 173–80. For Europe's attitude in the 1830s, see Roger, *The American Enemy*, 53.

13. See "Frenchmen in America, 1776–1783," in Echeverria's *Mirage in the West*, 79–115.

14. See Moreau-Zanelli, *Gallipolis*, 414–15.

BIBLIOGRAPHY

Primary Sources

Chateaubriand, François-René de. *Voyage en Amérique*. 1827. In *Œuvres complètes de Chateaubriand*, vols. 6–7, edited by Henri Rossi. Paris: Honoré Champion, 2008.

———. *Mémoires d'outre-tombe*. 1848. Books 6–8. Edited by Jean-Claude Berchet. Paris: Le Livre de poche, 1989.

Crèvecœur, Michel-Guillaume Saint-John de. *Lettres d'un cultivateur américain*. 2 vols. Paris: Cuchet, 1784. Facsimile edition, with an introduction by G. Bertier de Sauvigny. Geneva: Slatkine Reprints, 1979.

———. *Lettres d'un cultivateur américain*. 3 vols. Paris: Cuchet, 1787.

———. *Voyage dans la Haute Pensylvanie et dans l'État de New York*. 1801. Edited by Françoise Plet. Preface by Bernard Chevignard. Presses Universitaires de Vincennes, 2002.

———. *Voyage dans la Haute Pensylvanie et dans l'État de New York, par un membre adoptif de la Nation Onéida, traduit et publié par l'auteur des Lettres d'un cultivateur américain*. 3 vols. Paris: Édition Marandan, an IX [1801].

Lezay-Marnésia, Claude-François-Adrien de. *Letters Written from the Banks of the Ohio*. 1792. Edited by Benjamin Hoffmann. Translated by Alan J. Singerman. University Park: Pennsylvania State University Press, 2017.

Secondary Sources

Allemagne (d'). *Nouvelles du Scioto ou relation fidèle du voyage et des infortunes d'un Parisien qui arrive de ces pays-là, où il était allé pour s'établir*. Paris: Lenoir et Leboucher, 1790.

Andrieux, François-Guillaume-Jean-Stanislas. "Les Français aux bords du Scioto, épître à un émigrant pour Kentucky." 1790. In *Letters Written from the Banks of the Ohio*, 1792, edited by Benjamin Hoffmann and translated by Alan J. Singerman, 117–22. University Park: Pennsylvania State University Press, 2017.

Anonymous. *Le Parlement de Paris établi au Scioto, Sur les bords de l'Oyo, et se trouve à Paris: chez tous les marchands de nouveautés*. Bibliothèque nationale, Lb 39 9346, 1790.

Anonymous. *Lettre écrite par un Français émigrant sur les terres de la Compagnie du Scioto à son ami à Paris*. Bibliothèque nationale, Pb 1599, New York, May 23, 1790.

Anonymous. *Nouveau prospectus de la Compagnie du Scioto, avec plusieurs lettres écrites du Scioto même*. Paris: Prault, 1790.

Anonymous. *Prospectus pour l'établissement sur les rivières d'Ohio et de Scioto en Amérique*. Paris: Prault, 1789.

Barbé-Marbois, François. *Histoire de la Louisiane et de la cession de cette colonie aux États-Unis de l'Amérique septentrionale; précédée d'un discours sur la constitution et le gouvernement des États-Unis*. Paris: Firmin-Didot, 1829.

Bartram, William. *Travels Through North and South Carolina, Georgia, East and West Florida, the Cherokee Country, the Extensive Territories of the Muscogulges or Creek Confederacy, and the Country of the Choctaws. Containing an Account of the Soil and Natural Productions of Those Regions; Together with Observations on the Manners of the Indians*. Philadelphia: James and Johnson, 1791.

Bouhours, Dominique. *Les Entretiens d'Ariste et d'Eugène*. 1671. Edited by Bernard Beugnot and Gilles Declercq. Paris: Champion, 2003.
Brackenridge, Hugh Henry. *Modern Chivalry: Containing the Adventures of Captain John Farrago and Teague O'Regan, His Servant.* 1792–1815. Edited by Ed White. Indianapolis: Hackett Press, 2009.
Brissot de Warville, Jacques-Pierre. *Examen critique des Voyages dans l'Amérique septentrionale de Monsieur le marquis de Chastellux, ou Lettre à Monsieur le marquis de Chastellux, dans laquelle on réfute principalement son opinion sur les Quakers, sur les Nègres, sur le Peuple et sur l'Homme.* London, 1786.
———. *Mémoires sur ses contemporains et la Révolution française, publiés par son fils.* 4 vols. Paris: Ladvocat, 1830–32.
———. *Nouveau voyage dans les États-Unis de l'Amérique Septentrionale, fait en 1788.* 3 vols. Paris: Buisson, 1791.
Buffon, Georges-Louis-Leclerc de. *Animaux de l'Ancien continent.* 1761. In *Histoire naturelle, générale et particulière, avec la description du Cabinet du Roi.* 36 vols. Paris: Imprimerie royale, 1749–88. Vol. 9. 56–83.
———. *Animaux du Nouveau Monde.* 1761. In *Histoire naturelle, générale et particulière, avec la description du Cabinet du Roi.* 36 vols. Paris: Imprimerie royale, 1749–88. Vol. 9. 84–96.
———. *Les Animaux communs aux deux continents.* 1761. In *Histoire naturelle, générale et particulière, avec la description du Cabinet du Roi.* 36 vols. Paris: Imprimerie royale, 1749–88. Vol. 9. 97–128.
———. *De la Dégénération des animaux.* 1766. In *Histoire naturelle, générale et particulière, avec la description du Cabinet du Roi.* 36 vols. Paris: Imprimerie royale, 1749–88. Vol. 14. 311–14.
Casanova, Giacomo. *Histoire de ma vie.* Edited by Jean-Christophe Igalens and Érik Leborgne. 2 vols. Paris: Robert Laffont, "Bouquins," 2013–15.
Champlain, Samuel de. *Voyages et Descouvertes faites en la Nouvelle-France par le sieur de Champlain.* Paris: Claude Collet, 1620.
Charlevoix, Pierre François Xavier de. *Histoire et description générale de la Nouvelle France, avec le journal historique d'un voyage fait par ordre du roi en l'Amérique septentrionale.* 1744. 3 vols. Montréal: Éditions Élysée, 1976.
Chastellux, François-Jean de Beauvoir, marquis de. *Voyages de M. le Marquis de Chastellux dans l'Amérique septentrionale dans les années 1780, 1781 et 1782.* 2 vols. Paris: Prault, 1788–91.
Chateaubriand, François-René de. *Atala.* 1801. In *Œuvres romanesques et voyages.* Vol. 1. Edited by Maurice Regard. Paris: Gallimard, "Bibliothèque de la Pléiade," 1969.
———. *Correspondance générale.* 8 vols. Paris: Gallimard, 1977–2010.
———. *Essai sur les révolutions. Génie du christianisme.* 1797/1802. Edited by Maurice Regard. Paris: Gallimard, "Bibliothèque de la Pléiade," 1978.
———. *Itinéraire de Paris à Jérusalem.* 1811. In *Œuvres romanesques et voyages.* Vol. 2. Edited by Maurice Regard, 679–1343. Paris: Gallimard, "Bibliothèque de la Pléiade," 1969.
———. *Les Natchez.* 1827. Edited by Gilbert Chinard. Baltimore: Johns Hopkins University Press, 1932.
———. *Œuvres complètes.* 31 vols. Paris: Ladvocat, 1826–31.
———. *Œuvres complètes de M. le Vicomte de Chateaubriand.* 36 vols. Paris: Pourrat Frères, 1836–39.
———. *Voyage au Mont-Blanc.* 1805. In *Œuvres complètes de Chateaubriand.* Vols. 6–7. Edited by Henri Rossi. Paris: Honoré Champion, 2008.
Cloots, Anacharsis. *Écrits révolutionnaires, 1790–1794.* Edited by Michèle Duval. Paris: Éditions Champ libre, 1979.
Columbus, Christopher. *The Journal of Christopher Columbus.* Edited and translated by Cecil Jane. New York: Bonanza Books, 1989.

Condorcet, Marie-Jean-Antoine-Nicolas de Caritat, marquis de. *Writings on the United States.* Edited and translated by Guillaume Ansart. University Park: Pennsylvania State University Press, 2009.
Cooper, James Fenimore. *The Letters and Journals of James Fenimore Cooper.* Edited by James Franklin Beard. Cambridge, Mass.: Harvard University Press, 1960.
Crèvecœur, J. Hector St. John de. *Crèvecœur's Eighteenth-Century Travels in Pennsylvania and New York.* Translated by Percy G. Adams. Lexington: University of Kentucky Press, 1961.
———. *Letters from an American Farmer and Other Essays.* 1782. Edited by Denis D. Moore. Cambridge, Mass.: Harvard University Press, 2013.
———. *More Letters from the American Farmer: An Edition of the Essays in English Left Unpublished by Crèvecœur.* Edited by Dennis D. Moore. Athens: University of Georgia Press, 1995.
———. *Saint-John de Crèvecœur, Voyage aux grandes salines tyroliennes de Reichenhall.* 1808. Edition, notes, and introduction by Bernard Chevignard and Angela Kuhk. Munich: Kommission für Bayerische Landesgeschichte, 2003.
———. *Sketches of Eighteenth-Century America.* New Haven: Yale University Press, 1925. Edited by Henry L. Bourdin, Ralph H. Gabriel, and Stanley T. Williams. New York: Benjamin Bloom, 1972.
———. *Traité de la culture des pommes de terre et de différents usages qu'en font les habitants des États-Unis d'Amérique, par un normand qui a résidé longtemps et parcouru les différentes provinces de ce continent.* Caen: Leroy, 1782.
Cutler, Manasseh. *An Explanation of the Map Which Delineates That Part of the Federal Lands Comprehended Between Pennsylvania, West Line, the Rivers Ohio and Scioto and Lake Erie, Confirmed to the United States by Sundry Tribes of Indians, in the Treaties of 1784 and 1786, and Now Ready for Settlement.* Salem: Dabney and Cushing, 1787.
Desportes, Philippe. *Choix des poésies de Ronsard, Du Bellay, Baïf, Belleau, Du Bartas, Chassignet, Desportes, Régnier.* Edited by Gérard de Nerval. Paris: Bureau de la Bibliothèque choisie, 1830.
Diderot, Denis. *Œuvres complètes.* Edited by Jules Assézat and Maurice Tourneux. 20 vols. Paris: Garnier, 1875–77.
Diderot, Denis, and Jean le Rond d'Alembert, eds. *Encyclopédie, ou dictionnaire raisonné des sciences, des arts et des métiers.* Edited by Robert Morrissey and Glenn Roe. Chicago: University of Chicago ARTFL Encyclopédie Project, 2017.
Dillon, Henriette Lucy, marquise de La Tour du Pin. *Mémoires de la Marquise de la Tour du Pin.* Paris: Mercure de France, 1979.
Du Bellay, Joachim. *Les Regrets.* 1558. Edited by Samuel de Sacy. Paris: Gallimard, 1967.
Fénelon, François de Salignac de la Mothe. *Les Aventures de Télémaque.* 1699. Edited by Jeanne-Lydie Goré. Paris: Classiques Garnier, 2009.
Fontanes, Louis de. *Œuvres de M. de Fontanes.* 2 vols. Paris: Hachette, 1839.
Franklin, Benjamin. *Avis à ceux qui voudraient s'en aller en Amérique.* Paris, 1784.
Grimm, Friedrich Melchior. *Correspondance littéraire, philosophique et critique.* 16 vols. Edited by Maurice Tourneux. Paris: Garnier Frères, 1877–82.
Jefferson, Thomas. *Notes on the State of Virginia.* 1785. Edited by Frank Shuffelton. London: Penguin Classics, 1999.
———. *The Papers of Thomas Jefferson.* 41 vols. Edited by Julian P. Boyd et al. Princeton: Princeton University Press, 1950–2015.
Lafayette, Gilbert du Motier, marquis de. *Mémoires, correspondance et manuscrits du général Lafayette, publiés par sa famille.* 6 vols. Paris: H. Fournier aîné, 1837.
Lafitau, Joseph-François. *Mœurs des Sauvages américains comparées aux mœurs des premiers temps.* 1724. 2 vols. Excerpts edited by Edna H. Lemay. Paris: Maspero-La Découverte, 1983.
Lahontan, Louis Armand de. *Dialogues de Monsieur le Baron de Lahontan et d'un sauvage.* 1704. Edited by Henri Coulet. Paris: Desjonquères, 1999.

La Rochefoucauld-Liancourt, François-Alexandre-Frédéric, duc de. *Voyages dans les États-Unis d'Amérique, fait en 1795, 1796 et 1797*. 8 vols. Paris: Du Pont, Buisson, Pougens, 1799.
Ledoux, Claude-Nicolas. *L'Architecture considérée sous le rapport de l'art, des mœurs et de la législation*. 2 vols. Paris: Printed by the author, 1804.
Léry, Jean de. *Histoire d'un voyage faict en la terre du Brésil*. 1578. Edited by Frank Lestringant. Paris: Livre de poche, 1994.
Lescure, Mathurin de. *Mémoires sur les Assemblées parlementaires de la Révolution*. 2 vols. Paris: Firmin-Didot, 1881.
Lezay-Marnésia, Albert de. *Mes souvenirs: À mes enfants*. Blois: E. Dezairs, 1851.
Lezay-Marnésia, Claude-François-Adrien de. *Le Bonheur dans les campagnes*. 1785. Paris: Royez, 1788.
———. *Discours de réception à la Société royale des Belles-Lettres de Nancy, le 20 octobre 1767*. Paris: Quillau Libraire and Dessain Junior, 1767.
———. "Épître à mon curé." 1775. In *Essai sur la nature champêtre*, 185–91. Paris: Prault, 1787.
———. *Essai sur la minéralogie du bailliage d'Orgelet en Franche-Comté, lu dans la séance publique de l'Académie des Sciences et des Arts de Besançon, le 5 décembre 1778*. Besançon: Charmet and Mérigot Jeune, 1778.
———. *Essai sur la nature champêtre*. Paris: Prault, 1787.
———. *L'Heureuse famille, conte moral*. Geneva: Leclerc, 1766.
———. *Idée d'un député du bailliage d'Aval sur la permanence de l'Assemblée nationale*. S.l., s.d. British Library (FR 7428), 1789.
———. "Les Lampes, allégorie." *Journal de Paris* 118 (April 27, 1788).
———. "Maraudeur." *Journal Encyclopédique*, July 15, 1759.
———. "Maraudeur"/"Voleur." In Denis Diderot and Jean le Rond d'Alembert, eds., *Encyclopédie, ou dictionnaire raisonné des sciences, des arts et des métiers*, edited by Robert Morrissey and Glenn Roe. Chicago: University of Chicago ARTFL Encyclopédie Project, 2017.
———. *Les Paysages, ou essai sur la nature champêtre, poème*. Paris: Louis, 1800. [This volume also contains: *Apelle et Campaspe, ballet héroïque; Pièces fugitives; L'Heureuse famille, conte moral;* and *Les Lampes, allégorie; Épître à mon curé*.]
———. *Plan de lecture pour une jeune dame*. Lausanne: A. Fischer and Luc Vincent, 1784; Paris: Louis, 1800. [This volume also contains *Voyage au Pays de Vaud; Lettre à M. de V.; Pensées littéraires, morales et religieuses; L'Héroïsme de la charité; Lettre à M. Audrain à Pittsbourg; Dialogue entre Buffon et Bailly;* and *Discours de réception à la Société royale des Belles-Lettres de Nancy*.]
Mazzei, Filippo. *Recherches historiques et politiques sur les États-Unis de l'Amérique Septentrionale*. 4 vols. Paris: Froullé, 1788.
Mercier, Louis-Sébastien. *Mon bonnet de nuit*. 4 vols. Neuchâtel: Imprimerie de la Société typographique, 1784.
Mondésir, Édouard de. *Souvenirs d'Édouard de Mondésir, 1789–1811*. Edited by Gilbert Chinard. Baltimore: Johns Hopkins University Press, 1942.
Montaigne, Michel de. *Essais*. 1580–88. Edited by Jean Balsamo, Catherine Magnien-Simonin, and Michel Magnien. Paris: Gallimard, "Bibliothèque de la Pléiade," 2007.
Montesquieu, Charles-Louis de Secondat, baron de La Brède et de. 1734. *Considérations sur les causes de la grandeur des Romains et de leur décadence*. Edited by Catherine Volpilhac-Auger. Paris: Gallimard, 2008.
More, Thomas. *The Yale Edition of the Complete Works of St. Thomas More*. Edited by J. H. Hexter and Edward J. Surtz. New Haven: Yale University Press, 1965.
Moreau de Saint-Méry, Médéric-Louis-Élie. *Voyage aux États-Unis de l'Amérique, 1793–1798*. Edited by Stewart L. Mims. New Haven: Yale University Press, 1913.
Pauw, Cornelius de. *Recherches philosophiques sur les Américains ou mémoires intéressants pour servir à l'histoire de l'espèce humaine*. 1768. 2 vols. Paris: Jean-Michel Place, 1990.

Prévost, Antoine-François. *Cleveland.* 1731–39. Edited by Jean Sgard and Philip Stewart. Paris: Desjonquères, 2003.

———. *Manon Lescaut.* 1731. Edited by Frédéric Deloffre and Raymond Picard. Paris: Gallimard, 2008.

Rousseau, Jean-Jacques. *Les Confessions.* 1782–89. In *Œuvres complètes,* vol. 1. Edited by Bernard Gagnebin and Marcel Raymond, 1–656. Paris: Gallimard, "Bibliothèque de la Pléiade," 1959–95.

———. "Discourse on Inequality." 1755. In *The Major Political Writings of Jean-Jacques Rousseau,* edited and translated by John T. Scott, 37–152. Chicago: University of Chicago Press, 2012.

———. *Émile, ou de l'éducation.* 1762. In *Œuvres complètes,* vol. 4. Edited by Bernard Gagnebin and Marcel Raymond, 53–869. Paris: Gallimard, "Bibliothèque de la Pléiade," 1959–95.

———. *Julie ou la Nouvelle Héloïse.* 1761. In *Œuvres complètes,* vol. 2. Edited by Bernard Gagnebin and Marcel Raymond, 1–794. Paris: Gallimard, "Bibliothèque de la Pléiade," 1959–95.

———. *Narcisse ou l'amant de lui-même.* 1753. Edited by Henri Coulet. Paris: Desjonquères, 2008.

———. *Les Rêveries du promeneur solitaire.* 1782. In *Œuvres complètes,* vol. 1. Edited by Bernard Gagnebin and Marcel Raymond, 999–1099. Paris: Gallimard, "Bibliothèque de la Pléiade," 1959–95.

Roux. *Le Nouveau Mississippi ou les dangers d'habiter sur les bords du Scioto, par un patriote voyageur.* Paris: Jacob-Sion, 1790.

Sabran, Éléonore de, and Stanislas de Boufflers. *Le Lit bleu: correspondance de la Comtesse de Sabran et du Chevalier de Boufflers.* Edited by Sue Carrell. Paris: Tallandier, 2009.

Sade, Donatien-Alphonse-François de. *Œuvres.* Edited by Michel Delon. 3 vols. Paris: Gallimard, "Bibliothèque de la Pléiade," 1990–98.

Saint-Lambert, Jean-François de. *Les Saisons.* Amsterdam: s.n., 1769.

Saint-Pierre, Bernardin de. *Correspondance de J.-H. Bernardin de Saint-Pierre.* Paris: Louis-Aimé Martin, 1826.

———. *Études de la Nature.* 1784–88. Edited by Colas Duflo. Saint-Étienne: Université de Saint-Étienne, 2007.

———. *L'Arcadie et l'Amazone.* 1788. Edited by Raymond Trousson. Genève: Slatkine Reprints, 1980.

———. *Paul and Virginia.* 1787. Translated by John Donovan. London: Peter Owen, 2005.

Scève, Maurice. *Œuvres poétiques complètes.* Edited by Bernard Guégan. Geneva: Slatkine Reprints, 1967.

Spinoza, Baruch. *Éthique.* 1677. Edited and translated by Charles Appuhn. Paris: Vrin, 1977.

Thevet, André. *Le Brésil d'André Thevet, Les Singularités de la France Antarctique.* 1557. Edited by Frank Lestringant. Paris: Editions Chandeigne, 1997.

Tocqueville, Alexis de. *De la Démocratie en Amérique.* 1835–40. Edited by Eduardo Nolla. Paris: Vrin, 1990.

———. *Writings on Empire and Slavery.* Edited and translated by Jennifer Pitts. Baltimore: Johns Hopkins University Press, 2001.

Tocqueville, Alexis de, and Gustave de Baumont. *Correspondance d'Alexis de Tocqueville et de Gustave de Beaumont.* 3 vols. Edited by André Jardin. Paris: Gallimard, 1967.

Vail, Eugène A. *De la littérature et des hommes de lettres des États-Unis d'Amérique.* Paris: Charles Gosselin, 1841.

Volney, Constantin-François de. *Les Ruines, ou Méditation sur les révolutions des Empires.* Paris: Desenne, Volland, Plassan, 1791.

———. *Tableau du climat et du sol des États-Unis d'Amérique.* 2 vols. Paris: Courcier, 1803.

Voltaire. *L'Ingénu.* 1767. Paris: Gallimard "Folioplus classiques," 2004.

———. *Philosophical Letters: Or, Letters Regarding the English Nation.* 1734. Edited by John Leigh. Translated by Prudence L. Steiner. Indianapolis: Hackett, 2007.

Complementary Works

Balzac, Honoré de. *Le Père Goriot*. 1835. Paris: Gallimard, "Folio," 1971.
Baudelaire, Charles. *Œuvres complètes*. 2 vols. Edited by Clande Pichois. Paris: Gallimard, "Bibliothèque de la Pléiade," 1976.
Dos Passos, John. *U.S.A.* New York: Library of America, 1996.
Duhamel, Georges. *Scènes de la vie future*. 1930. Paris: Mercure de France, 1962.
Faiguet de Villeneuve, Joachim. "Moraves ou frères unis." In Denis Diderot and Jean le Rond d'Alembert, eds., *Encyclopédie, ou dictionnaire raisonné des sciences, des arts et des métiers*. Edited by Robert Morrissey and Glenn Roe. Chicago: University of Chicago ARTFL Encyclopédie Project, 2017.
Fitzgerald, Francis Scott. 1936. *The Crack-Up*. Edited by Edmund Wilson. New York: New Directions, 2009.
Freud, Sigmund. "Negation." 1925. In *The Standard Edition of the Complete Psychological Works*, vol. 19. Translated and edited by James Strachey, 235–42. London: Hogarth, 2001.
Herodotus. *Histoires*. 10 vols. Translated and edited by Philippe-Ernest Legrand. Paris: Les Belles Lettres, 1932–54.
Lawrence, David Herbert. *Studies in Classic American Literature*. 1923. Edited by Ezra Greenspan, Lindeth Vasey, and John Worthen. Cambridge: Cambridge University Press, 2003.
Lévi-Strauss, Claude. *Tristes tropiques*. Paris: Plon, 1955.
Mabanckou, Alain. *Bleu-Blanc-Rouge*. Paris: Présence africaine, 1998.
Mallarmé, Stéphane. *Œuvres complètes*. Edited by Bertrand Marchal. Paris: Gallimard, 1998.
Mercier, Alfred. *L'Habitation Saint-Ybars, ou maîtres et esclaves en Louisiane, récit social*. 1881. Montréal: Guérin, 1989.
Nietzsche, Friedrich. *Seconde considération intempestive: de l'utilité et de l'inconvénient des études historiques pour la vie*. 1874. Translated by Henri Albert. Paris: Garnier Flammarion, 1988.
Pinchot, Gifford. *The Training of a Forester*. Philadelphia: J. B. Lippincott Company, 1917.
Pindar. *Olympian Odes, Pythian Odes*. Translated by William H. Race. Cambridge, Mass.: Harvard University Press, 1997.
Plato. *Sophiste*. Translated by Émile Chambry. Paris: Flammarion, 1985.
Proust, Marcel. *Du côté de chez Swann*. 1913. Edited by Antoine Compagnon. Paris: Gallimard, "Folio Classique," 1988.
———. *Le Temps retrouvé*. 1927. Edited by Pierre-Louis Rey, Pierre-Edmond Robert, Jacques Robichez, Brian G. Rogers. Paris: Gallimard, "Folio Classique," 2002.
Tesson, Sylvain. *L'Axe du loup: De la Sibérie à l'Inde, sur les pas des évadés du Goulag*. Paris: Pocket, 2006.
Wyss, Johann David. *Le Robinson suisse, ou Journal d'un père de famille naufragé avec ses enfants*. 1812. 4 vols. Translated by Isabelle de Montolieu. Paris: Arthus Bertrand, 1814.

Literary Studies

ON ST. JOHN DE CRÈVECŒUR

Books

Chevignard, Bernard. *Michel Saint-John de Crèvecœur: Au miroir de la mémoire*. Paris: Belin, 2004.
Crèvecœur, Robert de. *Saint-John de Crèvecœur, sa vie et ses ouvrages*. Paris: Librairie des Bibliophiles, 1883.
Mitchell, Julia Post. *St. Jean de Crèvecœur*. New York: Columbia University Press, 1916.
Philbrick, Thomas. *St. John de Crèvecœur*. New York: Twayne, 1970.
Rice, Howard C. *Le Cultivateur américain, étude sur l'œuvre de Saint-John de Crèvecœur*. Paris: Honoré Champion, 1933.

Articles and Chapters

Adams, Percy G. "Crèvecœur and Franklin." *Pennsylvania History* 14 (1947): 273–79.
———. "The Historical Value of Crèvecœur's *Voyage in la Haute Pensylvanie et in New York*." *American Literature* 25 (1953): 152–68.
Chevignard, Bernard. "Confusion, fusion, diffusion: les variations révolutionaires de Saint-John de Crèvecœur." *Revue française d'études américaines* 40 (1989): 141–48.
———. "Entre débris et débuts: le *Voyage dans la Haute Pensylvanie et dans l'État de New York* de Saint-John de Crèvecœur (Paris: an IX-1801)." In *Les Débuts de siècles*, edited by Terence McCarthy, 119–29. Dijon: UFR de Langues et Communication, 2000.
———. "From Nantucket to Bermuda: Saint-John de Crèvecœur's Isles and Illusions." In *Literary Archipelagoes/Archipels littéraires*, edited by J.-P. Durix, 109–18. Dijon: Éditions universitaires de Dijon, 1998.
———. "La pomme de terre de Saint-John de Crèvecœur: un fruit de rêve et de raison (1782)." *Papilles* 10–11 (1996): 119–22.
———. "Une pomme de terre à la sauce américaine: le *Traité de la culture des pommes-de-terre* de Saint-John de Crèvecœur." *Mémoires de l'Académie des Sciences, Arts et Belles-Lettres de Dijon* 131 (1990): 45–55.
———. "Saint John de Crèvecœur en Bavière (1808–1809), ou l'Amérique retrouvée." In *Éclats de Lumière: Mélanges en l'honneur de Paul Sadrin*, edited by Louise Godard de Donville and Jacques Poirier, 173–90. Dijon: Association Bourguignonne d'Études Linguistiques et Littéraires, 2001.
———. "*Saint-John de Crèvecœur*. Letters from an American Farmer *et* Lettres d'un cultivateur américain: *Genèse d'une œuvre franco-américaine*." 3 vols. Atelier national de reproduction des thèses. Lille: Université de Lille III, 1989.
———. "Saint-John de Crèvecœur's 'Silent Voices,' or the Rustle and Rumble or Ruins." *Interfaces: Image Texte Langage* 19–20 (2001–02): 51–65.
———. "Les Souvenirs de Saint-John de Crèvecœur sur Mme d'Houdetot." *Dix-Huitième siècle* 14 (1982): 243–62.
———. "St. John de Crèvecœur à New York en 1779–1780: Un manuscrit inédit." *Annales de Normandie* 33 (1983): 161–73.
———. "St. John de Crèvecœur in the Looking-Glass: *Letters from an American Farmer* and the Making of a Man of Letters." *Early American Literature* 19 (1984): 173–90.
Cunliffe, Marcus. "Crèvecœur Revisited." *Journal of American Studies* 9 (1975): 129–44.
Derail-Imbert, Agnès. "Letters from an American Farmer: une Amérique sans histoire." *Revue française d'études américaines* 118 (2008): 10–29.
Fichtelberg, Joseph. "Utopic Distresses: Crèvecœur's *Letters* and Revolution." *Studies in the Literary Imagination* 27 (1994): 85–101.
Hoffmann, Benjamin. "Crèvecœur: The Art of Equivocation." In *Versailles and the American Revolution*, edited by Valérie Bajou, 147–49. Paris: Gourcuff Gradenigo, 2016.
Jehlen, Myra. "J. Hector St. John de Crèvecœur: A Monarcho-Anarchist in Revolutionary America." *American Quarterly* 31 (1979): 204–22.
Monette, Pierre. "Une utopie problématique: les *Letters from an American Farmer* de St. John de Crèvecœur." *Figura: Textes et Imaginaires* 3 (2001): 71–102.
Traister, Bryce. "Criminal Correspondence: Loyalism, Espionage and Crèvecœur." *Early American Literature* 37 (2002): 469–96.
White, Ed. "Crèvecœur in Wyoming." *Early American Literature* 43, no. 2 (2008): 379–407.
———. "Introduction to and Translation of Hector St. John de Crèvecœur's 'Origin of the Settlement at Socialburg.'" *Early American Literature* 7, no. 1 (2009): 235–41.

ON LEZAY-MARNÉSIA

Books

Bonnel, Roland. *Éthique et esthétique du retour à la campagne au XVIIIe siècle: l'œuvre litteraire et utopique de Lezay-Marnésia, 1735–1800.* New York: Peter Lang, 1995.

Bourget-Besnier, Élisabeth. *Une famille française sous la Révolution et l'Empire: la famille de Lezay-Marnésia.* Paris: Printed by the author, 1985.

Veyre, Marius. *La Maison de Lezay-Marnésia, 1240–1884.* Strasbourg: Brant, 1958.

Articles and Chapters

Bonnel, Roland. "Lezay-Marnésia, seigneur, poète et paysan, 'lit' Clarens." *Études Jean-Jacques Rousseau* 8 (1996): 121–41.

———. "Le soc s'est ennobli sous les mains d'un bon roi"–lumières, nature et bonheur à la veille de la Révolution ou réaction nobiliaire? Le cas de Lezay-Marnésia." In *Lumen: travaux choisis de la Société canadienne d'étude du dix-huitième siècle* 12 (1993): 139–47.

———. "Sur les rives de l'Ohio: la cité utopique de Lezay-Marnésia." *Lumen: travaux choisis de la Société canadienne d'étude du dix-huitième siècle* 13 (1994): 43–59.

———. "Le traitement de la nature dans *Le Bonheur dans les campagnes*." In *Facets of the Eighteenth Century: Descriptive, Social and Normative Discourse*, edited by Roland Bonnel, 109–18. North York: Captus University Publications, 1991.

Hoffmann, Benjamin. "Bâtir des châteaux en Amérique : utopie et retraite dans les *Lettres écrites des rives de l'Ohio* (1792)." *Dix-Huitième Siècle* 48 (2016): 311–24.

Roulin, Alfred. "*Le Voyage au Pays de Vaud de M. de Lezay (1799–1800)*." *Revue historique vaudoise* 55 (1947): 175–91.

ON CHATEAUBRIAND

Books

Antoine, Philippe. *Les Récits de voyage de Chateaubriand: Contribution à l'étude d'un genre.* Paris: Honoré Champion, 1997.

Bazin, Christian. *Chateaubriand en Amérique.* Paris: Table ronde, 1969.

Bédier, Joseph. *Études critiques.* Paris: Armand Colin, 1903.

Berchet, Jean-Claude. *Chateaubriand.* Paris: Gallimard, 2012.

Cavallin, Jean-Christophe. *Chateaubriand mythographe: Autobiographie et allégorie dans les Mémoires d'Outre-Tombe.* Paris: Honoré Champion, 2000.

Chinard, Gilbert. *L'Exotisme américain dans l'œuvre de Chateaubriand.* Paris: Hachette, 1918.

Clément, Jean-Paul. *Chateaubriand: biographie morale et intellectuelle.* Paris: Flammarion, 1998.

Fumaroli, Marc. *Chateaubriand: Poésie et Terreur.* Paris: Fallois, 2003.

Lebègue, Raymond. *Aspects de Chateaubriand: vie, voyage en Amérique, œuvres.* Paris: Nizet, 1979.

Levaillant, Maurice. *Splendeurs, misères et chimères de Monsieur de Chateaubriand, d'après des documents inédits.* Paris: Albin Michel, 1948.

Mourot, Jean. *Le Génie d'un style: Chateaubriand, rythme et sonorité idans les Mémoires d'outre-tombe.* Paris: Armand Colin, 1960.

Painter, George D. *Chateaubriand: une biographie. Les Orages désirés (1768–1793).* Translated by Suzanne Nétillard. Paris: Gallimard, 1979.

Reboul, Pierre. *Chateaubriand et le conservateur.* Lille: Presses Universitaires de Lille, 1973.

Richard, Jean-Pierre. *Paysages de Chateaubriand.* Paris: Seuil, 1967.

Sainte-Beuve, Charles Augustin. *Chateaubriand et son groupe littéraire.* 1860. 2 vols. Edited by Maurice Allem. Paris: Garnier Frères, 1948.

Articles and Chapters

Antoine, Philippe. "Le paysage américain chez Chateaubriand." In *Enfance et voyages de Chateaubriand, Armorique, Amérique*, Actes du colloque de Brest, September 1998, edited by Jean Balcou, 47–60. Paris: Honoré Champion, 2001.

Barberis, Pierre. "Les réalités d'un ailleurs: Chateaubriand et le *Voyage en Amérique*." *Littérature* 21 (1976): 91–104.

Bassan, Fernande. "Le vertige du temps dans les récits de Chateaubriand de son voyage en Amérique." *Bulletin de la Société Chateaubriand* 41 (1999): 96–101.

Bédé, Jean-Albert. "L'Itinéraire spirituel de Chateaubriand en Amérique." *French Review* 49, no. 6 (May 1976): 985–1000.

Bédier, Joseph. "Chateaubriand en Amérique: réplique à un contradicteur." *Revue d'Histoire littéraire de la France* 1 (1901): 80–109.

———. "Chateaubriand en Amérique: Vérité et fiction." *Revue d'Histoire littéraire de la France* 4 (1899): 501–32.

———. "Chateaubriand en Amérique: Vérité et fiction (Suite)." *Revue d'Histoire littéraire de la France* 1 (1900): 59–121.

Berchet, Jean-Claude. "Le voyageur et le poète: Chateaubriand et la découverte des mondes nouveaux." *Bulletin de la Société Chateaubriand* 35 (1992): 35–39.

Butor, Michel. "Chateaubriand et l'Ancienne Amérique." *Nouvelle Revue Française* (December 1–January 1, 1963–64): 1015–31. Reprinted as "L'influence de l'Amérique sur l'œuvre de Chateaubriand." In *Répertoire II*. Paris: Minuit, 1964. 152–92.

Cabanès, Jean-Louis. "L'encadrement du voyage en Amérique dans les *Mémoires d'outre-tombe*." *Littérature* 32 (1995): 61–67.

Cavallin, Jean-Christophe. "Chateaubriand mythographe: autobiographie et injonction du mythe dans les *Mémoires d'outre-tombe*." *Revue d'Histoire littéraire de la France* 6 (1998): 1087–98.

Chaouat, Bruno. "À vau-l'eau: l'Amérique désécrite de Chateaubriand." *French Forum* 25, no. 3 (2000): 277–89.

Chevignard, Bernard. "Chateaubriand et Crèvecœur aux chutes du Niagara." In *Chateaubriand 98*, edited by Jacques Gury, 123–33. Rennes: Institut culturel de Bretagne, 1999.

Chinard, Gilbert. "Chateaubriand en Amérique: quelques nouvelles sources des *Natchez* et du *Voyage*." *Modern Philology* 9, no. 1 (1911): 129–49.

Degout, Bernard. "De la remémoration d'outre-tombe: à propos du 'Journal sans date' du *Voyage en Amérique*." *Bulletin de la Société Chateaubriand* 41 (1998): 102–08.

———. "Les voyages de Chateaubriand. L'Amérique." *Magazine littéraire* 366 (June 1998): 36–38.

Dick, Ernst. "Quelques sources ignorées du *Voyage en Amérique* de Chateaubriand." *Revue d'Histoire littéraire de la France* 2 (1906): 228–45.

Didier, Béatrice. "Voyages croisés." In *Chateaubriand Mémorialiste, colloque du cent cinquantenaire (1848–1998)*, edited by Jean-Claude Berchet and Philippe Berthier, 59–68. Genève: Droz, 2000.

Dobie, Madeleine. "La rhétorique du rapprochement in l'*Itinéraire de Paris à Jérusalem*." *Revue des Sciences Humaines* 247 (1997): 63–87.

Faguet, Émile. *Dix-Neuvième Siècle: Études Littéraires*. Paris: Lecène, Oudin et Cie, 1890.

Fumaroli, Marc. "Chateaubriand et Rousseau." In *Chateaubriand: Le tremblement du temps*, Colloque de Cerisy directed by Jean-Claude Berchet and Philippe Berthier, 208–09. Toulouse: Presses Universitaires du Mirail, 1994.

Hazard, Paul. "Chateaubriand et la littérature des États-Unis." *Revue de littérature comparée* 8 (January-March 1928): 46–61.

Hoffmann, Benjamin. "Chateaubriand, Crèvecœur, and the Twilight of Native American Civilizations." *Loxias* 56 (2017): 14 pp.

Hollier, Denis. "French Customs, Literary Borders." *October* 49 (1989): 40–52.

———. "Incognito." *Revue des Sciences Humaines* 247 (2007): 25–43.

Lebègue, Raymond. "Les Avatars du voyage de Chateaubriand en Amérique." *Revue des travaux de l'Académie des Sciences morales et politiques* 130 (1977): 93–103.
———. "Chateaubriand, révélateur de l'Amérique." *Cahiers du Sud* 357 (1960): 173–82.
———. "Encore les visites de Chateaubriand à Washington." *Studi Francesi* 22 (1978): 401–04.
———. "Réalités et résultats du voyage de Chateaubriand en Amérique." *Revue d'Histoire littéraire de la France* 6 (1968): 905–33.
Lefort, Claude. "Mort de l'immortalité?" In *Le Temps de la Réflexion*, 171–201. Paris: Gallimard, 1982.
Martino, Pierre. "À propos du *Voyage en Amérique* de Chateaubriand. Le manuscrit des *Natchez*, son histoire, son contenu. La visite à Washington." *Revue d'Histoire littéraire de la France* 3 (1909): 429–78.
———. "Le voyage de Chateaubriand en Amérique: essai de mise au point." *Revue d'Histoire littéraire de la France* 2 (1952): 149–64.
Moussa, Sarga. "Un voyage dans l'*Itinéraire*. Lamartine contradicteur de Chateaubriand." *Bulletin de la Société Chateaubriand* 50 (2008): 93–102.
Redman, Harry Jr. "Jusqu'à ce que la preuve irrécusable paraisse: l'Amérique, Washington et Chateaubriand." *Nineteenth-Century French Studies* 20, nos. 1–2 (Fall-Winter 1991–93): 1–14.
Reichler, Claude. "Le deuil et l'enchantement dans les textes américains." In *Chateaubriand, le tremblements du temps*, edited by Jean-Claude Berchet and Philippe Berthier, 155–75. Toulouse: Presses Universitaires du Mirail, 1994.
———. "Raison et déraison des commencements." *Revue des Sciences Humaines* 247 (1997): 153–79.
Riberette, Pierre. "Chateaubriand et Beltrami." *Bulletin de la Société Chateaubriand* 35 (1992): 40–47.
Riffaterre, Michael. "De la structure au code: Chateaubriand et le monument imaginaire." In *La Production du texte*, 127–51. Paris: Le Seuil, 1979.
Stathers, Madison. *Chateaubriand et l'Amérique*. Grenoble: Allier frères, 1905.
Switzer, Richard. "Chateaubriand's Sources in the *Voyage en Amérique*." *Revue de littérature comparée* 42 (January-March 1968): 5–23.
Viatte, Auguste. "Chateaubriand et ses précurseurs français d'Amérique." *Études françaises* 4 (1968): 253–61.
Zimra, Clarisse. "La vision du Nouveau Monde de Chateaubriand à Beaumont: pour une étude de forme de l'exotisme." *French Review* 49 (1976): 1001–24.

Complementary Literary Studies

Adams, Percy G. *Travelers and Travel Liars, 1660–1800*. Berkeley: University of California Press, 1962.
Aldridge, Alfred Owen. "Le problème de la traduction au XVIIIe siècle et aujourd'hui." *Revue belge de philologie et d'histoire* 39 (1961): 747–58.
Ansart, Guillaume. "From Voltaire to Raynal and Diderot's *Histoire des deux Indes*: The French *Philosophes* and Colonial America." In *America Through European Eyes: English and French Reflections on the New World from the Eighteenth Century to the Present*, edited by Aurelian Craiutu and Jeffrey C. Isaac. University Park: Pennsylvania State University Press, 2009.
Apostolidès, Jean-Marie. "L'altération du récit: Les *Dialogues* de Lahontan." *Études françaises* 22, no. 2 (1986): 73–86.
Aron, Robert, and Arnaud Dandieu. *Le Cancer américain*. 1931. Lausanne: L'Âge d'homme, 2008.

Aronson, Nicole. "Chastellux et Brissot: deux images de l'Amérique au dix-huitième siècle." *French Review* 49, no. 6 (1976): 960–71.
Bourdin, Philippe, and Gérard Loubinoux. *La Scène bâtarde: entre Lumières et romantisme.* Clermont-Ferrand: Presses Universitaires Blaise Pascal, 2004.
Chinard, Gilbert. *L'Amérique et le rêve exotique dans la littérature française aux XVIIe et XVIIIe siècles.* 1918. Genève: Slatkine reprints, 2000.
Darnton, Robert. *George Washington's False Teeth: An Unconventional Guide to the Eighteenth Century.* New York: W. W. Norton, 2003.
Debaene, Vincent, and Jean-Louis Jeannelle. "Où est la littérature ?" *Fabula/Les colloques, L'Idée de littérature dans les années 1950,* June 2004.
Frangsmyr, Tore, and John L. Heilbron, Robin E. Rider, eds. *The Quantifying Spirit in the Eighteenth Century.* Berkeley: University of California Press, 1990.
Funke, Hans-Günter. "L'évolution sémantique de la notion d'*utopie* en français." In *De l'utopie à l'uchronie: formes, significations, fonctions,* edited by H. Hudde and P. Kuon, 19–37. Tübingen: Gunter Narr Verlag, 1988.
Gallagher, Catherine. "What Would Napoleon Do? Historical, Fictional and Counterfactual Characters." *New Literary History* 42, no. 2 (Spring 2011): 315–36.
Genette, Gérard. *Figures III.* Paris: Seuil, 1972.
Gohin, Ferdinand. *Les Transformations de la langue française, pendant la deuxième moitié du XVIIIème siècle (1740–1789).* Paris: Éditions Belin Frères, 1903.
Grosclaude, Pierre. *Malesherbes: Témoin et interprète de son temps.* Paris: Fischbacher, 1961.
Guion, Béatrice. "Langue et nation: l'invention du siècle de Louis le Grand." *Revue Française d'Histoire des Idées Politiques* 36 (2012): 347–63.
Guyot, Alain. *Analogie et récit de voyage: Voir, mesurer, interpréter le monde.* Paris: Classiques Garnier, 2012.
Hibberd, John. *Salomon Gessner: His Creative Achievement and Influence.* Cambridge: Cambridge University Press, 1976.
Hoffmann, Benjamin. "Posthumous Louisiana: Literary Reinvention of Louisiana in Alfred Mercier's *The Saint Ybars Plantation* (1881)." *Southern Quarterly* 53, no. 2 (Winter 2016): 164–81.
Jackson, Heather. *Those Who Write for Immortality: Romantic Reputations and the Dream of Lasting Fame.* New Haven: Yale University Press, 2015.
Jeanneret, Michel. "Léry et Thevet: comment parler d'un monde nouveau ?" In *Mélanges à la mémoire de Franco Simone,* vol. 4, 59–72. Genève: Slatkine, 1983.
Jullien, Dominique. *Récits du Nouveau Monde, les voyageurs français en Amérique de Chateaubriand à nos jours.* Paris: Nathan Université, 1992.
Jungo, Michel. *Le Vocabulaire de Pascal, étudié dans les fragments pour une Apologie.* Paris: Éditions d'Artrey, 1950.
Kavanagh, Thomas M. "Boufflers's *La Reine de Golconde* and the Conte philosophique as an Enlightenment Form." *French Forum* 23, no. 1 (January 1998): 5–21.
———. "Casanova's Autobiography of Chance." In *Chance, Culture, and the Literary Text.* Edited by Thomas Kavanagh. Ann Arbor: *Michigan Romance Studies* 14 (1994): 151–72.
———. *Esthetics of the Moment: Literature and Art in the French Enlightenment.* Philadelphia: University of Pennsylvania Press, 1996.
Kerbrat-Orecchioni, Catherine. "Des usages comiques de l'analogie. Comparaison et métaphore: fonctionnement sémantique et pragmatique." *Folia linguistica* 15 (1981): 163–84.
Knee, Philip. "Wolmar comme médiateur politique." In *Lectures de la Nouvelle Héloïse.* Edited by Ourida Mostefai. Ottawa: *Pensée Libre* 4 (1993): 117–27.
Lestringant, Frank. *L'Atelier du cosmographe, ou l'image du monde à la Renaissance.* Paris: Albin Michel, 1991.
———. "Le déclin d'un savoir: La crise de la cosmographie à la fin de la Renaissance." *Annales: Économies, Sociétés, Civilisations.* 46e année, 2 (1991): 239–60.

———. "Rhétorique et dispositif d'autorité dans le texte cosmographique de la Renaissance." *Littérature* 32 (1978): 3–26.
Luna, Marie-Françoise. *Casanova mémorialiste*. Paris: Honoré Champion, 1998.
Mathy, Jean-Philippe. *Extrême-Occident: French Intellectuals and America*. Chicago: University of Chicago Press, 1993.
Miller, Christopher L. *The French Atlantic Triangle: Literature and Culture of the Slave Trade*. Durham: Duke University Press, 2008.
———. "'Slaves' in My Family: French Modes of Servitude in the New World." In *Caribbean Globalizations, 1492 to the Present Day*, edited by Eva Sansavior and Richard Scholar, 105–26. Liverpool: Liverpool University Press, 2015.
Minois, Georges. *L'Âge d'or, histoire de la poursuite du bonheur*. Paris: Fayard, 2009.
Montalbetti, Christine. *Le Voyage, le monde et la bibliothèque*. Paris: Presses Universitaires de France, 1997.
Morrissey, Robert. *The Economy of Glory: From Ancien Régime France to the Fall of Napoleon*. Translated by Teresa Lavender Fagan. Chicago: University of Chicago Press, 2013.
Prasad, Pratima. *Colonialism, Race, and the French Romantic Imagination*. New York: Routledge, 2009.
Racault, Jean-Michel. *Nulle part et ses environs: Voyage aux confins de l'utopie littéraire classique (1657–1802)*. Paris: Presses de l'Université de Paris-Sorbonne, 2003.
———. *L'Utopie narrative en France et en Angleterre, 1675–1761*. Oxford, UK: Voltaire Foundation, 1991.
Roger, Philippe. *The American Enemy: The History of French Anti-Americanism*. Translated by Sharon Bowman. Chicago: University of Chicago Press, 2005.
Ruyer, Raymond. *L'Utopie et les utopies*. Paris: Presses Universitaires de France, 1950.
Samuels, Maurice. *The Spectacular Past: Popular History and the Novel in Nineteenth-Century France*. Ithaca: Cornell University Press, 2004.
Sayre, Gordon M. *Les Sauvages Américains: Representations of Native Americans in French and English Colonial Literature*. Chapel Hill: University of North Carolina Press, 1997.
Tinguely, Frédéric. "Jean de Léry et les vestiges de la pensée analogique." *Bibliothèque d'Humanisme et Renaissance* 57, no. 1 (1995): 25–44.
Trousson, Raymond. *Voyages aux pays de nulle part, histoire littéraire de la pensée utopique*. Bruxelles: Université de Bruxelles, 1999.
West, C. B. "La Théorie de la traduction au xviiie siècle." *Revue de Littérature Comparée* 12 (April-June 1932): 330–55.
Yee, Jennifer. *Exotic Subversions in Nineteenth-Century French Fiction*. Oxford, UK: Legenda, 2008.

Historical Studies

Ammon, Harry. *The Genêt Mission*. New York: W. W. Norton, 1973.
Auricchio, Laura. *The Marquis: Lafayette Reconsidered*. New York: Alfred A. Knopf, 2014.
Carcassonne, Élie. *Montesquieu et le problème de la constitution française au xviiie siècle*. 1927. Genève: Slatkine Reprints, 1970.
Carré, Henri. "Les Émigrés français en Amérique, 1789–1793." Paris: Chaix, 1898.
———. *La Noblesse française et l'opinion publique au xviiie siècle*. Paris: Champion, 1923.
Certeau, Michel de. *The Writing of History*. 1975. Translated by Tom Conley. New York: Columbia University Press, 1988.
Chevignard, Bernard. "D'une révolution à l'autre: les consuls de France aux États-Unis, 1783–1789." *Revue Tocqueville* 9 (1987–88): 63–81.
Chinard, Gilbert. *Les Amitiés américaines de Madame d'Houdetot, d'après sa correspondance inédite avec Benjamin Franklin et Thomas Jefferson*. Paris: Librairie Ancienne Édouard Champion, 1924.

Clarke, T. Wood. *Émigrés in the Wilderness*. New York: Macmillan, 1941.
Cleland, Hugh G. "John B. C. Lucas, Physiocrat on the Frontier." *Western Pennsylvania Historical Magazine* 36 (March 1953): 1–15.
Clément, Jean-Paul. "Lezay-Marnésia. Pour une France américaine ? Des limites de la liberté." *Revue des deux mondes* (February 2009): 115–26.
Clements, William M. *Native American Verbal Art: Texts and Contexts*. Tucson: University of Arizona Press, 1996.
Craiutu, Aurelian. *A Virtue for Courageous Minds: Moderation in French Political Thought, 1748–1830*. Princeton: Princeton University Press, 2012.
Craiutu, Aurelian, and Jeffrey C. Isaac, eds. *America Through European Eyes: English and French Reflections on the New World from the Eighteenth Century to the Present*. University Park: Pennsylvania State University Press, 2009.
Craiutu, Aurelian, and Jeremy Jennings, eds. *Tocqueville on America After 1840: Letters and Other Writings*. Cambridge: Cambridge University Press, 2009.
Cullen, Jim. *The American Dream: A Short History of an Idea That Shaped a Nation*. Oxford: Oxford University Press, 2003.
Cunliffe, Marcus. "European Images of America." In *Paths of American Thought*, edited by Arthur M. Schlesinger Jr. and Morton White, 492–514. Boston: Houghton Mifflin, 1963.
Debray, Régis. *Contretemps*. Paris: Gallimard, 1992.
Desan, Suzanne. "Transatlantic Spaces of Revolution: The French Revolution, *Sciotomanie*, and American Lands." *Journal of Early Modern History* 12 (2008): 467–505.
Diesbach, Ghislain de. *Histoire de l'émigration, 1789–1814*. Paris: Grasset, 1975.
Duchet, Michèle. *Anthropologie et histoire au siècle des Lumières*. 1971. Paris: Albin Michel, 1995.
Duprat, Catherine. *"Pour l'amour de l'humanité.": Le Temps des philanthropes: La Philanthropie parisienne des Lumières à la Monarchie de Juillet*. Vol. 1. Paris: Comité des Travaux historiques et scientifiques, 1993.
Echeverria, Durand. *Mirage in the West: A History of the French Image of American Society to 1815*. 1957. New York: Octagon Books, 1966.
Echeverria, Durand, and Everett C. Wilkie Jr. *The French Image of America: A Chronological and Subject Bibliography of French Books Printed Before 1816 Relating to the British North American Colonies and the United States*. 2 vols. Metuchen: Scarecrow Press, 1994.
Eckert, Allan W. *That Dark and Bloody River*. New York: Bantam, 1995.
Ekberg, Carl J. *A French Aristocrat in the American West: The Shattered Dreams of De Lassus de Luziéres*. Columbia: Missouri University Press, 2010.
Faÿ, Bernard. *L'Esprit révolutionnaire en France et aux États-Unis à la fin du xviiie siècle*. Paris: Édouard Champion, 1925.
Figueiredo, Yves. "Aux sources du débat écologique contemporain: l'expérience américaine." *Revue française d'études américaines* 109 (September 2006): 69–82.
Furet, François, and Mona Ozouf, eds. *Dictionnaire critique de la Révolution française*. Paris: Flammarion Champs, 1992.
Furstenberg, François. "The Significance of the Trans-Appalachian Frontier in Atlantic History." *The American Historical Review* 113, no. 3 (June 2008): 647–77.
———. *When the United States Spoke French: Five Refugees Who Shaped a Nation*. New York: Penguin Press, 2014.
Garvey, Todd, and Alison Dolan. "Presidential Claims of Executive Privilege: History, Law, Practice, and Recent Developments." *Congressional Research Service* (2012): 1–42.
Gauchet, Marcel. *Le Désenchantement du monde: Une histoire politique de la religion*. Paris: Gallimard, 1985.
Glazer, Nathan. *We Are All Multiculturalists Now*. Cambridge, Mass.: Harvard University Press, 1997.

Griffiths, Robert Howell. *Le Centre perdu: Malouet et les "monarchiens" dans la Révolution française*. Grenoble: Presses Universitaires de Grenoble, 1988.
Harsanyi, Doina Pasca. *Lessons from America: Liberal French Nobles in Exile, 1793–1798*. University Park: Pennsylvania State University Press, 2010.
Havard, Gilles, and Cécile Vidal. *Histoire de l'Amérique française*. Paris: Flammarion, 2005.
Jacobs, James R. *The Beginning of the U.S. Army, 1783–1812*. Princeton: Princeton University Press, 1947.
Jameson, Fredric. *Archaeologies of the Future: The Desire Called Utopia and Other Science Fictions*. London: Verso Books, 2007.
Jones, Robert. *The King of the Alley: William Duer, Politician, Entrepreneur, and Speculator, 1768–1799*. Philadelphia: American Philosophical Society, 1992.
Labbé, François. *Anacharsis Cloots, le Prussien francophile: Un philosophe au service de la Révolution française et universelle*. Paris: L'Harmattan, 1999.
Lerner, Gerda. *Why History Matters: Life and Thought*. Oxford: Oxford University Press, 1997.
Liebersohn, Harry. *Aristocratic Encounters: European Travelers and North American Indians*. Cambridge: Cambridge University Press, 1998.
Lilti, Antoine. *Figures publiques: L'Invention de la célébrité (1750–1850)*. Paris: Fayard, 2014.
Lopez, Claude-Anne. *Mon Cher Papa: Franklin and the Ladies of Paris*. New Haven: Yale University Press, 1990.
McDermott, John Francis. "John B. C. Lucas in Pennsylvania." *Western Pennsylvania Historical Magazine* 21 (September 1938): 209–30.
McNally, Michael D. *Honoring Elders: Aging, Authority, and Ojibwe Religion*. New York: Columbia University Press, 2009.
Moreau-Zanelli, Jocelyne. *Gallipolis: Histoire d'un mirage américain au XVIIIème siècle*. Paris: L'Harmattan, 2000.
Olson, James S., and Raymond Wilson. *Native Americans in the Twentieth Century*. Urbana: University of Illinois Press, 1986.
Piketty, Thomas. *Capital in the Twenty-First Century*. Cambridge, Mass.: Harvard University Press, 2014. Translated by Arthur Goldhammer.
Rémond, René. *Les États-Unis devant l'opinion française, 1815–1852*. Paris: Armand Colin, 1962.
Rice, Howard C. *Barthélémi Tardiveau, a French Trader in the West*. Baltimore: Johns Hopkins University Press, 1938.
Sergeant Childs, Frances. "Fontaine Leval, a French Settlement on the Maine Coast, 1791." *Proceedings of the American Antiquarian Society* 51 (April-October 1941): 187–222.
Slotkin, Richard. *Regeneration Through Violence: The Mythology of the American Frontier, 1600–1860*. Middletown: Wesleyan University Press, 2000.
Soboul, Albert. "Anacharsis Cloots, l'orateur du genre humain." *Annales historiques de la Révolution française* 239 (1980): 29–58.
Sollors, Werner. *Beyond Ethnicity: Consent and Descent in American Culture*. Oxford: Oxford University Press, 1987.
Vardi, Liana. *The Physiocrats and the World of the Enlightenment*. Cambridge: Cambridge University Press, 2012.
Weber, Max. *L'Éthique protestante et l'esprit du capitalisme*. 1905. Paris: Gallimard, 2004.

INDEX

Note: Page numbers in italics refer to figures; those followed by n refer to notes, with note number.

L'Action des principes de la religion et de, la véritable philosophie (Lezay-Marnésia), 89
Adams, John, 86
Adams, Percy G., 63
adaptation method of translation, Crèvecoeur's *Lettres* and, 26–27
Adventures of Télémaque (Fénelon), 12
advertising function of posthumous accounts
    definition of, 6
    Lezay-Marnésia's *Letters* and, 96–97, 106, 123
    Lezay-Marnésia's *Nouveau prospectus* and, 92
A la recherche du temps perdu (Proust). See *In Search of Lost Time* (Proust)
Alembert, Jean le Rond d', 80, 107, 130
Algeria, Chateaubriand on French conquest of, 164, 208n135
Aline, reine de Golconde (*Aline, Queen of Golconde*, Boufflers), 100–101, 103–4
alterity
    Amerindian, Lezay-Marnésia's negation of, 100–102
    analogic understanding as rejection of, 157, 158–59
    and French anti-Americanism, 184, 185–86
    French perception of, in America, 154–55, 182–83, 184, 185
America, French views on
    and America as alterity, 154–55, 182–83, 184, 185
    and America as mobile sign, 181, 182, 183
    evolution from idealized past of Europe to its disquieting future, 181, 183, 184
    French Revolution and, 182, 183
    idealization of, as result of great distance, 3–4
    as land of opportunity, 4
    as utopia, 4
    See also anti-Americanism; philo-Americanism
American Dream
    Chateaubriand on death of, 178
    Crèvecoeur on death of, 41
    as part of Golden Age in Crèvecoeur's America, 41
    as unnecessary to French after French Revolution, 182
Americanization, French fear of, 184–85
Amerindians
    attacks on Ohio and Kentucky Territory settlers, 86–87, 199n31
    perceived affinity of European nobles with, 99
    resistance to US expansion, 2
    Tocqueville on, 9
    translation of Bible into Natick language as monument to, 66, 73
    See also noble savage concept; *entries under* Chateaubriand, François-René de; Crèvecoeur, Michel-Guillaume Saint-John de; Lezay-Marnésia, Claude-François-Adrien de
Aminta (Le Tasse), 108
analeptic function of posthumous accounts, 12
    in Chateaubriand, 146, 147–50, 163–64, 167–73, 181–82, 206n72
    definition of, 6
analogy, as path to understanding
    vs. aesthetic of convergence, 160–62
    Chateaubriand's rejection of in *Mémoires d'outre-tombe*, 156–59
    Chateaubriand's use of, in *Itinéraire de Paris à Jérusalem*, 157
    and ethnocentrism, 157, 158–59
Andrieux, François, 114–15
"Anecdote of the Sassafras and the Wild Vine" (Crèvecoeur), 37–38, 38–39
"Anecdote of the Wild Dog" (Crèvecoeur), 28–30, 32, 102
Ansart, Guillaume, 104–5
anti-Americanism
    characteristics of, 210n1

Chateaubriand and, 173, 175, 180
evolution of eighteenth-century philo-Americanism into, 181–83
perceived characteristics of American culture in, 185–86
and perception of America as model of undesirable future, 184–85
and US culture as other, 184, 185–86
Atala (Chateaubriand)
on Amerindians, 71
anachronistic aesthetic of, 145
Chateaubriand's transport of manuscript from England, 134
critics on veracity of, 128
on French loss of American colonies, 147, 184
model for Atala in, 172–73
shell fragment intercepted by manuscript of, at siege of Thionville, 133
success of, 76
writing of, 132–33
Atlantic crossing, time required for, 3
and inaccuracy of descriptions of America, 3–4
Audrain, M., Lezay-Marnésia and, 121
Avis à ceux qui voudraient s'en aller en Amérique (Franklin), 4
L'Axe du Loup (Tesson), 12

Baillet, M., 92
Balzac, Honoré de, 54
Barbé-Marbois, François, 1, 149
Barlow, Joel, 82, 83
Barth, comte de, 97
Bartram, William, 63, 128, 137, 141–42, 143, 205n45
Bassan, Fernande., 128
Baudelaire, Charles, 176, 177, 184
Bazin, Christian, 125
Beaumarchais, Pierre, 101
Beauvau, Prince and Princess of, 25, 27
Bédier, Joseph, 128
Beltrami, Giacomo Constantino, 128, 142, 143
Berchet, Jean-Claude, 128–29, 170, 176
Bergasse, Nicolas, 24
Bethlehem, Pennsylvania, Moravian community at
French admiration for, 107–8
history of, 107
as model for Lezay-Marnésia's ideal community, 105, 107, 108–10; and Golden Age, hope for, 108; Lezay-Marnésia's idealization of, 105, 110–11; as proof of Lezay-Marnésia's patriarchal model, 105, 107, 108; removal of equality from model, 109–10; similarities to Lezay-Marnésia's program and, 109
Beyond Ethnicity (Sollors), 43–45
Bleu-Blanc-Rouge (Mabanckou), 12
Bonaparte, Napoleon, 21, 59, 65, 147, 149, 155, 164
Le Bonheur dans les campagnes (Lezay-Marnésia), 79, 80–81, 99, 104
Bonnel, Roland Guy, 15, 80
Bornet, Claude, 43
Boufflers, Stanislas de, 80, 81, 98
See also *Aline, reine de Golconde* (Boufflers)
Brackenridge, Hugh Henry, 113
Brissot de Warville, Jacques-Pierre
Chastellux and, 108
and circular interplay of New World expectations and experience, 31–32
Crèvecoeur's correspondence with, 48
and Crèvecoeur's idealized America, 36–37
on Crèvecoeur's melancholy, 24–25
defense of Crèvecoeur against critics, 78
and fictionality of Crèvecoeur's farmer persona, 60
on French colonies in America, 88
motives for visiting America, 139
Bucolics (Virgil), 108
Buffon, Georges-Louis-Leclerc de, 77–78
Butler, Richard, 83, 87

"Des Cannibales" (Montaigne), 30
Capital in the Twenty-First Century (Piketty), 179
Carré, Henri, 105
Carver, Jonathan, 143
Casanova, Giacomo, 61–62
Castries, Charles-Eugène-Gabriel de la Croix, Marquis de, 25, 47
Certeau, Michel de, 73–74
Cerutti, 80
Chamfort, Sébastien-Roch Nicolas de, 80
charity, and renewal of feudal relations, Lezay-Marnésia on, 80
Charlevoix, Pierre-François-Xavier de, 128, 143
Chastellux, marquis de, 107–8, 109, 139

228 ~ INDEX

Chateaubriand, François-René de
  alternative destinies as central theme in, 126–27
  on America: as ancient land of lost civilizations, 155; expectations vs. reality of, 11; role of, in regeneration of France, 184
  on Amerindian decline: causes of, 73; and effort to preserve memory through writing, 11, 66, 73, 75, 76; European influence as cause of, 153, 155; as harbinger of American decline, 177; and inevitable annihilation, 74; and lost languages, 150; as presage of French future, 152–56; as reflection on human impermanence, 146; as warning to France, 76
  on Amerindians: account of, as posthumous representation, 76; affinity with French, 153; disappointment in, 9; encounter with, in *Atala*, 71; fascination with, 11; and implied superiority of European culture, 75; influence of, 9; and search for Northwest Passage, 129; as well-informed, 142–43
  and anti-Americanism, 173, 175, 180
  appeal of ancient things to, 66
  as contemporary of American and French revolutions, 10
  and Crèvecoeur, familiarity with, 11
  on Crèvecoeur's *Voyage dans la Haute Pensylvanie*, 66
  on decline of civilizations, inevitability of, 152–53, 155
  on decline of France, 76, 146–47, 152–56
  diplomatic career of, 154, 207n99
  doxological America in, evolution of, 7
  exile in England, 133, 134
  final pessimism about America, 173–80
  on French culture, self-interest's triumph over duty in, 155–56
  and French imperialism, support for, 150, 151–52, 163–65, 208n135
  on French language, 150, 151–52
  and French Revolution, 55, 130, 131, 133, 154, 205n23
  on human inability to see future, 75
  influence of Crèvecoeur on, 125
  influence on Lévi-Strauss, 165–66
  interest in America, 129
  loss of manuscripts of French Revolution, 133
  Montesquieu and, 130
  and New France colonies: analeptic speculations about alternative futures based on, 147–50, 163–64; and French language, perpetuation of, 150; nostalgia for, 146–47, 184; pride in French glory reflected in, 149–50
  and Northwest Passage, search for, 129–31, 145, 167; and potential alternative futures, 126, 131
  parallels in work of, 159
  philo-Americanism of, and travelers' disappointment at reality, 186
  and polar conquest, plans for, 11
  posthumous America in, 15, 127, 131–32, 140; anachronisms in, 138–39, 145–46, 167–71; analeptic function of, 146, 147–50, 163–64, 167–73, 181–82, 206n72; and intrusion of fictional elements over time, 131–32; as meditation on what could have been, 150; reinvention of, over years before publication, 180; and role of America in regeneration of France, 184; specular function of, 146–47, 152–56; as unrecoverable ghost, 138
  recollections in, as either philosophical or affective, 161–62
  return to France after exile, and manuscripts abandoned in England, 134
  and Rousseau, influence of, 170
  scholarship on, 12–13
  and sharks, story of swimming near, 124–26
  ties to Lezay-Marnésia's and Crèvecoeur's works, 8, 11
  tragic consciousness of time in, 137–38
  ultimate insignificance of human achievement as common theme in, 126
  and use of fictional sources, 63
  on writing and memory, 6
  See also *Atala* (Chateaubriand); *Mémoires d'outre-tombe* (Chateaubriand); *Les Natchez* (Chateaubriand); *Voyage en Amérique* (Chateaubriand); *other specific works*
Chevignard, Bernard, 14, 17, 23, 26, 48
chiasmus
  in life of Lezay-Marnésia, 120–21
  in work of Crèvecoeur, 60, 121
chrysogenous aristocracy in America, Chateaubriand on, 178–79, 209n160

cities, US, rapid growth of, 2
civilization(s)
  American, French perception of, 42, 58
  Chateaubriand on inevitable decline of, 152–53, 155
  Crèvecoeur on American contributions to, 42
  US, as other for French, 183, 184, 185
  See also Amerindians; *Mémoires d'outre-tombe* (Chateaubriand), on American decline
Clavière, Étienne, 24
Cleland, Hugh G., 203n136
climate, as cause of American decline, Chateaubriand on, 179–80
Cloots, Anacharsis, 85
Club des Impartiaux, 114
Code Noir (Black Code), Colbert and, 151
Colbert, Jean-Baptiste, 151
colonization, French, Chateaubriand's support for, 150, 151–52, 163–65, 208n135
  See also New France colonies
Columbus, Christopher, 8
  New-World reports by, as descriptions on his expectations rather than reality, 95–96
commemorative function of posthumous accounts, 6
  in Chateaubriand, 132, 134, 135–38
  in Lezay-Marnésia, 123
conservation movement
  Crèvecoeur and, 67
  vs. preservation movement, 68
Cooper, James Fenimore, 142, 176
Copley, John Singleton, 125, 204n4
cosmography
  borrowed erudition as characteristic of, 141–42
  characteristics of, 140–41
  Chateaubriand's *Voyage en Amérique* as work of, 140–43
Craiutu, Aurelian, 146, 181
Crèvecoeur, Guillaume-Alexandre "Ally" (son), 19, 20, 23
Crèvecoeur, Guillaume-Augustin de (father), 17
Crèvecoeur, Mehetable Tippet (wife), 19, 23
Crèvecoeur, Michel-Guillaume Saint-John de
  on America: ambivalent attitude toward, 121; expectations vs. reality of, 11
  on Americans' as unworthy of free government, 48

on Amerindians: ambivalent view of, 69, 72; contact with, 18; destruction of, as warning to France, 76; ecumenical relations with settlers, 29–30, 31, 32, 193n70; effort to preserve memory of through writing, 11, 66, 67, 70–76; empathy with, 70, 71–73, 75; fascination with, 11; hypocrisy of Christian treatment of, 73; inability to foresee future, 69; inevitable annihilation of, 70, 73, 74; inferiority to Europeans, 69, 70, 71; as inhabitants of the present, 69, 75; lack of permanent monuments made by, 69, 74–75; languages, lack of abstract words in, 71, 72; as portrayal of expectations, 102; as posthumous representation, 67, 73, 74–75, 76; praise for eloquence of, 72; and preservation of Amerindian toponyms, 70; rejection of sedentary lifestyle by, 69, 72; as Rousseauian noble savages, 28–30, 31; spread of views across several characters, 70; and translation of Christian texts into Amerindian languages, 73; white colonists' responsibility for annihilation of, 67, 69, 70–71
attack on, in Lezay-Marnésia's *Letters*, 77, 78
attractiveness of ancient things to, 66
career of, 18, 19, 23
as contemporary of American and French revolutions, 10
correspondence, with son Ally, 20
creativity of, as nostalgic impulse of second self, 17, 21, 25, 35–37, 37–39
criticisms of, 77, 78
and ecological thought, 67–69
and English, excellent command of, 19, 20
on Federalist-Antifederalist debate, 52–53
as French Consul in New York, 25, 27, 37, 47–48, 60, 121, 130, 193n58
and French language: difficulty of re-learning, 19–20, 27; turn to writing in, after *Letters*, 20–21
and French Revolution, 24–25
on French Revolution, damage done by, 60–61
greater knowledge of America that Lezay-Marnésia or Chateaubriand, 18, 19
and Greycourt estate, purchase of, 19

Crèvecoeur, Michel-Guillaume Saint-John de *(cont'd)*
   and happiness, as alway "before," 123
   and idealized view of US, exploitation for book sales, 4
   and Lezay-Marnésia, influence on, 122
   on liberty, Americans' abuse of, 46–47
   life of: in Canada, 18; destruction of farm and death of wife, 192n48; in English colonies, 18–23; English pseudonym adopted by, 18–19; family and early life, 17; residence in England, 17–18; return to France, 19, 20–21, 24; wife and children, 19
   Madame d'Houdetot and, 25, 47, 191n17
   Malesherbes and, 130
   on Napoleon, 21, 65
   on newness of America, 7
   philo-Americanism of, and travelers' disappointment at reality, 186
   and physiocratic theory, 53
   posthumous America in, 15; as combination of collective image and individual nostalgia, 32; Crèvecoeur's lack of interest in return to, 60; as doubly fictionalized, 39, 63–64; as doubly posthumous, 64–65; as dream world of refuge, 60, 61, 62; and France as symbolic double of United States, 54, 58–59, 65; as Golden Age, 39–41; as idealization, 35, 138; masquerading as direct reporting, 36; vs. pessimism of his correspondence, 36; as response to nostalgic impulse, 32, 36–37; and role of America in regeneration of France, 184; specular function of, 154; as type of publicity, 32
   reputation of, 14
   and Revolutionary War losses, effect of, 35
   scholarship on, 13
   ties to Lezay-Marnésia' and Chateaubriand's works, 8, 11
   Turgot and, 53
   and War of Independence, 22–23, 24–25, 35, 41, 51
   and War of Independence, imprisonment during, 22–23; metaphysical crisis prompted by, 23, 24, 52–53; period of anguish following, 24–25; release, 23; as source of literary creativity, 16–17, 23–24; and splitting of self into two, 16–17, 22, 23–24, 25, 51
   work of, as chiasmus, 60, 121
   and writing, discomfort with, 27
   See also *Letters from an American Farmer* (Crèvecoeur); *Lettres d'un cultivateur américain* (Crèvecoeur); *More Letters from the American Farmer* (Crèvecoeur); *Sketches of Eighteenth-Century America* (Crèvecoeur); *Voyage aux grandes salines tyroliennes de Reichenhall* (Crèvecoeur); *Voyage dans la Haute Pensylvanie et dans l'État de New York depuis l'année 1785 jusqu'en 1798* (Crèvecoeur)
Cronique de Paris, 85
Cullen, Jim, 35, 54
Cunliffe, Marcus, 31–32

Davies, Thomas, 24
Davis, Lockyer, 24
Debray, Régis, 186
deception
   in hopes for France and America, Lezay-Marnésia on, 119
   and idealization of posthumous representations, 9, 123, 131, 167
   by land speculators, *See* Scioto Company
   Lezay-Marnésia's state of denial and, 117–18
   by writers on America, Lezay-Marnésia on, 77, 78
Découverte des sources du Mississippi et de la Rivière sanglante (Beltrami), 142, 143
Degout, Bernard, 136, 137
deism, Crèvecoeur's Socialbourg and, 51
De la littérature et des hommes de lettres des États-Unis (Vail), 175, 177
Delawares, attacks on Ohio and Kentucky Territory settlers, 86–87
Desan, Suzanne, 104, 114
Description of the Soil and the Productivity of this Portion of the United States (Scioto Company), 83
descriptions of America, inaccuracy of
   delay in communication between US and France and, 3–4
   rapid cultural change and, 1, 2–3, 189n11
Le Désenchantement du monde (Gauchet), 167
Desmoulins, Camille, 85
Dialogues de Monsieur le Baron de, Lahontan et d'un sauvage (Lahontan), 30

INDEX   231

Dictionnaire philosophique (Voltaire), 107
Diderot, Denis, 33, 80, 104, 107
Didier, Béatrice, 172
Didier, Pierre-Joseph, 92
Dillon, Henriette Lucy, marquise de la Tour du Pin, 86
Discours sur l'origine et les fondements de l'inégalité parmi les hommes (*Discourse on the Origin and Foundations of Inequality Among Men*, Rouseau), 8, 28, 31
Discovery of the Sources of the Mississippi and of the Bloody River (Beltrami), 142, 143
disenchantment, illusions about America and, 8, 167, 209n144
The Disenchantment of the World (Gauchet), 167
Dobie, Madeleine, 163, 164
Dom Juan (Molière), 101
doxological America
  changes over time in, 32
  in Chateaubriand, evolution of, 7
  Columbus's reports on New World and, 95–96
  Crèvecoeur and, 32
  definition of, 6–7
  French Revolution and, 7
  gaps between referent and, 6
  as Golden Age, 7
  interplay with actual experiences, in accounts of New World, 31–32
  in Lezay-Marnésia's letters from America, 79, 95, 96–97, 102–3; basis in hopes rather than reality, 89, 92–95, 103
  national variations in, 32
  in posthumous representations of America, 6
  slow reconfiguration of, 7
  See also advertising function of posthumous accounts
Duhamel, Georges, 184–85
Dupaty, Jean-Baptiste Mercier, 80

Echeverria, Durand, 41–42, 60, 182, 210n3
ecological thought, Crèvecoeur and, 67–69
elegy, and posthumous representations of America, 6
  in Chateaubriand, 152, 165, 173, 184
  in Crèvecoeur, 17
  in Lezay-Marnésia, 80, 120, 121–22
emigration to America
  by Chateaubriand, 36, 129–30, 205n23

  of Crèvecoeur's family, 18
  Crèvecoeur's warnings on, 117
  as escape from French Revolution, 36, 82, 87, 96, 130, 205n23
  as escape from poverty, 41
  Franklin's encouragement of, 4
  French criticisms of, after Revolution, 114–15
  Girondins' views on, 88
  by Lezay-Marnésia, 79, 87
  Lezay-Marnésia's promotion of, 118, 120–21, 123
  See also Saint-Pierre settlement, Lezay-Marnésia's plans for; utopian project on Ohio River, Lezay-Marnésia's plans for
Encyclopédie of Diderot and d'Alembert
  Lezay-Marnésia and, 80
  Malesherbes and, 130
  on Moravian community in Bethlehem, 107
Enlightenment thought
  Crèvecoeur's Socialbourg and, 51
  progressive paradigm of New World and, 42
En Lisant en écrivant (Gracq), 38
Eprémesnil, Jean-Jacques Duval d', 85, 86, 105, 113–14
"L'Esquisse du Fleuve Obyo et du Pays de Kentuckey" (Crèvecoeur), 83–84
Essais (Montaigne), 169, 171
Essai sur la nature champêtre (Lezay-Marnésia), 79, 109
Essai sur les moeurs et l'esprit des nations (Voltaire), 107
Essai sur les revolutions (Chateaubriand), 133
Essay on Rural Nature (Lezay-Marnésia), 79, 109
Essay on the Manners and Spirit of Nations (Voltaire), 107
Ethics (Spinoza), 161
L'Étudiant étranger (Labro), 12, 54
exoticism of America
  Chateaubriand and, 18
  Crèvecoeur and, 43, 123
  French, of nineteenth century, 4
  Lezay-Marnésia and, 123
exoticism of Amerindians, Lezay-Marnésia and, 101

Faguet, Émile, 128
Fantanes, Louis de, 80

Faÿ, Bernard, 76
Federalist-Antifederalist debate, Crèvecoeur on, 52–53
Fénelon, François, 12
fictionalization
  in Chateaubriand, 63, 131–32, 137
  in Crèvecoeur, 39, 59–60, 63–64
  in Lezay-Marnésia, 89, 92–95
Figueiredo, Yves, 68
Fontanes, Louis de, 167
The Foreign Student (Labro), 12, 54
France
  decline of, Chateaubriand's fear of, 76, 146–47, 152–56
  hopes for American colonies sympathetic to Revolution, 88
  imperialism, Chateaubriand's support for, 150, 151–52, 163–65, 208n135
  See also America, French views on; emigration to America
Franklin, Benjamin
  comtesse d'Houdetot and, 191n17
  Crèvecoeur and, 18, 25, 41, 63
  emigration of French couple and, 120
  and idealized view of US, encouragement of, 4
"The French on the Banks of the Scioto, Epistle to an Emigrant to Kentucky" (Andrieux), 114–15
French Revolution
  Chateaubriand and, 55, 130, 131, 133, 154, 205n23
  Crèvecoeur and, 24–25
  Crèvecoeur on damage done by, 60–61
  and France as new world of liberty and equality, 114–15
  and French view of America, 182, 183
  Lezay-Marnésia and, 55, 82, 87, 88–89, 113–14
  Lezay-Marnésia's Saint-Pierre settlement as uchronotopia recreating France without, 112–14
  and reconfiguration of doxological America, 7
Fumaroli, Marc, 154
Furstenberg, François, 147

Gauchet, Marcel, 167
Genêt, Edmond-Charles, 88
Genette, Gérard, 206n72
Génie du christianisme (Chateaubriand), 66, 140–43
Georgics (Virgil), 33, 108

Girondins
  censure of Lezay-Marnésia's *Letters*, 15, 76, 87–88
  hopes for American colonies sympathetic to Revolution, 88
Golden Age
  comparisons of US to, 4
  Crèvecoeur's posthumous America as, 39–41, 55–56, 181; destruction of with War of Independence, 41; in Early Republic, 55–56, 58–59; economic opportunity as necessary condition for, 41; and necessity of isolated autonomy, 39–41; and role of America in regeneration of France, 184
  doxological America as, 7
  Lezay-Marnésia on, 89, 107, 108, 122–23, 184
  and utopia, fusion of, 40
  Voltaire on Penn and, 107
Gracq, Julien, 38, 49
Grimm, Friedrich Melchior, 80
guidebooks, characteristics vs. travel narratives, 139–40
Guyot, Alain, 96

Hamilton, Alexander, 86
Happiness in the Countryside (Lezay-Marnésia), 79, 80–81, 99, 104
The Happy Family (Lezay-Marnésia), 80, 120
Hazard, Paul, 175
Hemingway, Ernest, 12
Henry, Patrick, 52
Herodotus, 158
Hesiod, 39
L'Heureuse Famille (Lezay-Marnésia), 80, 120
Histoire de ma vie (Casanova), 61–62
history, vs. posthumous account, 5
Hollier, Denis, 131
Homer, 108
Houdetot, Elisabeth-Françoise-Sophie-Lalive de Bellegarde, Comtesse de, 19–20, 25, 27, 47, 191n17

idealization of America
  in Crèvecoeur, 21–22, 26, 33–34, 35, 36–37, 37–39, 138
  French distance from America and, 3–4
  in French view of America as France's past, 181, 183, 184
  in Lezay-Marnésia, 78–79, 105, 110–11, 138
  posthumous America as, 5–6

in posthumous representations, 9, 123, 131, 167
Rousseau and, 4
Illusions perdues (Balzac), 54
imagination, truth of, Chateaubriand on, 143–46, 166–67
immigration
　origins of migrants, 2
　and population growth, 2
In Search of Lost Time (Proust), 38, 49, 160
Irving, Washington, 176
Isaac, Jeffrey C., 146, 181
Itinéraire de Paris à Jérusalem (Chateaubriand)
　and aesthetic of convergence, 160
　on civilizations, destruction of, 155
　evocation of memories from, in *Mémoires d'outre-tombe*, 159–60, 163, 208n121
　use of analogy in, 157

Jefferson, Thomas, 47, 63, 86, 175, 177, 191n17, 203n135
Jehlen, Myra, 22
Journey in Upper Pennsylvania and the State of New York from 1785 to 1798 (Crèvecoeur). See *Voyage dans la Haute Pensylvanie et dans l'État de New York depuis l'année 1785 jusqu'en 1798* (Crèvecoeur)
Julie ou la Nouvelle Héloïse (Rousseau)
　aesthetics of, Crèvecoeur's adoption of in *Lettres*, 4
　on appeal of country life, 80
　aristocratic paternalism in, 81
　comtesse d'Houdetot and, 191n17
　echoes of, in Lezay-Marnésia, 79
　and idealized view of US, 4
　influence on Lezay-Marnésia, 80, 81
Jullien, Dominique, 8

Kléber, Jean-Baptiste, 164
Krugman, Paul, 210n174

Labro, Philippe, 12, 54
Lacretelle, Louis de, 19, 27, 34, 193n58
Lafayette, Gilbert du Motier, marquis de, 47, 107, 123
Lahontan, Louis Armand de, 96, 143
"Les Lampes" (Lezay-Marnésia), 79
La Rochefoucauld family, Crèvecoeur and, 25
La Rochefoucauld-Liancourt, François-Alexandre-Frédéric, 2–3, 139

la Tour du Pin, marquise de. See Dillon, Henriette Lucy, marquise de la Tour du Pin
Launey, Emmanuel-Henri-Louis-Alexandre, comte d'Antraigues, 105
law of suspects, Lezay-Marnésia and, 88
Le Page du Pratz, Antoine-Simon, 143
Léry, Jean de, 30, 142, 158
Lestringant, Frank, 140
Letters from an American Farmer (Crèvecoeur)
　on Amerindians, effort to preserve memory of, 66
　in anthologies of American literature, 20
　attacks on Crèvecoeur in, 77, 78
　on bees, and struggle for existence in nature, 33
　and Crèvecoeur's nostalgia, 17
　Crèvecoeur's turn to writing in French following, 20
　dedication to abbé de Raynal, 47
　differences from *More Letters* and *Sketches*, 21
　farmer in, readers' confusion of with Crèvecoeur, 20, 191n22
　as idealized account of American farm life, 21–22
　interpretation of, in tandem with French version, 14
　Lezay-Marnésia on fabrications in, 11
　as literary, not documentary, account, 21
　on newness of America, 7
　publication of, 24
　translation into French, 19
　on translation of Christian texts into Amerindian languages, as type of monument, 73
　on War of Independence, 22
　"What is an American?" (Letter III), 20
　See also *Lettres d'un cultivateur américain* (Crèvecoeur)
Letters Written from the Banks of the Ohio (Lezay-Marnésia), 95–104
　on America as lost paradise, 120
　on Amerindians: and circular interplay of New World expectations and experience, 102; condescendence toward, 99; expected dominion over, 96; and Lezay-Marnésia's privilege, 99–100; literary models for, 100–102; as natural colonial subjects, 98–102; negation of alterity in, 98, 100–102;

Letters Written from the Banks of the Ohio (cont'd)
  rewriting of, to fit his expectations, 99–100, 100–102; visit from Huron queen and party, 97–102
  attack on previous literary descriptions of North America, 77–78
  attack on Scioto Company in, 106
  on Bethlehem, Pennsylvania, as model community, 105, 107, 108–10; as Golden Age, 108; idealization of, 105, 110–11; as proof of Lezay-Marnésia's patriarchal model, 105, 107, 108; removal of equality from model, 109–10; similarities to Lezay-Marnésia's program, 109
  censure by Girondins, 15, 76, 87–88
  claimed accuracy of, 78
  condescendence toward Americans in, 98
  first letter, 97–104
  and hope for revival of Old World through New, 76
  on Lezay-Marnésia's despair in New World, 121–22
  literary qualities of, 10
  on Monsieur and Madame Pintreaux, 120–21, 122
  portrait of America in: criticisms of, 78; as idealized, 78–79, 105, 110–11
  posthumous representation of America in: advertising function of, 96–97, 106, 123; as descriptions on his expectations rather than reality, 95, 96–97, 103
  publication history of, 76, 87, 89
  on realities of settlers' life, 98
  reception of, 14–15
  Saint-Pierre as addressee of, 105, 112, 119
  on Saint-Pierre settlement, plans for: Bethlehem, Pennsylvania, as model for, 105, 107, 109–11; as both reality and imaginary emotional escape, 117–19; comparison to Islands of the Blessed, 118–19; as idealization, 110–11; isolation of community within Pennsylvania, 115–17; land for, 112; Lezay-Marnésia's Freudian denial about, 118; naming of, 109; plans for expansion into Northwest Territory, 112, 115; as potential reality and imaginary emotional escape, 111–12; precise calculations used to project practicality of, 117; and proposed peaceful relations with France, 115; removal of equality from Bethlehem model, 109–10; Saint-Pierre's earlier plan as model for, 105, 108; as uchronotopia recreating France without Revolution, 112–14
  on "salad-bowl" theory, 15, 116–17
  second letter, 104–19
  third letter, 119–23
  three letters of, 89
  and uchronical genre, 15
  on utopian project, possibility of continuing, 106–7
"Letter to Monsieur Audrain, Merchant in Pittsburg" (Lezay-Marnésia)
  addition to second edition of *Reading Program*, 89–90
  on American Golden Age, as available only in posthumous representation, 122–23
  gap between writing and publication of, 102–3
  on Lezay-Marnésia's utopian community, as no longer possible, 111
Lettre écrite par un Français émigrant sur les terres de la Compagnie du Scioto à son ami à Paris (*Letter Written by a Frenchman Immigrating to the Lands of the Scioto Company to his Friend in Paris*), 91–92, 94
Lettres d'un cultivateur américain (Crèvecoeur), 1784 edition
  aesthetics of, influence of French political context on, 25
  on Amerindians: ecumenical relations with settlers, 29–30, 31, 32, 193n70; and portrayal of expectations, 102; as Rousseauian noble savages, 28–30, 31
  "Anecdote of the Sassafras and the Wild Vine," 37–38, 38–39
  "Anecdote of the Wild Dog," 28–30, 32, 102
  on autonomy as condition for Golden Age, 40
  on bees, and struggle for existence in nature, 33–34
  as boundary of this study, 1
  composite form of, 14
  and construction of French doxological America, 32

contrasting of present war with idealized past in, 37–39
Crèvecoeur's losses as motive for therapeutic writing, 35–36, 37–39, 40
Crèvecoeur's translation from English, 19, 25; and adaptation method of translation, 26–27; addition of pastoral tone to, 33–34; additions of material to, 26–27, 38, 192n54, 194n95; aesthetics of Rousseau's *Nouvelle Héloïse* and, 28; and *francisation* of text, 26, 27–30, 31, 32, 35; French support for American rebels as context for, 25; friends' help and influence on, 27, 33, 193n58; and idealization of text, 26, 33–34, 35; introduction of deism and theodicy to, 34; and invocations of Rousseau's state of nature, 27–30, 31, 32; and struggle to re-learn French, 27; as type of publicity, 32
dedication to Lafayette, 47
on economic opportunity, as necessary condition for Golden Age, 41
on family insularity, as condition for Golden Age, 39–40
as idealized account of American life, 21–22, 26, 33–34, 35
illustrations in, 42–43, 43
and interplay of expectations and actual experiences, 31–32
interpretation in tandem with English version, 14
on link between farmer's identity and land ownership, 35
as literary account, 21
marketing of, exploitation of idealized view of US in, 4
on newness of America, 7
and nostalgic paradigm of New World, 17, 32, 35–36, 42
paternity and family as theme in, 40
politics of, influence of French political context on, 25
posthumous representation of America created by: Crèvecoeur's lack of interest in return to, 60; and double updating of past, 39; as dream world of refuge, 60; factors shaping, 26, 32; as Golden Age, 39–41, 55–56, 181; as idealization, 35; masquerading as direct reporting, 36; as response to

nostalgic impulse, 36–37; as type of publicity, 32
Proust and, 38
published copy of, as Crèvecoeur's recreation of stolen manuscript, 34–35
and Saint-John, relation of Crèvecoeur to, 196n180
scholarship on, 13–14, 26
shadow of Crèvecoeur's losses hanging over, 35–36
"Story of André l'Hebridéen" (Crèvecoeur), 40
success of, in Europe, 4
temporal strata in, 36–37, 39
use in Scioto Company advertisements, 83–84
writing of, 25–26
See also Letters from an American Farmer (Crèvecoeur)
Lettres d'un cultivateur américain (Crèvecoeur), 1787 edition, 41–54
additions to, 27, 38, 42
"Combat Between Two Snakes," 54
and Crèvecoeur as French Consul, embrace of Patriot cause by, 47–48
on Early Republic, concerns about challenges faced by, 53–54
on Federalist-Antifederalist debate, 52–53
"5th Anecdote," 125
on human penchant for destruction, 54
illustrations in, 42–47, 44, 45
influence on Chateaubriand, 125
on liberty, as necessary for Golden Age, 46
progressive paradigm of New World in, 42; and American as model of European future, 42; coexistence with nostalgic paradigm, 42, 47–48, 48–51, 53–54; in final letters on Early Republic, 51–54; vs. pessimism of Crèvecoeur's correspondence, 48; political necessity of embracing, 47–48
and Revolutionary War as end of Golden Age, 51
"Sketch of a Journey by Ménéssink . . . ," 51
"Sketch of the Destruction of the Settlements . . . ," 51
on Socialbourg, establishment and demise of, 49, 50–51
structure of: apparent lack of temporal or thematic order, 48–49; and coexistence of nostalgic and progressive

236 ~ INDEX

Lettres d'un cultivateur américain (cont'd)
  paradigms, 53–54; as echo of Crèvecoeur's split self, 51; and imperative of proliferation, 49; and letters on colonial life, war-related letters as commentary on, 50–51; restructuring of earlier draft as clue to, 49–50
  on US cultural homogeneity, difficulty of achieving, 46–47
Les Lettres écrites des rives de l'Ohio (Lezay-Marnésia). See *Letters Written from the Banks of the Ohio* (Lezay-Marnésia)
Lettres persanes (Montesquieu), 130
Lettres philosophiques (Voltaire), 107
Lévi-Strauss, Claude, 165–66, 167, 168, 209n138
Lezay-Marnésia, Adrien de (son), 87, 88, 120
Lezay-Marnésia, Albert-Madelaine-Claude de (son), 84, 87, 97, 98, 101, 102, 110
Lezay-Marnésia, Claude-François-Adrien de
  on America: ambivalent attitude toward, 121; expectations vs. reality of, 11; Golden Age imagined in, 89, 107, 108, 122–23; as new, better France, 121, 181, 184; and travelers' disappointment at reality, 186
  American letters of, 89–90
  on Amerindians: and circular interplay of New World expectations and experience, 102; condescendence toward, 99; desire to preserve record of, 11; expectations for dominion over, 96; fascination with, 11; and Lezay-Marnésia's privilege, 99–100; literary models for, 100–102; as natural colonial subjects, 98–100, 98–102; natural politeness of, 98; negation of alterity in, 98, 100–102; preconceptions about, 96; rewriting of, to fit his expectations, 99–100, 100–102; visit from Huron queen and party, 97–102
  appeal of country life to, 80
  on autocratic government, necessity of, 81
  Brackenridge's *Modern Chivalry* on, 113
  character of, 110
  and circular interplay of New World expectations and experience, 31–32
  and Club des Impartiaux, 114
  as contemporary of American and French revolutions, 10
  Crèvecoeur and, 11, 77, 78, 122
  on democracy, impracticality of, 81
  and denial, 118, 121
  doxological America in, 79, 95, 96–97, 102–3; basis in hopes rather than reality, 89, 92–95, 103
  erudition of, 80
  and French feudal aristocracy, support for return of, 81
  friends of, 80
  and happiness, as alway "before," 123
  influence of Crèvecoeur on, 122
  influence of Lahontan on, 96
  influence of Montaigne on, 96
  influence of Montesquieu on, 81
  influence of Rousseau on, 79, 80, 81, 96, 104
  influence of Voltaire on, 101
  life of, 81–89; army career of, 79–80; on Azile farm in Pittsburgh, 87, 120, 121; death of, 89; financial ruin of, 89; and French Revolution, 55, 82, 87, 88–89, 113–14; literary career of, 80; married life at Château de Moutonne, 80; political career in France, 81–82; return to France, 87–88, 120–21; return to France, melancholy following, 87, 120, 122–23
  and moderate reform, support for, 81, 82
  paradoxical view of US political climate, 82
  posthumous America in, 15; advertising function of, 92, 96–97, 106, 123; commemorative function of, 123; as descriptions on his expectations rather than reality, 95, 96–97, 103; as idealized, 138; Lezay-Marnésia's politics and, 103–4; mythical past as model for future in, 105; and role of America in regeneration of France, 184; specular function of, 154
  scholarship on, 13
  and Scioto Company, attack on, 106
  ties to Crèvecoeur's and Chateaubriand's works, 8, 11
  on women's education, 109
  works by, 79, 80
  See also *Letters Written from the Banks of the Ohio* (Lezay-Marnésia); Saint-Pierre settlement, Lezay-Marnésia's plans for; utopian project on Ohio River, Lezay-Marnésia's plans for

INDEX 237

liberty, Crèvecoeur on Americans' abuse of, 46
Liebersohn, Harry, 99
Literature and Literary Figures in the United States (Vail), 175, 177
Locke, John, 192n52
Logan (Indian chief), lament of, 177
Lost Illusions (Balzac), 54
Louisiana literature of nineteenth century, and posthumous representations of America, 9
Louisiana Purchase, 2
Louis XVI, trial of, 130
loyalists, Crèvecoeur's leanings toward, 22–23, 40

Mabanckou, Alain, 12
Mackenzie, Alexander, 165, 204–5n19
Madison, James, 86
Malesherbes, Chrétien-Guillaume de Lamoignon de, 130
Mallarmé, Stéphane, 144
Mariage de Figaro (Beaumarchais), 101
Martini, Pietro-Antonio, 43
Mathy, Jean-Philippe, 6–7
Mazzei, Filippo, 78
McDermott, John Francis, 203n136
melting pot
  Crèvecoeur's formulation of concept, 116
  evocation of, in frontispiece to Crèvecoeur's 1787 *Lettres d'un cultivateur américain*, 46
  salad bowl model as alternative to, 203n129
Mémoires (Brissot de Warville), 24–25
Mémoires de ma vie (Chateaubriand), 162
Mémoires d'outre-tombe (Chateaubriand), 156–80
  aesthetic of convergence in, 157; characteristics vs. analogy, 160–62; and common linking term, 160–62; and convergence of memories with observations, 159–60, 163, 208n121; political significance of, 163–65
  on America character, and degeneration of talent, 176–77
  on American aristocracy, development of, 178–79
  on American decline: and American language, increasing poverty of, 176; Chateaubriand's lack of direct evidence for, 180; climate-based causes of, 179–80; excesses of philosophical liberty as cause of, 180; growth of selfishness and, 177, 179; as inevitable, 176–77; lack of literary or artistic accomplishment, 175–76; and loss of equality, 178–79; practical, material bent of character and, 175–76; radical decline over time, 174, 186; rampant commercialism and, 177–78, 179
  on American language, decline of, 176
  on Amerindians: decline of, as harbinger of American decline, 177; effort to preserve memory of through writing, 66
  and analogy as path to understanding, rejection of, 156–59
  as boundary of this study, 1
  and burden of recording actual and alternative destinies, 126–27, 129
  on chrysogenous aristocracy in America, 178–79, 209n160
  and evolution of Chateaubriand's doxological America, 7
  first view of America in, and aesthetic of conversion, 159–60
  on France's colonial project: continuity of, in New World and Middle East/Africa, 163–65; narrator's travels as reflection of, 164–65
  on French Revolution, 55
  on futility of immortality through works, 67
  homological relationship between history of author and epoch in, 162–65
  on languages, inevitable loss of, over time, 66–67
  literary qualities of, 10
  on lost "primitive life" of America, 8
  on manuscripts written in America, 132–33
  mix of dream and reality in, 173
  on Napoleon, 65
  on Niagara Falls, 162–63, 164
  nostalgia for sixteenth century in, 131–32, 165–73; and anachronistic vocabulary, 167–71; and Chateaubriand as Don Quixote figure, 170–71, 172; and double memory of actual trip and desired visit to pristine wilderness, 167–73; and quotations, blurring of time periods through, 171–73; and regret at missing initial contact with New World, 165–67; simplicity of first European visitors and, 165

Mémoires d'outre-tombe (cont'd)
   posthumous America in, 127; analeptic function of, 167–73 (*See also* nostalgia for sixteenth century in, *above*); and reinvention over years between experience of America and publication, 180
   scholarship on, 13
   on search for Northwest Passage, 130
   sources for, 128
   swim with sharks incident in, dubious reality of, 125–26
   synoptic vision of Chateaubriand's life in, 159
   temporal strata in, 36
   and triumph of poet over traveler, 129
   veracity of travels describe in, critical investigations into, 127–29
   on Villeneuve's use of analogy, 157–59
   writing of, 207–8n112
mercantile spirit of America, Chateaubriand on, 177–78, 179
Mercier, Alfred, 9
Mercure de France, 11, 19, 34
Mersenne, René de, 127–28, 145
Miller, Christopher L., 153
Mirage in the West (Echeverria), 182
Mitchell, Julia Post., 61
Modern Chivalry (Brackenridge), 113
Molière, 101
Mondésir, Édouard de, 124, 204n2
Montaigne, Michel de, Chateaubriand and, 30, 96, 141, 169, 171
Montesquieu, Charles-Louis de Secondat, baron de La Brède et de, 81, 130
More, Thomas, 109
Moreau de Saint-Méry, Médéric-Louis-Élie, 139
Moreau-Zanelli, Jocelyne, 80, 85, 86
More Letters from the American Farmer (Crèvecoeur), 21, 39
motives for travel in America, 129–30
A Moveable Feast (Hemingway), 12
Muir, John, 68
My Memories (Albert de Lezay-Marnésia), 87, 97, 101

Naigeon, Jacques-André, 33
Les Natchez (Chateaubriand)
   American research for, 129
   Chateaubriand's abandonment of manuscript in England, 134
   on decadence of French civilization, 154
   doubling of Chateaubriand's persona in, 134–35
   model for Céluta in, 172–73
   Montesquieu's *Lettres persanes* and, 130
   writing of, 132–33
Nettancourt-Vaubécourt, Marie-Claudine de, 80
Néville, M. de, 34
New France colonies
   Chateaubriand on: analeptic speculations about alternative futures based on, 147–50, 163–64; and French language, perpetuation of, 150; nostalgia for, 146–47, 184; pride in French glory reflected in, 149–50; *See also* Saint-Pierre settlement, Lezay-Marnésia's plans for; utopian project on Ohio River, Lezay-Marnésia's plans for
New World
   creation of prior to discovery, 31–32
   expectations about, circular interplay with actual experiences, in travel narratives, 31–32, 102
   newness of: as already lost in posthumous representations, 8; emphasis of French observers on, 7
   nostalgic paradigm of, in Crèvecoeur, 17, 32, 35–36, 42
   progressive paradigm of, in Crèvecoeur, 41–42; and American as model of European future, 42; coexistence with nostalgic paradigm, 42, 47–48, 48–51, 53–54; in final letters on Early Republic, 51–54; vs. pessimism of Crèvecoeur's correspondence, 48; political necessity of embracing, 47–48
   sixteenth-century reports on, 30
Noailles, Louis-Marie-Marc-Antoine de, 2, 199n12
noble savage concept
   in Crèvecoeur, 28–30, 31
   development of, 30–31
   in Lezay-Marnésia: and Amerindians as natural colonial subjects, 98–100; negation of Amerindian alterity in, 100–102
   and perceived affinity with nobles of Europe, 99
Northwest Ordinance of 1787, 86
Northwest Passage, 204–5n19
   Chateaubriand's search for, 129–31, 145, 167; and potential alternative futures, 126, 131

Northwest Territory
　history of, 112, 199n12
　planned expansion of Lezay-Marnésia's Saint-Pierre settlement into, 112, 115
　See also utopian project on Ohio River, Lezay-Marnésia's plans for
nostalgia
　in Chateaubriand: for lost manuscript of *Voyage en Amérique*, 134; for New France colonies, 146–47, 184; for sixteenth-century America, 131–32, 165–73
　in Crèvecoeur: coexistence with progressive paradigm, in 1787 *Lettres*, 42, 47–48, 48–51, 53–54, as creative impulse, 17, 21, 25, 35–37, 37–39; and New World portrayal, 17, 32, 35–36, 42; and posthumous America, 32, 36–37
　as element in posthumous representations of America, 5, 9
　in Lahontan, for feudal nobility, 30–31
Nouveau prospectus de la Compagnie du Scioto (1790)
　citing of Crèvecoeur in, 92
　letters by Lezay-Marnésia in, 89, 92–95; advertising function of, 92; and critical need to attract settlers, 94–96; and doxological America, presentation to readers, 95; as fictions based on his hopes, 89, 92–95; influence of, 95; on Scioto lands as Promised Land, 94
　letters by others in, 92
　new wave of settlers enticed by, 95
　as response to criticisms of first prospectus, 90–92

Ohio Company, 83, 199n29
Ovid, 39

Painter, George D., 128, 129, 130
Paintings of American Nature (Chateaubriand). See *Tableaux de la nature américaine* (Chateaubriand)
panegyric, Crèvecoeur and, 47
Pascal, Blaise, 192n47
pastoral tone, Crèvecoeur's addition to *Lettres* translation, 33–34
Paul et Virginie (Saint-Pierre), 105, 108
Pauw, Cornelius de, 77–78
Penn, William, 107

Pennsylvania, religious and civil liberties in, as model for *philosophes*, 104–5
　See also Bethlehem, Pennsylvania
Philbrick, Thomas, 17–18
philistinism in United States, Chateaubriand on, 175–76, 179
philo-Americanism
　as admiration for idealization of what no longer exists, 186
　basis in posthumous representation, 186
　of eighteenth century: assumption of American anteriority in, 183–84; evolution into anti-Americanism of nineteenth century, 181–83; and role of America in regeneration of France, 184, 210n01
　waning of, with experience of American reality, 186
physiocratic discourse, 53
Piketty, Thomas, 179
Pinchot, Gifford, 68
Pintreaux, Jean-Baptiste-Charles Lucas des, 120–21, 122, 203–4nn135–136
Plan de lecture pour une jeune dame (Lezay-Marnésia). See *Reading Program for a Young Lady* (Lezay-Marnésia)
Playfair, William, 82, 83
Plet, Françoise, 13
posthumous America
　application of concept to other fields, 11–12
　as basis of philo-Americanism, 186
　and breaches of truth, 5
　in Chateaubriand, 15, 127, 131–32, 140; anachronisms in, 138–39, 145–46, 167–71; analeptic function of, 146, 147–50, 163–64, 167–73, 181–82, 206n72; and intrusion of fictional elements over time, 131–32; as meditation on what could have been, 150; reinvention of, over years before publication, 180; and role of America in regeneration of France, 184; specular function of, 146–47, 152–56; as unrecoverable ghost, 138
　corpus of works chosen to illustrate, 8–11
　in Crèvecoeur, 15; as combination of collective image and individual nostalgia, 32; Crèvecoeur's lack of interest in return to, 60; as doubly fictionalized, 39, 63–64; as doubly posthumous, 64–65; as dream world of refuge, 60, 61, 62; and France as

posthumous America (cont'd)
   symbolic double of United States, 54, 58–59, 65; as Golden Age, 39–41; as idealization, 35, 138; masquerading as direct reporting, 36; vs. pessimism of his correspondence, 36; as response to nostalgic impulse, 36–37; and role of America in regeneration of France, 184; specular function of, 154; as type of publicity, 32
   definition of, 5
   dialectic flow of loss and resurrection in, 6
   vs. elegy, 6
   evolution of, 9–10
   functions of, 6
   vs. historical accounts, 5
   in Lezay-Marnésia, 15; advertising function of, 92, 96–97, 106, 123; commemorative function of, 123; as descriptions on his expectations rather than reality, 95, 96–97, 103; as idealized, 138; Lezay-Marnésia's politics and, 103–4; mythical past as model for future in, 105; and role of America in regeneration of France, 184; specular function of, 154
   nostalgia as element in, 5, 9
   as retrospective idealization, 5–6
   See also advertising function of posthumous accounts; analeptic function of posthumous accounts; commemorative function of posthumous accounts; specular function of posthumous accounts
Préface testamentaire (Chateaubriand), 174
preservation movement
   vs. conservation movement, 68
   Crèvecoeur and, 67–68
Prospectus pour l'établissement sur les rivières d'Ohio et de Scioto en Amérique (*Prospectus for the Colony on the Ohio and Scioto Rivers in America*, Scioto Company), 82–84
Proust, Marcel, 38, 160, 162
Pumpkin Fields, Battle of, 201n79
Putnam, Rufus, 97, 202n93

Raynal, Guillaume-Thomas-François, 47, 175
Reading Program for a Young Lady (Lezay-Marnésia), 80, 109
   See also "Letter to Monsieur Audrain, Merchant in Pittsburg" (Lezay-Marnésia)
Reading Writing (Gracq), 38
Recherches historiques et politiques sur les États-Unis (Mazzei), 78
Recherches philosophiques sur les Américains ou mémoires intéressants pour servir à l'histoire de l'espèce humaine (de Pauw), 78
reenchantment, analeptic representations and, 167
regeneration, American as land of, 46, 104, 184
Reichler, Claude, 132, 153
Rémond, René, 3, 4
René (Chateaubriand), 134
Restoration, Chateaubriand on, 154
Rêveries du promeneur solitaire (*Reveries of the Solitary Walker*, Rousseau), 170
Révolutions de France et de Brabant, 85
Rice, Howard C., 26, 43, 60–61
Riffaterre, Michael, 6, 161–62
Roger, Philippe, 186
Ronsard, Pierre de, 172
Rossi, Henri, 139, 143, 154
Rousseau, Jean-Jacques
   and Chateaubriand, influence on, 170
   comtesse d'Houdetot and, 191n17
   and Lezay-Marnésia, influence on, 79, 80, 81, 96, 104
   Malesherbes and, 130
   shock at Vincennes prison, 192n47
   on state of nature, 28, 31, 193n68; Crèvecoeur's invocation of, in *Lettres*, 27–30, 31; imitators' recasting as real historical period, 31
   and values of *Contrat social*, 81
   See also Julie ou la Nouvelle Héloïse (Rousseau)
The Route of the Wolf (Tesson), 12

Sade, Donatien-François-Alphonse de, 38
Saint Clair, Arthur, 87, 106, 199n31, 200nn50–51
Sainte-Beuve, Charles Augustin, 127–28
Saint-Lambert, Jean-François de, 27, 33, 80, 191n17, 193n58
Saint-Pierre, Bernardin de, 80, 105, 108, 112, 119
Saint-Pierre settlement, Lezay-Marnésia's plans for

Bethlehem, Pennsylvania, as model for, 105, 107, 109–11
  as both reality and imaginary emotional escape, 117–19
  comparison to Islands of the Blessed, 118–19
  as idealization, 110–11
  isolation of community within Pennsylvania, 115–17
  land for, 112
  Lezay-Marnésia's Freudian denial about, 118
  naming of, 109
  plans for expansion into Northwest Territory, 112, 115
  as potential reality and imaginary emotional escape, 111–12
  precise calculations used to enforce practicality of, 117
  and proposed peaceful relations with France, 115
  removal of equality from Bethlehem model, 109–10
  Saint-Pierre's earlier plan as model for, 105, 108
  as uchronotopia recreating France without Revolution, 112–14
Saisons (Saint-Lambert), 33
salad bowl theory, 203n129
  Lezay-Marnésia on, 15, 116–17
Samuels, Maurice, 148
Sayre, Gordon M., 73
Scènes de la vie future (*Scenes of Future Life*, Duhamel), 184–85
Scioto Company, 82–84
  advertisements by, 83
  Bissot on, 88
  deceptive representation of lands sold by, 83, 91–92
  founding members of, 82
  land-purchase scheme of, 82–83
  Lezay-Marnésia's criticisms of, 106, 121
  refusal to refund investors' money, 87
  reliance of word of mouth from first settlers, 83, 91–92
  use of Crèvecoeur excerpts in ads by, 83–84
  See also *Description of the Soil and the Productivity of this Portion of the United States* (Scioto Company); *Nouveau prospectus de la Compagnie du Scioto* (1790); *Prospectus pour l'établissement sur les rivières d'Ohio et de Scioto en Amérique* (Scioto Company)
Seasons (Saint-Lambert), 33
Seton, William, 23
Sketches of Eighteenth-Century America (Crèvecoeur)
  "Anecdote of the Wild Dog" in, 28
  differences from *Letters from an American Farmer*, 21
  more-realistic focus on problems of American farmer, 21
  "Sketch of the Obyo River and of the Kentucky Region" (Crèvecoeur), 83–84
slavery
  in eighteenth-century Americas, 86
  French, Colbert and, 151
  and Northwest Ordinance of 1787, 86
social classes in America, Chateaubriand on, 178–79
Société des Vingt-Quatre (Society of the Twenty-Four), 84–85, 87, 95, 97
Société Gallo-Américaine, 24
Sollors, Werner, 43–45
Souvenirs (Albert de Lezay-Marnésia), 87, 97, 101
The Spectacular Past (Samuels), 148
specular function of posthumous accounts, 12
  in Chateaubriand, 146–47, 152–56
  in Crèvecoeur, 54, 58, 154
  definition of, 6
  in Lezay-Marnésia, 154
speech, characteristics vs. writing, 73–74
Spinoza, Baruch, 161
state of nature
  development of concept, 30–31
  in Rousseau, 28, 31, 193n68; Crèvecoeur's invocation of in *Lettres*, 27–30, 31; imitators' recasting as real historical period, 31
"Story of André l'Hebridéen" (Crèvecoeur), 40
Story of My Life (Casanova), 61–62
Switzer, Richard, 128

Tableau du climat et du sol des États-Unis d'Amérique (Volney), 143
Tableaux de la nature américaine (Chateaubriand), 132–33
Target, Gui-Jean-Baptiste, and Crèvecoeur's translation of *Lettres d'un cultivateur américain*, 27, 193n58
Tasso, 108

Tesson, Sylvain, 12
Thevet, André, 142, 157, 206n55
Tocqueville, Alexis de, 8, 9, 179, 210n173
   See also *Voyage au Lac Oneida* (Tocqueville)
topography, vs. cosmography, 141
touristic guides, characteristics vs. travel narratives, 139–40
Traité de la culture des pommes de terre (Crèvecoeur), 20, 53
Traité sur la tolérance (Voltaire), 107
translation, transposition vs. adaption methods of, 26–27
transposition method of translation, 26
travel narratives
   bibliographies of, 10
   characteristics vs. guidebooks, 139–40
   interplay of expectations and actual experiences in, 31–32
   as intertextual, 11
   lack of literary pretensions in most of, 10
Travels in America (Chateaubriand). See *Voyage en Amérique* (Chateaubriand)
Travels Through North and South Carolina (Bartram), 63
Treatise on Potato Farming (Crèvecoeur). See *Traité de la culture des pommes de terre* (Crèvecoeur)
Treatise on Tolerance (Voltaire), 107
"Les Treise Chapitres du Troisième Volume du Cultivateur Américain" (Crèvecoeur), 49–50, 187–88
Tristes tropiques (Lévi-Strauss), 165–66
trolique, Crèvecoeur on, 40
truth, scientific vs. imaginative, Chateaubriand on, 143–46, 166–67
Turgot, Anne-Robert-Jacques, 53, 195n58
Turgot, Étienne-François, 53

uchronia, Lezay-Marnésia's Saint-Pierre settlement and, 113, 148
uchronical genre, 203nn122–23
   Chateaubriand's *Voyage en Amérique* and, 148–50
   definition of, 15
   Lezay-Marnésia and, 15, 113, 148
   need for retrospective analysis and, 148
uchronotopia, Lezay-Marnésia's Saint-Pierre settlement as, 112–14
United States
   growth of population, 2
   growth of territory, 1–2, 189n5
utopia

Crèvecoeur's Socialbourg as, 50–51
   French view of America as, 4
   and Golden Age, fusion of, 40
   Lezay-Marnésia's Saint-Pierre settlement as, 113
Utopia (Moore), 109
utopian project on Ohio River, Lezay-Marnésia's plans for
   acreage purchased by Lezay-Marnésia, 95
   Amerindian possession of land for, 83, 86–87, 91, 97, 201n79, 203n121
   collapse of, 106
   complete separation from France, 88
   French criticism of, 114–15
   and French Revolution, flight from, 82, 88
   ideas of, in *Le Bonheur dans les campagnes*, 80–81
   importance of, 4
   land purchased for, 84, 199n36
   Lezay-Marnésia's large investment in, 95
   Lezay-Marnésia's travel to site of, 86, 97
   membership requirements for, 84
   and mistaken beliefs about region, 82, 83
   and *Nouveau prospectus de la Compagnie du Scioto*, 89, 92–95
   and outlawing of slavery in Northwest Territory, 86
   persistence in, after initial setbacks, 106
   planned social stratification in, 85
   and realities of settlers' life, 97, 98
   recruitment of indentured workers for, 86
   religious character of, 84
   as renewal of European feudalism, 80–81, 82
   and Scioto Company land sales, 82–84, 87, 88, 199n29
   and Society of the Twenty-Four, 84–85

Vail, Eugène A., 175, 177
Vergennes, Charles-Gravier de, 34, 105
Villèle, Joseph de, 154, 207n99
Virgil, 33, 108
visitors to America, range of motives in, 139
Volney, Constantin-François
   on Amerindians, 71
   appeal of ancient things to, 66
   criticisms of Crèvecoeur and Lezay-Marnésia, 78, 198n7
   motives for visiting America, 139

and New World high society, 2
weather tables by, 143
Voltaire, 80, 101, 107
Voyage au Lac Oneida (Tocqueville), 9
Voyage au Mont-Blanc (Chateaubriand), 160
Voyage aux grandes salines tyroliennes de Reichenhall (Crèvecoeur), 20
Voyage dans la Haute Pensylvanie et dans l'État de New York depuis l'année 1785 jusqu'en 1798 (Crèvecoeur)
   American as mythical French past in, 54, 58–59, 65
   on Amerindian languages, lack of abstract words in, 71, 72
   on Amerindians: ambivalent view of, 69, 72; Crèvecoeur's empathy with, 70, 71–73, 75; destruction of, as warning to France, 76; effort to preserve memory of through writing, 66, 67, 70–76; hypocrisy of Christian treatment of, 73; inability to foresee future, 69; inevitable annihilation of, 70, 73, 74; as inhabitants of the present, 69, 75; intellectual inferiority to Europeans, 69, 70, 71; lack of permanent monuments made by, 69, 74–75; as posthumous representation, 67, 73, 74–75, 76; praise for eloquence of, 72; and preservation of Amerindian toponyms, 70; rejection of sedentary lifestyle by, 69, 72; spread of views across several characters, 70; and translation of Christian texts into Amerindian languages, 73; white colonists' responsible for annihilation of, 67, 69, 70–71
   on attractiveness of ancient things, 65–66
   Chateaubriand essay on, 11
   and Crèvecoeur's nostalgia, 17
   Early Republic as Golden Age in, 55–56, 58–59
   and ecological thought, 67–68
   on farmers as destroyers, 68
   fictional account of Franklin speech in, 63
   as fictional creation from fragmented memories and sources, 59–60, 63–64
   on forests of America: need to preserve, 67, 68–69; white colonists as responsible for disappearance of, 67
   fragmented narration and geography of, 64–65
   France as possible US future in, 54, 58–59, 65
   on French Revolution, 55–56
   on human inability to see future, 75
   as intended fourth book of *Lettres*, 38
   and melancholy meditation on time and destiny, 75
   on Napoleon, 21
   opposition of America and negative Other of Europe in, 58–59, 65
   overlapping temporal strata in, 62
   Plet edition of, 13
   poor sales of, 76
   posthumous representation of America in: as doubly fictionalized, 63–64; as doubly posthumous, 64–65; as dream world of refuge, 61, 62
   publication of, and fictional status as issue, 60
   scholarship on, 13
   shipwreck trope in preface of, 55, 64, 65
   sloppy use of sources in, 63
   "Tale of a Flight into the Appalachians During the War of Independence," 56–57
   temporal strata in, 62
   writing of, 20
Voyage en Amérique (Chateaubriand), 132–56
   on American character, likely changes in, 173
   on Amerindian decline: European influence as cause of, 153, 155; as presage of French future, 152–56; as reflection on human impermanence, 146
   on Amerindians: affinity with French, 153; lost languages of, 150
   anachronistic aesthetic in: critics' failure to recognize, 145–46; as reenactment, 138–39; and truth of the imagination, 145–46, 166–67
   borrowed erudition in, 141–43
   on Chateaubriand's preference for forests over cities, 146–47
   as commemorative representation of America, 132, 134, 135–38
   as cosmographical account, 140–43
   on decline of civilizations, inevitability of, 155
   and evolution of Chateaubriand's doxological America, 7
   heterogeneous subject matter in, 141

Voyage en Amérique (cont'd)
   as inventory of facts about America, 141
   "Journal sans date" section of: alternative copy of, 136–37; borrowings from Bartram's *Voyages* in, 137, 205n45; and intrusion of fiction into memory, 137; past in, as unrecoverable ghost, 137–38; as reconstructed memory of aged writer, 135–38; three voices in, 137; tragic consciousness of time in, 137–38
   literary qualities of, 10
   manuscript of, as twice-lost and twice-written, 132–34
   meditations on alternative destinies in, 126
   multiple voices in, 132
   and New France colonies: analeptic speculations about alternative futures based on, 147–50, 163–64; specular function of encounters with remnants of, 146–47, 152
   on Niagara Falls, 146–47
   nostalgia for earlier period in, 131–32, 146
   original manuscript of: Chateaubriand's nostalgia for, 134; irreplaceable authenticity of, 133–34
   posthumous America in, 132, 140; analeptic function of, 146; as reenactment, 138–39
   "Present State of the Savages of North America," 154–55
   publication of, 154
   as pure travel narrative devoid of guidebook characteristics, 140
   as return to origin as person and writer, 126
   scholarship on, 13
   second manuscript of, Chateaubriand's abandonment in England, 134
   swim with sharks incident in, dubious reality of, 125–26
   and truth of imagination vs. scientific truth, 143–46, 166–67
   uchronic speculation in, 148–50
   uneventful travel depicted in, imaginative embellishment of, 144–45
   "updates" added to, as more information from old sources, 142–43
   voice of both aged writer and novice author in, 134–35
   writing of, 132–33
Voyages (Bartram), 137

Wabash, Battle of, 87, 106, 199n31, 200nn50–51
War of Independence
   Crèvecoeur and, 22–23, 24–25, 35, 41, 51
   Crèvecoeur's imprisonment during, 22–23; metaphysical crisis prompted by, 23, 24, 52–53; period of anguish following, 24–25; release, 23; as source of literary creativity, 16–17, 23–24; and splitting of self into two, 16–17, 22, 23–24, 25, 51
Washington, George, 47, 51–52, 86, 141, 177, 200n51
Watson and the Shark (Copley), 125, 204n4
Weber, Max, 167, 209n144
White, Edward, 20, 50
A word to those who would like to go to America (Franklin), 4
writing, characteristics vs. speech, 73–74
The Writing of History (Certeau), 73–74
Wyandots, attacks on Ohio and Kentucky Territory settlers, 86–87

Yellowstone national park, preservation movement and, 68

www.ingramcontent.com/pod-product-compliance
Lightning Source LLC
Chambersburg PA
CBHW021400290426
44108CB00010B/322